ENGLISH DOLLS

Doll Pottery Co. Ltd.

POLLOCK'S DICTIONARY OF
ENGLISH DOLLS

Planned by Marguerite Fawdry

Research by Deborah Brown and Sarah Postgate

Edited by Mary Hillier

Robert Hale Ltd
London

CONTENTS

First published 1982 by Robert Hale Limited
Clerkenwell House, Clerkenwell Green, London EC1R 0HT

© Pollock's Toy Museum 1982
ISBN 0 7091 9940 6
Designed by Melvyn Gill ARCA

Printed in Great Britain by
St Edmundsbury Press, Bury St Edmunds, Suffolk
Bound by Woolnough Bookbinding Ltd.

INTRODUCTION

The English have never been recognised as one of the greatest doll-making nations of the world. The crown would go to Germany, pre-eminent in this as in other toy-making production. Very beautiful dolls were also made in Paris in the 19th century and probably nowadays, in the field of plastics, the greatest output of mass-manufactured dolls comes from U.S.A. Nevertheless there were certain especial types of doll for which England was very famous in the past and they were produced curiously enough (by a rough but recognisable division) at four specific periods and in four different materials!

From an early date, certainly the 16th century, wooden, papier mâché and moulded clay dolls were known in Europe. They were both imported and made in England. Records show that finely dressed 'babies' (the earlier name for a child's play doll) were sold annually at the big open air fairs, especially St. Bartholomew's, London in September. By the late 17th century such finely carved wooden dolls as 'Lord and Lady Clapham' were on sale, splendidly costumed and accoutred, and this product of the turner's skill continued through the 18th century until the import of foreign dolls seems to have usurped it.

From the early 19th century the art of wax-modelling was adapted and developed for play-dolls and the masters of such craft seem all to have resided in London, though some of them certainly, such as the Montanari and Pierotti families, had European antecedents. The English wax doll was very realistic and comparatively expensive, having head and limbs shaped from wax poured into moulds and usually real hair, eyebrows and eyelashes. Some of Queen Victoria's numerous progeny produced in effigy were marketed as the "Royal Baby" and introduced the vogue for baby dolls. (As distinct from the rather adult types presented by French and German makers up to the 1850 period.)

Dolls with china heads were certainly most popular during the latter half of the 19th century and the competition between French and German makers was very keen. The skilful artists who designed figurines produced some outstandingly beautiful doll faces, and when the 1914-18 war broke out and Staffordshire potters were challenged to make doll heads to replace the European imports, the results were often ludicrous. But the study of the English pottery doll is an interesting one, a collecting field in itself. Though some of the heads are crude or homely in feature they are rare and desirable since they were made only for a short period. Not many firms lasted for long after the Armistice.

Just before the War period (1914-18) various English firms had taken up the production of 'soft' toys with stuffed fabric—possibly the enormous popularity of the Teddy bear inspired makers to try and discover other 'winners' as well as their own version of a Teddy. Mascot dolls became popular during the War such as 'Fumsup' patented by Hamleys. "Thumbs Up" had the same optimistic significance as the Victory V sign in the Second World War. Various women's organisations undertook toy-making with the increased call-up of man power from factories.

With the end of the war and the impetus the home trade had received through a ban on German toys, some of these 'back-room' traders with clever artists designing for them became well-established and concentrated especially on dolls which portrayed well-known figures. Some were from the currently popular cinema (Charlie Chaplin, Felix the Cat, Jackie Coogan, Popeye the Sailor Man etc) or from strip cartoons in comics and newspapers: (Pop; Pip, Squeak and Wilfred; Rupert; Buster Brown). Other dolls represented characters renowned in public life: the little Princesses, Elizabeth (now Queen) and Margaret Rose, were of course especial favourites and the child film star Shirley Temple.

Obviously the four interesting aspects of doll manufacture I have outlined (wood, wax, china, rag) are not the whole of the story and there were various interesting individual inventions, some of them very short-lived in production and scarcely extending beyond the period of their patent. There are still many people alive who can recall the methods and history of past doll making and they have been invited to share their memories of places and personalities, artists and techniques.

The Dictionary does contain references to various foreign makers and firms and this is necessary for various reasons. Before the 1914/18 war there was a vast influence on toys from the continent of Europe. Foreign agents were established in London as a link to a factory in Germany, or a London merchant (such as J. Cremer) scoured European toy areas and returned with the ingredients for doll making, such as china heads, glass eyes etc, to be made up in England. When the First World War broke out some German merchants were interned here and later on organised an English trade (e.g. Kohnstam), even bringing German labour over to teach workers their craft. Finally, and importantly, some German makers, of famous toy-producing families, fled here from the Hitler purge of Jewish families and they added immensely to our English trade: men such as Philipp Ullmann from Nuremberg (Mettoy) and H. Schelhorn from Sonneberg (Telitoy). Even our new found china doll manufacture in the Potteries during the Great War owed much to the Germans, as existing German dolls were largely used as models.

Among the lists of patents for doll inventions registered in London some foreign names are included: this was done to protect their inventions from piracy in England. The whole question of patents registration is puzzling, since some of the names entered are those of agents rather than inventors, or of firms who marketed the doll rather than the actual manufacturer (e.g. Hamley's London shop). The existence of a patent does not always establish that a doll was produced commercially and many curious inventions intrigue us that seem doubtful since actual examples have never come to light. They perhaps proved unpopular, uneconomic or were made on a very small scale.

Finally it should be stressed that this present volume is the accumulation of research and study carried out over years by the staff of Pollock's Toy Museum plus the contribution of various private collectors interested in the project. In pooling our findings it has been our wish to establish a sort of national archive of doll lore whilst there are still veterans from the trade who can confirm facts. No doubt the story is unfinished and it will be left to future collectors to add further interesting facts and discover intriguing examples of English dolls from the past.

Publisher's Note

Because many companies changed their names frequently and products, too, were subject to variations in spelling e.g. Mr Jollyboy/Mr Jolliboy, some apparent inconsistencies may occur in the dictionary.

AABA. 1907. Trademark. See **James, Arthur William.**

AA SCOUT. 1930. See **Road Patrol Scouts.**

A & A MERCHANDISING CO. LTD. c1941. 1 Lauderdale Court, Aldergate, London EC1. From 1941 new factory at 51, Clarendon Road, London, W.11. Made dolls and soft toys. 1941 Fully jointed dolls with china and unbreakable heads. In 1953 advertised character dolls, baby and art dolls and soft toys. Obtained patent no. 626901 with N. Quinn for a movable eye lid for an eye in 1946, and no. 646745 relating to construction of eye in 1948. Trademark "A & A. Products".

'A1' DOLLS & TOYS. c1922. Brand name of Dean's Rag Book Co. Firm's trademark consisted of letter 'A' and '1' with words 'A 1' Quality and 'A 1' Value, plus earlier picture of two dogs tugging at a rag book. 1923 range included Dressed Disc Doll series, Sunbonnet babies, Cherub series, Kuddlemee dolls, Wendy, dressed, and her equivalent sold as a rag doll sheet.

ABBA DOLLS. Introduced 1978. Character merchandised dolls of famous Abba singing group dressed in authentic outfits used by the group. Dolls are fully jointed with rooted hair. Produced in Hong Kong for Lesney Products & Co. Ltd. Range comprises Anna, Frida, Bennie and Bjorn.

ABBEY HOUSE MUSEUM. Kirkstall, Leeds. Only a fifth of this enormous collection can be shown at any one time, and the displays are continually changed. Almost every kind of toy and game from the 18th century to the present day is represented, and a selection of modern toys is added each year. The doll collection includes a two-foot wooden doll from the Stuart period which has an elaborate stumpwork contemporary costume; and a Victorian doll, wearing a silk dress with a flowing train, which has a wardrobe of 8 dresses complete with underwear and accessories.

ABRAHAMS, HYMAN A., & SONS. 1913. At 30 St. Bride Street, London, EC. A wholesale company, selling dolls and toys of British manufacture. 1917 range included 'My Kiddie'—a doll in a white silk frock, 'British Babes'—stockinette dolls, 'Circus Girl'—a jointed clockwork dressed doll which gave an acrobatic display. Were also agents for Leda dolls. See **Fretwell Toy Manufacturing Co.**

Far right: Cut-out paper doll and dresses published by Rudolph Ackermann, 1830

Below and right: English dolls advertised by Hyman A Abrahams in 1916-17.

ABRAHAMS (TOYS) L. D. LTD. London. 1917. Dolls, toys and games wholesaler and importer. Stocked British Babies, Baby Bunting and Daddy-Long Legs.

ACKERMANN, Rudolph. 1764-1834. A German who opened a print shop in London in the late 18th century. He introduced lithography to England and translated a work by its inventor, Alois Senefelder. Some of the finest and earliest sets of paper doll dressing games are credited to him. There were *Poupée Modèle* (1830) card figures, 8½ ins. high, with 5 costumes hand-coloured cut-out etchings. Also (1819) *Interchangeable Ladies* and *Interchangeable Gentlemen* and *Endless Metamorphoses*, hand-coloured aquatints on little dissected cards of a type very much copied afterwards. See **Faulkner & Co. Ltd., C. W.**

THE ACORN TOY CO. LTD. c1944. 2, 4 and 4a Chillingworth Road, Holloway Road, London, N7. Made toys and dolls, Registered trademark of acorn on oak leaf, 31st October 1944. no. 632,399

ACTION GIRL. 1971. Fully articulated Palitoy doll with 14 joints. Can be posed in any position and has various outfits. In 1974 Dancing Action Girl was introduced; dressed in ball gown, she dances to specially composed pop record.

ACTION MAN. 1966. Male Palitoy doll with various outfits and accessories. Voted the toy of the year for 1966 by the National Association of Toy Retailers in England.

ACTIVE SINDY. 1975. A new Sindy doll by Pedigree, designed to capture nearly every possible human movement. She is dressed as a ballet dancer. See **Sindy Dolls; Pedigree Soft Toys Ltd.**

ADART, LTD. See **Photographic Dolls.**

ADLON WALKING DOLL. 1923. Unbreakable doll with stuffed body and papier mâché head and limbs, dressed in various cotton outfits and fitted with a 'ma-ma' voice. When held by the hand, the doll can be made to walk realistically. Sizes: 20″ and 24″. Sold by Whyte, Ridsdale.

ADORA TOYS LTD. London. 1945. Made dolls and toy animals. Registered trade mark 'Adora', Nos. 642, 199, 22nd November 1945. See **Thomas Industries (London) Ltd.**

ADVERTISING DOLLS. Dolls made to promote the name of some commercial product, e.g. Betty Oxo (for Oxo), made by Dean's; Bisto Kids by Cerebos; Miss Sue, a printed rag doll, made by Dean's to advertise Sue Flakes Beef Suet; the Wounded Soldier made by Dean's for Boots the Chemist;

The 'Adlon' walking doll with fitted 'mama' voice, sold by Whyte, Ridsdale & Co. Ltd., 1923

the first injection moulding machines to make injection moulded combs and by 1947 they were the largest comb manufacturers in England. In 1948 they were producing plastic dolls with movable arms and legs. The company expanded and ceased to be the Kove family concern; by 1957 they went public and became Airfix Industries. In 1962 they took over Semco Ltd., a doll-producing firm, but ceased manufacture in 1967 although they still retained the name. Airfix re-entered the doll market in 1976 with two rag dolls, Sweet Dreams and Lil' Sweet Dreams, which were manufactured in Taiwan, and 'Walking Baby Loves You', manufactured in Hong Kong. In 1977 they introduced 'Summertime Girls', a range of three fashion dolls and clothes sets, and 'Farrah', another fashion doll copying the features of Farrah Fawcett-Majors, the American actress of T.V's 'Charlie's Angels' fame. These dolls are manufactured in Hong Kong.

AIR HOSTESS. Introduced 1976. Dressed doll from Matchbox Disco Doll range made in Hong Kong for Lesney Products and Co. Ltd.

AIRMAN. Made by Dean's Rag Book Co. in 1917. Styled with patent 'Tru-to-Life' or ordinary flat face. Trench coats were supplied separately.

ALABASTER. Material of ancient Babylonian doll with movable arms in the British Museum. A translucent form of gypsum, the variety found near Paris was extensively used for the preparation of plaster of Paris. 18th century dolls referred to as 'alabaster' were probably moulded from this material; for instance, the "poupards" and a 4-foot-high doll called "Le Grand Courrier de la Mode", sent from Paris to London to display fashion.

In 1789 Miss Dorothea Herbert compiled, at the age of 19, a little manuscript book for the amusement of her nine brothers and sisters. It was based on her childhood diaries, and in it it recalls how in 1777 she and her mother made a trip to the fashionable watering-place of Bath, and brought back to Ireland a large alabaster doll. 'We now', she wrote, 'had another addition to the family which afforded the young folk much amusement. We christened her Miss Watts, after one of the beautiful Miss Wattses of Pill'. She was obviously a fashionable-looking doll, perhaps made of wood with a face of moulded plaster.

ALBANY TOY COMPANY. c1919. Manufactured soft toys and dolls.

ALBECK, PAT. See **Cuckoobird.**

ALDERSON, M. W. Obtained patent no. 14511 relating to arrangement of dolls' hands so that small objects could be held in them. September 1890.

Jimmy Whiteshine for advertising a polish. Other firms adopted a doll as a mascot or trademark: e.g. Robertson's jams, with the famous golliwog.

AEROLITE. 1923. Trademark for printed rag dolls, registered by Chad Valley. Series included Peggy, Sonia, Peter Pan, Pixie, Red Cloud.

AILION, J., & CO. 1936. At 44 Hatton Garden, London E.C.1. Doll and toy wholesalers and agents. In 1936 they advertised

Hungarian costume dolls, Czechoslovakian costume dolls and Gypsy dolls, possibly made by Toy Time Toys Ltd., for whom they were agents c1937.

AIRFIX PRODUCTS LTD. 1939-1977+. 1945 at 5 & 6 Eden Street, London, NW1. By 1955 at Haldane Place, Garratt Lane, London, SW18. The company was formed in 1939 by Mr Nicholas Kove for the manufacture of rubber toys filled with air. During the war years the firm made rattles and saw-cut plastic combs. Later they installed some of

The original Alice in Wonderland.
Photograph of Alice Liddell by Lewis Carroll

ALDIS, FREDERICK. 1878-1901. 61, 63 &
65 Buckingham Palace Road, London SW.
& 10-13 Belgrave Mansions, London, SW.
Doll maker and doll importer. Sold Pierotti
dolls.

ALDON STUDIOS. 1921. See **Zobeide.**

ALERT DOLL. c1916. See **Lindop, W.**

ALDRED, Thomas. 1881-1903. London.
Made and imported dolls; used Pierotti wax
heads for some of his dolls.

ALICE. 1952. See **Pin-Up Dolls.**

ALICE. 1961. A Palitoy Petalskin vinyl doll
with long rooted hair, blonde or brunette. 3
sizes, 13″, 15″ and 17″. A 'Belinda' range doll.

ALICE IN WONDERLAND DOLLS.
Dolls made after Lewis Carroll's book was
published in 1865. The dolls were modelled
on the illustrations by Sir John Tenniel.

ALICE IN WONDERLAND. 1973. 23″
walking talking Palitoy doll, based on the
film, wearing traditional blue dress and
pinafore. At the touch of a button, the doll
told stories lasting 1 minute and featuring
the voice of actress Fiona Fullerton, star of
1972 film 'Alice's Adventures in Wonderland'.

Prototype of 'Alice', designed by Faith Eaton.
One of a set commissioned by
H.M. Government to accompany a gift of
books by Lewis Carroll to the
Toy Museum in New Delhi.

ALLAM, Miss Ruth. 1939. 39 Glenthorne Road, Hammersmith, London, W6. Recorded in 'Kelly's Street Directory' as doll repairer in 1939.

ALLBRIT DOLLS. See **All British Doll Manufacturing Co.**

ALL BRITISH DOLL MANUFACTURING CO. June 1915—c1919. Addresses: 5, 7 & 9 Carver Street, Sheffield and 202 Brookhill, near Sheffield. Firm began by making rag dolls; it soon extended to produce jointed dolls in papier mâché or kid, with sleeping, winking, etc. eyes. In 1917 became sole owner of Eugene Sandow's patent for a 'physical exerciser' in form of a doll or toy, e.g. Boy Scout, Dolly Dimple, and Teddy Spring Bear. Also made human and mohair dolls' wigs. Trade mark: 'Allbrit'.

ALLEN, FREDERICK H. LTD. 1941. 3 The Broadway, London, N11. Wholesaler of toys and dolls.

ALLWIN. 1935. Trade mark of Richards, Son and Allwin.

Shirley Temple doll and trade mark of Richards, Son & Allwin, 1936

ALMAR DOLLS LTD. Est. 1964. 5a Gransden Avenue, London, E8. Directors: Albert and Mary Dorsett. Manufacturers of military and traditional costume dolls. 1966 range includes English and Scottish soldiers, Beefeaters, Policeman, Scottish Girl Pipers, Bride Doll. All 7½" tall, costumes designed by Mary Dorsett. Retail 15s to 25s. 1968 range includes: London Cockney Boy and Girl, Union Jack & Union Jill. 1973 range includes Henry VIII and his wives. 1974 range includes Austrian Boy and Girl and Miss Spain. In 1975 the company introduced a 'Make your own Traditional Costume Doll' kit, containing 8" doll with sleeping eyes and movable arms, material and glue etc. 8 different models: Horse Guard, Rifle Guard, Scots Girl Drummer, Irish Colleen, Scots Piper, Beefeater, Girl Piper and Welsh Girl.

ALPHA CHERUB DOLLS. 1935. Trade mark no. 561,979 registered by J.K. Farnell & Co. Ltd., for dolls on August 2nd 1935. The dolls Tennis Girl, Farm Boy, Village Belle etc. were soft, life-like replicas of real children dressed in contemporary children's clothes (1935). Retail price 15s 11d.

ALPHA 'JOY DAY' DOLLS. 1935. range of 6 dolls including Sailor Boy, Dutch Girl, School Girl. Retail price 9s 11d. Made by J.K. Farnell & Co. Ltd.

ALPHA PICCANINNIES. 1936. Nigger doll series comprising 6 styles. J.K. Farnell & Co. Ltd.

ALPHA SMILERS. 1935. Range of 6 dolls: Airman, Sailor, Sweep, Dutch Boy, Soldier and Page Boy. 2s.11d each. J.K. Farnell & Co. Ltd.

ALRESFORD CRAFTS LTD. The Town Mill, Alresford, Hampshire. Soft toy company founded by John Jones. In 1977 the company employed a ceramics manager from Stoke-on-Trent and branched out into the manufacture of English porcelain dolls with soft cloth bodies.

AMALGAMATED IMPEX (LONDON) LTD. c1949. 19 Russell Street, London, WC2. Wholesaler or distributor of baby doll (produced by Simpsons of Surrey) representing Prince Charles, elder son of Queen Elizabeth II of England.

AMANDA DOLL Registered trademark for dolls. See **Kove, Nicholas.**

AMANDA JANE LTD. Halfway Bridge, Petworth, West Sussex. The firm was founded in 1952 by Conrad and Elsin Rawnsley who operated from a flat in Great Portland Street, London, W1. originally designing and making dolls' shoes, boots and accessories for West End stores. In 1957 the company moved to Sussex and expanded their activities to the making and

'Alpha Cherub' dolls made by J K Farnell & Co. Ltd., 1935

wholesaling of vast varieties of dolls' clothes and accessories including brushes, combs, umbrellas, jewellery, hats, socks and stockings. At this time they had 100 items in their range. In 1963 the ownership/management changed hands and from this point onwards, the company specialised in the production of one small doll called 'Amanda Jane' and a small range of about 20 different outfits for her. No individual accessories were sold. In 1972 the company introduced an 'Amanda Jane Baby' doll. In 1977 their range comprises the two dolls, each with its own range of outfits and each with 1 to 2 main accessories. 40-45% of the company's production is for export.

AMARA DESIGNS (POTTERS BAR) LTD. Unit 4, Alston Works, Alston Road, Barnet, Hertfordshire. Toy, puppet and rag doll manufacturers. 1975 range includes souvenir rag dolls: Policeman, Beefeater, Guardsman and Welsh Girl in traditional costume.

AMERICAN KIDDIE. 1918. Soft stuffed stockinette doll made by Fretwell Manufacturing Co.

AMERSHAM WORKS LTD. See **Rees, Leon**

AMY JOHNSON DOLL. Amy Johnson (1903-41) was a pioneer aviator. She made the first solo flight from Britain to Australia in 1930. In the war she flew transport planes, but disappeared presumed crashed.

ANGEL, L. V. & NUNN, G.L. 241 Great Homer Street, and 8 Ellerslie Road, Tuebrook, Liverpool. Obtained patent no. 114, 327 for manufacture of moulded or cast composition dolls or toys in June 1918. See **Nunn & Smeed.**

ANGELO DOLL. 1907. See **Gibbons, Charles Kendrick.**

ANITA. 1946. Doll made by Unity Pack Co.

ANKIDOODLE. 1927. Trade mark no. 478,714 registered by John Jacoby Ikle Ltd. London, for dolls, games and toys.

ANNA. 1978. See **Abba Dolls.**

ANNA and HAPPYTIME. 1977. See **Pedigree Soft Toys Ltd.**

ANNE. 1948. 3″ high plastic doll with movable arms and legs, made by Airfix Products Ltd.

ANNE, PRINCESS. Many dolls were made with likeness of Elizabeth II's daughter born in 1952. A portrait doll in wedding dress was produced by Honor Wilson after a model by Jane McSweeny 1973.

ANNE BATHTIME SET. 1955. 12″ Palitoy doll complete with bathtub, "totty" pot, feeding bottle, powder, soap and sponge.

Applehead Pedlar Doll, 1830

ANN PARKER DOLLS. See **Parker, Ann.**

APPLEHEAD PEDLAR DOLLS. Pickled or dried apples were often used by country people to make heads for dolls. The apples were carved to indicate features and then were dipped in vinegar, lightly salted and air-dried on a stick propped in a bottle neck. When dry and leathery after about 3 to 6 weeks, the faces could be painted and the stick served as a base for a rudimentary body. See **Emergent Dolls** and **Home Made Dolls.**

ARMITAGE, H. K. 1925. Haddington, Scotland. Obtained patent no. 254,105 for a diving doll on June 25th, 1925.

ARNOLD, M.O. 1904. 4 Corporation Street, Manchester. Obtained patent no. 11356 for a mechanical doll on wheels on May 17th, 1904. Also obtained patent no. 13824 for improvements in doll bodies containing phonographs, in 1908.

ARRETON MANOR. Near Newport, Isle of Wight. Besides much else of interest, this Jacobean manor house has an extensive display of toys. There are about 100 dolls in superb condition and beautifully dressed, including French fashion dolls and English wax dolls, two of which were made by Pierotti. There are also dolls' accessories and dolls' clothes.

ART DOLLS. Miniature models by J.S. Sant, 17 Coleman St, London EC2. made from wax over plaster: Salome, Du Barry, Daphne Priscilla and also a mechanical walking Felix 1924.

The Nell Foy Co. Church St, Chelsea 1918 made wax statuettes and dolls with a waxed finish over composition head representing famous actresses: Doris Keane as she appeared in Romance; Gaby Deslys in The Fairy Queen. Also Character dolls. See **Nellfoy & Co.; Sant, J.S.**

ART FABRIC MANUFACTURING CO. Established 4 November 1913-1916. 75 Queen Victoria Street, London, EC. Made rag dolls and toys. Took over business of Art Fabric Mills, Textile Novelty Co., British Rag Doll Co. and Shynall Rag Doll Co. in November, 1913.

ART FELT DOLLS. See **Felt.**

ARTHUR ASKEY DOLL. c1942. Character doll based on 'big-hearted' Arthur Askey, popular radio comedian of the era. Made by Dean's Rag Book Co Ltd., under licence held by W.O.P. Gibb, Brownlow House, 50-51, High Holborn, London, WC1.

ARTISTIC DOLLS LTD. c1946. Doll manufacturer. 144 Holland Park Avenue, London, W11.

ART MASTER OF CHELSEA LTD. 1975. 1 Commerce Road, Brentford, Middlesex. Manufacturers of art and craft products. In 1975 introduced Costume Doll Kits to their range. Individual kits contain a 9″ doll with fabric, trimmings, patterns and glue to make costumes. Range comprises 18 different kits, 9 historical and 9 national costumes.

ART PLASTICS LTD. c1950. Aycliffe, London, South Shields, Durham. Made unbreakable dolls in 'art plastics'—baby dolls, dressed jointed dolls, girl dolls, 13 to 20 inches high. Distributors: J. Cowan (Dolls) Ltd.

ART STATUE CO. c1918. 14 Featherstone Buildings, High Holborn, London, WC1. Made complete dolls or parts in type of unbreakable composition named 'Tuftex'. 1918 advertisement shows baby dolls, fitted with glass eyes. Also made toys.

Arthur Askey dolls, 1942

ART TOY MANUFACTURING CO. LTD. c1919. In 1919 at 46 Fitzroy Square, London, W1. In 1920 at 71b Gowan Avenue, Fulham, London, SW6. Toy and doll manufacturers. Made 'Bathing Jeff' and 'Misska' dolls—kapok-stuffed, plush-covered soft dolls in various colours. According to a trade magazine, buyers said Misska was a potential rival to the Teddy Bear. Made 'Misska' Dutch Boys and Pierrots, also tea cosies surmounted by a miniature 'Misska' doll in 1920. Trade mark: 'Bathing Jeff' no. 398, 924 registered on 30 December, 1919.

ASSAEL, Gabriel Mentech. 1919-1925. 66 Highbury Grove, London, N1. Showrooms Byron House, 2 & 4 Finsbury Street, London, EC. Wholesaler of English and French dolls and toys, manufacturer of dolls. Changed firm's name to Assael's United Agencies before 1945.

ASTON & CO. c1949. Basingstoke. Advertised miniature crinoline dolls in pastel wools, 3½″ tall.

ASTON HALL. Trinity Road, Birmingham. One room, arranged as a Victorian nursery, has typical toys and children's furniture including a pedlar doll and a rocking horse.

Art Fabric Mills rag dolls, 1912

ATKINSON, A. & CONWAY, M. Obtained patent no. 14959 on 4 July 1904, for a jointed doll riding on a bicycle.

ATKINSON, Mrs Sue. 7 Park Drive, East Sheen, London. Attempt to produce a loveable modern play doll led to the making of Emma, 22″ Victorian type rag doll with embroidered face, wool ringlets and removeable clothes. Later teamed up with Nyna Denby who contributed painted felt mask for large cloth doll inspired by Mary in "The Secret Garden". Resin was used for moulding "Georgina", an Armand Marseille type doll with cloth body, followed by a French bébé style dressed Kate Greenaway in modern materials. 1975.

ATLANTIC RUBBER CO. LTD. c1923. Address 167 Moorgate, London, EC2. Manufacturers. Registered 'Toggy' trade mark no. 437, 414 for toys, 22 May, 1923.

ATLAS MANUFACTURING CO. 1916. Stanley Row, Woodford, London NE. Produced simple stuffed dolls and dressed animals.

ATTWELL, Mabel Lucie. An artist born in London 1879. (d. 1964). The plump and impish little children which filled her story books and postcards were popular with toy designers. Models were made up for Chad Valley in fabric and for Cascelloid Co. in rubber and celluloid. The postcards were issued by Valentine's, Dundee, Scotland and were

'Sophie', 'Emma' and 'Georgina': rag dolls made by Sue Atkinson, 1979

'Hygienic' rag dolls designed by Mabel Lucie Attwell for Chad Valley, c. 1920

especially successful as they appeared during the 1914-18 war when people needed to correspond in absence. In consequence mascot dolls such as Diddums, Little Happy and Fumsup (trademark registered by Hamley's) also sold very well. See **Cascelloid; Chad Valley; Hamley Bros.**

AUDLEY END HOUSE. Saffron Walden, Essex. Visitors to this palatial Jacobean mansion should look out for a large Georgian dolls' house on display there.

AUNT SALLY. An early form of fairground amusement: a lifesize puppet made of wood, depicting an old woman. (*Aunt* stood for any old crone in Shakespearian times and *Sally* meant to throw). The game was to hurl heavy sticks and knock off her nose or a clay pipe from her mouth. Wooden toy dolls were sold during the '20s but the aim was to throw rings on to a wooden pipe like a hoopla.

AUSTIN GRAY LTD. Langdon Road, Highgate, London; from 1934 Derby Road, East Sheen, London, SW14. Made soft dolls including cabaret and art dolls, e.g. Beach Belle, Sailor. Also made soft toys and novelties. 1936 range includes 'Saucy Joyce', a soft doll with goo-goo eyes.

B.U.T. LTD. c1936. 518 Caledonian Road, London, N7; also from 1949 at Pickering Street, Essex Street, London, N1. Doll manufacturers, wholesale and export. Had German factory, Edmund Edelmann of Sonneberg. Made (possibly in Germany) 'Hansa Dolls' brand of character dolls, baby dolls (1936); a jointed composition doll 'Baby Shirley' with sleeping eyes and lashes (1948). Firm's additional premises acquired in 1949 in order to install up-to-date machinery probably for injection moulding of plastics.

BABA DOLLS. 1936. Doll series made by Dean's Rag Book Co. Ltd.

BABBLING BABY. 1970. 18″ talking baby doll, made by Palitoy. It makes baby noises using record mechanism contained in its back, powered by 1½ volt battery.

BABES IN THE WOOD. 1916. See **Tah Toys.**

BABETTE. 1926. See **Dean & Son Ltd.**

BABETTE. c1931. Soft felt doll with hand-painted face, advertised as "just as stylish and just as attractive as the best Italian dolls" and much cheaper. Made by Leon Rees & Co.

BABS. 1927. Velvet cuddly doll by Mabel Bland-Hawkes.

BABS. 1933. Soft doll made of wool plush with "natural baby face". Made by J. K. Farnell & Co.

BABS. 1936. Baby doll with soft body, unbreakable head, sleeping eyes and movable limbs. East London Toy Factory Ltd.

BABS. 1955. A 'Roddy' plastic baby doll 13″ to 21″ in a short dress with puffed sleeves, and a sunbonnet. Made by D. G. Todd & Co. Ltd.

BABY. See **Doll.**

BABY. Introduced 1920. Fully jointed composition doll with china head and glass eyes, in 3 sizes. 5 styles of mohair wigs. Dressed in white, lace-trimmed dress with wide sash. Dummy in mouth. Made by Speights Ltd.

BABY. 1937. See **Spear, J. W., & Sons**

BABY ALIVE. Introduced 1974. Soft cuddly Palitoy baby doll who 'eats' her 'food' like a real baby. 9 different types of 'food' provided.

B.U.T. 'Baby Shirley', 1948

'Babette'. Leon Rees & Co., 1931

BABY ANGEL. 1967. Baby doll in 24″ high chair, complete with bowl, cup and feeding bottle. Manufactured by Rosebud Mattel Ltd.

BABY BETTY. 1928. Life-like kapok-stuffed doll made by Dean's Rag Book Co. with hand-painted face, glass eyes and finely modelled velvet limbs. Dressed in long organdie robe with lace insert. Made in 3 sizes: 14 ins, 16 ins. and 20 ins.

BABY BOY. 1919. Doll in muslin robe made by Three Arts Women's Employment Fund Toy Industry.

BABY BUNNY. 1916. See **Tah Toys.**

BABY BUNTING. Dolls made by firms to represent the nursery rhyme character, presumably a first soft toy for an infant: Bunting is an old form of endearment for a plump little child and the doll usually wore either a fur or woolly all-in-one outfit with rabbit ears. The lullaby is old and variously written:

> Bye, baby bunting
> Daddy's gone a-hunting
> Gone to get a rabbit skin
> To wrap the baby bunting in.

In Scotland it reads "lammie's skin": See **Abrahams (Toys) Ltd; Dean's Rag Book Co. Ltd; Hawksley & Co. Ltd; Hughes & Sons; Worthing Toy Factory.**

BABY BUNTING. 1923. doll based on the 'baby dressed in rabbit skin' from the nursery rhyme song. Made by Dean's Rag Book Co. Ltd. The doll has a 'Tru-to-life' face and patent 'Evripose' joints. Assorted shades of mohair plush, stuffed with down. 10″, 12″ & 15″.

BABY BUNTY. Soft plastic doll with detachable soother, price 6d. Sold by Val Green, 1948.

BABY CARROTS. c1916. See **Houghton, Elizabeth Ellen.**

BABY DOLL CO. LTD. 1949. 3 Oxford Street, London, WI. Manufacturers and dealers in dolls, toys and novelties.

'Baba'. Dean's Rag Book Co., 1936

'Babs'. J K Farnell & Co. Ltd., 1933

'Baby Bunting'. Dean's Rag Book Co., 1923

BABY DOLLS. 1928. Made by Dean's Rag Book Co. Stuffed kapok and dressed in knitted Shetland suits with ribbon trim. 14″, 16″ and 20″.

BABY FIRST LOVE. 1974. Moulded vinyl baby doll with floppy limbs and head who 'behaves just like a real tiny baby before muscles have developed.' Made by Pedigree Dolls Ltd.

BABY FIRST STEP. 1967. Blonde-haired walking doll made by Rosebud Mattel Ltd.

BABY GIRL. 1919. Doll in muslin dress made by Three Arts Women's Employment Fund Toy Industry.

BABY JONATHAN. 1977. Doll made by H. Schelhorn & Co.

BABYKINS. 1962. Chiltern 'suck-thumb' vinyl doll. Fully jointed with sleeping eyes and soft curled lashes and rooted honey-coloured washable hair. It comes in dress, romper suit or swaddling clothes with blanket 15″ & 21″. Made by H. G Stone & Co. Ltd.

BABY LOVE. 1972. Palitoy doll range consisting of 3 dolls and play sets: 'Avril's Bathtime', doll with bathtime and feeding accessories; 'Connie in her Carrycot', doll with bedtime accessories; and 'Lisa's Trousseau', a baby doll with outfits.

BABY MARY. 1934. Excella range doll made by L. Rees & Co. Ltd.

BABY MAYBE. 1967. 14″ Palitoy doll.

BABYMINE. c1927-c1939. Range of baby dolls dressed in baby clothes, made by Norah Wellings. Registered design no. 723 934.

BABY NORENE. c1934. Range of high class soft dolls made by Norah Wellings.

BABY PEGGY. 1924. Stuffed rag doll made by Dean's Rag Book Co. Ltd., in the likeness of the American child film actress Diana Cary, known as 'Baby Peggy'.

BABY ROYAL. 1923. Life size baby doll by Mabel Bland-Hawkes

BABY SHIRLEY. "Mama" doll with sleeping eyes and eyelashes and dressed in organdie, silk, velvet or cotton. Made by B. U. T. Ltd in 1948.

BABY TENDER LOVE. 1972. Doll by Mattel Ltd.

BABY TODDLES. 1932. A British-made doll. According to 'Games and Toys' for June 1932, 'A handsome production retailed at remarkably cheap prices and a credit to British Manufacture'.

BABY VAMP. 1921. See **Lawton Doll Co.**

BABY WALK ALONE. Introduced 1967. Battery-operated walking doll 15″ tall with golden hair. Walks in baby fashion when button in back is pressed. Made by Pedigree Dolls Ltd.

Baby doll. Dean's Rag Book Co.,1928

Baby doll in long clothes. Dean's Rag Book Co., 1928

BAILEY, Doris Sylvia, BAXTER, Sarah Jane. 1916. Longton, Staffordshire. Obtained patent no. 102797 on 20th July, 1916 for coating doll parts with wax. Busts, bodies, arms and legs were first fired and painted; then the unglazed porcelain, earthenware or plaster of Paris was dipped in transparent wax and heated to 250 degrees. After draining and cooling, it was dipped again for a second coat and finally, in order to produce a glossy appearance, it was dipped into cold water.

BAILEY POTTERIES LTD. c1940. Duke Street, Fenton, Stoke-on-Trent. Pottery which made dressed and undressed "Lo-La" dolls; also doll's heads and limbs.

BAILEY'S AGENCIES LTD. c1946. Wholesaler of dolls, toys and games.

BAIRNTOYS. 1920. See **Foster, Blackett & Wilson Ltd.**

BAKELITE XYLONITE LTD. Coalville, Leicestershire. Originally British Xylonite Ltd. In 1937 took over Cascelloid Ltd. and Palitoy Production. In 1968 sold toy division, Palitoy, to General Mills Inc. of U.S.A. See **Cascelloid.**

BAKER, CHAS. W. 1916. 36a Northampton Street, Essex Road, London, N. Manufacturers' representative for dressed and undressed dolls with china heads and wigs and other games and toys. He was related to Miss Rebecca Baker of London, SE14, who was listed as a toy maker in 1918.

BALL JOINTS. See **Joints.**

BAMBETTA. 1936. Doll made by Chad Valley.

BAMBINA DOLLS. 1932. Series of soft dolls with jointed velveteen limbs and painted features. Can be dressed and undressed. Designed by Mabel Lucie Attwell; manufactured by Chad Valley Ltd.

BAMBINO. c1916. See **Houghton, Elizabeth Ellen.**

BANTOCK HOUSE MUSEUM. Bantock Park, Wolverhampton. This museum has a good display of tourist, ethnographic and folk dolls to complement its collection of conventional play dolls. Most doll types are represented—early wooden dolls, papier mâché, wax, porcelain, rag, bisque, celluloid and composition.

BARBER, V. S. 1932. London. Obtained patent no. 388951 on 20th April, 1932, for a doll 'comprising an articulated trunk and a series of interchangeable heads, the limbs being permanently attached to the trunk. The trunk and limbs conform to the actual shape of the human figure, and the heads are each complete and represent characters or features. Means are provided for detaching and for securing any one of the heads to the trunk'.

'Baby Peggy' - the American child film actress Diana Cary

Doll made by Sunlight, Sieve & Co., and advertised by C W Baker, 1916

BARKER, Florence Annie (née Rees). The Oaks, Huddersfield Road, Mirfield, Yorks, January 9 1905: patent 7899 for dolls made of fabric and filled with rose petals, lavender, etc and dressed to represent the plant involved. Trademark: circle containing E and eye.

BARRETT, L. Obtained patent no. 420, 361 for a doll which has a sound-producing apparatus combined with or adjacent to it, March 28th, 1933.

BARTHOLOMEW BABIES. The name for brightly dressed dolls sold at the Annual Bartholomew Fair celebrated at Smithfield, London from the 12th century. 17th century Customs records show that wooden toys and "Babies and puppets for children" were imported from Europe, as well as "Babies' heads of earth the dozen". But it is assumed that many of the Bartholomew babies were English wooden dolls. They are mentioned often in literature.

> "Her petticoat of satin
> Her gown of crimson tabby
> Laced up before, and
> spangled o'er
> Just like a Bartholomew
> Baby"

(1683 Wit and Drollery).
"Packed up like a Barthol'mew baby in a box": 1638. A character in Ben Jonson's play "Bartholomew Fair" (1614) speaks of the dolls as both male and female: See **Clapham Dolls.**

BARTHOLOMEW, Marjorie Lilian. Manufacturer and merchant of 2, Westbury Lane, Buckhurst Hill, Essex. Registered 'Marty' Trademark no. 795, 588 for dolls and soft toys, September 18th, 1959.

BARTLEY, Ena Marjorie. 34 Wake Green Road, Moseley, Birmingham 13. Merchant. Registered trademark 'Rhythmbar' no. 717, 606 on May 8th, 1953, for dolls, soft toys and card games.

BARTON, John. 1847—56. 2 Constitution Road, Gray's Inn Road, London. Wax doll maker. 1852-55.

BATGER. 'Confectioners and Chocolate makers since 1748', Ratcliff, London E. In 1915 were making wax and composition dolls with well-moulded features, also Christmas stockings and crackers.

BATHING JEFF. Rag doll made by Art Toy Manufacturing Co. Ltd. 1919.

BATHTIME BABY SETS. 1955. Palitoy range of various dolls and bath accessories including 'Babs', and 8″ vinyl flexible doll plus bathtub, comforter, feeding bottle, toilet accessories and tea set.

BATT, JOHN & CO. London doll-maker. Registered trademark 1883: a Bat.

Above: Advertisement in Games & Toys, October 1922

Below: Bartholomew Fair, 1721. Part of a drawing on a fan.

BATTS, Thomas. Also known as BETTS. See **Betts.**

BAUMAN, Victor. 1900-18. 1900 at 2 Bunhill Row, London, EC. 1918 at 29 Fann Street, London, EC1. Composition doll maker and wholesaler.

BAYLY, J. P. Obtained patent no. 15610 on October 2nd 1890, for attaching limbs of dolls and animals and other moving figures.

BAZZONI, Anthony. 1826-55. At 128 High Holborn, London. 1868: 14 Queen's Square, London WC. c1843-1878. Made wax, composition and 'speaking dolls'. Claimed to be inventor and sole maker in London of the 'speaking' doll, in interview with Henry Mayhew in the Morning Chronicle, c1850.

BEACH BABY. 1932. Soft stuffed doll with velvet limbs, dressed in pretty print dresses. Manufactured by Dean's Rag Book Co. Ltd.

BEACH BELLE. Art doll made by Austin Gray Ltd., 1934.

BEACH, M. P. Obtained patent no. 211,602 for sponge-stuffed doll covered with turkey towelling. December 1st, 1922.

BEAKY-BA. 1912. Registered trademark for dolls and toys: See **Eisenmann & Co.**

BEAN DOLLS. See **Burbank Toys.**

BEAUTY DOLL. 1921. See **Lawton Doll Co.**

BEAUTY-SKIN DOLL. c1948. Made by Pedigree Soft Toys Ltd. 'Beauty Skin' was the name given to new 'lightweight rubber skin', of latex rubber, which was washable and unbreakable, and used for body and limbs. The doll had a stuffed body and injection-moulded plastic head with sleeping eyes and lashes. The head was designed by a sculptor who specialized in dolls.

BEAUTY SPOTS or PATCHES. Following the current fashion, dolls of the late 17th. and early 18th. century often have painted beauty spots. In 1660 the diarist Pepys recorded "My wife seemed very pretty today, it being the first time I had given her leave to wear a black patch". The affectation of a 'mole' to offset beauty seems to have originated in Classical times, and was fashionable in 17th. century French court circles. When Charles I married Henrietta Maria in 1625, fashion spread to England. Patches were of velvet or taffeta and in a variety of shapes, even a coach and horses! As a candlelight adornment they also had a language of sentiment according to where they were fixed on the face.

BE-BE (DOLLS) LIMITED. c1941. 13 Church Street, Ringstead, Kettering, Northamptonshire. Manufacturers of soft toys and dolls. In 1950 the 'Blue Ribbon' Playthings range included hardbody dolls which were for export only. Registered trademark 'Comfy-Glow' no. 760,390 on December 11th, 1956 for teddybears, dolls and puppets. The company was still in existence in 1976, producing a range of soft toys, nightdress cases and musical push-along toys.

BECK BRIGHT. 1966. Zany, long-legged doll with wide skirt forming a nightdress case. Made by Dean's Childsplay Toys Ltd.

BECKINGTON PRAM, DOLLS & TOY MUSEUM. Beckington, near Frome, Somerset. The 17th century mansion houses a good collection of toys, dolls in period costume and baby carriages.

BECK, Isabelle and Hedy. See **Eye Manor.**

BEDFORD MUSEUM. The Embankment, Bedford. This old-style museum has a varied assortment of exhibits, including a small collection of dolls and toys. There is a wax fairy doll in original clothes and some tiny 1930's dolls.

BEDINGTON LIDDIATT & CO. LTD. Established 1911. 4-7 Chiswell Street, 2 New Zealand Avenue, Barbican, London, EC. 1913 at 22-3 Hamsell Street, Jewin Street, London, EC. 1919 at 16-18 Bayer Street, Golden Lane, London, EC1. Manufacturers and merchants of games and toys and agents for American and Japanese dolls and toys. In 1917 they produced Plastolite dolls' heads. They used the trademark 'Tessted

---

THE

SPEAKING DOLL!

A. BAZZONI,

MANUFACTURER OF WAX & COMPOSITION DOLLS,

AND

Maker of the Speaking-Doll,

No. 128,

High Holborn.

RESPECTFULLY informs the juvenile portion of the Female Nobility, Gentry, and the Public, that after a succession of experiments, he has finally succeeded in imparting the wonderful Faculty of SPEECH to his DOLLS, which for neatness of Workmanship, and elegance of Costume, defy competition. For the unprecedented patronage with which he has been honoured, he returns his grateful acknowledgments; it will be his undeviating study to merit a continuance of their kind Favours.

LINES ON THE SPEAKING DOLL.

IN modern times "Inventions" are the rage,	With modest aspect charm the raptur'd sight,
And scheming minds in mighty tasks engage;	And many a *Miss* has kiss'd them with delight.
Steam-boats, *Steam-coaching*, and the brilliant blaze	"Papa!" "Mama!" his little Nymphs exclaim,
Of *Gas*, are wonders of these pregnant days;	And with their own proclaim their maker's fame.
Newspapers, too, the terror of bad Kings,	Unlike those figures which were made of old,
Are work'd by *Steam*, as swift as Morning's wings,	Unseemly shap,d, and in their features bold,
Old England's glory is maintain'd by *vapour*,	Mere rough-hewn blocks, like Otaheite's Gods,
And *Steam* will keep it longer than her *Paper*.	Before whose *Majesties* that *nation* nods!
Blest Peace continue our fair Isle to guard,	Ye rising Fair, to Merit give its due,
The Arts to prosper, Genius to reward;	BAZZONI's Art has giv'n a Treat to you.
If *Foes* should threaten, soon they'd be undone,	Nature his copy, he has giv'n it just—
They'd dread the pow'r of our *Percussion Gun.*	The perfect semblance of the human bust.
No plan like this e'er mov'd BAZZONI's mind,	And what sweet Miss in all her blooming charms
To Peace and Arts from infancy inclin'd.	Would not embrace his Smilers in her arms?
In nightly study its sole aim to reach—	For to be sage, the Muse (though rather droll),
His DOLLS have now the Faculty of SPEECH!	Infers that Miss who "dearly doats" on Doll,
They are as comely, and as bright and fair,	Imbibes a love, as tender as 'tis true,—
As e'er was Beauty in the balmy air;	A love to kindred which is justly due!

LEWIS AND CO. PRINTERS, 96, BUNHILL ROW.

Toys', and in March 1932 they registered the trade mark 'Baby Dimples' no. 530, 377 for dolls produced by the American firm E.I. Horsman Company. See **Plastolite.**

BEDSIE. 1971. See **Ploppy Character Dolls.**

BEDTIME BABY DOLLS. 1928. Cuddly little dolls made by Dean's Rag Book Co. Dressed in neat little sleeping suits of pink and blue 'fluffdown' cloth 14″, 16″ and 20″.

BEEFEATER DOLL. A rag doll in the likeness of a Beefeater of the Tower of London. Made by Dean's Rag Book Co. in 1953, the year of Queen Elizabeth II's Coronation. Also Guardsman, Peeress and London Policeman in same series.

BELINDA. 1949. All-rubber doll with movable head and limbs (the latter are detachable and replaceable) and sleeping eyes. Made by North's Rubber Co. Ltd.

BELINDA. 1960. 17″ Palitoy sports girl doll, made of Petalskin vinyl, with ponytail-style rooted hair and sleeping eyes. 'A typical modern Miss' in brushed nylon sweater and trousers, shoes, socks and earrings.

BELISHA BEA CONEY. 1935. Bunting-type doll with rabbit ears made by Dean's Rag Book Co. Ltd.

BELL BOY. 1929. Hotel bell boy doll with bell in his hand. Made by Dean's Rag Book Co. Ltd.

BELLE. 1922. See **Lawton Doll Co.**

BELLES OF BRIGHTON. 1955. 28″ walking dolls made by Pedigree. Dressed in specially designed clothes. Dolls walk, talk, sit, stand or sleep and have Saran hair which can be brushed or combed.

BELL & FRANCIS. Established 1906. 1' Willowbrook Grove, Trafalgar Road, London, SE. 1910. Premises at 29 Bread Street, London, EC. Advertised various rag dolls and cloth dolls stuffed with Swedish wood-wool, a product for which they were the agents. 1915: 'Munition' doll—a doll dressed as a girl ammunition maker, with protective overall and mob cap. Also Red Cross Nurse, Dutch Girl, Red Riding Hood, Baby doll and Pierrot at 1s retail. Empire doll, Khaki soldier, French Soldier at 1s 6d retail. In 1920 advertised unbreakable composition dolls—dressed baby dolls with soothers and undressed baby and girl dolls.

BELL (TOYS AND GAMES) LTD. c1942—. Primus House, Willow Street, London, EC2. Made toys, games and dolls. 'Bell' trademark. 1945 lines include a paper dressing doll with 8 different outfits.

'Beauty Spots or Patches'. 1690-1700. English or Scottish lady - carved wooden head, wooden body, jointed legs.

BELL, W. Obtained patent no. 111,745 relating to mechanism for moving dolls' eyes, January 9th 1917.

BELLOID CO. LTD. 1948. Downpatrick, Northern Ireland. Advertised hard-bodied baby and boy dolls, also dolls' heads. P.V.C. baby dolls, glass eyes & mama voices.

BENCO DURA. Mark on pateless shoulder heads made by the Dura Porcelain Co.

BENDA, A. Obtained patent no. 2283 relating to stringing of dolls' and animals' heads and limbs, October 13th, 1858.

BENDYKINS. 1965. Bendy range doll, see **Newfeld Ltd.**

BENJAMIN, Henry Solomon. Milton House, 8-9 Chiswell Street, London EC2. Wholesaler and agent for English and continental toy manufacturers. 1917: registered trademark 'Victory' for fully jointed, sleeping eye doll.

BENNETT, Jill and ERLAND, Susan. 4 Ruvigny Gardens, Putney, London SW15. Since 1974 have produced an individual range of dolls, period doll houses and dolls in appropriate settings. The dolls with heads, hands and feet are of porcelain with real hair and joints that make them bend and turn correctly. Mainly two sizes: 1″ (often used as dolls' house dolls) and 8½″. Also a less specialised range: "Standard Victorians"— Father, Mother, son and daughter.

Right: Trade mark regd. H S Benjamin,

'Victory Doll'

Bell & Francis Ltd., 1916. China heads and rag bodies.

BENNIE. 1978. See **Abba Dolls.**

BERCOVITCH, L. W. & S. and ANNIS-ON, J. H. 33 Downing Street, Ardwick, Manchester. Doll manufacturers. Registered trademark, 'Bersonian'. No. 437,068 on May 11th, 1923 for dolls.

BERGMAN, FRITZ & CO. 1903-11. 47 Milton Street, London, EC. Wholesale doll-makers.

BERGMAN, KLEEMAN & CO. 1912-13. Doll manufacturers and distributors. 68 Milton Street, London, EC. & 7 Butler Street, London EC.

BERGNER, C. Obtained patent no. 27919 for dolls constructed in two parts, so that several faces can be fixed to one body, December 2nd, 1904.

BERSONIAN. See **Bercovitch, L. W.**

BESWICK, J. W. 1915. Longton, Staffordshire. Dealt in pottery dolls' heads.

BETHNAL GREEN MUSEUM. Cambridge Heath Road, London, E2. A section of the Victoria and Albert Museum situated in East London and specialising in toys and dolls.

BETSY. 1967. Small pedigree doll with bendable limbs and 3 outfits. Retail 9s 11d.

BETTS, Thomas 1879-1912. 1881 at 150 St. John's Road, Hoxton, London, N. 1891-1912 at 12 de Beauvoir Road, London, N. Made wax and/or composition dolls. Mrs Marion Betts was his successor at the same address from 1907-12. In 1881 Miss H. Spratt, doll maker, was listed at the Hoxton address.

BETTY BLUE. 1913. 'Tru-to-Life' rag doll made by Dean's Rag Book Co. Ltd. 20″ high, 'a chubby little lady with auburn hair, blue eyes and delicate blue underclothes.'

BETTY OXO. c1936. Advertising doll obtained from Oxo Ltd. of London in exchange for Oxo cube wrappers or equivalent number of Oxo bottle metal caps. Made by Dean's Rag Book Co. Ltd. A stuffed fabric doll with printed features and limbs covered in velvet and metal pinned to body. Dressed in pink velvet jacket and hat. Height 16½″. Oxo also had 'Little Miss Oxo' specially made for it.

BEXOID CHERUB. 1935. New born baby doll made from Bexoid safety plastic material. Made by Cascelloid Ltd.

BHANKAWALA. 1910. registered trade mark for dolls. See **Sherwood, Katherine Mary.**

BIANCHI, P. 1855. London. Made wax dolls.

BIDDLE, L. Obtained patent no. 23621 for a smoking doll. Instead of tobacco, disinfectant was used. October 13th 1897.

BIDDY & BUTCH. 1955. Comic rubber dolls manufactured by Young & Fogg Rubber Co. Ltd.

BIERER, F. L. Registered trademark for rubber toys 1908 (Girl's Head)

BIFFY. 1973. See **Ploppy Character Dolls.**

BIG BABY DOLL. 'Knockabout' toy made by Dean's Rag Book Co. 1908. Described as biggest seller of knockabout toys by 'Toys and Fancy Goods Trader' magazine. Produced as 'Tru-to-Life' rag doll in 1913, it was life-size with curly brown hair, blue corset and underclothes painted on and could be dressed in baby's clothing.

BILLIE BIMBO. 1926. Doll made by J. K. Farnell & Co. Ltd.

BILL THE SAILOR. Celluloid doll, price 1s. Sold by Cascelloid Ltd. 1939.

BILTOYS. See **Bonnan, Lewis**

BINGS LTD. c1912+. 25 Ropemaker Street, London, EC. London branch of German doll and toy manufacturers. On March 1st, 1912 they registered the trademarks 'Sunshine Girl' no. 340,760 and 'Sunshine Kid' no. 340,761 for dolls and toys. In 1915 they were producing jointed nursery rhyme dolls and animals, including Jack & Jill, 10 Little Niggers, Mother Hubbard and dog, Mary had a little lamb, Jack Horner and Little Miss Muffet and spider. Each figure came complete with rhyme book; wholesale price from 7s 6d to 78s per doz.

'Binkie Babs'. Ken Donald Mfg. Co. Ltd., 1935

BINKIE BABS. 1935. Soft doll made from Art Silk locknit fabric with soft skin finish, kapok filled, featherweight. Sizes 12″, 14″, 15″, 18″ and 20″. Colours Jubilee Blue, Margaret Rose and Marina Green. Retail price from 2s.11d. H. M. Queen Mary purchased one at the British Industries Fair. Made by Ken Donald Manufacturing Co. Ltd.

BIRMINGHAM CITY MUSEUM & ART GALLERY. Birmingham, Warwickshire. This museum houses the Pinto collection of Wooden Bygones and includes many interesting dolls and toys.

BISHOP, W. H. & CO. 11 Edmund Place, Aldersgate, London EC. Sold dressed dolls & large jointed dolls.

BISHOP'S HOUSE. Meersbrook Park, Sheffield. This is a late 15th Century timber-framed domestic building, with later additions. There is a children's room with a constantly changing display of toys dating from 1800 onwards.

BISTO KIDS. c1948. Trademark nos. 660, 302 registered for games and playthings by Cerebos Ltd., Cerebos House, Victoria Road, London NW10. Advertising boy and girl dolls based on Cerebos' posters by Will Owen of two street urchins with noses in the air sniffing the aroma of Bisto. Composition heads and shoulder plates stuck on to fabric bodies.

BITTY DOLLS. 1971. See **Ploppy Character Dolls.**

BJORN. 1978. See **Abba Dolls.**

Right: Bisque baby doll, unglazed, intaglio eyes, 'made in England'.

Bings' Nursery Rhyme Dolls, 1915

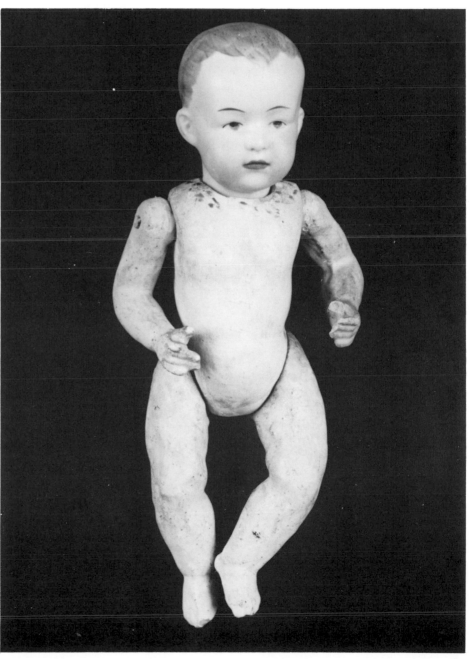

BLACK DOLLS. 'Down the Ratcliffe High-way is an old marine store And a big black doll hangs out at the door.' This rhyme from the Ingoldsby Legends refers to the black wooden dolls which once hung outside shops selling muslins and other West Indian pro-duce. Over the years the wares in these dockland shops changed character and they became known as 'marine' stores, selling candles, second-hand goods, old bottles, rags and bones. The dolls hanging outside as shop signs also went down the social scale: clothed only in a bundle of old rags, they were however like Janus two-faced, looking both up and down the street. London cock-neys called this type of shop sign doll a 'moggy'.

At the Edward Lovett exhibition of Folk Toys and Emergent Dolls held at Car-diff in 1914 one of these black dolls was on show; also a doll made from an ox's blade bone and draped in old rags, which was used as a sign for a Portsmouth marine store. In the same exhibition were examples of the better-known carved wood 'Black Boys' holding or standing by rolls of tobacco, which used to stand outside snuff and tobac-co stores.

Very occasionally other 18th and 19th century black wooden or wax dolls are found, often dressed as pedlars.

English dolls' heads made in the Potter-ies during the First World War sometimes have a brown finish, reflecting no doubt their imperial connections. Later dolls using a composition of plaster and resin have European features but much darker com-plexions; while plastic dolls made after World War II sometimes have more marked ethnic features and can be jet-black. Between the wars a great number of soft rag dolls were made from what was then called 'nigger brown' velveteen. In recent years dolls such as the 'Sasha' dolls have been made in an intermediate milky coffee colour, presuma-bly for the wider international market.

See **Dean's Rag Book Co.; Farnell, J. K. & Co.; Golliwogg; Merrythought; Negro Dolls; Piccaninnies; Pixie and Dixie; Three Arts Women's Employment Industries; Todd, Daniel G.; Topsy; Trendon Toys; Tyneside Toys; Wellings, Norah; Woolly Wally; Woombo; Zulu.**

Dark brown wax doll

Advertisement in Games & Toys, June 1921

Black wax Pedlar Doll, 1840

BLACK McCOY. 1976. Fully jointed Cowboy doll from Western range of Fighting Furies series by Lesney Products and Co. Ltd. Made in Hong Kong.

BLACKPOOL BELLE. 1921. See **Lawton Doll Co.**

BLAISE CASTLE MUSEUM. Henbury, Bristol. A branch of Bristol City Museum, Blaise Castle has an extensive collection of 19th century toys, with some 18th century dolls and early 20th century soldiers.

BLAKE BROS. 1918-21. 1918—160 Shepherd's Bush, London, W6. 1920—142 Kingsland High Street, London, NE. Dollmaker.

BLAND-HAWKES, Mabel. 1918. 190 Lavender Hill, Clapham Junction, London SW11. Designer and manufacturer of soft dolls and mascots. She obtained patent no. 125525 on May 15th, 1918 for the articulation of the limbs on soft-bodied dolls. In 1921 she advertised special 'Light weight Fairies' and Father Christmas dolls (for Christmas trees), and 'Fluff', a knockabout cuddly doll in coloured stockinette trimmed with brushed wool. "Over 300,000 dolls sold since August 1920." In 1923 'Baby Royal', a life-size baby doll in long clothes, 'Little Lady Anne', a "smartly dressed doll", and 'Tutenkamen', a mascot doll. In the same year Miss Bland-Hawkes applied for a patent for a jointed washable cuddly toy which could float. In 1927 popular lines included 'Toots' a "dainty creation in silk, trimmed with marabout"; 'Hazel', a summer doll in finished silk, with rosebud trimming, 'Babs', a cuddly doll in velvet; 'My Dollie's Nana'; and 'Little Miss Vogue', in assorted coloured velvets trimmed with white plush, an example of which was purchased by Queen Mary at the British Industries Fair.

BLUEBELL DOLLS. See **Todd, Daniel G.**

BLUE JOHN POTTERY LTD. Union Street, Hanley, Stoke-on-Trent, Staffordshire. Pottery firm which took up manufacture of dolls and heads intended for home and export markets in c1940. Produced six sizes of dolls (30cm-60cm) and baby dolls. In April 1942 British Board of Trade banned further production of dolls by Potteries firms.

BLUE RIBBON PLAYTHINGS: See **Be-Be (Dolls) Ltd.**

BLUESTOCKING DOLLS. Trademark no. 379, 471 registered for dolls by John Green Hamley, Toy merchant, of 86 High Holborn, London, WC1. August 22nd, 1917.

BLUESTOCKING KID. 1917. Educational doll whose removable clothes were printed with alphabet. Sold by Hamley's Bros.; made by Harwin & Co. Ltd.

BLUETT, Thomas. 1856. 1 Nelson Square, Blackfriars Road, London. (Kelly's Directory). Made wax and composition dolls.

BLYTHE. 1973. Small Palitoy doll whose eyes can be made to change colour when a cord is pulled. Has 12 outfits and 4 wigs.

BLYTON, Mary Enid. Born 11th August 1897, Dulwich, London. Froebel training at St. Christopher's School, Ipswich 1916. Died 28 November 1968. From about 1917 besides contributing to Arthur Mee's Children's Encyclopaedia she wrote over six hundred books. Her most popular nursery character was Little Noddy, who first appeared in 1949 and was illustrated by Harmsen van der Beek. Noddy was produced as a doll in fabric, in metal and in plastic.

BOASE, Elizabeth. 9 Grafton Street, London, W. Registered 'The Soldier's Baby' trademark no. 363, 480, September 15th, 1914 for dolls.

BOBICHE. 1925. Al doll by Dean's Rag Book Co. Ltd, with up to date 'bobbed' hair and dainty undies. 12″

BODIES. (Construction, material etc) The first shaped dolls would seem to have been one-piece, either fashioned from fabric, hand-carved wooden stump dolls or single section moulds from clay or wax. All of these types were probably made in mediaeval England. Sir Walter Raleigh is reported as carrying "puppets and babes" to America in 1585 as gifts for Indian children, and we can presume they were of turned wood with painted features. Poplar seems to have been the usual material. Doll bodies fashioned from oak are usually adaptations of some earlier use such as chair leg or bannister rail. Arms were made of sewn leather with carved wooden hands and nailed to the shoulder joint. Wigs of real human hair were made and nailed to the pate. Legs were fashioned from wood and slotted to the hip section. Usually such dolls were roughly finished in the body section, as they were intended to be dressed. By the end of the 18th. century moulded plaster faces were sometimes attached to the head, to avoid the labour of hand-carving details of brow, nose, chin, cheeks, etc. Clothing would often seem to have been made up from snippets of materials left from some other dressmaking, so the full skirts of the dolls were often in varied

'Bluestocking Girl', 1919

strips. (See Letitia Penn Doll). Later dolls with heads and limbs of wax, either poured or dipped papier mâché, had bodies of stitched fabric stuffed with wool, moss, bran or flock. German wax dolls are usually found with sawdust or coarse hay stuffing.

Dolls made up during the 1914/18 period with pottery heads are found with machine-stitched fabric bodies and often rather crude articulation.

BOLLING HALL MUSEUM. Bradford 4, Yorkshire. This museum has a small representative toy collection including about 30 dolls (and dolls' clothing), two of which are probably late 18th century. There is one doll's house and a large collection of doll's house furniture.

BONNAN, Lewis. Greenford, Middlesex. Registered trade mark 'Biltoys' no. 632055 for dolls on October 13th, 1944.

BONNEDOL. c1918. Series of character dolls with moving heads and limbs made by Frederick Cooper & Sons Ltd.

BONNY. 1935. Soft doll dressed in assorted coloured prints. Made by Dean's Rag Book Co. Ltd.

BOOFUL BABY BEANS. 1971. See Ploppy Character Dolls.

BO-PEEP. 1919. See Harwin & Co. Ltd.

BOROUGH BRITISH DOLLS. c1915-17. In 1915 at 276 Clapham Road, London, SW. 1917 moved to 1 Lansdowne Road, South Lambeth, London, SW8. Made dressed and undressed baby dolls with china heads and arms, lightweight stuffed bodies and original hand-made wigs, and dressed character dolls in Allies' uniforms and peasant costumes.

BORTHWICK, Jessica. See Nellfoy & Co.

BOUCHET, A. In 1851 was awarded an honourable mention for his representation of the Great Exhibition with moving figures and various dolls.

BOUDOIR DOLLS. Dolls designed for adult women. In 1910 Paul Poiret, the couturier, suggested that fashion-conscious women should carry dolls. Such figures were especially costumed by Paquin and Madame Lanvin and copied by other designers. The dolls were usually in the form of long-limbed women with silk- or fabric-covered faces. Boudoir dolls were made in England by several firms during the 1920s, notably Dean's 1928 'Smart Set' dolls, including a duchess in leopard skin coat. Long-legged adult-type dolls were in production until 1938 when pierrot costume dolls became popular. Chad Valley called this type of fashion doll "Sofa dolls for the sophisticated Miss of 1935."

BOULT, A. J. and GAY, W. ALFRED. Patent 11063 June 1893. Doll with container fitted with a series of small metal rods. As the toy is moved about a marble inside rolls, striking musical notes.

BOULT, A. K. Obtained patent no. 13084 relating to fixing hair to doll's heads, September 27th, 1887.

BOW BELLE. Dressed girl rag doll with large bow in her hair, made by Dean's Rag Book Co. c1920.

BOWDEN, J. Obtained patent no. 24523 relating to dancing doll operated by water wheel, November 21st, 1898.

BOWERS, C. E. Obtained patent no. 448, 591 for doll containing sound device, July 19th, 1935.

BOWES MUSEUM. Barnard Castle, Co. Durham. The toy collection includes a rare 'Ondine' clockwork swimming doll of the kind first patented in 1876, and a group of wax figures in 17th Century Slavonic costume forming a wedding scene. There are also several doll's houses.

BOY DOLLS. See **Boy Scout; Boy Sprout; British and Colonial Novelty Co.; Buster Brown; Canada's Victory; Peter Pan; Genital Dolls.**

BOY SCOUT. Physical exerciser doll made by All-British Manufacturing Co. 1917.

BOY SPROUT. 1914 Boy doll made by Dean's Rag Book Co.

BRADGATE. Wholesale division of Palitoy Ltd. from January 1971.

BRADLEY & GALZENATI. 1913-17. In 1917 at 80-90 Milton Street, London, EC. Made dolls' heads.

BRANDT, R., & CO. (MFG) LTD. 1949. 220-24 Pentonville Road, London, N.1. Manufacturers of nylon eyelashes for dolls in black or brown or other shades.

BRAXTED DOLL INDUSTRY. c1918-23. Braxted Park, Witham, Essex. Made 'original' dolls with composition heads and limbs. 1923 lines include an all-leather doll and carved wood dolls.

BRENDA. 1952. See **Pin-Up Dolls.**

BRENTLEIGH DOLLS. 1940. See **Howard Pottery Co. Ltd.**

BRER RABBIT. 1918. See **Tah Toys Ltd.**

BRIDE DOLLS. Dolls are often found dressed in fragments of material actually used in the past for a wedding gown. Some-times wax dolls were framed as commemoratives of such an occasion, and if a family history attaches it is a useful guide to the dating of a doll. The Victoria and Albert Museum has a series of dolls from the Powell family (of which Chief Scout Baden Powell was one of the famous descendants). They were dressed by hand to represent contemporary dress, a tradition begun in 1754 by Laetitia Clark. In 1761, she married and became Mrs Powell. A doll dressed for that year wears a silk brocade, reputedly from her wedding dress. Other members of the family continued to make bride dolls from their wedding dresses down to 1912. Commercially dressed Bride dolls were also popular in Victorian times, chiefly as Wedding Breakfast decorations. Sometimes the bridegroom also figures in the group.

BRIERLEY, W. Obtained patent no. 10100 for making dolls' and puppets' heads by uniting stamped pieces of metal. August 7th 1886.

BRIGITTE. 1978. New name given to Matchbox Disco Girl doll Britt.

BRINGLEE. See **Models (Leicester) Ltd.**

BRINSLEY, W. H. & E. R. Obtained patent no. 172, 073 relating to joint for doll's limbs and body, August 20th, 1920.

BRISTOL. See **Blaise Castle Museum.**

BRITAIN, WILLIAM (BRITAINS LTD). Hornsey, London N19. A family business established in the 1870s when they produced some clever hand-dressed mechanical toys and dolls. The firm still exists but mainly manufactures plastic miniatures: toy soldiers, zoo sets. farm animals etc.

BRITANNIA TOY CO. Established 1915. 87 Great Eastern Street, London EC. From 1943 at Alliance Works, Windus Road, London N16. Doll & toy manufacturers.

BRITEYES DOLLS. c1952. Doll range manufactured by The Britannia Toy Co. Ltd. Patent Nos. 642846-663954.

BRITISH ARTWARE LTD. 1941. 91-93 Brollo Bridge Road, Acton, London W.3. 1947. 45, Beaumont Road, Chiswick, London, W4. Doll and toy manufacturers.

BRITISH BABIES. c1917. Four dressed stuffed stockinette baby dolls, 'George' for England, 'Andrew' for 'Scotland, 'David' for Wales and 'Patrick' for Ireland. Retail price 4s 6d each. Designed by E. E. Houghton of Shanklin Toy Industry Ltd.

BRITISH & COLONIAL NOVELTY CO. c1921. Made stuffed dolls with sleeping eyes, celluloid character dolls and cheap teddy bears.

BRITISH DOLL MANUFACTURING CO. 1914-19. 82 Liverpool Road, Stoke-on-Trent, Staffordshire. Mr C. J. Bisson, proprietor of Staffordshire Small Wares Co. at above address, began to manufacture character dolls in 1914. Range included policemen, nursery rhyme characters, and servicemen. Dolls had china heads and stuffed bodies.

Left: Wax doll, stuffed rag body wearing ivory silk dress. A contemporary label attached to the petticoat reads 'Mrs Powell, wedding suite 1761'.

BRITISH DOLL & NOVELTY CO. c1916. San Toy Works, Western Road, Merton, Surrey. Made bisque dolls and jointed dressed and undressed dolls with porcelain socket heads.

BRITISH DOLLS LTD. During the First World War Miss M. Moller acquired showrooms at 153 Cheapside, London EC2. for the promotion and sale of dolls made by the Shanklin and the Nottingham Toy Industries. Miss Moller's firm was first called British Toys, subsequently British Dolls Ltd. Under this title she set up a factory at Greenwich in 1920 which took over most of the lines developed by the Nottingham Toy Industry. In 1921, however, the manufacture of Houghton stockinette dolls was in turn taken over by Roberts Brothers of Gloucester.

BRITISH INDOOR PASTIMES LTD. c1947. 150 Southampton Row, London, WC1. 6-10 Wakefield Road, London, N15. Doll and toy distributors. Lines include the 'Mormit' series of plastic dolls made by Morris Mitchell & Co.

BRITISH JOINTED DOLL CO. c1920. 10 & 11 Etloe Terrace, Church Road, Leyton. Made jointed composition dolls and own wigs.

Stockinette doll made by Mrs Houghton, 1920 and sold by British Dolls Ltd.

Below: British Doll Mfg. Co., 1917

BRITISH NATIONAL DOLLS LTD. Before September 1933 in Cricklewood, London. From September 1933 at 4-8 Hutton Grove, Finchley, London N. & 99 Fore Street, London, EC2. By 1942 at Acton Lane, Harlesden, London, NW10. Doll manufacturers. 1933 made dolls with china heads. 1934 made new born baby dolls—'Sunshine Babs', and character dolls with wigs and 'chubby' china headline—'Chubby' 'the Wonder Doll of 1934'. In 1942 the firm claimed to be the first to manufacture composition dolls using mass production methods. 1947 lines include 'hard-to-break' sleeping eye character and baby dolls. In July 1947, the firm registered the trade mark 'Skintex', no. 661049 for dolls, and in July 1948, together with E. Ainley, they obtained patent no. 642,065 for the design of the doll's eye.

Right and below: China-headed dolls marked B.N.D. Composition bodies
Below right: B.N.D. china head

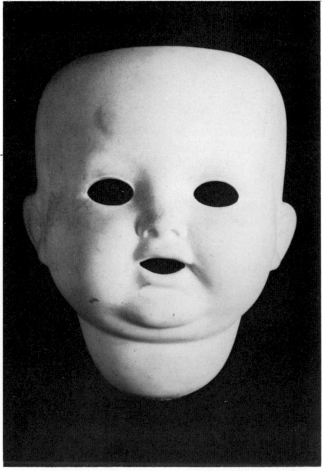

BRITISH NOVELTY CO. 1916. At 228 Morning Lane, Hackney, London NE. c1920 at Willesden Lane, Kilburn, London, NW6. Made dolls and toys, In 1916 they were making rag dolls (6d & 1d lines), dressed and undressed china head dolls, character dolls e.g. Russian national costume girl, also large artistic caricature dolls; in 1920 'nankeen' (cotton cloth) hair-stuffed dolls with sleeping and stationary eyes.

BRITISH NOVELTY WORKS LTD. 1915-21. 2-14 Newington Butts,, London SE. Toy and doll manufacturers. Firm owned by Dean's Rag Book Co. Ltd. Registered trade mark 'B.N.W.' no. 365,840 on February 9th, 1915 for toys and dolls. 1921 lines include 'The Coogan Kid', a doll based on the popular child film star of the period, Jackie Coogan (American). The doll was dressed in a red jersey with brown velvet pants and a green velvet cap, and was of 'Evripose' construction with patented flexible limbs.

BRITISH PRODUCTS MANUFACTURING CO. 1918-21. 3 Great Titchfield Street, London, W1. Made composition and other types of dolls. The firm was owned by the Salzedo Brothers who in 1920 were agents for Steevans Mfg. Co. and Tatchbrook Toy Factory. Trademark 'B.P.M.C.' Dolls.

B.P.M.C. doll, 1919

BRITISH RAG DOLL CO. Before 1913. London. Made rag dolls. In November 1913 the firm was taken over by Art Fabric Manufacturing Co. Ltd.

BRITISH TEXTILE NOVELTY CO. Before 1913. Made rag dolls. In 1913 the firm was taken over by Art Fabric Manufacturing Co.

BRITISH TOY CO. LTD. See **Potteries Toy Co.**

BRITISH TOYS LTD. 1917. Showrooms: 153 Cheapside, London, EC2. Factory from 1920 at Greenwich. Director: Miss M. Moller, who represented three firms: The Nottingham Toy Industry Ltd—dolls; Shanklin Toy Industry Ltd—"Houghton" dolls; Pyram Toys—toy animals. Company became British Dolls Ltd. in 1920.

BRITISH UNITED TOY MANUFACTURING CO. 1912. Showrooms: 118 Fore Street, Cripplegate, London, EC. Factory: Union Works, Southey Road, South Tottenham, Middlesex. Made variety of dolls, teddy bears and animals mounted on cam wheels. Used trademark 'Omega'.

BRITOY LTD. c1947. Hinckley, Leicestershire. Made composition dolls with sleeping eyes, 'long sweeping lashes', with voices and 'superb dressing'. 1950 range included dolls dressed by 'leading continental dress designer'

BRITT. c1974. Articulated Palitoy doll.

BRITT. See **Lesney Products & Co. Ltd.**

BROGDEN, James. 1835-40. 5 Cross Street, Hatton Garden, London. Made composition dolls.

BROHEAD, S. Obtained patent no. 16700 for walking toys, especially dolls, July 28th 1902.

BRONYX. 1919. Tradename used by Dolls Supplies Ltd.

BROOKE, A. G. 14 January 1888. Patent no 616 for a phonograph doll. Sound issued through a tube in the crown of the head.

BROOKS, John. 1835. London. Made dolls.

BROTHERS & BABINGTON LTD. 1942. 1 & 2 Cynthia Street, Pentonville Road, London, N1. Manufacturers of dressed dolls.

BROWNE, Thomas. Patented a fabric doll stuffed with disinfected flock and resembling a Polynesian islander. 6th January 1899.

BROWNIE. See **Cox**

BRUGIER, Charles Abram. 1815-21. London. Made mechanical walking dolls. Charles Brugier was a member of the famous Swiss watchmaking firm.

Stockinette doll made by Mrs Houghton, 1918, and sold by British Toys Ltd.

BRYAN, F. Bartholomew Close, London E.C. Trade mark a grasshopper.

BUBBLES. 1936. Soft stuffed doll made in fluffy nap cloth. Colours pink and sky. Mfd. by Dean's Rag Book. Co. Ltd.

BUBBLES. 1938. Boy doll with plastex head described as 'The Angel Child'. Registered design no. 824,205 by Cascelloid Ltd.

BUBBLES. 1955. 'Roddy' plastic baby doll, 11" to 21" tall, with blonde curly hair and a short dress with puffed sleeves. Made by D. G. Todd & Co. Ltd.

BUBBLES AND SQUEAK. (The Quant Kids) Introduced 1975. Sister and brother dolls with outfits designed by Mary Quant in 10 styles. Manufactured by Model Toys Ltd. Supplied by Flair Toys Ltd.

BUBBLY KIDDIE. Soft boy doll with fair curly wig, made by Fretwell Toy Manufacturing Co. 1918. Registered trademark no. 661753

BUCHERER, A. Obtained patent no. 177, 739 for doll's ball-and socket joints, June 20th, 1921.

BUCKINGHAM (LONDON) LTD. 418 Edgware Road, London, W2. Registered 'Monica' trademark no. 659948 for dolls, July 11th, 1947.

BUCKLAND, Edmund. 1840-43. 12 Carburton Street, Fitzroy Square, London, W1. Made dolls.

'Fondle Dolls' by A J Burman, from the British Cavalcade series, 1935

BUCKMASTER, George Henry. See **Smith, W. H. & Sons.**

BUDDY. 1936. Soft cowboy doll mfd. by Merrythought Ltd.

BUMBLY. Trademark for dolls, soft toys and toy animals registered on November 20th, 1953 by Michael Bentine Enterprises Ltd., of 129 Mount Street, Berkeley Square, London, W1.

BUN DOLLS. See **Edible Dolls**

BUNNY HUG. 1913. Registered trademark for dolls, puppets and toys. See **Eisenmann & Co.**

BUNNYMUM. 1928. Fur-clad doll with rabbit ears, made by W. H. Jones Ltd.

BUNTY DOLL. 1955. Plush material doll with flexible mask face and ribbon bow at neck. Has painted eyes. Made by Palitoy.

BURBANK TOYS. Burbank House, Rixon Road, Northants. Member of the Dunbee-/Combex/Marx group. Fairytale and Nursery Rhyme characters filled with beans. Stuffed and talking toys and puppets. Rupert, Pooh, Buzby, Teddy Bears, Wombles and Walt Disney characters 1978. 'Country Miss' Rag Dolls.

BURGESS, S. H. Sold Pickett's phonograph figures which are fitted beside gramophone record and dance. They have British patent. Also 'Slymphs'—dolls with long wire limbs which can be manipulated, so become 'great mimics': intended as mascots, table decorations, for dinner parties etc. (1921)

BURLEY, George. Southward, Surrey. Exhibited dolls at London Exhibition 1862.

BURMAN LTD., J. & A. J. 1919-1976. 1919 at 32 Whitecross Street, London EC1. Doll and toy manufacturers. In 1919, their Zoo Toy Co. lines included jointed dolls, dressed and undressed, mascots and plush toys. 1956 lines include the 'Cuddly Doll', 10" high in various colours of silk plush. The firm's brand name is 'Fondle Toys'. 1956 address was 9-11 London Lane, London, E8. In 1958 the firm changed its name to Fondle Toys Ltd., with premises at 440 Kingsland Road, Hackney, London.

BURNELL & HOCKEY, J. 15th June 1906. Crouch End, Middlesex. Patent no. 13745 for a rag doll of printed pattern, and sewed-together sections which when stuffed enabled the doll to sit down.

BURROWS TOY MUSEUM. The Octagon, 46 Hilsom Street, Bath, Somerset. One of the newest toy museums, its collection ranges from the products of prestige manufacturers to the humblest penny toy, and covers the past century and a half.

BURTOYS MANUFACTURING CO. c1950. 7 Charleville Road, London, W14. Dollmakers. (Kelly's Directory).

BUSTER c1949: See **Playlastic Toy Co. Ltd.**

BUSTER BROWN. A child character invented by strip cartoonist Richard Felton Outcault for the New York Herald, 1902. Hamley Bros registered the name for a doll 1904. Deans produced a 12" doll to coincide with release of six Buster Brown films. The star had bobbed flaxen hair, a tunic suit, patent shoes and a dog. (1923)

BUTLER, Charles. c1826-48. Made dolls. 1826 at 18 Aylesbury Street, Clerkenwell, London. 1848 at 8 Chapel Row, Exmouth Street, London.

BUTTERFLY SERIES. 1908. Registered trademark for toys and dolls. See **Eisenmann & Co.**

C.C. 1920. Mechanical Charlie Chaplin doll made by Foster, Blackett & Wilson Ltd.

C Q DOLLS INDUSTRY. Southampton Referred to in Games and Toys, February 1920.

CABARET. Stuffed fabric dolls made by Austin Gray Ltd. 1934.

CABBAGERINO. See **Dakin, Margaret Ann.**

CAMBRIDGE COUNTY FOLK MUSEUM. Many rooms of toys and bygones including early dolls bought or found in Cambridge, local basket-ware, doll furniture. Dolls' house and furniture made by local carpenter.

CAMI DOLLS: 1935. Doll range made by Dean's Rag Book Co. Ltd.

CAMOUFRAGE. 1921. China character doll made by Dolls' Accessory Co.

CANADA'S VICTORY. Unbreakable dolls with composition heads and fully jointed limbs. They were advertised in June 1919 and were stocked in London by C. Britton, 47 Milton St, London EC2. Many of these dolls were boy dolls, dressed in boys' shirts and tunics, and could be 'profitably retailed from 2/- each'.

'Cuddles', made in Canada by The Reliable Toy Co., 1935.

CANADIAN DOLLS. Already before the First World War Canada had a small indigenous toy industry, but with the absence of German competition after 1914, a great boom in toy manufacture took place. Large quantities were exported to Britain and by 1919 Harrods were ordering £1,500 worth of dolls for the Christmas sale. A few bisque heads were made after the discovery in 1919 of kaolin in Hastings County, Ontario but the majority of dolls were made from a composition material using the abundant wood waste. One of the largest exporters was Mr E Roy Clarke of the Dominion Toy Mfg Co Ltd, Toronto who commenced making his unbreakable knock-about dolls in 1911 with a range of ten or twelve models. By 1920 he was producing 200 different lines. Another Canadian firm was the Reliable Doll Factory of Toronto, started in 1920. By 1939 they were the largest users of corn starch in Canada, corn starch and wood flour being two of the basic ingredients used to mould the dolls. The Reliable Doll Factory made baby dolls, teenage dolls and ventriloquists' dummies, imported by Eisenmann & Co. Ltd. Canadian dolls were labelled: Dominion, Made in Canada.

CANADIAN UNBREAKABLE DOLLS. In June 1946 soft dolls with Canadian un-

breakable heads were being manufactured in Eire by Gaelterra Eireann. Made in three sizes 16½″, 18″, 19½″. Sold by Graham Bros. Endell St, London.

CANNON DOLLS. See **Kent Toy Works.**

CANNON, James. 1952-5. 25 Fleet Street, Farringdon Street, London. Dollmaker.

CAPTAIN HOOK. 1975. See **Fighting Furies.**

CAPTAIN PEGLEG. 1975. See **Fighting Furies.**

CAPTAIN SCARLETT. 1967. 12″ jointed male doll based on character in T.V. adventure puppet series. Also made as a 4½″ figure in bendable limbs. Manufactured by Pedigree Dolls Ltd.

CARESSE. 1936. Soft stuffed doll with fabric mask, made by Chad Valley.

CARIAD. Trademark no. 783,521 for dolls. Registered November 3rd, 1958 by manufacturer Thomas Garrie Falconer trading as Garrie Thomas, of Caerffynon Hotel, Talsarnau, Merioneth, N. Wales.

Injection moulding at Britannia Works of Cascelloid Ltd., 1938.

CARICATURE DOLLS. Dolls or mascots based on characters from cartoons or book illustrations. Made of many different materials and included fabric dolls and china figurines.

CARINA. 1936. Doll made by Chad Valley.

CARLTON WARE. See **Wiltshaw & Robinson Ltd.**

CARNABY KATE. Introduced 1968. 28″ rag doll with long legs, vinyl face, painted eyes, fly-away hair in blue, lemon or pink. Dressed in green felt mini-jacket with contrasting collar and cuffs. Made by Rosebud Mattel Ltd. Retail £3.12s.6d.

CARRY-ME-CASE DOLL SET. 1958. Small plastic attaché case containing doll and complete outfit. 2 sets in pale blue, ivory and red. First set includes 8″ Delite doll with knickers, socks, shoes, straw hat, dress, piqué coat, housecoat, nightgown and coathangers. Retail price 29s 11d. The second set contains a 13″ vinyl doll with rooted hair and knickers, socks, shoes, piqué print dress and hat, floral print dress, nightgown, négligé, mules and coathangers. Retail 75s. Manufactured by Lines Bros.

CARTER, H. W. & CO. LTD. 1951. The Royal Forest Factory, Coleford. Gloucestershire. Fruit Juice manufacturers who registered the trademark 'Quoshiwog' no. 696701 on March 12th, 1951 for soft toys and dolls, probably used for promotional purposes.

CARTOON. See **Little Tich; Margot and Midget; Pop.**

CARTWRIGHT, A. S. LTD. Est. 1880. Ford St, Birmingham. Chief product: rubber baby 'dummies' which gave rise to the name 'Holdfast', later used for all sorts of toys and dolls.

CASCELLOID. The firm originated in humble premises at Britannia Street, Leicester (1919). The founder, Mr A. E. Pallett, produced small fancy goods and toys such as windmills and rattles, using an early plastic material manufactured from casein or erinoid and celluloid. After moving to new premises at Cobden Street he produced fairground Kewpie dolls. They owned their own printing plant and made advertising novelties also. Cascelloid Ltd. became a subsidiary of British Xylonite Ltd in 1937 and with additional finance and Mr Pallett

as Managing Director they acquired new factory premises at Abbey Lane, Leicester and a new factory at Coalville for the manufacture of Palitoy dolls. These dolls (named after A. E. Pallett) were fitted with 'Bexoid' heads (a new type of celluloid) on hygienic soft bodies. Bexoid was a new safety material, unbreakable and non-inflammable, which was used for Palitoy dolls from 1937. Bunty cuddly dolls, Betty dolls with glass eyes, Tony with boy head; Anne with girl head and the Dinky baby dolls. Bexoid cherub with 'soother' Novelty dolls included Diddums, Cupid dolls, Mickey Mouse and other Walt Disney characters. In 1937 when the new factory opened they produced a comprehensive Coronation range. Within 4 days of the abdication of Edward VIII the firm had switched to pictures of the new King and Queen. Composition dolls were made with Plastex (1940), a new plastic material.

Two 'Palitoy' dolls made by Cascelloid Ltd. in 1937, with 'Plastex' heads and soft rag bodies stuffed with flock.

1968 Palitoy was acquired by General Mills of America and manufactured such popular models as Tressy, Tiny Tears, Action Man, Tippy Tumbles, Katie Kopycat, Striker and Pippa. Various patents were taken out by the firm for improvement or variations in doll making. July 1939 535611; April 1941 535811; March 1942 543756; October 1946 618338; March 1947 623238; September 1948 644965; June 1949 662811; including one for a 'wetting' doll.

CASDON DOLLS. See **Cassidy Bros. Ltd.**

CASSIDY BROS. LTD. Casdon Works, Mitcham Road, Marton, Blackpool, Lancashire. Doll manufacturers. 1971 lines include 'Casdon' all-vinyl dolls, and a 15″ Moppet doll with movable arms and legs, rooted, washable nylon hair and sleeping eyes. 1973 lines include 'Belinda Bathtime', an 8″ doll with feeding bottle, polythene bath and potty. 'Bernie and Bath', 12″ soft vinyl baby doll with rooted hair, plus accessories.

Left: 'Bubbles', the Angel Child, regd. design no. 824,205.

CASTLE TOY CO LTD. 1941. Crown Works, 54a High Street, South Norwood, London, SE25. Toy and doll manufacturers. In 1955 produced Shirley dolls.

CAUGHLEY. Early pottery established at Broseley in Shropshire, demolished in 1814 by John Rose of Coalport who acquired it from Thomas Turner in 1799. Fragments excavated in pre-1799 strata at the site included, according to an article in Antique Collector by James H. Ruston, a 'small, unglazed, undecorated, shod right foot, the manufacture of which had not been completed as it was in biscuit state. Foot was undoubtedly intended for a doll, as a groove was to be cut in the calf to enable it to be tied to a cloth body below the knee. It is reasonable to presume from this that arms and heads as well were made at Caughley.'

CAULDON POTTERIES. Staffordshire 1774-1925. On the authority of G. J. V. Bemrose, Curator of Stoke-on-Trent Mu-

Right: 'Rags', the Bad Boy of a good family, regd. design no. 824,207.

seum it is said that Messrs Ridgeway manufactured dolls at the Cauldon works at Shelton during the 19th century. The pottery founded at the end of the 18th century was taken over by Brown, Westhead and Moore when John Ridgeway retired in 1859. Cauldon also took over the Corona potteries owned by S. Hancock Sons. See: **Hancock** and **Tam-o-Shanter.**

CAVERSHAM DOLL. **See Hazel, H. J.**

CECILLE. 1926. See **Rees, Leon**

CECILY DOLL. 1918. Registered trademark for dolls. See **Edwards & Pamflett.**

CECILY. c1914. Dolls heads made by Doll Pottery Co.

CELIA. 1952. Pedigree doll. See **Pin-Up Dolls.**

CELLALAINE CO. 1919-21. 5 & 7 Mare Street, Hackney, London, E8. Made rag dolls with celluloid faces and stuffed plush animals.

CELLULOID. The patent name given by Hyatt Brothers in U.S.A. to a synthetic material for use in making dental plates (July 12 1870, 105,338). The substance, made of camphor, nitrocellulose and alcohol, had been prepared previously in England but the Hyatt Bros developed various uses at their Celluloid Novelty Co, including doll-making. Manufacturers all over the world used celluloid but eventually a campaign against the dangerous, inflammable nature of the material made celluloid toys unpopular. See **Erband, S. & Son; Ivorine Manufacturing Co.; Lee, A. H. & Sons Ltd.; Moritz & Chambers Ltd.; Punfield, F. W.; Tattersall, J; Whyte, Ridsdale & Co.**

CELLULOID DOLLS. See **British & Colonial Novelty Co.; Cascelloid; Graham Bros.; Henreck, S.; Ivorine Manufacturing Co.; Lee, A. H. & Sons Ltd.; Maden, J. H.; Punfield, F. W.; Tattersall, J. Ltd.; Xylolith.**

CESAR, C. F. Patent for the articulation of doll limbs. 12 January 1949, 656434.

CESAR, S. S. 1952. 111 Crundale Avenue, Kingsbury, London, NW9. Dolls' hair manufacturers. 1952 advertising double gloss hair, straight and curly with fire-resisting properties.

'Palitoy' novelty celluloid dolls made by Cascelloid Ltd., 1939.

Cecily Dolls.

CHAD VALLEY. 1823. Still in existence. The firm originated with a lithographic, printing and bookbinding business owned by Anthony Bunn Johnson, Lichfield St, Birmingham. The firm moved in 1860 to new works in George St, Birmingham where stationers' sundries were produced besides general printing. When the firm moved to the village of Harbourne near Birmingham in 1897 the new factory was beside a stream called the Chad which eventually gave the name Chad Valley (1919 registered). Management was by Johnson's sons and grandsons who introduced a range of boxed games. In 1915 they acquired a further factory in the old Harbourne Institute and finally a building at Wellington (Salop) to be devoted to the production of soft toys and dolls. They absorbed other factories such as Isaacs of Birmingham who had patented 'bounding' animals under the brand name of Isa toys.

Joseph Johnson, 1842-1904, founder of the Chad Valley Company.

Chad Valley's 'Scots Girl', from the series 'A Cavalcade of the Empire's Toys', 1935 (King George V's Jubilee Year).

Chad Valley, 1939.

'Monica', 22 ins., 1932.

Chad Valley specialised in promotional toys, subjects already popularised commercially in film cartoons, newspaper strips or book characters. One of the first was Bonzo, the famous bull terrier pup drawn by G. Studdy for the Daily Sketch. At the 1920 British Industries Fair Chad Valley hired a dwarf dressed in a Bonzo suit to amuse King George V and Queen Mary. Chad Valley's reputation was established by very high quality of materials and workmanship. They listed Teddy Bears, mascot dolls, boudoir dolls with long legs, nursery rhyme characters and stuffed animals made from plush, velvet, felt and other fabrics, hygienically stuffed. A series of Mabel Lucie Attwell dolls was produced during the twenties based on characters popular in 'annuals' and post cards. They were in three sizes, 14½″ to 18½″.

1925 Chad Valley produced a children's magazine Happyland, 3d. per copy. Patents 235424, 237250, 255184 1924/5 dealt with a doll's head of stiffened fabric with inserted glass eyes. A model of little princess Elizabeth (1930) was sold at one guinea at the expressed wish of her parents, The Duke and Duchess of York, who thought the doll should not be too expensive for people of average means. Dressed in pink, blue or yellow (her mother's favourite colour). In the same year 1930 the A. A. and R. A. C. agreed to models of their Road Patrol Scouts being marketed.

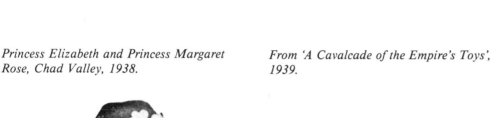

Princess Elizabeth and Princess Margaret Rose, Chad Valley, 1938.

From 'A Cavalcade of the Empire's Toys', 1939.

A.A. Road Patrol Scout, 1930.

'Bambina' doll, with fully-jointed velveteen limbs, 1936.

In 1931 the Company acquired the toy manufacturing business of Peacock & Co. Ltd. of London, and in 1938 it was granted the Royal Warrant of Appointment, 'Toymakers to Her Majesty the Queen'. In 1946 Waterloo works was taken over for the mass production of rubber toys and dolls. 1950 saw the end of the firm as a private family business and it was declared a Public Company. In 1954 Chad Valley acquired Roberts Bros. (Gloucester) Ltd., manufacturers of "Glevum" toys and games. By 1960 the Company was operating 7 factories and employing about one thousand people. In the 1970s the Chad Valley Co. changed hands a number of times until it was finally acquired by General Mills U.K. Ltd.

From 'A Cavalcade of the Empire's Toys', 1935.

From 'A Cavalcade of the Empire's Toys', 1932.

'Bambina' doll, with fully-jointed velveteen limbs, 1936.

Chad Valley's 'Snow White', 1938 (Pollock's Toy Museum).

Chad Valley doll, 1935.

Chad Valley doll dressed in orange felt (Faith Eaton Collection).

Nurse doll, labelled 'Chad Valley Hygienic Toys, made in England, the Seal of Purity'. Pressed felt mask and jointed velveteen body with swivel neck (Faith Eaton Collection).

CHAMBERLAIN, Neville. 1938. Doll representing the English Prime Minister dressed as a fisherman in tweeds, deer-stalker hat, Wellington boots and holding a rod and looking "as if a real big 'un had just got away". Also dressed in black morning coat and striped trousers, as if addressing the House. The doll faces were made with a new flexible material. Dolls were designed by Eric Sutton, and his firm J. K. Farnell & Co. manufactured them.

CHAMBERLAIN, Neville. Hand-made doll depicting Chamberlain the English Prime Minister after his historic meeting with Adolf Hitler in 1938. (Worthing Museum)

CHAMPIONS. 1977. See **Pedigree Soft Toys Ltd.**

CHAPMAN, Constance Mary. "Roedean", Glossop Road, Sanderstead, Surrey. Designed doll called 'Wallypug', Registered 1906. The Wallypug of Why was a fantasy creature invented by G. E. Farrow and illustrated by Harry Furniss (1895).

CHARACTER CRAFTS LTD. Vale Industrial Estate, Spilsby, Lincolnshire. Toy and doll manufacturers. 1973 lines include 'Miss Nobody', a soft character doll with interchangeable features. All faces, clothes and wigs can be peeled off, and expressions changed by pressing different features, thus creating a new character. The doll is 61cm high.

CHARACTER DOLLS. Writing in Games and Toys 1920, the Editor said "The traditional doll with pink cheeks and blue eyes is doomed. The modern child wants new sensations, it wants its bathing baby, its airman, its U-boat commander and it wants each in appropriate costume." Curiously prophetic of Action Man, Play People, etc.

See **Bland-Hawkes, Mabel; Burman, J. & A. J.; British Novelty Works; Dean's Rag Book Co. Ltd.; Ellison, Rees & Co.; Hamley Bros.; Hansen, Laurie & Co. Ltd.; Pop (Daily Sketch); Stone, H. G. & Co. Ltd.; Wellings, Norah; Wonderland Toymaking Co.**

See also **Advertising Dolls; Arthur Askey; Charlie Chaplin; Lambeth Walkers; Little Tich; Lloyd George; Lord Kitchener; Miller, Gertrude; Royal Dolls.**

CHARLES, Prince. 1949. Sleeping baby doll 'royally' dressed, produced by Simpsons of Surrey shortly after the birth of Prince Charles, and sold by Amalgamated Impex (London) Ltd.

CHARLIE CHAPLIN. 1920. See **Foster, Blackett & Wilson Ltd.** and 1928, **Sant, J.S. Ltd.**

CHARLIE CHAPLIN DOLL. 1916. See **Huvan Manufacturing Co.** also **Abrahams**

A 'Bairntoy' mechanical Charlie Chaplin doll, made by Foster Blackett & Wilson Ltd., 1920.

CHARLIE CHAPLIN. 1920. Rag doll made by Dean's Rag Book Co. Ltd, complete with walking stick. Reissued 1982 for export.

CHARLOTTE: See **Tricia Dolls.**

CHARSTONE, W. J. Patented a movable mannequin: from pivoted lever a doll on three wheels was motivated. Patent 1702 January 1902.

CHATTY-CATHY. 1962. A Rosebud talking doll, which says 10 phrases including 'My name is Rosebud' and 'Do you like my dress?' Made with exclusive Mattel patented talking unit. Doll has English, Dutch or Swedish speaking unit. Made by Rosebud Dolls Ltd. Retail price £5 19s 6d.

CHEERFUL TEARFUL. 1967. Blonde plastic baby doll, whose facial expression can be made to alter by means of a mechanism operated by the movement of her left arm. 'I smile, I pout, and I cry real tears.' Made by Rosebud Mattel Ltd.

CHELMSFORD MUSEUM. Oaklands Park, Chelmsford, Essex. Various toys and dolls, particularly from the bequest of a local resident Mrs Spalding of Chelmsford, including papier mâché tumbler dolls.

Charlie Chaplin, Dean's Rag Book doll, 1919.

CHELSEA ART DOLL MAKERS. For the Coronation of Elizabeth II in 1953 many Souvenirs were made. The project was under the supervision of the Council of Industrial Design at the instigation of the Board of Trade. To make an approved model permission had to be obtained from the Committee. A doll created by Major Puslowski, 21 Carlyle Square, London, SW3 showed the Queen in the famous coronation robe designed by Norman Hartnell and it won much praise for its beauty and accuracy. Major Puslowski had come to England with the Free Polish forces and served as Aide-de-Camp to the Commander. It was he who had the honour to present two Polish dressed dolls to the little English princesses at Windsor Castle during the war. The Coronation model was his idea but the actual fine sculpture was done by Bruckner, the kid bodies tailored by Miss Tearle of Leicester and various pieces of the metal crown, orb and sceptre made in Spain with semi-precious stones as jewels. The bead work and decoration of the gown material also were worked in Spain where labour was cheap. The porcelain heads and limbs were potted in Staffordshire. The finished doll cost $100 but it was hardly profitable. It was 16″ high. Models were also made of Prince Philip, Princess Anne and Prince Charles. Later, characters from Alice in Wonderland and Danny Kaye as Hans Christian Anderson. Most of these collector's pieces were bought by Americans. In 1956 the Coronation doll won the prize as champion doll at an Exhibition in Selfridge's held on behalf of the National Fund for Polio Research. Gradually the project was dropped as the orders did not support the supply. All models are rare collector's pieces.

CHERUB. 1936. See **East London (Federation Toy) Factory.**

CHERUB DOLL. See **Isaacs, Abraham**

CHERUB DOLL JENNY. A 'True-to-Life' baby doll manufactured by Dean's Rag Book Co. Ltd. In 1923 a small girl entered a snapshot of her doll in a real life 'happy baby' competition organised by the manufacturers of a food for infants, and won a prize. The Cherub Jenny doll had a brother, 'Cherub Johnny'. They came in three sizes, 10½″ 13″, and 16″. There were also tiny 3″ 'boy' and 'girl' Cherubs in art silk suits or dainty embroidery frocks and bonnets.

CHERUB DOLL SERIES. Dolls made by Palitoy in 1937 from the safety plastic material Bexoid—fitted with glass eyes by a new patent process. Complete with a dummy.

This is to certify that

_____

has acquired a Miniature Figure of Her Majesty Queen Elizabeth II. in Coronation Robes.

Chelsea Art Doll Makers

Certificate No. ....

CHESHAM BRAND DOLL. Marketed by Ellison, Rees & Co, Basinghall St, London and Chesham. Trade mark Ellarco 1916. Cloth body with shoulder head, from English potteries. They sold another model called Dolleries.

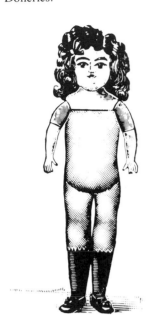

Chunky toys, 1914-18.

CHILTERN DOLLS. Doll range manufactured by H. G. Stone & Co. Ltd., a subsidiary company of L. Rees & Co. Ltd. The dolls were vinyl with saran hair, sleeping eyes and soft eyelashes, and were dressed in a wide variety of dresses. Also sold undressed and in a better series of nylon dresses. 1962 Baby doll range included an 11″ Ballerina doll and Lullaby soft-bodied baby doll. In 1967 the company was acquired by Chad Valley.

CHINA. The term properly applies to porcellanous doll heads for which kaolin clay was used and the finished product was either glazed or left in the bisque state. The majority of such products came from Germany or France but it is rumoured there was a limited English output in the 18th/early 19th century. See **Caughley, Coalport.** When the 1914 war broke out pottery firms in Staffordshire were instructed to make doll heads after the German type and many firms were involved. See **Pottery** for detailed list. The heads and limbs were made from feldspar.

CHINN, H. T. 30th June 1924. Pat. No. 226 448 for doll provided with simultaneously moving arms and hair, operated by rods in holes in the body.

CHOOSY SUSIE. 1967. Bluebell range doll who shakes and nods her head and has washable nylon hair. Made by D. G. Todd & Co. Ltd.

CHRISTIANSEN, B. K. March 1926. Pat. No 264361, relating to "dolls with movable limbs against a spring pressure through the intermediary of bell crank levers actuated by pressure members extending through some part of the doll".

CHRISTIE, Walter Edward. 41 Charterhouse Square, London, E.C. A merchant who registered the trade mark—a picture of a pair of kid gloves—no. 298,740 for dolls on December 10th, 1907.

CHRISTMAS TREE DOLLS. March 1922. 'Special Light Weight Fairies & Father Christmases for Christmas Trees' advertised by Miss Mabel Bland-Hawkes, 190 Lavender Hill, London SW. See: **Bland-Hawkes, Mabel.**

CHRISTOPHER. 1918. Soft boy doll designed by Elizabeth Ellen Houghton.

CHUBBY GIRL DOLL. 1968. 15″ soft vinyl toddler doll, with movable limbs, sleeping eyes and rooted hair. White and negro doll.

'CHUBBY' THE WONDER DOLL. See **British National Dolls Ltd.**

CHU CHIN CHOW. 1922. Pottery mascot doll dressed in silk with moving arms, earrings and pigtails. Probably made by S. Hancock & Sons and sold by Hamley Bros.

CHUCKLES. c1937. Baby doll series with plastex heads dressed in long and short clothes. Made by Cascelloid Ltd.

CHUCKLES. 1970. Laughing doll by Pedigree.

CHUMMY. See **Tiny Tot Toy Co. Ltd.**

CHUNKY. Small articulated wooden dolls made by disabled soldiers in the Lord Roberts Memorial Workshops 1914-18.

CHURCHILL, James. 1852-55. Oakley Street, Lambeth, London, SW. Made composition dolls.

CILLY BILLY. See **Hamley Bros.**

CINDERS. Model doll made with long grey plush. Sizes 10″-60″. Manufactured by Norah Wellings 1929.

CINETTE. See **Herzog, Rae**

CLAIRE. Introduced 1975. 18″ Matchbox doll with blue sleeping eyes and rooted hair. Flared trousers and tie-up jacket. Made in Italy for Lesney Products & Co. Ltd.

CLAPHAM DOLLS. At an auction sale on 19 April 1974 a collection of dolls were sold at Sotheby's by auction. A pair of late 17th century wooden dolls made history when they were sold for £16,000. They were bought by a Swiss collector but later when this amount was collected by public subscription she generously ceded her claim to the dolls and they were taken by the Victoria and Albert Museum in London. Ten other dolls from this same family collection and a miscellaneous pile of clothing went to Switzerland. There were four early papier mâché dolls, three 18th century wooden ones and three foreign wax dolls, all in a remarkable state of preservation. See: **Clapham, Lord and Lady.**

The famous 'Lord and Lady Clapham' were accompanied by ten other dolls, from the same family collection. These consisted of four papier mâché dolls, three 18th century wooden dolls and three foreign wax dolls. Their state of preservation is remarkable. Wooden dolls were made on the turner's lathe, horizontally as with chairlegs, the limbs of material or jointed wood being added separately to the skittle-shaped head and body. The papier mâché dolls could be reproduced more cheaply and quickly by using moulds, originally also made from a wooden pattern. The finished torso was especially suitable for dressing as a fashionable doll and only the exposed head and shoulders was carefully painted and adorned with a wig of real hair. One papier mâché doll retains her original costume. A further two have been recostumed at a later date, one as a Canoness of St. Augustine in full choir robes and winter cloak, the other as a Choir Nun of one of the Benedictine Orders. Private collection.

Late 17th Century doll, wood and papier mâché, part of the Clapham Collection.

The same doll dressed in the habit of a choir nun of the Benedictine Order.

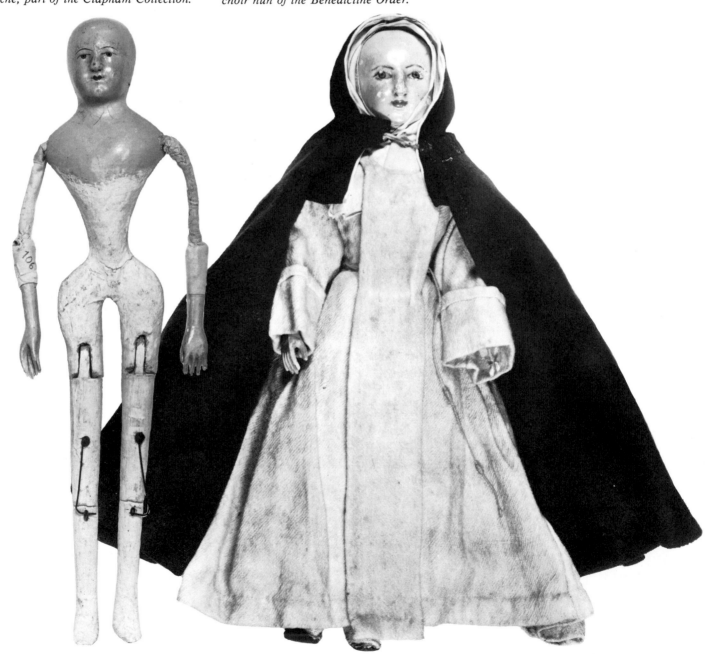

CLAPHAM, LORD AND LADY. The name given to two remarkable wooden dolls 22 inches high and dressed in late 17th century costume. The man wore a coat of scarlet wool with cuffs and buttons matching his waistcoat and breeches of silver tissue. His white silk stockings were knitted with red clocks and tops and held by a light blue ribbon garter. Metal buckles decorated his hand sewn leather shoes and his wig was made of natural hair. His accessories included a 3-cornered hat made of black felt with silver braid and silver sequins and the maker's name inside: T. Bourdillon, Hosier & Hatter to his Majesty, No 14 Russell St Covent Garden. Also a night shirt of plain linen, kid gauntlets, a purse holding silver pennies, a Banyan (informal wear) of salmon pink satin with a semi-naturalistic floral pattern in purple, pale blue, emerald green, lime green, orange and deep pink.

Lady Clapham wore a mantua of white Chinese export silk damask trimmed with silver gilt English bobbin lace. and with silver braid. Underneath she had a quilted linen petticoat and undershift of plain lawn. Her stockings resembled her husband's but her shoes were of white silk brocaded in silver. Her head-dress was wired in the fashion of the age and made from spotted lawn with pink ribbons and English bobbin lace lappets. Both dolls were seated in their own chairs of caned beech wood and elmwood with a small footstool of stuffed silk.

Lady Clapham's married state was proclaimed by a little gold wedding ring and she held a unique carnival mask with a crystal bead at the mouth (method of holding it in place). Lord Clapham wore a sword and scabbard of fine miniature quality.

The name is thought to have come from Clapham near London where the first owners lived. The pedigree has been traced back through the Cockerell family to a direct descendant of Samuel Pepys the diarist. It was to Clapham Samuel Pepys returned and where he died in a friend's house. His favourite nephew John Jackson had a house in Clapham and it seems likely that the doll collection belonged to his children, since one of his daughters, Frances Jackson, married a Cockerell. (John Jackson was the son of Samuel Pepys's sister Pauline.) See **Wooden Dolls.**

Lord and Lady Clapham.

CLARK, W. Obtained British patent for a walking doll, spring motivated with a step by step motion. no. 1664 Patent 2672 1862 for a new doll. Patent 1068, 1865 for a recipe for composition dolls heads using glue 4lb, nutgall etc 3oz, glycerine 8oz, acid 1lb.

CLARKE, NICHOLLS & COMBE. Hackney Wick, Middlesex 1870. Dolls, toys and edible figures.

CLARKSON, T. C. Surrey. Obtained British doll patents 1867 and 1876 Pat. No 2630 for dolls made of West Indian Corkwood, made by covering a mould with netted fabric, cementing on sheet cork with india rubber solution and covering the whole with leather, calico or felt, the surface of which may be painted or enamelled after the removal of mould.

CLASSIC. Proprietary name given to dolls made by Messrs Speight, Classic Works, Dewsbury, Yorks. Registered 1917 also the name Kidette (referring to washable kidette body).

'Classic' doll, 1919, model no. 3003 A/D. Hair-stuffed body, composition limbs, mohair wig.

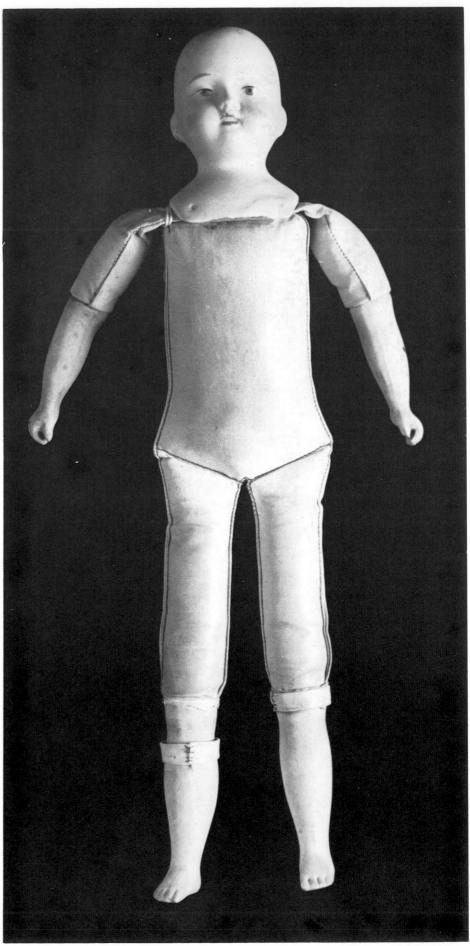

China head and limbs, body made of a washable, oilcloth type of material, 'Classic'

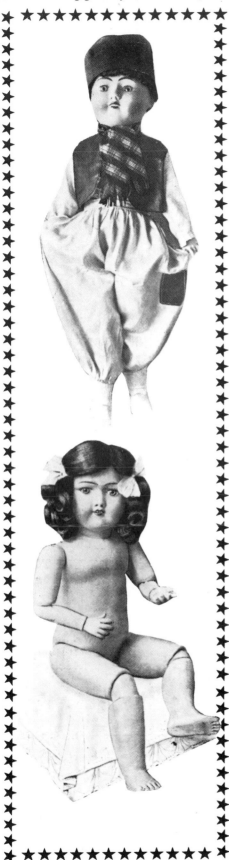

'Classic' Dutch Boy, 1920. China head, fixed or moving glass eyes, mohair wig.

'Classic' kidette doll, fully-jointed, washable body; best English china heads with veined glass eyes; the forearms and lower limbs finished in compo.

CLAVELL, J. Doll patents taken out in 1866 (no 2897) for a dancing doll and 1867 (1334) for an articulated doll with swivel neck.

CLEMENTS, Reginald Arthur. 24th Feb 1958. Pat. No 826818. Patent for dolls' eyes for insertion in a fabric or other flexible material.

CLEVER KERRY. Introduced 1973. Palitoy talking doll whose voice mechanism is activated by touching a number of important trigger spots on the doll. Dressed in pink silky dress with lace frills.

CLIFFE CASTLE MUSEUM. Keighley, Yorkshire. Interesting local collection of antique dolls including pedlars and dolls made from flax.

CLOTHES-PEG DOLLS. The Childrens Newspaper edited by Arthur Mee in 1924 gave these instructions for making clothes-peg dolls: 'The common round clothes-peg is a convenient article to adapt so as to make tiny dolls or figures. The split end serves for legs, and the body and head are all there ready made, so that the work is simple and easy. Then clothes-pegs are cheap, so that we can use a good many of them without incurring much expense, and that fact is an important consideration if we have not much pocket-money. If we prefer it, instead of making dolls we may make a small army of soldiers.

A clothes-peg will not stand steadily on its legs, so we must therefore provide supports by which our dolls or soldiers may stand upright. These supports may be small pieces of cardboard, or thin wood or cork, about the size of a half-penny, as seen in the pictures. A tack or two driven through the support into the bottom of the legs will serve the purpose.'

Then there are many ways in which we can decorate or dress our clothes-pegs, so as to make them look realistic. Black ink is the plainest form of decoration we can apply, and the first two pictures show clothes-pegs finished in this way. One is a circus clown and the other is a nigger with a fool's cap, which is made from a piece of paper twisted into shape. If we wish to give colour to some of our dolls, we can easily do so by using our box of paints, and there is room for display of skill even in such a simple thing as this. If we begin to put dresses on our clothes-pegs, tissue paper is at once the cheapest and easiest material to work. In pictures 3 and 4 we see a man and a woman clothes-peg dressed in tissue paper. They look quite handsome if the work is neatly done. The man has a tall hat, which is made from cork stuck upon the head. There are many other varieties of dress that will suggest themselves as we experiment with the pegs, and it is always better to devise different styles than to copy something exactly as before.

CLOWN (DANCING). 1926. Made by A. J. Holladay & Co Ltd, 3 Aldermanbury Road, London EC. One of a series of dancing puppet figures. These were often used by buskers to entertain theatre queues. A. J. Holladay & Co Ltd marketed 'Givjoy' toys. See **Jollyboy; Dancing Dolls.**

CLOWN DOLL. 1925. Manufacturer Alfred Goldsmith, 55 Whitecross St, London

CLOWN PRINCE. c1916. See **Huvan Manufacturing Co.**

COALPORT CHINA. See **Caughley.**

COBO DOLL. 1880. Made in Guernsey by by Alice Hurays and Judy Guilles. These dolls were made of painted calico stuffed rock hard with sawdust. They were called 'Cobo-Alice' or 'Cobo-Judy'.

CODEG. Trade name of Cowan de Groot & Co, a large import and manufacturing firm. See **Cowan de Groot.**

COHN, Margarete. 1940. At 40 Streatleigh Court, Streatham High Road, London SW16. A German girl who attended art school in Berlin in 1917 but exhibited her work at the British Industries Fair in 1936. Her first dolls were caricatures of her

Clothes-peg dolls.

friends, then she made some to advertise a brand of knitting wool, making fantasy figures from hanks and skeins of wool. She registered the trademark 'Grecon' no. 611, 679 in England on May 2nd, 1940 for her flexible miniature dolls made of wire and wool, which were subsequently advertised by A. Barton & Co. (Toys) Ltd. as being suitable for dolls' houses (1952). Examples of her dolls are in the Worthing Museum.

COLCHESTER MUSEUM. The Museum at the Castle, Colchester, Essex has an interesting collection of clay figurines discovered at various times during the excavation of Roman graves. They date from about 50 AD and when found in the graves of children it has been surmised they are toys and dolls, but they may also have been supplication statues with religious significance. Some seem to have holes which would have been used for stringing as puppets. Also, a collection of dolls and toys is housed in Colchester at the Holly Trees Museum.

COLEMAN, CECIL LTD. Founded 1905. by Mr Sidney Coleman, 130 Pentonville Road, London. 'Peter Pan' trademark. Manufactured toys, indoor games, Christmas crackers and fabric dolls with buckram masks. 1929 advertised 'Sleeping Pop-eye China doll by permission of King Features Syndicate Inc and "Diddums" dressed China doll by permission of Mabel Lucie Attwell.'

COLLEEN. Irish girl doll designed by Mabel Lucie Attwell: Chad Valley 1933/4. 19" high. A series using same face included Nurse, Scots Girl and Policeman.

COLLEEN DOLLS. 1931. Manufactured by Dean's Rag Book Co. 1931.

COLLINS & ROBINS. London 1916. Doll makers 36 Beech St, Barbican, London EC.

COLOMBO, John. London 1843-1848. Doll maker.

'Colleen', Dean's Rag Book Co., 1931.

COLOMBO, William. 1856-68. 37 Winchester St, Pentonville, London. Dollmaker.

COLONEL BOGEY. Doll produced by George Lawrence Nunn.

COLONIAL DOLLS. In 1917, obviously with patriotic impetus, Messrs Dean's Rag Books were supplying Colonial Dolls in tropical kit and Airman dolls, wearing Trench coat with patent 'Tru-to-life' faces and dolls' coats. See **Dean's Rag Books.**

COLONIAL AND OVERSEAS EXPORT COMPANY LTD. 15a Bury Street, Guildford, Surrey. Merchants and manufacturers. Registered trademark 'Wynjoy' no. B614,688 on April 10th, 1941 for soft dolls and soft toy animals, all for export.

COLWELL, W. E. 3rd August 1927. Patent no 282305. Walking toy mechanism.

COMFY-GLOW. See **Be-Be (Dolls) Ltd.**

COMMEMORATIVE DOLLS.

COMMEMORATIVE DOLLS. Dolls have often been costumed to represent some historical character or perhaps celebrate some important moment of history. Pedlar dolls often are found with a real name and licence no. and there were many representations of Queen Victoria and Albert and later of Princess Alexandra dressed in some mode pictured by a contemporary artist. At the 1851 Exhibition Mme Montanari put on show wax dolls representing the royal family, and there were several famous wax doll makers who modelled 'Royal Babies'—a fact they were able to celebrate almost yearly. See **Edwards, John; Pierotti.** Mrs Peck, a later wax modeller, made Lloyd George at his marriage.

Wax dolls were quite often used to commemorate some personal celebration such as marriage or a personal loss such as the death of a child. These memorials are usually preserved in a glass case or beneath a glass dome.

Small dolls might be used for various purposes connected with advertising or sport, theatre etc. Little celluloid dolls with blue-coloured pom-poms and tipped miniature oars were regularly sold as favours for the Oxford and Cambridge boat race.

The small china doll tucked on a spring in a mock Gladstone bag (see illustration) was given away as a souvenir of the first performance of 'The Importance of Being Earnest' by Oscar Wilde. The cheap stoneware doll was obviously moulded for this especial purpose and is not merely a made-up novelty using some contemporary small doll.

COMPOLITE AND COMPOLENE.

c1916. Unbreakable materials for doll making. See **Miller, J. P. & Co.** Dolls designed by Helen Fraser Rock for the Nottingham Toy Industry had bodies made of 'Compolite' (a lightweight composition).

COMPOSITION.

COMPOSITION. A class of unbreakable dolls made from a variety of materials and a succession of recipes. Papier mâché and composition dolls were no doubt originally created by doll makers who wanted a cheap and easily moulded material for the mass production of doll heads.

The material could vary from a primitive papier mâché (literally chewed paper) either soaked in water to form a sort of paste; or laminated with a surface applied with paint or gesso to secret formulas employing a pulp base with a filler and a fixer. Either type could be used with a mould to make a mask. Then more sophisticated forms of papier mâché used various additives and hardeners. The pulp base of fibrous form beaten with water could be shredded paper, saw-dust, or leather waste shavings etc—many variations being recognised according to the locality of the manufacture. The 'filler' to give stability

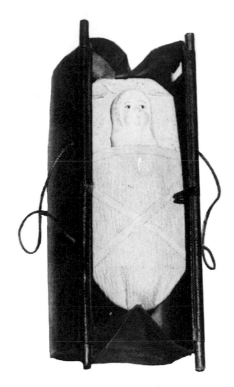

might be sand, plaster, or flour, often with addition of a chemical deterrent to vermin which might be tempted to gnaw the finished goods. Finally the fixer was strong glue or gelatinous substance which could dry rock hard and give the unbreakable quality. The processes of moulding goods in 'composition' were introduced to Europe from the East in the early Middle Ages; and doll heads, puppet heads and masks were probably produced from that time.

In the Clapham collection of dolls are late 17th century examples nicely modelled and decorated.

COMPOSITION DOLLS.

COMPOSITION DOLLS. See **Angel & Nunn; Bluett, T.; Braxted Doll Industry; British National Dolls Ltd.; Compolite; Dean's Rag Book Co.; Hallett, W.; Ideal Dolls Ltd; Lawton Doll Co.; Longbottom, J.; Models (Leicester) Ltd; Tuftex Co.**

COMPRESSED CARD BODIES.

COMPRESSED CARD BODIES. Manufacturer Ilford Doll & Toy Co. 267-273 Ilford Lane, Ilford. 1920 advertisement reads 'Jointed dolls, compressed card bodies sleeping eyes in 3 sizes ½d 1d and 2d dolls.'

CONCHIE DOLL.

CONCHIE DOLL. In January 1918 it was reported that Conchie Dolls (representing conscientious objectors to fighting in the 1914-18 war) had made an appearance in the shops, but were not popular. 'We can scarcely imagine any healthy-minded child harbouring a toy of this kind' declared the Toy and Fancy Goods Trader in January 1918. There is no detail of the maker.

CONEY KID.

CONEY KID. 1936. Plush doll made by Dean's Rag Book Co. Ltd.

CONFECTIONERY CONTAINERS.

CONFECTIONERY CONTAINERS. Dolls made in costume by Mabel Bland-Hawkes 1922 and mounted on a round box for sweet containers.

CONNIE AND HER CARRY-COT.

CONNIE AND HER CARRY-COT. 1972. Made by Palitoy Ltd.

CONSTERDINE, Herbert.

CONSTERDINE, Herbert. Littleborough, Lancashire. Obtained British patent no. 4586 on February 27th 1903 for a doll imitating an acrobat by means of pin joints with a spring wire.

COOGAN KID.

COOGAN KID. See **British Novelty Works Ltd.**

The child film star Jackie Coogan in 'The Kid'; and the rag doll made by The British Novelty Works (i.e. Dean's Rag Book Co.), 1921.

COOK, Henry & SOLOMON, John.

COOK, Henry & SOLOMON, John. Barbican Court, London, E. Made soft toys and dolls, notably Fluff-Fluff and Fluffy-Ruffles in 1908.

COOKMAN, Winifred F.

COOKMAN, Winifred F. 1935. At 244a High Street, Croydon, Surrey; 1939 at 28 Morland Road, Croydon, Surrey. Largest manufacturer in the country of dolls' bed sets and clothes. Every article hand-cut.

COOPER, FREDERICK & SONS CO.

COOPER, FREDERICK & SONS CO. Registered on March 19th, 1917. 5, Dyers Buildings (Bonnedol Works) Holborn, London, E.C.1. Manufacturers and dealers of leather goods, dolls, dolls' clothing and dolls' houses. Made 'Bonnedol' series of character dolls and composition dolls with 'mama' voices.

CORA. 1927. Soft doll made by Norah Wellings. A Cora doll was given to Her Majesty Queen Mary in 1927 when she visited the Victoria Toy Works, Wellington. Height of doll 17 inches dressed in Victorian style. Felt face, glass eyes, moveable joints, real hair wig. The dolls had fine characterisation and were designed from life: See **Wellings, Norah.**

CORN DOLLY. Traditional straw decorations made at harvest time with the last sheaf reaped. Sometimes called kermaiden and associated with ancient pagan rites of fertility. Corn dolly making is now carried on as a hobby and in a great variety of types. An interesting collection of straw dolls made by apprentices to the straw hat industry is shown at Luton Museum: See **Luton.**

CORNELIUS, W. H. LTD. Established c1918. 1955 at Mappin House, 156-162, Oxford Street, London, W1. 1978 at 419 Old Kent Road, London, SE1. Manufacturers and importers of toys and dolls. 1976 selling 'Liza Jane' range of cheap dolls manufactured in Hong Kong.

CORNISH MUSEUM. Lower Street, East Looe, Cornwall. This museum illustrates the life and culture of Cornwall and has as a section devoted to games and pastimes. There is a set of Victorian Punch and Judy Puppets in original costumes, and a collection of home made dolls' hats and shoes c1918.

CORONATION BABE. 1937. Dean's Rag Book Company. This fabric doll was 23″ high; in patriotic colours, she wore long fair plaits and a beret. "The Doll they made a song about."

CORONATION DOLLS. 1937. Messrs J. K. Farnell & Co Ltd, Alpha Works, Acton Hill, London W3. A centre piece of this toy firm's exhibit at the Toy Fair 1937 was a set of dolls representing HM King George VI in Grenadier, Air Force and Scots Guards uniforms. Farnells made a variety of soft toys and character dolls. They had also prepared a Coronation version of the Duke of Windsor as King Edward VIII. See **J. K. Farnell & Co.**

CORONATION TARIFF. In 1937 an 100% tariff was imposed on imported Coronation goods since it was felt buyers should hesitate to buy foreign goods for such a festivity.

COSY KIDS. 1920. Rag dolls manufactured by Dean & Son with 'Tru-Shu' feet. Dressed in coats, bonnets and gaiters. These dolls are somewhat like the American 'Campbell kids'. See **Dean's Rag Book Co.**

'Coronation Babe', 23″ high, Tru-to-life face, 1937 (Pollock's Toy Museum).

COUNTESS. 1920. Classic doll by Speights Ltd.

COUNTRY GIRL. 1920. Classic doll by Speights Ltd.

COUNTRY MISS RAG DOLLS. See **Burbank Toys.**

COWAN DE GROOT & CO. 1919. At City Chambers, 13 City Road, London EC. 1922: 14 Bunhill Row, London, EC1. 1943: 110 Leonard Street, London, EC2. 1977: Wakefield House, Chart Street, London, N1. Toy importers and factors. Founded in 1919 by S. D. Cowan and A. de Groot. 1919 sold 'Britannia' dressed and undressed dolls. December 1929 registered trademark 'Sonny Boy' no. 509,016 for dolls. Used trademark 'Codeg'. In 1960 the company became public, controlling 16 subsidiaries manufacturing and importing a wide variety of electrical and household goods as well as toys.

COWAN, J. (DOLLS) LTD. 1955. At 18-20 Tabernacle Street, London, EC2. Agents and distributors for doll manufacturers. Sold Jayco Dolls, were sole distributors in the British Isles for Roddy dolls manufactured by D. G. Todd & Co. Ltd., and in 1941 became sole agents for Goss China Co. Ltd. dolls. See **Doll Industries Ltd.**

COWAN, S. D. During 1914-18 war founded a doll factory in Ireland producing cheap dolls. Originally apprenticed to Zimmer. See **Zimmer** and **Cowan de Groot.**

COWHAM, Hilda. Professional name of Hilda Gertrude Lander, 65 High St. Marylebone, London W. An artist and illustrator of children's books, particularly annuals. She was known for an almost caricature type figure with long thin black legs and decorative costumed child. The typical Hilda Cowham dolls were promoted by Dean & Son in 1915 and given prominence when Queen Mary bought some examples. They were advertised as play dolls, display dolls and in miniature form, for holding menus, calendars etc.

Both boy and doll models were made and as an advertising promotion Dean's showed at the British Industries Fair in 1915 at a group entitled "Hilda Cowham Kiddies at School. Mademoiselle cheeking the teacher." See also **Dean's Rag Book Co. Ltd.**

Hilda Cowham also designed a doll for Messrs Laurie Hansen & Co. Ltd., 9-15 Whitecross St, London EC1. The doll was made in two patterns: one had eyes wide open and one nearly closed which 'altered the whole expression of the face', long legs, one size but various dresses, and different wigs. See **'Tru-to-life' Rag Dolls.**

Rag doll designed by Hilda Cowham for Laurie & Hansen, 1916.

Doll designed by Hilda Cowham, with china or composition head, for Laurie & Hansen, 1918.

Hilda Cowham 'Kiddies', designed for Dean's Rag Book Co., 1917.

COX, Palmer. An artist and author who produced books about the Brownies published in America but drawing largely on his earlier life in his homeland Scotland. The Brownies were produced in various doll forms including rag dolls on material printed by the Arnold Print firm Massachusetts 1893.

COXETER, Clara 1865. At 38 Newman Street, London, W. 1870. At 38 Store Street, Bedford Square, London, WC. Made dolls.

THE CRABAT SHAPE CO. 158 South gate Road, Dalston, London. Advertised in Feb., 1917 British made rag dolls.

CRAWLING DOLL. A doll imitating the act of a baby crawling over the floor. See **Stranders & Perry; and A. V. Newton.**

CRAZY HORSE. 1976. Fully jointed Cowboy doll from Western range of Fighting Furies series by Lesney Products & Co. Ltd. Made in Hong Kong.

CRECHE DOLLS. Models made for Christmas crib scenes from various materials such as wax, carved wood and terracotta. Dolls also dressed for this purpose as religious figures and angels.

CREMER & SON. 1862-73. London toy shop at 210 Regent Street. Cremer acted as an agent for many continental sources and also sold Pierotti dolls. He had a special department for conjuring and provided salon entertainment and even the Xmas show for the sick children of Great Ormond St. Hospital (1867). He was praised for his responsibility in organising the toy section of the 1871 Exhibition.

According to a Canadian historian, Professor A. K. Adamson, "Recent research into the life of Gladstone shows that in 1867, when in opposition, he was so riled by the taunts of his rival Disraeli that his reason was affected. More than once he ordered the entire stock of Cremer's toy shop to be delivered to his home. Mrs Gladstone had to act swiftly to countermand the orders".

CREST CHINA. See **Carlton Heraldic China; Goss, W. H. & Co.; Hewitt & Leadbeater.**

CRIES OF LONDON. See **Cuckoobird.**

CROLLY DOLLS. See **Gaeltarra Eireann.**

CROPPER, B. Obtained patent no. 407176 in February, 1933 for a doll constructed in two parts, hinged and connected together, one part being a box or container and the other forming a lid. The meeting edges of two parts were provided with a sliding clasp fastener.

CROWN POTTERY. The Royal Crown Pottery Co. Advertised in 1918 dolls' tea services and dolls.

CROWN STAFFORDSHIRE PORCELAIN CO. LTD. Minerva Works, Fenton, Stoke-on-Trent (est 1801). Design nos. 654305 and 654736 registered by Doll Pottery Co. Ltd. 1916. Company reported as making fully-jointed dolls 1919 (Pottery and Glass Record).

CROWTHER, C. WHITELEY & BURTON, W. J. 24th August, 1943. Patent no. 567949. A facial representation has eye holes through which can be seen the pupils, located at a slight distance between the plane of the holes, thus imparting to the eyes an appearance of following a passer-by looking at the face.

CRY BABY. 1924. See **Worthing Toy Factory**

CRY BABY BEANS. 1973. See **Ploppy Character Dolls.**

CRYER & NAYLOR. 1802-5. At 206 Whitecross Street, London. Made dolls.

'Cry Baby', china head, stuffed body and legs, sold by J.W. Lawrence, 1916.

CRYING DOLLS. Reports exist of 'crying' dolls available in England as early as 1700 but a good account is given by Mayhew in 1850 of the doll maker Bazzoni of High Holborn who invented a lifelike voice box for a doll saying Papa and Mama. He said he sold rather more than a dozen at 'six guineas apiece'. It was probably a bellows and reed contraption resembling the invention of Maelzel who patented a talking doll in 1824 (English patent). See also **Phonograph dolls.**

CUBBY. 1973. See **Ploppy Character Dolls.**

CUCKOOBIRD. Peckham Bush, Tonbridge, Kent. Soft toy and doll manufacturers. 1972 lines include 'Cries of London'— small printed cotton dolls in blue, pink, turquoise or yellow, filled with lavender, designed by Pat Albeck from the Royal College of Art. Some of the firm's products are made only for sale in National Trust Houses.

CUDDLEY COO. 1931. Range of dolls. See **Merrythought.**

CUDDLEY-ONES. c1917. Series of soft stockinette dolls designed by Mrs Elizabeth Ellen Houghton and manufactured by the Three Arts Women's Employment Fund Toy Industry.

CUPID. See **Kohnstam, M. & Co.**

CUPID DOLLS. The first British-made celluloid Cupid dolls were manufactured by Palitoy 1937. See **Cascelloid.**

CURLING, Robert Sumner. 70 Duke Street, London, W. A barrister who in January 1916 registered the trademark 'The Papooski' no. 371,224 for dolls.

CURLY LOCKS. A soft, cuddly, featherweight doll. Down-stuffed with Tru-to-Life mask. Made by Dean's Rag Book Co. Ltd. 1923.

CUTIE. 1921. See **Lawton Doll Co.**

CUT OUT CLOTH DOLLS. All types of animals and dolls designed on material and realistically printed. They could be cut and sewn to make an attractive rag toy. See **Dean's** and **Rag Dolls**

CUPID DOLLS. Manufacturer Lawton Doll Co, 37-40 Station Road, Blackpool 1921. Also 57-59 Neal Street, Long Acre, London WC2. Mascot dolls with goo-goo eyes and tutu dress. The firm had a capacity output of 12,000 dolls a week.

Also made statuary and art productions at 35, Clerkenwell Close and 14 Sans Walk. Material for dolls was chiefly wood fibre, making them unbreakable. Manufactured in huge presses.

CUT OUT PAPER DOLLS. See **Dean's Rag Book Co. Ltd; Fell, J. C.; Gibson, E. T.; Spear, J. W. & Sons; Tuck, Raphael.**

CYGNET. 1958. Registered trademark for dolls and other toys. See **Simpson, Fawcett & Co. Ltd.**

DADOOWALA. 1910. Registered trademark for mechanical doll. See **Sherwood, Katherine Mary.**

DAGMAR, MARGOT, LTD. 10 The Little Boltons, London, SW10. Doll and puppet manufacturers and merchants. Registered trademark 'Rainbow', no. 791,829 on 8th June, 1959 for dolls and puppets.

DAILY SKETCH & SUNDAY GRAPHIC LTD. 200 Grays Inn Road, London WC1. Publishers. Registered trademark 'Pop' no. 512,473 on 29th April, 1930, for toy dolls and sporting articles in the form of character reproductions.

DAINTY MAY. c1922. Doll manufactured by Dennis, Malley & Co. Ltd.

DAISY. Introduced 1972. 9″ fashion doll, with movable head, waist, arms, legs and knees. Over 30 outfits designed by Mary Quant, well-known English fashion designer who rose to fame in the 'swinging' 60's. Manufactured by Model Toys Ltd. In the autumn of 1974 over 40 new Mary Quant designed outfits were introduced; also new Daisy accessories.

DAISYCROFT STUDIOS. 1938. Kiln Road, Thundersley, Essex. Manufacturers of dolls' masks, at prices competitive with those of imported masks. 'Foreigners used to have monopoly on dolls' masks in earlier period, but today firms make them for their own dolls.' (James & Co. 1938.)

DAISY DOLLS or JUNE BABIES. c1918. Made by Nottingham Toy Industry Ltd. Range includes 'Joyce & Josylin', dressed, with china heads and limbs; 'Peter & Pauline' with 'Compolite' bodieso No. 56 girl doll in simple muslin dress and sash; No. 55 girl doll, in silk dress with ribbon around her hair.

DAKIN, Margaret Ann. 1922. Church Hall, Broxted, Dunmow, Essex. Registered trademark 'CABBAGERINO' no. r 0,458 on 5th September, 1922 for toys and dolls.

DALLIMORE, W. H. Obtained patent no. 21268 on November 8th 1893 for dolls which are caused to move by two wires, the limbs and head being jointed to a plate. The ends of the wires are bent round a connecting piece to the head, which is caused to move from side to side when the wires are pulled alternately.

DANCING DOLLS. Manufactured by Dean's Rag Book Co. Ltd. Extremely popular line in 1928. 'The antics and attitude of the figures when danced singly or in couples are beyond description!'

'Unique as a window display not requiring elaborate fittings. An effective method is to fix a cord five feet above floor level and another cord 9 inches from one of the fixed

'Daisycroft' brand of doll masks, 1938.

ends. Pulling upon this causes the dolls to perform realistically, as each pair is supplied with a cord attachment on the end of which is fixed a small ring. The extended cord is passed through this ring and adjusted so that the dolls' feet just touch the ground.' (Games & Toys, 1928.)

Dancing dolls worked on a cord were a popular street entertainment in London in 18-19th centuries. A sort of miniature loose limbed puppet, they were jiggled about on a cord attached at one side to a small post on a wooden plank and at the other to the foot or knee of the performer. In Hogarth's Southwark Fair Print, 1773, a young lad is represented working them and accompanying the dance on crude bagpipes. In a print of 1835 a boy performs on pipe and drum and they are entitled "London Dancing Dolls".

A patent taken out in London (No. 6198) 14th March 1904 by H. P. Rugg registered a dancing doll mounted on a stick which jigged on a tapped board in the style of such traditional home-made dolls as "Peter Waggies", the North country term for such types. They were usually made of a skittle-shaped body with very loosely jointed legs and arms

which could perform a mad jive.

Dean's dancing dolls included Bunty and Bobby with rabbit heads, 1928. See **Action Girl; Bowden, J.; Burgess, A. H.; Clavell, J.; Dunn, W.; Gray, W.; Jollyboy.**

Dancing animals, 1928. Pat. no. 33981

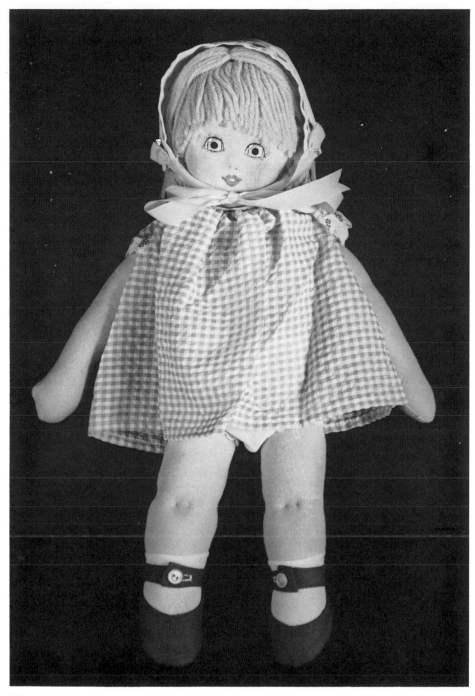

Mary Dean rag doll, 1975.

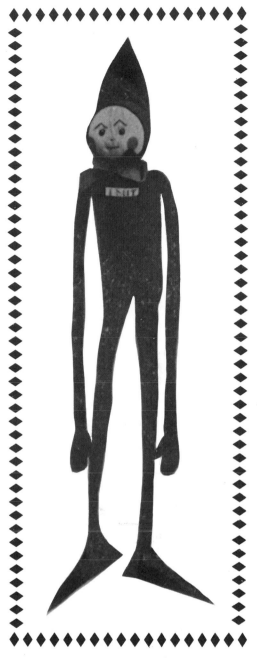

'I Mit' doll, 1919, Darenta Toy Works.

DANIELS, Miss E. M. See **Jungle Toys.**

DANNY. Introduced 1975. 18″ Matchbox cuddly boy doll, soft-bodied with sleeping eyes and rooted hair. Vinyl face and hands. Made in Hong Kong for Lesney Products & Co. Ltd. and stuffed and assembled in U.K.

DAPHNE. See **Art Dolls**

DAREDEVIL. Introduced 1974. 9″ articulated male doll with various adventure outfits. Made by Model Toys Ltd.

DARENTA TOY WORKS. c1919. Vickers House, Broadway, London, SW1. Doll and toy manufacturers; proprietors, Vickers Armstrong. Made comic figures with long, fabric-wired limbs, dressed and undressed, such as Frolix and I Mit figures.

DARLING. 1936. Baby doll with soft body, unbreakable head, sleeping eyes, and movable limbs. Manufactured by The East London Toy Factory Ltd.

DARTFORD MUSEUM. Market St, Dartford, Kent. Dolls, toys, costume on show.

DASHING DAISY. Introduced 1975. A new Daisy doll with more articulated movement; also has horse and sporting outfits designed by Mary Quant. Manufactured by Model Toys Ltd.

DAVIS, Alfred. c1850. Houndsditch, London. Imported and assembled china-headed dolls to be hawked in the London streets.

DAZZLE-DAZZLE DOLL. 1919. Doll from 'Classic' registered range. 16″ high with china head and glass eyes. 5s 11d. 'Dazzling effect of striped dress'. See manufacturers, **Speights Ltd.**

DEAN, H. S.. See **Dean's Rag Book Co. Ltd.**

DEAN, Mary. 1975. At Flat 1, Bottisham Hall, Bottisham Park, Cambridge. Makes 'Lisa' rag dolls with faces of moulded cloth in the traditional manner of 75 years ago.

DEAN & SON LTD. 52-54 Southwark St., London SE1. The printing and publishing firm of Dean & Son has been established in the City of London since the 18th century, first in Threadneedle Street and later on Ludgate Hill, near the centre of the printing trade. Dean's were among the first to produce children's books designed for entertainment as much as for instruction: pictorial alphabets, for instance, or Perrault's fairy tales with liberal illustration and a minimum of text. From the 1840s onwards they produced all kinds of movable-flap and three-dimensional books, strung together with ribbons: a typical example was 'Dissolving Pictures of Things Worth Knowing', published in 1862.

Colouring by hand with stencils gave way around 1870 to oil colour printing and soon afterwards the experiment was made of pasting the printed pages on to calico to strengthen them (as is done with maps). In 1901 this process was superseded in turn by direct printing on to 'holland' calico.

Dean's first rag book title was 'The Life of Bold A.B. on his Ship in the Rolling C.' The colours were fast, the product certified as hygienic. The pages could be washed without damage, and sucked with impunity: perfect, in fact, for children who, in the words of the rag book's originator, 'wear their food and eat their clothes'.

In 1926, from Debrett House, 29 King Street, London WC2, Dean's produced a series of books in the shape of a doll, 25 in high, that could be played with. The series comprised Nanette, Minette, Babette and Odette, at 2s 6d each. In 1928 came a series of books shaped like dolls, and called Nono, Lulu, Rosine and Lucette. The body of the doll opened to form an attractive book; while its head and legs were jointed inside the back cover and could be moved to any position.

Over the past forty years Dean & Son have published a wide variety of doll dressing and other novelty books.

Dean and Son Ltd. is no longer connected with Dean's Rag Book Company and Dean's Childsplay Toys Ltd., but is part of a large complex of publishing firms. Since 1958 however they have acted as sole agents for Merrythought Ltd., and the soft toys produced by this firm are on show at Dean & Son's Ltd. headquarters at 52-4 Southwark Street, London SE1.

DEAN'S CHILDSPLAY TOYS LTD. c1960. 17-18 Tower Street, Rye, Sussex. Subsidiary company of Dean's Rag Book Co. Ltd. Soft toys and wood toys etc. 1966 lines include 'Penny', a washable rag doll, 13″ tall, with ponytail hairstyle of nylon yarn, a gay coloured reversible frock. Also 'Gloria', 18″ rag doll, 'sister' to Penny.

Jointed doll book, Dean & Son. (A book and a movable doll combined. The body of the doll opens and inside is an illustrated book. The head and legs of the doll are attached to the back cover. Four books in the series: Nono, Lulu, Rosine, Lucette)

DEAN'S RAG BOOK CO. LTD. A subsidiary of Dean & Son Ltd., founded in 1905 to print rag books and dolls at 18, Paternoster Square, London, EC. c1915 Factory at 2-14 Newington Butts, London, SE. Showrooms at 160a Fleet Street, London, EC. c1923 Offices and Factory at Elephant and Castle London, SE1. c1925 Showroom at 29 King Street, Covent Garden, London, WC2. c1934 Showroom at Ludgate Hill, London EC4. c1936 Factory at High Path, Merton, London, SW19. 1960

Tru-to-life doll with wig, Dean's Rag Book Co., 1922.

Nanette, Minette, Babette and Odette: four doll books published by Dean & Son, 1926.

onwards 17-18 Tower St, Rye, Sussex. Publishers and toy and doll manufacturers.

On 25th November, 1908 H.S. Dean obtained patent no. 25452 for dolls of printed or coloured fabrics, cut in 6 parts, sewn together and stuffed.

Registered trademark (picture of two dogs fighting over a rag book) no. 319,017 on 8th December, 1909, for toys, dolls, toy animals, birds and other toy figures. Registered trademark 'Fuz Buz' no. 354,125 18th August, 1913 for dolls, puppets and toys. In 1913 they introduced a collection of thirty 'Tru-to-Life' face rag dolls.

On 1st June, 1915 H. S. Dean obtained patent no. 8118 for dolls, puppets, figures, toy animals etc. of inflatable and uninflatable portions enclosed within a fabric or other cover shaped to the outline of the complete article.

With A. L. Wheeldon, they obtained patent no. 100469 on 17th March, 1916 for the manufacture of stuffed dolls and toy animals etc. in which the 'sheet material forming the front and back of the foot is formed with extension pieces, so that by sewing the sheets together and drawing in a central portion, a complete foot is formed'. Also with A.L. Wheeldon, they obtained patent no. 105888 on 14th February, 1917; 'Material for making a stuffed doll is shaped so as to form a skirt or other garment in one therewith.'

Products included 'Knockabout Toys' (coloured printed cloth sheets, various subjects, 'Big Baby Doll' the most popular); 1915 'Gilbert the Filbert, King of all the Knuts'; c1921 A1 range of toys and dolls (A1

Louise Heard wearing a dress made entirely from Dean's Rag Books sewn together. The books were published in 1922.

Part of a display of Dean's Rag Book Co.'s series of national costume dolls, Bethnal Green Museum, November 1923.

63

being the symbol of Dean's quality) including during the following years felt-dressed Posy Dolls and Posy Buds, Doll with the disc (with patent Tru-to-Life face), 'Evripoze' dolls, Princess dolls; c1925, Luvly Dolls, Smart Set Dolls, Frilly Dolls; c1929 'Modern Beau Brummel' with eye-glass, spotted bow tie, cut away jacket, cane and hat, etc., 'Domestic Utility Dolls', 'Baby Bunting Dolls'; 'Goo-Goo Petlings' designed by Grace Wiederseim in 1913-14 and Pauline Guilbert series of dolls, followed by Hilda Cowham rag dolls, one of which Queen Mary ordered, Moppietops, Pierrette, Sambo, Dinah, Boy Sprout, Sarah Starer, Nautical Nancy, Joyful Joey, Shrieking Susan, Rag Time and many others.

Dean's Rag Book have over the years commissioned a number of artists to design books and dolls for them, many being well-known in other fields: for instance Hilda Cowham, an illustrator of children's books, and John Hassall, a cartoonist. Grace Wiederseim's dolls and animals are all characterised by their large goo-goo eyes, whereas the dolls and bonbonnières of the French designer Pauline Guilbert are more conventionally pretty. Other designers who worked for Dean's Rag Book include Cecil Aldin, Stanley Berkley and David Brett.

In 1935, Dean's Rag Book Co. and Dollies Ltd. joined to form Dean's Dollies Ltd., a new company.

In 1972 Dean's Rag Book Co. merged with Dean's Childsplay Toys and Gwentoys and premises were opened at Pontypool, Gwent. The old premises in Rye, Sussex finally closed in January 1982. Dean's recent productions include 'Teddie and Peggy' rag dolls (1980), designed by Grace Wiederseim and originally produced in 1912; 'Mignonne' doll, originally produced in 1920 and reproduced in 1980 specially for the Church of England Children's Society; 'Dismal Desmond' (1981) originally produced in 1923; 'Charles and Diana' Royal Engagement Souvenir dolls (cut-out sheets) designed by Sylvia Rosemary Willgoss and produced in 1981; 'Charlie Chaplin' doll, reproduced 1982 for export only, originally produced in 1920. Future productions will include a *new* 'Mr Golly' in made-up and do-it-yourself form.

'The Doll with the Disc', 1922. Tru-to-life face. Made in 3 sizes and dressed in 13 different styles.

'Dutch Girl', patent 'Evripoze' doll, 1922. The series comprised 30 national costume models.

'Sunshine Doll', dressed in picture frock, 1929.

'The Doll with the Disc', Dean's Rag Book Co., 1922. Tru-to-life face made in 3 sizes and dressed in 13 styles.

'Travel Tot', Dean's Rag Book Co.'s 'A I Doll's, 1929.

'Miss Moppietopps', Dean's Rag Book Co., 1914.

DEAN'S A1 DOLLS & TOYS

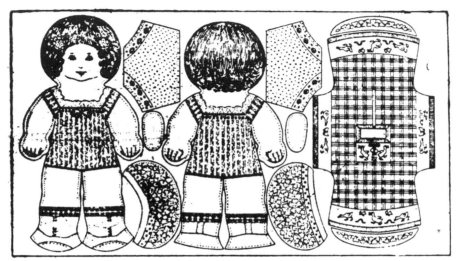

A 1 Doll Sheet, 'Wendy and her Wardrobe', 1923. To be cut out and sewn.

'Peggy' and 'Teddy', designed by Grace Wiedersheim for Dean's Rag Book Co. in 1912 and re-issued by Dean's Childsplay Toys Ltd. in 1980.

'Dolly Dips', the sea-side doll, Dean's Rag Book Co., 1917. Made with flat or Tru-to-life face.

DEAN'S RAG BOOK CO., LTD.

NURSERY NOVELTIES

The New Series of Dolls, Tea Cosies and Bonbonnières from original designs by Pauline Guilbert *the famous French Artist*

¶ Nursery Novelties appropriately describes this series of Dolls, Tea Cosies and Bonbonnières, in as much that it is a striking departure from anything that has been produced hitherto.

¶ The quaint and pleasing originality of the artist is faithfully reproduced and displayed to the utmost advantage in the " Edition de Luxe" on Satin, the effect of the harmonious and delicate colouring being greatly heightened by the rich sheen of the material.

¶ The embracing of three distinct articles in this one series affords an exceptionally wide scope so far as sales are concerned ; for instance, where a Doll may not appeal, there is every possibility of a customer purchasing a Nursery Tea Cosy, or Bonbonnière, and *vice versa*.

¶ As a means of conveying small gifts of Confectionery, Jewellery or Perfumery, the Bonbonnières cannot be excelled, a neat box being provided for the purpose in the base of each figure, whilst the Tea Cosies give just the requisite finishing touch to the table at the Nursery Tea Party.

¶ Every "Pauline Guilbert" Figure bears the Artist's facsimile signature (a specimen of which is given above), also a certificate of guarantee of Hygienic Manufacture.

JOSEPHINE

Retail Prices

"EDITION DE LUXE" ON RICH SATIN
:: — ::

Small Dolls - 2/6 each
Large Dolls - 3/6 each
Bonbonnières
Small - - - 3/- each
Large - - - 4/- each
Tea Cosies - 4/- each
(Large size only)

ENTIRELY BRITISH MANUFACTURE.

Exceptionally advantageous Trade Terms

MIGNONNE

Retail Prices

STANDARD EDITION ON COTTON CLOTH
:: — ::

Small Dolls - 1/6 each
Large Dolls - 2/6 each
Bonbonnières
Small - - - 2/- each
Large - - - 3/- each
Tea Cosies - 3/- each
(Large size only)

WASHABLE INDESTRUCTIBLE HYGIENIC.

Full Particulars furnished upon application

Trade Mark — Registered in all Countries

 SMALL :: ::   SIZE :: ::

ANTOINETTE   **MARGUERITE**   **EUGÉNIE**

DEAN'S RAG BOOK Co., Ltd.,

Toy Dept., 18 Paternoster Square, London, E.C.

:: ::   DEAN'S RAG BOOK CO., LTD.   :: ::

Dean's Rag Book 'Nursery Novelties', 1912.

Dean's patent Tru-to-life rag doll, 1913.

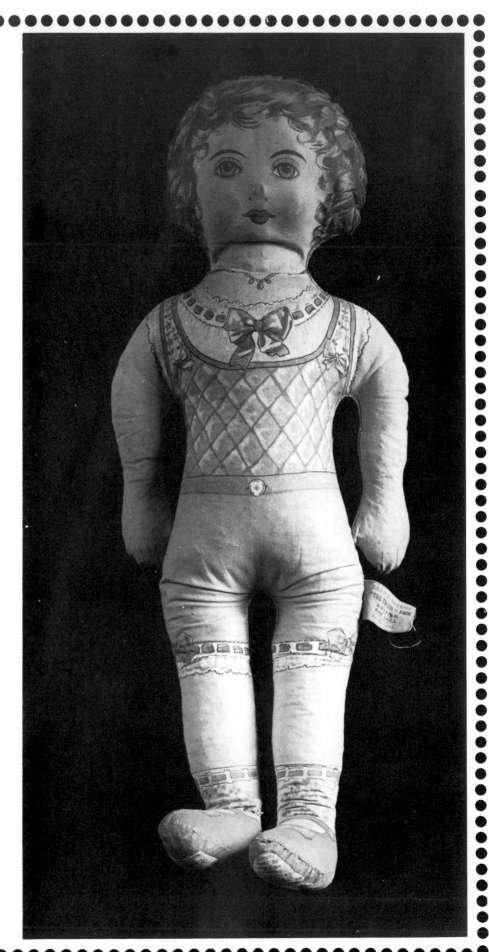

Dean's 'Knockabout' doll, 1908.

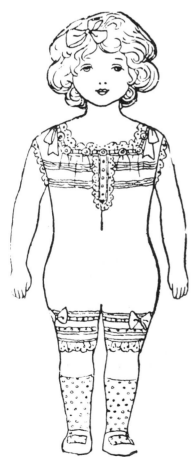

'Bell Boy', 1929.

'Trike Boy', 1929.

*'Smart Set' doll,
1927, 22 ins.*

*'Frilly Doll', 1927. Made in 8 sizes,
12½ ins. to 36 ins.*

'Scooter' doll, 1929.

'Poppy', 'Rose' and 'Daisy' - three Posy dolls, 1925, dressed in soft felt. 12 different flower patterns, each made in 3 sizes: 13 ins., 17 ins., 22 ins.

'Gem' doll, 1932, with different jewelled necklaces.

'Peter' and 'Patsy', wearing romper suits, 1933.

'Princess' dolls, 1925. Made in 7 sizes,
from 10 ins. to 36 ins. Down-stuffed bodies,
velveteen dresses in 6 different colours,
trimmed with white bear plush (Pollock's
Toy Museum).

'TommyFuzbuz', 1914. Part of a set of ra[g]
doll ninepins, with fur busbies, sold boxe[d]
with a soft ball covered in wool net plus
a little book.

'Popeye', the sailor man, based on a strip
cartoon figure. Dean's Rag Book Co. 1935.

'Sam', of 'Pick up tha musket' fame.
Dean's Rag Book character doll, 1936.

'Punch', a stuffed
puppet, made by [?]
1930.

'Puckaninny', 1936.

Mickey Mouse.

'Flo, the girl in the little green hat', 1933.
Made in 3 sizes.

onette-type
ag Book Co.,

'Henry', 1936. Based on a popular cartoon
character.

DEBBIE. 1960. A 20″ teenage vinyl doll with stitched-in wig, blonde ponytail or wavy brunette, and sleeping eyes. Wardrobe includes: embroidered nylon dress, underskirt, panties, bra, silk stockings, high-heeled shoes, and earrings. Made by Palitoy.

DEBUTANTE DOLLS. 1960. Pedigree range of 20″ vinyl 'Mannequin' dolls including 'Louretta' at 87s 6d, 'Theda' at 110s and 'Bridesmaid' at 99s 6d.

DEE. 1972. Matchbox Disco Doll.

DEICHMANN, A. O. W. Obtained patent no. 346878 for a miniature doll which produces various facial expressions, 30th January, 1930. Obtained patent no. 363847 on 5th January, 1931 for 'a figure used as a toy for advertising purposes, or for trick films'.

DELCO DOLLS. See **Dell & Co.**

DELITE DOLLS. c1949. Injection-moulded Pedigree dolls, with moving limbs and body, and head with sleeping eyes, 'good dress styles'. Heights 16″ and 10″.

DELL & CO. c1917-30. At 288 Amhurst Road, Stoke Newington, London, N16. c1919 at 1A Colverstone Crescent, London, E8. c1930 Showrooms at 45-51 Church Row, Bethnal Green, London, E2. Made dolls. 1917 rag and china-head dolls, dressed and undressed. 1930 Delco series of 'unbreakable composition dolls with movable eyes'. 'Delco Beauty', 'Delco Special' and 'Delco Princess'.

DELMACOL. Brand name and trademark of Dennis, Malley & Co. Ltd.

DELTA DOLLS LTD. Before 1948 at Riverside Works, Borough Road, Wallasey, Cheshire. From April 1948 at 19-21 Baker Street, Liverpool 6. Made jointed hard-bodied dolls with sleeping eyes and eyelashes. Together with D. Cohen, obtained patent no. 621332 on 19th February, 1947 for a sleeping eye unit.

DE LUXE DOLLS 1960. Pedigree range of fully-jointed vinyl dolls with sleeping eyes and eyelashes, rooted Saran hair, lace-trimmed petticoat and panties, white nylon socks and plastic shoes. Range includes Dorcas at 57s 6d, Eleanora at 65s, Miranda at 63s. The dolls have special make-up effects and varnished finger nails.

DE LUXE TOY CO. LTD. Westmoreland Road, Kingsbury, London, NW9. American-owned toy and doll manufacturers and an associate company of the Lines Bros. group. 1963 lines include Suzy Smart the talking school doll, (voice mechanism made in America): 'She recites, she spells, she adds! she has her own desk and chair, blackboard and easel, pencil, schoolbook, chalks and blackboard eraser!' The doll is 25″ tall with washable rooted hair. In 1964 a new division was formed called 'Topper Toys'; lines included 'Penny Brite', an 8″ flexible doll with 6 different outfits. Also 'Schoolroom' and 'Beauty Parlour' accessory sets.

DENNIS MALLEY & CO. LTD. 14 Heathman's Yard, Parsons Green, London, SW6. & Walton House, 1 Newman Street, London, W1. c1921 at 7 Hamsell Street, London, EC. Import, export and general merchants. Owned factories in Germany: Delmacol Catterfeld Puppenfabrik and Delmacol Neustadt Puppenfabrik. 'Delmacol' was the brand name for their dolls. Also made 'Dainty May' and 'May Blossom' lines. Registered trade mark for latter: no. 430,728, on 21st October, 1922.

DENYS FISHER TOYS LTD. Thorp Arch Trading Estate, Boston Spa, Yorkshire. Toy and doll manufacturers. In 1968 took over Wendy Boston Playsafe Toys and in 1974 took over the production of Bluebell dolls. 1976 range includes 'Dusty', the air hostess doll, and many baby dolls with action features. 1976 Wendy Boston/Bluebell series includes a large selection of dressed and undressed dolls from 12″ to 25″ tall.

DERBYSHIRE COUNTY MUSEUM. Sudbury Hall, Derbyshire. The collection includes some Victorian dolls.

DESDEMONA. Introduced 1969. 14″ walking Palitoy doll with black glancing eyes.

DESTINY ANGEL. 1967. 4½″ doll with bendable limbs based on character in T.V. adventure puppet series. Manufactured by Pedigree Dolls Ltd.

'Diamond' dolls and dolls' heads advertised by The Diamond Tile Co. Ltd., 1941.

DEW, S. T. & TRAUTMANN, F. O. Obtained patent no. 188960 on 23rd November, 1921, for a skipping doll.

DIAMANT, L. c1924. At Spitalfields, London, E1. Manufacturer of cheap jointed dolls, baby dolls and teddy bears.

DIAMOND DOLLS. See **Diamond Tile Co. Ltd.**

DIAMOND POTTERY CO. LTD. 1908-1925. Brook St, Shelton. During the 19th century, Brook St. Shelton, on the outskirts of Hanley, Stoke-on-Trent, was the home of four or five small pottery firms. In 1892 the firm of Wood and Thompson which was listed as occupying No. 1 Brook St. was replaced by the Pearl Pottery Co. Sixteen years later, in 1908, the Pearl Pottery Co. moved across the road and installed themselves in the Brook St. works. They still retained the premises at No. 1 and formed a subsidiary company, the Diamond Pottery Co. to run the pottery they had just vacated.

In 1935 the Pearl Pottery closed. Its premises were taken over by the New Pearl Pottery and in 1936 the shares of this new company were acquired by the New Hall Pottery, famous in the last century for hard paste porcelain.

In 1940, the Brook St. Works were damaged by fire bombs and in 1947 the New Hall Pottery sold the site and itself went into liquidation ten years later in April 1956. Brook St. is now called Century St., and by 1957 all potworks had disappeared except the Diamond Tile Co. Ltd., who occupied No. 1 Brook St. Probably they continued making tiles after the doll industry petered out.

In her book "English Dolls", published in 1955, Mrs Alice Early reported a recollection from a pottery worker who had joined the Empire Porcelain Co. in 1916. She remembered several factories which had made doll parts. She thought the doll making was continued up to 1940 when "the Pearl Pottery" was taken over by the War Department.

A great number of English-made pottery dolls are marked D.P.C., and there is confusion as to whether the initials stand for Diamond Pottery Co., or Doll Pottery Co., which worked between 1916-1922. All variations of the D.P.C. mark are shown under the Doll Pottery Co. of Fenton, Staffs, since in Pollock's Toy Museum most dolls so marked resemble the dolls actually advertised in 1917 by the Doll Pottery Co.

DIAMOND TILE CO. LTD. Founded 1933. Brook Street, Hanley, Stoke-on-Trent, Staffordshire. Manufactured earthenware dolls and heads for a limited period. 1941 advertised Diamond Dolls in 3 sizes: 37cm, 42cm, and 52cm; with matt, bright or negro finish. Also dolls' heads for soft-bodied dolls. In 1943 doll production stopped because the firm was producing without a government licence. One of the partners at this time was a Mr Thompson, a name connected in late 19th century with the premises occupied in Brook St by the Diamond Pottery Co. So possibly the two firms were connected.

DIANA. 1952. Pedigree doll. See **Pin-Up Dolls.**

DICKINS, H. M. Obtained patent no. 322222 on 31st August 1928, relating to a stuffed figure toy.

'Diddums' - Mabel Lucie Attwell postcard.

Hamley's novelties, 1921: 'Fums Up' with assorted wigs and ribbons, in 3 sizes, and 'Diddums' mascot 'Miss Dainty', dressed in silk in assorted colours.

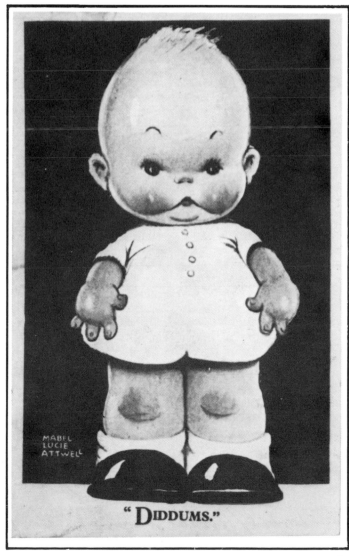

"DIDDUMS."

DICKINSON, W. A. & LYXHAYR MANUFACTURERS LTD. Obtained patent no. 28358 on 16th December, 1911, for using 'Lyxhayr' as a stuffing for dolls.

DIDDUMS. See **Hamley Bros.**

DIDDUMS. c1939. Dressed china doll designed by Mabel Lucie Attwell and manufactured by Cecil Coleman Ltd.

DIDDUMS AND HAPPY. Dolls designed by Mabel Lucie Attwell, manufactured by Cascelloid Ltd.

DIETRICH, T. G. Obtained patent no. 165352 on 28th September, 1920, relating to production of articulated limbs for sheet metal dolls of different patterns.

DILLY DICK. 1917. Character doll made by Tah Toys Ltd.

DIMPLE. 1935. Baby doll made by Dean's Rag Book Co. Ltd.

DINAH. Doll made by Dean's Rag Book Co. Ltd.

DINKIE. 1919. 'Classic' doll made by Speights Ltd. with china head, composition arms and legs, dressed in a coat and hat of 'venta' cloth and carrying a white muff.

DINKIE DOLLS. 1926. A1 doll range comprising four 12″ models. Hygienically stuffed. Retail price 1s. Manufactured by Dean's Rag Book Co. Ltd.

DINKY BABY DOLLS. See **Cascelloid.**

DINKY TOY. 1925. See **Jones, William Henry.**

DISCO GIRLS. See **Lesney Products & Co. Ltd.**

DISNEY. Walt Disney Film Corporation augmented its profits from film production by a large-scale merchandising programme, and by selling licences to manufacturers outside the U.S.A. The Disney licensing office in Wardour Street, London. was particularly busy during the years 1930 to 40. Film characters appeared as toys and dolls, on watches, T-shirts etc., thus ensuring a perennial popularity with the public. Dolls were made of Snow White, Pinocchio, Cinderella, Alice in Wonderland, Davy Crockett, Sleeping Beauty, Mary Poppins etc.

DIXIE. 1952. See **Saucy Walkers.**

DIXIE STYLE DOLLS. c1933. Black dolls manufactured by Merrythought Ltd. 'Dixie Bebe' and 'Patsie'.

DIXON, Elizabeth. 1811-14. At 7 Little Anchor, Tottenham Street, Shoreditch, London. Made dolls.

DIXON, John. 1808-50. At Old Bailey, London. Made dolls.

DIXON, T. A. 1918. Butts Works, Worcester. Doll manufacturer. Made unbreakable dolls of special composition, called 'Noxid'. Boy and girl dolls 'dressed in variety of costumes'.

DIZZY WHIZZ. 1959. Registered trademark. See **Sieki, Masa Roy; Roytoys.**

DODD, Isobel. 26 Fitzwilliam Square, Dublin, S. Ireland. Doll manufacturer. Registered trademark 'Durax' no. 389,648 on 28th March 1919, for dolls.

DODD, Thomas. 1914-18. Roxy factory, Lockett's Lane, Longton, Staffs. Made pottery parts for dolls.

'DOLAC'. See **Sissons Bros. & Co Ltd.**

'DOLFAM'. See **Perks, R. M.**

DOLGAR MANUFACTURING CO. 1939. Stourbridge, Worcestershire. Made dolls' wigs and clothes. A variety of clothes included see-through raincoats and waitress outfits.

The 'Dinkie' doll, Speight's Ltd., 1919

DOLL. O. E. D. definition is 'toy, baby, puppet'. 'The one word 'doll' is now left to describe all manner of children's toys and also earlier doll-like figurines or images from ancient times.'

However, in times past various other names were used for children's playthings in human form. In the 16th century children played with 'mammets', and in 1670 Dryden translated the Latin 'pupae' as 'baby-toys'. 'Poppets' was another popular term. Dolls have nearly always been feminine and therefore were given girl's names, one of which was Dorothy or 'Doll' for short; this term became increasingly popular in the 18th Century, and Pope in 1721 made reference to a jointed 'doll'. It is interesting to note that Punch and Judy men always refer to their puppets as 'dolls'.

DOLLERIES. See **Rees, Leon.**

DOLLIE DIMPLE. See **Hinde, John Lord.**

DOLLIES LTD. c1933. Bicester Road, Aylesbury, Buckinghamshire. Doll manufacturing company started by J. Kohnstam Ltd. c1933. Made 'Duckie' series of dressed and undressed dolls, including 'Non-inflammable, Indestructible, Washable' 22″ 'King Baby'; and specialising in the manufacture of unbreakable dolls' heads and other doll parts.

In 1935 Dollies Ltd. and Dean's Rag Book Co. Ltd. joined to form Dean's Dollies Ltd. See **Dean's Rag Book Co. Ltd.** and **Keen & Co.**

DOLL IN DOLL. See **Doll Industries Ltd.**

19th century child dollmakers.

Three dolls' heads made by Dollies Ltd., 1933. The first is marked 'Lucky', the other two 'Dollies'.

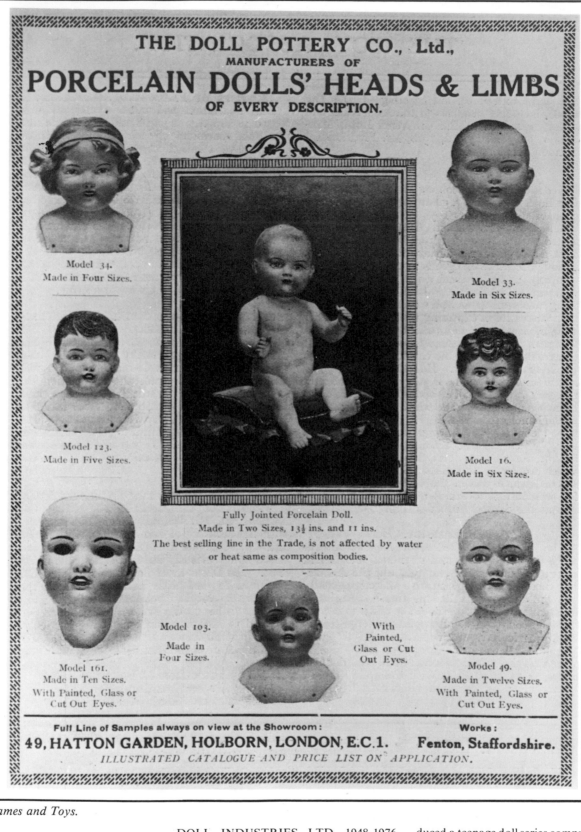

Advert., Games and Toys.

DOLL INDUSTRIES LTD. 1948-1976. c1948 at 148-50 High Road, Willesden, London, NW10. 1976 at 34 Brondesbury Park, London NW6. Doll manufacturers. Registered trademark 'Doll in Doll' no. 671,580 on 30th July 1948. In February 1949 the firm broke with J. Cowan, its distributor.

In November of the same year it introduced a teenage doll series comprising Bride, Gala Dress, Pompadour and Lady, trimmed with taffeta ribbon.

DOLLIT DOLLS 1906. See **Ivimey, Annie Alice.**

DOLL (JOINTED) BOOKS. See **Dean & Son Ltd.**

DOLL-MAKERS. (modern) *Porcelain-headed dolls, beautifully dressed:* Anne Parker, c/o Design Centre, London W1.; Helen Whateley, 13 High Street, Marlow, Bucks; Honor Wilson and Carolyn McSweeny, 1 Dentdale Drive, Knaresborough, Yorkshire; Jill Bennett and Susan Erland, 4 Ruvigny Gardens, Putney, London, SW15; Faith Eaton, Dollmaker's Circle.

China-headed Doll Kits: Camden Dolls 1975. Made by Maggie Granger and Rachel Waller.

Wax: Gilly Dolls, c/o Dollmaker's Circle, c/o Mrs June Hart, 6 Parklands, Rotcombe Lane, High Littleton, Nr. Bristol, Avon.; Margaret Glover, 42 Hartham Road, Isleworth, Middlesex; Myrtle Smith, 4 Bromley Road, Parsons Heath, Colchester, Essex.

The White Queen and The Red Queen from Alice Through the Looking Glass, with wooden heads and soft bodies. Made by Faith Eaton, 1975.

Resin Type: Nyna Denby, 49 Aldershot Road, Fleet, Hampshire; Sue Atkinson, 7 Park Drive, East Sheen, London SW14.

Wooden: Nell Dale, c/o Consumer Craft Council, London W1.; Sam Smith, c/o Design Centre, London W1.; Walter van Tinteren, 40 Mowbray Rd, Edgware makes reproduction 'Dutch' dolls.

DOLL POTTERY CO. LTD. Fenton, Stoke-on-Trent, Staffordshire. London Showroom (Green Bros. Agents) 49 Hatton Garden, London E.C. Company registered December 16th, 1915. Manufacturers of china dolls' heads and limbs of every description. Many of the better quality heads were made from classic designs by well-known artists. Special models were also made to customers' own registered designs. 'Striking features of the heads are the natural colour and expression. Each model is made in 5 or 6 sizes'. New models in April 1917 included pierrots, niggers and clowns. In February, 1920 'Games & Toys' advertised 'Fully-jointed Porcelain Doll made in three sizes: The best selling line in the trade, as it is not affected by water or heat (can be washed). Girl and Boy Babies: jointed arms; three models with fixed glass or sleeping eyes'. 'Cecily' was the trademark of some dolls' heads. In April 1922 the company advised 'Games and Toys' of its closure owing to its inability to compete with Germany.

DOLL REPAIR SERVICES. Dolls made from wood, wax or china were not particularly robust; if broken it was, however, and in certain respects still is, possible to repair them. A wooden doll can be repainted; a new limb can be carved for it; a new wig stuck on. With skill and patience broken bits of wax can be melted together again, china can be glued, or new heads and limbs be fitted on to old bodies. In the 19th and early 20th centuries every large toyshop had a doll-repairing service; and some shops advertised themselves as Dolls' Hospitals.

As long as it was possible to buy from the manufacturers all the necessary spare parts, repairs could be done.

Modern plastic dolls, however, are difficult and uneconomic to repair and Dolls' Hospitals have practically disappeared. But the growing interest in old dolls and the increasing number of serious doll collectors has led to the publication of books containing useful hints on doll repairs—notably those of Audrey Johnson.

DOLLS' ACCESSORY CO. c1917. Parkhall Works, Parkhall Street, Longton, Staffordshire. Manufacturers of dolls etc. Firm originally produced a wax-finish china head which was patented in 1916 by Doris Sylvia Bailey and Sarah Jane Baxter. This was made and fixed in the ordinary way, then dipped in wax, which gave it an appearance similar to the old wax doll. The idea was only a partial success and subject to considerable criticism, and was therefore scrapped. Ranges include 'Flesho' porcelain doll heads, 'Long Exposure' china doll (1919) 'I'se All Dicky'. In January 1921 stuffed body dolls 'Kydyte'(an imitation kid material) were produced, and china character dolls—'Profiteer', 'Goo-goo Smile' and 'Camouflage'.

DOLLS IN WONDERLAND. Seafront, Brighton, East Sussex. This is a superb collection of dolls by Mrs Vera Kramer, including one of the first bisque dolls made in England and the 'Bisto Kids' advertising dolls with composition shoulders-heads, created to promote the sale of Bisto gravy powder.

DOLLS MASKS (LONDON) LTD. 1952. At 68 Well Street, London, E9. Manufacturers of dolls' masks.

DOLLS, MESSRS. 1917. 55 Stone Street, Tunbridge Wells, Kent. Doll manufacturers. Made semi-dressed dolls 14″ high, with china heads and limbs and wigs, price 2s 6d, and stuffed dolls with handmade bodies and mask faces. Price 1s 6d.

DOLLS OF ALL NATIONS. 1960. Range of miniature life-like flexible figures 3 to 4 inches high, dressed in approximations of national costumes. The clothes were made of felts, silks, satins, cottons, and embroidered ribbons. Average retail price 4s 11d. Made by Dol-Toi Products (Stamford) Ltd.

DOLLS SUPPLIES LTD. 1915. At 1 Griffiths Street, Liverpool & Fleet Street, Liverpool. c1918 at 168 Mill Street, Liverpool. Established 1915, liquidated February 8th

Dolls' Hospital, Manchester, 1960 (Manchester Public Library).

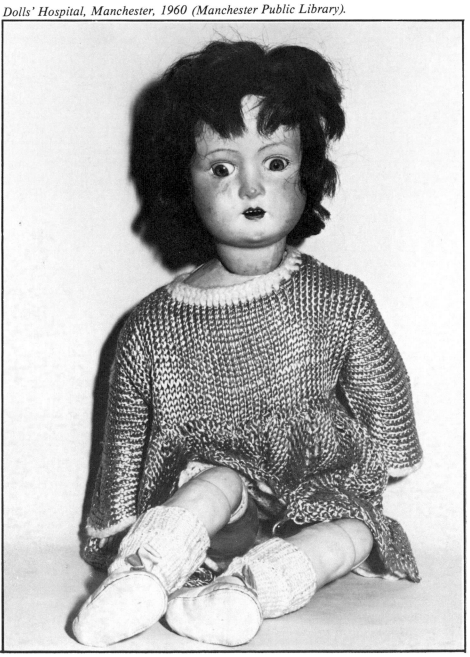

China-headed doll marked '161 D.P.C.' under an incised doll head on scroll mark (Speight's Classic mark). Fixed eyes, jointed composition body.

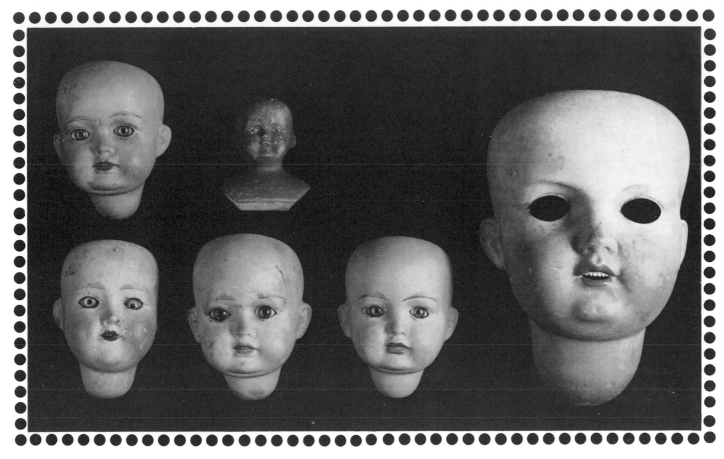

Dolls' heads marked 'D.P.Co.' First doll, bottom row, has vestige of Speight's Classic mark.

Head marked 'D.P.Co.' plus Speight's Classic mark. Painting unfinished. The composition body has wooden arms - possibly a wartime repair.

1921. Manufacturers of dolls' heads, limbs, jointed dolls and stuffed dolls and toys. Company was set up to use process patented by F. Wilkins on 30th July, 1915, no. 11064, for a doll provided with articulated limbs which are retained in their sockets by elastic springs. Company used 'Bronyx' trade mark.

DOLLY. 1928. Fully-jointed soft doll stuffed with java kapok, equipped with glass eyes and elaborately dressed. Made by Dean's Rag Book Co. Ltd.

DOLLY DEAR. Doll made by Textile Novelty Co.

DOLLY DENIM. 1976. Chad Valley doll.

DOLLY DIMPLE. Doll made by Nunn and Smeed. In Pollock's Toy Museum Collection.

DOLLY DIMPLE. 1914. See **Whyte, Ridsdale & Co.**

DOLLY DIMPLE. 1917. Doll made by the All British Doll Manufacturing Co.

DOLLY DIMPLE. 1920. See **East London (Federation Toy) Co.**

DOLLY DIMPLE. 1936. Made by J. Sear Ltd.

DOLLY DIPS. Rag doll made by Dean's Rag Book Co. in 1917. There are two patterns: one wears a bathing costume with a real skirt, the other is in a party dress, black stockings and shoes.

DOLLY DOLL CO. 1920. 108 Upper Street, London N1. Made dolls.

DOLLY-LOCKS. 1972. See **Wig World.**

DOLLYS-DOC. 1951. Registered trade mark for dolls. See **Woolley, A. G. Ltd.**

DOLPHITCH MANUFACTURING CO. LTD. 1915-19. 1915 At 16 Park Road, Acton, London W. 1916. 113a St. Aldate Street, Oxford. 1919 at Devinty Road, Oxford. Manufacturers of jointed composition dolls, rag-bodied dolls, character dolls, wax dolls etc. Principals: Mr and Mrs D. A. Fitch. Mr Fitch invented a special composition which possessed the property of setting with peculiar hardness. Dolls' accessories were also manufactured, including hats, wigs, shoes, socks, fur sets and muffs and dolls' trousseaux.

DOLRITE. Registered trademark. See **Michel-Levy, Fernande.**

DOL TOI PRODUCTS (STAMFORD) LTD. Established before 1949. 1954 at Uffington Road, Stamford, Lincolnshire. Manufacturers of dolls and dolls' house furniture. The factory first started in an ancient brewery in Stamford. It was taken over in 1949 by Mr C.W. P. Ibbotson. In 1954 the firm moved to a modern brick factory. 1959 range included a family of flexible dolls' house dolls, with lead feet and wire bodies, which could stand or sit. Range includes babies, young children, mothers and fathers, bridal groups, postmen, etc. dressed in real clothes of tweed, prints, cottons, silks and satins.

DOMESTIC UTILITY DOLLS. Doll range by Dean's Rag Book Co. Ltd.

DOMINO. 1972. Negro Matchbox Disco Doll. See **Lesney Products & Co Ltd.**

DOMINION BRAND. Dolls. See **Canadian Dolls.**

DONALD, Ken Mfg. Co. Ltd. 1935. 8-10 Johnson St, Commercial Road, London E1. Soft toy and doll manufacturers. See **Binkie Babs.**

DON BRICKS LTD. 1976. At 552 Kingsland Road, Walston, London E8. Previously E. M. Napier Ltd. Importers of rubber and soft dolls.

DONCASTER MUSEUM & ART GALLERY. Chequer Road, Doncaster, South Yorkshire. Two shop-window-type displays show Victorian and Edwardian dolls, a doll's house, toy theatre, board games, ships and other playthings.

DORA. 1924. 17″ doll made by Dean's Rag Book Co. Ltd.

DORA. 1935. Doll in 3 sizes, 13½″, 16″ and 19″ high. Can be brushed and combed. Two larger sizes fitted with Kleenagane face. Clothes take off. Range of linen prints with sun bonnet and shoes. Made by Dean's Rag Book Co. Ltd.

DOREEN DOLLS. 1931. Doll in dress and poke bonnet made by Dean's Rag Book Co. Ltd.

DORIC CHINA CO. c1924. At China Street, Fenton, Staffordshire. 1924-35 at High Street, Longton, Staffordshire. Taken over by Royal Albion China Co., 1935-1948. Made dolls until 1934 when fire destroyed the factory.

DORIS. c1923. See **Mann & Mann,** also **Whyte, Ridsdale.**

DOROTHEA. 1926. See **Wolstan Doll Co. Ltd.**

DOROTHY AND HER DRESSES. See **Spear, J. W. & Sons**

DOROTHY Dolls. See Manufacturers **Wolstan Doll Co. Ltd.**

DORRIE. 1935. Velvet doll in 7 sizes from 12″ to 30″ in 6 colours Made by Dean's Rag Book Co. Ltd.

DORRIS & Co Ltd. 1923. At 54 Mildmay Grove, London. Manufacturers of 'high grade dressed dolls and mascots'.

DORSETT, Albert & Mary. See **Almar Dolls Ltd.**

DOTS DOLLS. See manufacturers **Harwin & Co. Ltd.**

DOUGLAS, Anna Marie. Dalkeith House, Leamington, Warwick. Obtained patent no. 19850, on 18th October, 1894, for a dressed doll with a different head at each end; by turning the doll upside down the head could be changed.

DOUGLAS & HAMER. London 1843-1847. Made wax and composition dolls. Succeeded by William Hamer 1848-65.

DREYFUS, Miriam. 55 Seaside Road, Eastbourne, Sussex. Merchant. Registered trademarks 'Perry' no. 533,024 and 'Oppy' no. 533,025 on 30th June, 1932, for dolls and toys.

DRIAL, WILLIAM, PRODUCTS LTD. 6 The Mansions, Mill Lane, London NW6. Registered trademark 'Sweetheart Doll' no. 683359 on 21st October 1949.

DRUMMER BOY. 1915. See **Turton, W.S.**

DRYAD PEG DOLLS. In the 1960s Dryads, the craft suppliers' shop in London, made and sold several sizes of wooden dolls, somewhat similar to the traditional wooden 'Dutch' dolls. The arm and knee joints however were not fixed with tiny wooden pegs but with strips of metal, slotted into the wood and held in place by rather clumsy nails.

DU BARRY. See **Art Dolls; Sant, J. S. Miniature models.**

DUCHESS. 1920. Classic doll made by Speights Ltd.

DUCHESS DOLL. 1934. Doll made by Dean's Rag Book Co Ltd. Dressed in rich brocaded silk, lavishly trimmed with 'silkeen' plush in lovely shades.

DUCKIE DOLLS. See **Dollies Ltd.**

DUDU & ZUZU or ZULU. 1930. Soft nigger dolls made by Norah Wellings.

DULCIE. 1927. Doll made by Mabel Bland-Hawkes.

DUM TWEEDLE. Trademark no. 332,774 registered by Dean's Rag Book Co. on 13th April 1911, for rag dolls.

DUNLOP PRODUCTS. 1934. A subsidiary of Dunlop Rubber Co. Made hot water bottles in the shape of Red Riding Hood and animal shapes.

DUNN, W. Obtained patent no. 18814 on 20th September, 1901 for a doll made to dance by having its feet suspended from a spring above an electro-magnet.

DUNSTER. Somerset. See **Memorial Hall Museum.**

DURA PORCELAIN CO. Elm Street, Hanley, Stoke-on-Trent, Staffordshire. Established November 1915. Manufacturers of dolls' heads and limbs. 'Principal partners are the Hall Brothers, themselves practical potters. While they have specialised in the colouring and skin texture, the feature that is noteworthy is the eyes. These are finished in a brilliant enamel and are certainly an excellent substitute for glass.' (Games & Toys 1916.) Various styles of heads manufactured include: socket and shoulder; with painted hair or bald for wigs. Pateless shoulder heads marked Benco Dura.

DURAX. Registered trademark. See **Dodd, Isobel.**

DUTCH BOYS & GIRLS. 1920. Dolls dressed in national costume from 'Classic' range by Speights Ltd.

Dryad peg doll.

E. B. B. S. Ltd. Mark on 'one of the first bisque dolls made in England'. The bisque head is rough and has moulded painted hair. It is dressed in the blue hospital uniform of a wounded soldier of First World War and original tag at back says 'Plucky the Big Boy Blue, hero souvenir doll', made by Ellison, Rees & Co. The doll is on show at the 'Dolls In Wonderland' Museum, Brighton, Sussex.

EALON TOYS. See **East London (Federation) Toy Factory.**

EARTHENWARE DOLLS. 'Very popular during the 16th and 17th centuries. Probably imported into England from Germany and the Low Countries from the beginning of the 16th century'. (Eileen King's History of Dolls, 1978.)

EAST LONDON (FEDERATION) TOY FACTORY. c1915. Offices at 400 Old Ford Road, Bow, London. Factory at 45 Norman Road, Bow, London E. Made dolls and soft stuffed toys. Trademark 'Ealon Toys'. In 1915 made rag dolls with modelled faces, heads and arms (Japanese dolls and British babies); and dolls with wax and china heads and limbs, 'perhaps one of the most important lines emanating from this firm' (Toy Trader). In March 1920 lines included 'Little Black Sambo', 'Washey Dolly', 'Dolly Dimple', 'Jack and Jill' and 'Tumbling Doll'. In June 1933, the firm moved to 74-78 Bingfield Street, London N1. In 1936 range included dolls, soft-stuffed, with goo-goo eyes, 'Rattles' and 'Cherub'; a 'Baby Bunting Babs' type; and a toddler type doll in composition.

East London Toy Factory Ltd., 1936

EATES, Henry. 1894. London. Manufactured dolls.

EATON, Florence Emily. 1895-1904+. Tipperary and Dublin, Ireland. Began the Erin Doll Industry which made so-called composition dolls, and obtained three British patents for making dolls' heads. No. 897 15th January, 1895 relates to paper dolls; No. 7583 13th April, 1901 to dolls produced in dental enamel and coloured; No. 24846 16th November, 1904 to dolls' heads made of paper and finished off to resemble china. See **Irish Dolls.**

ECKART, Hans Englebert. 18-20 Barbican, London EC. Toy and doll importer. Registered trademark, a picture of a horse drawing a cart loaded with faggots, no. 335,363 on July 19th 1911 for dolls, toys and toy animals.

ECKART, Walter & ECKART, Ronald. 1920-5. London. Made dolls.

ECLIPSE DOLLS. c1918. See **Rochdale Doll Co.**

EDIBLE DOLLS. Jelly babies, sweets made out of coloured, fruit-flavoured jelly and shaped into baby figures. Gingerbread Men, ginger-flavoured biscuits made in the shape of human figures and animals since the 14th century.

Edward Lovett, in the catalogue of his 1914 exhibition of Folk Dolls, devoted a whole section to gingerbread dolls and moulds from all parts of England; and reported that the Bun Dolls were obtained in and around London. Eight of these bun dolls represented living people. Two other bun dolls from Yorkshire were dressed.

In the village of Biddenden in Kent white, spiced biscuits are still made every year to commemorate the Siamese twins Eliza and Mary, born in the village. See **Clarke, Nicholls & Combe.**

EDLIN'S. Rational Repository of Amusement Toy shop 37 Broad St, London. 1811-1850.

EDMUNDS, J. Henry. Jedmunds House, 428 Westbourne Avenue, London SE9. Importer. In January 1950, advertised 'New 22" Export Walking—Sleeping Mama Doll, with precision-built all-metal movement, "Jedmunds" everlast assembly and synchronized turning head, natural life-like expression, exquisitely designed dresses'. A composition doll with permed long curly wig, sunbonnet and pretty silky dress.

EDNA. 1935. Doll made by Dean's Rag Book Co. Ltd. Hand-painted face; blond, plaited hair, print frock and matching hat; black shoes tied with ribbons.

EDNA. 1955. Plastic walking doll which can sit, kneel and bend her legs in many life-like poses. Has sleeping eyes and eyelashes and is dressed in taffeta and floral waffle trimmed with lace, shoes and socks and a hand-curled combable wig on a hard plastic head. Manufactured by D.G. Todd & Co. Ltd.

EDUCATIONAL MUSEUM. Haslemere, Surrey. The collection includes a late Victorian doll's house, some 18th century dolls, and a wedding group of five late-19th century wax dolls.

EDWARDS, Charles. At addresses in Goodge Street, London W1. 1852-1868. Mrs Henrietta Edwards listed at same address from 1878-1891; they made wax-over-composition dolls.

EDWARDS, John. 1856-84. London. c1868 at 43-45 Waterloo Road, London. Made wax dolls. Thought to be the son of Charles Edwards. c1850 Edwards made a 'Royal Baby Doll', 15" high, marked with cipher E on its shoe. 1868. Listed as an inventor of the Exhibition rag dolls. Dolls were dressed or undressed; sold wholesale or for export. 1871. Showed a kneeling wax doll with inserted hair at the London Exhibition. 'The Graphic', 16th Dec., 1871 reported Edwards was manufacturing 20,000 wax dolls per week. "We are not a great toy making nation, but we admittedly beat the whole world in dolls." Some of his dolls were very expensive; one fine example cost £50.

EDWARDS & PAMFLETT. Mesdames. 1918-23. At 89-90 Milton Street, London EC2. Doll manufacturers. Made papier mâché jointed dolls, baby dolls in 6 sizes, boy dolls dressed in jersey suits and girl dolls in frocks, dressed dolls, sleeping-eyed dolls, and dolls in knitted clothing. Registered trademark 'The Cecily Doll' no. 382,079 on 22nd February, 1918.

EDWARDS, T. W. Obtained patent no. 21780 on 26th September, 1913 for fastening the parts of a stuffed-body doll.

EINCO. Trademark used by Eisenmann & Co.

EISENMANN & CO. Fuerth, Bavaria and London. c1882 Whitecross Street, London. 1891-1922 at 46 Basinghall Street, London EC. 1922 at 25 Ropemaker Street, London EC. Established in 1881 by Joe and Gabriel Eisenmann. Manufactured and distributed dolls. 'Joe Eisenmann was probably the most outstanding figure in the toy trade of this country, as witness his well known title "King of the Toy Trade". Up to the outbreak of war in 1914, he controlled the bulk of the toys imported into this country.' ('Toy and Fancy Goods Trader' Aug 1922.) The company obtained patent no. 20301 on October 7th 1905 for design of rag dolls' faces using moulded cardboard, covered by a layer of coloured gauze. Registered several trademarks for dolls and toys in Britain: 'Little Pet' in 1908; Butterfly Series in 1908; 'Kiddieland' in 1911; 'Hugmee' in 1912; 'Beaky Ba' in 1912; 'Bunny Hug' in 1913 and 'Floatolly' in 1914. 1975. Company still in existence at 36-42 Clerkenwell Road, London EC1. Trade mark 'Einco'.

ELEANOR WORKS. c1915. 44 Eleanor Road, Hackney, London. Manufacturers of dolls' masks, original makers of silk masks.

ELEGANT DOLLS. 1926. Dolls manufactured by Dean's Rag Book Co. Ltd.: 'The young lady of today', 'grown-up dolls' in twelve designs, 22″ high.

ELFIE. Registered trademark for dolls. See **Hamley Bros.**

ELITE. Trademark for dolls. See **Elite Doll Co.**

ELITE DOLL CO. Offices: 5 Morley Street, Tunstall, Staffordshire. Factory: Wesley Street, Tunstall, Staffordshire. Established 1915. Proprietor: W. J. Bailey. Doll manufacturers. Made 'Silver' series of sleeping dolls in 6 sizes fitted with china heads and limbs, fixed glass or painted eyes. The bodies were made of Egyptian cotton which bears a high silver lustrous gloss. 'The company was one of the first firms to introduce the sleeping eye doll in this country in competition with German lines.' Firm also made socket and shoulder heads in 8 sizes.

ELIZABETHAN HOUSE, THE. At 70, Fore Street, Totnes, Devon. A small collection of mostly 19th century toys including about 12 dolls and a fully furnished doll's house.

ELIZABETH, Princess. Character doll produced in 1930 by Chad Valley, dressed in organdie and silk dress with white kid shoes and necklace. Pink, blue and yellow dresses. 1 guinea only. 'England's most popular princess'.

ELLARCO. Trademark. See **Ellison, Rees & Co.**

ELLIOTT, Louise. 1970. Contemporary rag doll designer.

ELLISDONS. c1949. 246 High Holborn, London WC1. Sold dolls', 'mama' and 'cry' voices etc. to doll manufacturers. Also dolls' eyelashes.

ELLISON, REES & CO. 1916. At 45 & 46 Basinghall Street, London, EC. Factory: Chesham. Doll manufacturers. Trademark 'Ellarco'. Brand names 'Dolleries' and 'Chesham'. Lines include 'Impy', soft character doll, 'Union Jack Baby', and 'Plucky'. Unusually good bisque finish and moving eyes (eyes made in France). See **Rees, Leon.**

ELWICK, Mrs Helena. 1879. At 88 Clarendon Road, London W11. Made wax dolls.

EMDEE. Trademark for dolls and toys. See **Marcuse, Day & Co. Ltd.**

EMELL TOY MANUFACTURING CO. 1917-19. Upper Street, Islington, London, N. Proprietor: Marcus Littaur. Manufacturers of games, toys and dolls. Made the 'Rochdale' doll in various sizes, dressed and undressed. 1918: Made doll's house called the 'Palace', doll's villa, and a doll to go with it.

EMERGENT or EMERGENCY DOLLS. An expression coined by Edward Lovett. 'The emergent doll was one contrived for a child from any raw material at hand, probably in circumstances where the parents were too poor to buy a doll, or where it was left to the initiative of the child to make its own toys. Various articles were used, including clothes pegs, brushes, wooden spoons and even old bones, which were subsequently 'dressed' in scraps of rag and lace etc. See **Lovett, Edward** and **Home-made Dolls.**

'Emergent' doll, made from an old shoe (Museum of Childhood, Edinburgh).

EMLU DOLL & TOY CO. 1947.

EMMA & HER PONY. 1974. Palitoy articulated doll and model palomino pony.

EMPIRE PORCELAIN POTTERY. c1896-1964+. Empire Works, Stoke-on-Trent, Staffordshire. 1916-25: Made various sizes of dolls' heads in clay which were painted and then given a high glaze firing. The eyes were painted or were made of glass. Other factories made up legs, etc. Used the mark 'E.P. & Co. Stoke'.

ENID. 1952. Pedigree dolls. See **Pin-Up Dolls.**

ENGLISH COSTUME DOLLS. There is no recognisably distinctive English costume for doll-makers to copy. During the First World War, however, in response to the deeply patriotic feelings of the time, several manufacturers (notably Dean's Rag Book Co.) produced dolls wearing khaki uniforms, John Bull dolls sporting Union Jack waistcoats, and other military figures. Dolls dressed in 'sailor suits' were popular; also dolls in Scottish, Welsh and Irish traditional costumes.

In the 1930s Norah Wellings produced a series of British Sailors designed for sale on board the Cunard liners, a large 'Britannia' doll, and an airman doll, sold for the benefit of the RAF Benevolent Fund.

Various other attempts have been made to find costumes particular to England. A Quaker girl was popular during the early years of the 1914-18 war. Later efforts have centred more on traditional London characters: policemen, Lambeth Walkers, Beefeaters, Piccadilly flower-girls, and lavender-sellers (based on prints featuring old London street cries). Perhaps the most authentic of these are the Pearly dolls dressed by members of the Pearly Kings and Queens Association. Unfortunately the dolls dressed with loving care by such stalwart Pearly Queens as Mrs Beatrice Marriott, Mrs Tinsley, Mrs Golden and Mrs Rebecca Matthews were often quite unworthy of their beautifully made outfits. However Mrs Lily Lodge, the Pearly Queen of Lambeth, dressed for Pollock's Toy Museum before she died a series of little wooden 'Dutch' dolls, just as she used to do when she was a very young girl, as well as a large Armand Marseille doll in a replica of her own costume.

See **Dean's Rag Book Co.; Patriotic Dolls; Scottish Dolls.**

Dolls dressed by Lily Lodge as the Pearly King and Queen of Lambeth. The seed pearls and mother-of-pearl buttons are sewn with red cotton, in traditional patterns, on the black velvet outfits.

ENGLISH DOLL MANUFACTURING CO. 1916. At 279 Osmaston Road, Derby. Doll manufacturers. Dolls with china heads.

ENGLISH DOLL & TOY CO LTD. 1918. At 63 Branstone Road, Burton-on-Trent. Office: 48, Roberts Street, Sheffield. Doll and toy manufacturer. Firm took over company previously run by by J. F. Dunkerley at Branstone Road address.

ENGLISH DOLLS. A term applied to the early cut-out paper sheets with engraved figures and costumes produced by such firms as Ackermann in the late 18th century and copied by German firms in Nuremberg. See **Ackermann, Rudolph.**

A term loosely used for the purposes of this dictionary to class any dolls which were produced in England, sometimes with foreign components, or manufactured elsewhere in the British Isles (Ireland, Wales, Scotland).

Smaller doll: English china doll, with unmarked head on composition body (Faith Eaton).

Larger doll: English china doll head (unmarked) on soft body (Faith Eaton).

English china head marked 'C E T and Co.' Fixed glass eyes; composition body (Faith Eaton).

English china head, unmarked. Fixed glass eyes; strange body construction (Faith Eaton).

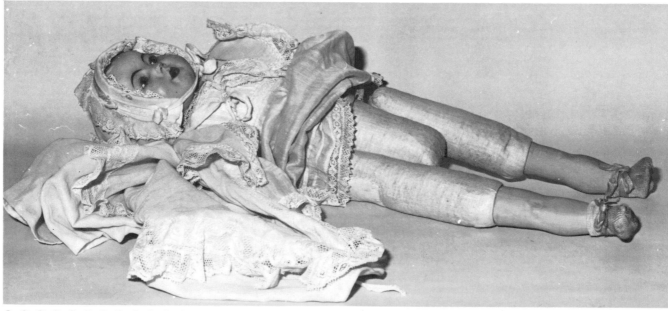

ERBIE BROWN. January 1929. Character doll made by Dean's Rag Book Co.

ERHARD, Stephen. Established 1887. 1891 at 2 Aldermanbury Postern, London. 1917 at 8 Bradford Avenue, Redcross Street, London EC. Doll and toy manufacturer and importer. 1891 made Nankeen dolls. 1915 advertised Red Cross Nurse doll with celluloid head, hair, movable limbs and squeaker. 1920 advertised Kewpie dolls.

ERIN. See **Eaton, F.E.**

ERLAND, Susan. See **Bennett and Erland.**

ESKIMO DOLLS. Eskimo dolls became popular during the period of Arctic exploration. The American R. E. Peary discovered the North Pole in 1909. See **J. Kamlish & Co; Layfield, J.; Timpo Toys; Hawksley & Co.; Terry, W. J.**

ESKIMO INTERLINING CO. LTD. 1947. At Devonshire Barley 'Mow Passage, London W4. In 1947 produced Eskimo Tot, a promotional Eskimo doll registered design no. 848043.

ESKIMO TOT. 1947. See **Eskimo Interlining Co. Ltd.**

ESMERALDA. Replica of lifelike doll which appeared with Jean Simmons and co-star Susan Stranks in J. Arthur Rank's film 'The Blue Lagoon' (1940's). Made by Cinemaster Products Ltd with the permission of J. Arthur Rank.

EUSTON, H. R. 1921. At 114/115 Fore London, EC. Manufacturer of dolls' accessories and agent for foreign dolls.

EVANS, A. E. Obtained patent no. 14240 on 8th October, 1915 for 'a toy that can be made to move with a rolling or swinging walk......'

EVANS, JOSEPH & SONS. 1868-81. London. Manufacturers and importers. Dolls with wax heads have been found with the mark of this company on their cloth bodies.

EVERREST. 1925. Trademark registered for dolls, games and toys. See **Seelig, William.**

EVRIPOSE or EVRIPOZE. c1921. Patented doll joints made by Dean's Rag Book Co Ltd.

EXELLA DOLLS. Novelty dolls made in 1934. See manufacturers **Rees, Leon.**

EYE MANOR. Leominster, Herefordshire. The collection includes some 18th and 19th century dolls, one being a pedlar woman doll with a baby. There is also a loan collection of 56 costume dolls made by Isabelle Beck and her mother, Hedy, which displays fashion from 1150 to 1955.

EYES, Dolls'. For the early wooden dolls eyes were usually painted, some of them very skilfully, with highlights added to give expression. Glass eyes for dolls were used by the 18th century and were made in England by the same artisans as produced glass eyes for taxidermy, model wax-figure making and human use. One of the earliest references is in an advertisement bill of the famous Waxworks show of Mrs Salmon for 1711: "Mrs Salmon sells all sorts of moulds and glass eyes and teaches the full art". Eyes made to open and shut and operated by a stiff wire passed through the body were in

'Eskimo Tot', a product of the Eskimo Interlining Co., 1947.

use by the end of the 18th century. See **Tussaud, Marie.**

Explicit details were contained in an article on the London Poor by Mayhew 1850. His informant refers to two people making glass eyes in London. Unfortunately he adds little to our knowledge of *how* they were made. He spoke of having been in the trade for 40 years and his father before him for 60 years, reported that some 24,000 dozen pairs of dolls' eyes were produced in London each year, many of them for export to America and France. He refuted the report he had sold £500 worth of eyes and said his largest order was for £50 worth from the Holborn doll maker (Bazzoni). Eyes were of two qualities, the best at 4d per pair and the common ones 5s. for twelve dozen: small hollow glass spheres coloured blue or black inside. ('Nothing goes down but blue eyes as the colour of the Queen's eyes is blue'). He added that the eye-maker must be a good chemist to know the action of metallic oxides on the fire, and that eyes were made both by blowing and by casting.

Sleeping eyes worked by counterbalance and flirting eyes were continental innovations introduced to England in the 1870s. British eye manufacturers include: Dale Glass Eye Co. Ltd. Angel House, Pentonville Road, London, N1.; M. Infield and

Advertisement in the Toy Trader, 1909.

Drielsma, 7 & 8 Albion Buildings, Aldersgate, London, EC.; National Doll and Glass Eye Manufacturing Co; Pache & Sons, Artificial Eye Makers, Birmingham. c1942; Weissbeck, H; Weston, S.

EYES RIGHT. c1917. Mascot doll made by Hancock & Sons and sold by Harwin & Co.

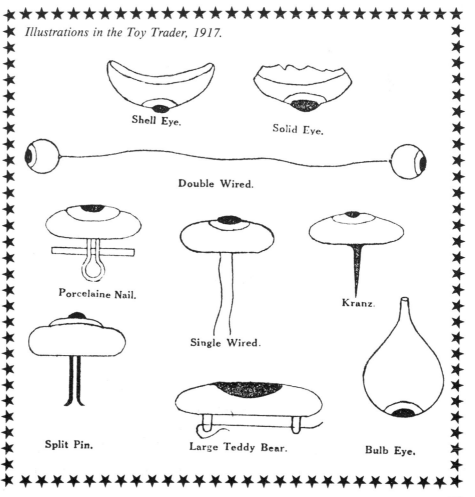

Illustrations in the Toy Trader, 1917.

Shell Eye.

Solid Eye.

Double Wired.

Porcelaine Nail.

Kranz.

Single Wired.

Split Pin.

Large Teddy Bear.

Bulb Eye.

FABER & FABER LTD. See **Pirate Twin, The.**

FAIRY DOLL. Sold by Hamley's. Made in wax for Christmas Trees, by Pierotti until 1926.

FAIRYLAND TOY MANUFACTURING CO. LTD. c1920. 10 d'Arblay Street, London W1. Made kapok-filled, hand-painted dolls, coon dolls, pierrots, pierrettes, character dolls (Luckikat, Susie, Sammie etc.)

FAIRYLITE. Registered trademark for toys and dolls. See **Graham Bros.**

FAIRY PRINCESS. 1956. Cut-out doll. See manufacturers **Philmar Ltd.**

FALCONER, Thomas Garrie. See **Cariad**

FALL-IN. A stuffed rag soldier doll marketed in 1915 by Hyman A. Abrahams. According to contemporary publicity, 'by moving the head the features change: saucy, impudent, coy, defiant, downcast are a few of the expressions that may be produced.' The same soldier appears in other advertisements with the label 'Territorial'.

FAMILY, The. c1917. See **Harwin & Co. Ltd.**

FANTASY DOLLS. A quote in Games & Toys 1923 reads "The London Lady, like her Parisian Sister, has caught the craze for carrying dolls. One doll is dressed in widow's weeds with tiny black veil over flaxen hair. The other is a fantasy doll with ugly face, sunken eyes with a vicious glint". Probably this is one of the weird side effects of the strong make-up of characters in popular films of the '20s.

FARMER'S BOY. 1916. See **Marcuse, Day & Co. Ltd.**

FARNELL, J. K. & Co. Ltd. 1871-1968. At Alpha Works, Acton Hill, London W3. Toy and doll manufacturers. The firm was founded in 1871 by Agnes Farnell. In the early days the firm was well known at home and abroad for the manufacture of soft toys and mascots. Originally natural skin and fur, such as monkey skin and squirrel fur, were used for models, but c1925, Miss Chloe Preston, the artist, was designing dolls and toys using modern materials.

1925 range included Dinkie and Blinkie, mascot pups, a cycling doll, Mumfie the baby elephant (world copyright); Zoo-zoo, a biscuit coloured monkey; and the Che-kee series of soft toy animals made from natural skins.

1926 lines included two Chloe Preston dolls; Billie Bimbo, Pal Peter, Miss Muffet and Peter Pan dolls.

In 1935 the firm registered the trade marks 'Alpha Cherub' and 'Joy Day' for dolls. Other Alpha ranges of the mid-30s

Pierotti wax Christmas Tree 'Fairy' doll.   Two baby dolls made by J.K. Farnell & Co., Ltd., 1937.

George VI in coronation robes. Made by J.K. Farnell & Co. Ltd., 1937.

FAVOURITE TOYS LTD. St. James Works, George Road, Holloway, London N7. Showroom: 1-2 Hanover Street, London, W1. Toy manufacturers. Director: Bert Collings. In 1968 another company was formed, Favourite Dolls Ltd., which commenced the complete manufacture of vinyl dolls. The first series 'New Trend' comprised 15″ all-vinyl dolls, produced in six different dress styles, and 14″ and 18″ standing dolls and baby dolls. Trademark 'Favourite'.

FELL, J. C. Obtained patent no. 25154 on 27th December 1894 for detachable paper garments for dolls.

Soft art felt doll made by A.J. Burman of Zoo Soft Toy Co., 1926.

included piccaninny dolls, smiler dolls and sofa dolls.

1936: Peter Pan doll, the royalties of which went to Great Ormond Street Hospital for Sick Children as part of the J. M. Barrie bequest.

1937: Coronation mascot doll of King George VI, also nightdress case dolls.

1938: provisional patent no. 25593 obtained for baby dolls made by a new process, light, soft and washable. These were introduced in 1939 as 'Rock-a-bye' baby dolls.

In 1966 A. E. B. Rose, the last of the firm's original directors died. In 1968 Farnell's was finally sold to a finance company.

FARRAH. 1977. See **Airfix Products Ltd.**

FASHION DOLLS. See **Boudoir Dolls; Sofa Dolls; Sindy Dolls.**

FATE LADY. A home-made fortune-telling doll. Instructions in Girls' Own Book 1858.

FAULKNER, C. W. & CO. c1900. London, EC. Publishing company which published 'Many Misfitz Folk', interchangeable paper people, designed in England and printed in Saxony.

Fashion doll, 1902. Dressed for Debenham and Freebody's in a smart strawberry tweed motoring outfit (Worthing Museum).

FELT. An ancient material used especially for hat making as it cannot fray, is readily dyed and cut, and can by steaming be shaped in various ways. Originally made from beaver hair or rabbit hair processed by pressure and by mixing with acidulated water; then, more cheaply but by similar process, mechanically produced from wool waste. This was known as 'Art Felt' and was used widely for doll and toy making, as it could be brightly coloured and strongly sewn, and was soft and pleasant to the touch. One great disadvantage is that felt is greatly loved by moths! English manufacturers of felt dolls include Chad Valley Co., Dean's Rag Book Co. Ltd., Farnell, J. K. & Co., Harwin & Co. Ltd., Wellings Norah.

FI-FI. A pinchushion mascot doll for adults made by Speights Ltd. 1920. China doll with 'goo-goo' eyes, dressed in satin and tulle evening dress, with satin headdress. 21s each.

FIFI DOLL. 1955. Manufactured by D. G. Todd & Co Ltd.

FIGHTING FURIES. Introduced 1975. Matchbox range of 2 male dolls, Captain Hook and Captain Peg Leg, and 6 adventure sets. The dolls are 9″ tall with fully articulated limbs, with the distinctive feature of sword-fighting and dagger-throwing arm movement. Manufactured by Lesney Products & Co. Ltd.

FILM STAR. Popular characters often appeared as dolls or mascots e.g. Charlie Chaplin, Jackie Coogan, Felix the Cat, Shirley Temple, Popeye the Sailor Man.

FINBURGH, Samuel & Co. 1909. At 63 Granby Row, Manchester. Calico printer. 1909 produced cut-out sheet for making up into a flannelette teddy bear. 1916 printed cut-out rag doll soldiers and rag dolls Sylvia, May, Cora and Agnes. 1917: printed calico doll clothes.

FIRTH, HARRY LTD. 1952. Exchange Mills, Frederick Street, Bradford. Dolls' hair manufacturers.

FISHMAN, S. Z. 21 & 23 Widegate Street, Bishopsgate, London, E1. General merchants. Registered trademark 'My Sweetie' no. 488303 on 8th February, 1928 for dolls and similar toys.

FITCH, Darrell Austen. 1909. At 15 Dorville Street, Ravenscourt Park, London. Obtained patent no. 2367 on 1st February, 1909 for dolls' eyes that moved from side to side by the pull of gravity on a weight. See **Dolphitch Manufacturing Co.**

FLAIR TOYS LTD. 1975. Company formed by Berwick Timpo Ltd., to sell dolls manufactured by their subsidiary, Model Toys Ltd. Lines include 'Daisy' the fashion doll, 'Havoc', Secret Agent doll, Daredevil etc.

FLAPPER DOLLS. Refers to long-limbed dolls dressed in smart young fashions of the 1920s. See **Boudoir Dolls** and **Sofa Dolls.**

FLAPPER, The. 1922. See **Lawton Doll Co.**

FLEET DOLLS. A sailor boy and two girls made by Nottingham Toy Industry Ltd., 1918.

'Sylvia', calico rag doll first printed in 1916 by Samuel Finburgh & Co., and reprinted by H M Stationery Office, 1975.

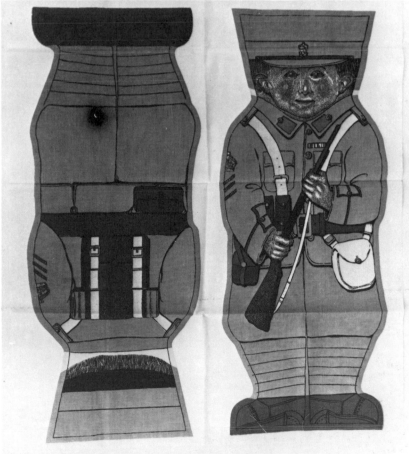

FLEISCHMANN, M. E. & S. See **Old Cottage Toys.**

FLESHO. Type of porcelain doll's head, made by Dolls Accessory Co. Ltd. c1917.

FLEXI. 1976. Brand name for dolls and soft toys made by Dean's Rag Book Co. Ltd.

FLIRTING EYES. Eyes that moved from side to side, popular from mid 19c to c1925. See **Fitch D.A.**

FLO. 1933. Comical negro doll, 'the girl in the green hat' in 3 sizes 12½", 14" and 16", made by Dean's Rag Book Co. Ltd.

FLOATOLLY. 1914. Trademark no. 359884 registered by Eisenmann & Co. of Fürth, Bavaria and 46 Basinghall Street, London E.C. Merchants for dolls, toy animals, puppets etc.

'Alice', printed calico rag doll sheet by Samuel Finburgh & Co., 1916.

Soldier doll, printed calico sheet by Samuel Finburgh & Co., 1915; reprinted by H M Stationery Office, 1975.

Felt doll with mohair wig (Pollock's Toy Museum).

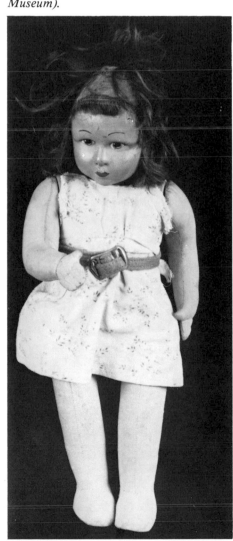

FLOPSIE. Trademark no. 400076 registered by William Henry Jones, toy merchant, of 11 Charterhouse Buildings, London EC1. for dolls, toys, puppets. 27th January 1920.

FLORENCE. Television character doll from children's series 'The Magic Roundabout', first shown in Britain c1967.

FLOSSIE. 1920. Classic doll by Speights Ltd.

FLUFF. c1921. 'Knockabout' doll designed by Mabel Bland-Hawkes. Stuffed with kapok and covered with coloured stockinette; satin face with hand-painted features and glass eyes, dressed in jumper and hat in stockinette, trimmed with brushed wool.

FLUFF-FLUFF. See **Cookman, Henry**

FLUFFY-RUFFLES. See **Cookman, Henry**

FLY DOLL. 1925. Sold by J. S. Sant. Plaster model 9″ high. Mounted on pedestal. Naked except for a Fig Leaf Calendar tied around waist and Hair in variety of colours, including green, blue and tango.

FOLLY DOLLS. 1924. Doll series made by Henry J. Hughes & Son.

FONDLE. 1956. Brand name of soft toys and dolls manufactured by Burman Ltd. Later known as Fondle Toys Ltd.

FORGET-ME-NOT. Trademark no. 381371 registered by Samuel Henry Ward of 19 St. Dunstan's Hill, London, EC3. Manufacturer of toys. 7th January 1918.

FORSTER, Thomas Streatham, London SW16. Obtained patent no. 10092 for India rubber dolls and dolls' parts cast in moulds. 6th March 1844.

FORTUNE-TELLING DOLLS. Dolls with skirts made of fortune-telling slips of paper.

FOSKETT & EDLER. 1887-95. 64 Fore Street, London EC. Made dolls and were manufacturers' agents for foreign dolls.

FOSTER, BLACKETT & WILSON LTD. 1920. Showroom at 121 Cheapside. London EC1. Manufacturers of wood and mechanical dolls and toys, and agents for manufacturers. Sole agents for Edwards & Pamflett. Trade name 'Bairntoys'. In 1920 produced 'C.C.', a mechanical Charlie Chaplin Doll.

FOXTON'S MANUFACTURING CO. London. 1918-21. Made dolls.

FRANCES. 1952. Pedigree doll: See **Pin-up Dolls.**

Fortune-telling doll, with hand-written fortunes on folded papers under the skirt (Bantock House Museum, Wolverhampton).

FRANKEL, Benjamin. Trading as B. Frankel & Co., 6 Cobb Street, London E1. Doll manufacturer. Registered trademark 'Key Products' no. 800197 on 9th January, 1950 for dolls.

FRANKLIN, J. G. & Sons. 1921. 11-17 Godstone Crescent, Dalston, London E.8 Rubber doll manufacturers. Used trademark 'Rubbadubdub'. Made inflatable rubber novelties with a valve, roly-poly clowns, dolls and animals.

FRANKS, Peggy. See **Hook & Franks Ltd.**

FRAZER ROCK, Helen. Doll designer for Nottingham Toy Industry c1916-c1920. Responsible for Frazer Rock Indestructible dolls, which had tough 'rock' china heads, 'compolite' and leatherette bodies, jointed limbs and fixed or sleeping eyes. Heads were modelled from real children: dolls were advertised as Helen's babies, 'The Real English Child Doll'. Modern dress styles were used.

FRETWELL TOY MANUFACTURING CO. 190 Lavender Hill, London S.W.11. Established 1917. Director: Miss Fretwell Soft toy and doll manufacturers. Registered trademarks 'My Kiddie' no. 660889 for 'soft stuffed dolls in superfine stockinette fitted with curly wigs and charmingly dressed in various coloured silk dresses,' and 'Bubbly Kiddie' no. 661753 for a soft boy doll with fair curly wig. Other lines included 'Cuddley' stuffed dolls covered with flesh-coloured stockinette, hand-painted features with googly eyes and 'artistic' silk clothes.

FRIDA 1978. See **Abba Dolls.**

FRIDO LTD. 1962. Victor Works, Houldsworth Street, Reddish, Stockport, Cheshire. Manufacturers of balls, toys and dolls. Makers of Frida dolls in Breon PVC. 1963 range includes Bride Doll, Nannie doll with piccaninny, Flower seller, Coloured nurse doll, Mammie doll, and Parisienne Maid. All dolls have movable eyes and rooted hair.

FRILLY DOLLS. 1927. Luxury doll range by Dean's Rag Book Co. Ltd. (Games and Toys March 1927 p.1.)

FROEBEL, Friedrich. 1782-1852. One of the great influences on the pattern of nursery toys and dolls. He wrote "Play is the early form of spiritual education—the world is displayed and revealed by Play". Teaching methods were altered and enlivened and interesting apparatus introduced to small children. He inaugurated the Kindergarten and induced F. A. Richter to make stone building bricks. English makers soon followed German lead. Dolls became more realistic and "cuddly", like real babies.

FROLIX. 1920. Long-legged wire and cotton figures, which bent into positions. Made by Darenta Toy Works.

FROZEN CHARLOTTES. Also called pillar dolls and bathing babies. China or bisque dolls made in one piece without joints; they were small, from ½" upward and generally female. Tiny 1" ones were used as surprise gifts in cakes and Christmas puddings.

FRY, Roger. London. Designed dolls for London Child's Welfare Exhibition 1914. He was a well-known artist and art critic.

FRYER, Thomas. 1915-16. 17 Pelham Street, London SW1. Distributed and repaired dolls.

FULLER, S. & J. 1810-1850. Temple of Fancy, Rathbone Place, London. Bookshop and publishers who produced apparently the earliest paper dolls intended for children. The well-known 'History of Little Fanny', 1810, consisted of a paper doll character who changed her outfit six times during the course of the moral tale. The movable parts—heads and costumes—were slotted into place by tags. This invention was quickly adopted in the U.S.A. and doll-dressing sets (of children only) are still popular today. One of the original 'History of Little Fanny' sets is still on display at Worthing Museum & Art Gallery.

FUMSUP. Trademark registered in Britain in 1914 and 1916 and in France in 1920 by John Green Hamley of Hamley Bros. A mascot baby doll with 'goo-goo' eyes and mop of hair giving the 'thumbs-up' for victory sign. Arms were jointed, legs moulded in one piece, made by S. Hancock & Sons. "Thumbs-up, over the top and the best of luck" was a 1914-18 slogan with reference to the terrible trench warfare in Flanders.

FUZBUZ. Trademark no. 354125 registered by Dean's Rag Book Co., for dolls, puppets and toys, 18th August, 1913. See **Tommy Fuzbuz.**

G.B. Mark on pottery doll in Mrs Mary Hillier's collection, possibly made by Hewitt & Leadbeater.

G. B. Mark on pottery doll in Pollock's Toy Museum collection, possibly made by Doll Pottery Co. for Speights Classic range.

G & S. Mark on doll in Pollock's Toy Museum Collection.

GAELTARRA EIREANN. 1944. Westland Row, Dublin, Eire. Doll manufacturers. Registered trademark 'Crolly' on 18th June, 1956, no B754,850 for dolls. 1946, made a range of stuffed rag dolls with Canadian unbreakable heads, marked 'Reliable'.

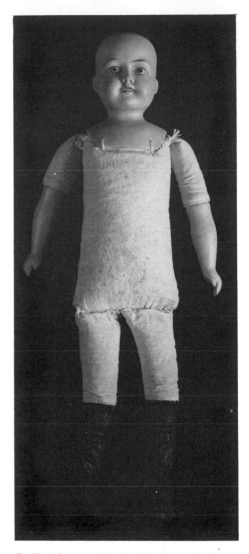

Doll with starched cloth body and china head, marked 'G.B. Made in England' (Pollock's Toy Museum).

Three sizes: 16½", 18", and 19½". 1967 range includes fully jointed dolls with rooted washable hair and sleeping eyes, from 12" to 28" tall. Collector's Piece dolls in traditional costumes, e.g. boy and girl from Connemara, Irish Fiddler and dancer, and replicas of leprechauns with rooted whiskers and traditional red cap. 1968 Crolly doll range includes 24" doll in Aran sweater and Donegal tweed skirt, fully jointed with washable, rooted and styled hair, 22" boy doll in blue denim jeans.

GAITY. Doll made by Bluebell Dolls Ltd. 1969. From 1974 was made by Denys Fisher Toys Ltd.

GAMAGE'S. London store. Holborn, 1910-1972. Sold all types of dolls and toys. Trademark Chantecleer for a soft toy.

GARDEN. 1927. Doll series made by Mabel Bland-Hawkes.

GARFIELD, JAMES & CO. 1920-1927. London. Doll and toy manufacturing company set up by Julius Kohnstam.

GARRIE, Thomas. See **Cariad.**

GATTER, Edward. 1884-87. 177 Walworth Road, London, SE. Made gutta-percha dolls.

GAY, Benjamin. London. c1836-1843. Made dolls. 1836-8 at addresses in Goswell Street, London EC.

GAY GADABOUT. Introduced 1970. 14″ walking and skating doll with rod and harness so as to propel her from behind, walking and skating with her own roller skates. Manufactured by Palitoy.

GEM DOLLS. 1932. Lucky birthday dolls, one for each month of the year and appropriately dressed in the colour of the jewel belonging to the month. Each doll wore a tiny necklace and pendant representing lucky birthstone. Height 16½ inches. Made by Dean's Rag Book Co.

GEMS, G. F. & NICKS, W. F. Obtained patent no. 14081 on 2nd July, 1908 for doll bodies: a series of solid discs. These are connected at the edges by a covering with a lining of silk or stockinette, the whole being collapsible in the manner of a concertina. Limbs etc, of similar or other construction may be attached.

GENITAL DOLLS. Trade term for boy dolls with male organ indicated as against "hermaphrodite" dolls, dressed as a boy but shaped like a girl. "Bibi" was a vinyl doll introduced in England in 1971 by Mr V. H. Howell of Don Bricks Ltd. Made in Spain but thought generally to be a "gimmick in poor taste".

GEORGE, John. 1894. At 116 Columbia Road, Bethnal Green, London NE. Made dolls.

GEORGETTE Doll. c1920. One of the 'Classic' series of dressed dolls by Speights Ltd. Georgette was a new material introduced in c1914.

GESSO. A fine plaster used to give coating to wooden heads.

GHOST OF CAPTAIN KIDD. 1976. Pirate doll from the Fighting Furies range made in Hong Kong for Lesney Products & Co. Ltd.

GIBBONS, Charles Kendrick. Surbiton, Surrey. Registered trademark for an Angelo doll, 1907.

GIBSON, E. T. Obtained patent no. 14496 on 30th July, 1895 relating to paper dolls. He made paper garments in parts, in such a way that change of costume could be effected by combining together different parts.

GIDDIKIDS. 1958. Registered trademark for dolls, games and playthings. See **Upperton, Patricia Gwendoline Elizabeth.**

GIFFORD, S. D. Obtained patent no. 9900 for mechanism of eyes and eyelids of dolls 1st May, 1906.

GIGGLY. 1920. Registered trademark. See **Jones, Edward Hazell.**

GILBERT THE FILBERT. Range of rag toys made by Dean's Rag Book Co. in 1921.

GILBERT, W. V. Patent no. 19728 in 1898 for cardboard cut-out dolls.

GILLIAN. 1956. See **Paliglide Walking Dolls.**

GINNY BABY. 1978. All-vinyl baby doll, drink/wet, 20 cms high. 2 hair colours and 2 dress colours. Made in Hong Kong for Lesney Products Co. Ltd.

GINSBERG & SMITH. 1946. 99 Charlotte Street, London W.1. Advertised hard-bodied dolls and dolls' heads, 'high-class' dolls in 1949.

GIPSY. Mark on doll in Pollock's Toy Museum Collection.

GIRL. Series of dolls dressed as River Girls, Gaiety Girls, Skating Girls, Seaside Girls. Made by Laurie Hansen, c1917.

'Georgette' doll, made by Speight's Ltd., 1919. 23 inches; china head; moving eyes; dressed in pink or blue georgette draped with white net.

GIRLY. 1928. Fully-jointed soft doll stuffed with Java Kapok. Glass eyes, elaborately dressed. Made by Dean's Rag Book Co. Ltd.

GIVJOY. See: **Holladay & Co.**

GLADEYE DOLL. 1916. See **Imperial Doll & Toy Co. Ltd.**

GLEVUM TOYS. See: **Roberts Bros.**

GLORIA and GLORIA PRINCESS. See **Wilson Bros. Ltd.**

GLOVER, Margaret. 42 Hartham Road, Isleworth, Middlesex. 1975 An artist craftswoman producing poured wax dolls in the traditional manner with soft fabric bodies. Inserted, rooted human hair is used for the wig; rooted eyelashes and brows and antique blown glass eyes confirm the care with which each model is made. Materials used for costume are all old and no man-made fibre is allowed. The dolls are rare collectors' items individually signed and dated by the artist. About 40 different types including 20″ negro girl, 20″ chinese girl, 19″ Japanese baby, and small 3″ and 8″ babies. Queen Victoria in Coronation Robes with crown and sceptre is 17″ high and another favourite is A. A. Milne's Christopher Robin, complete with Pooh Bear.

GOBLIN GOBBLERS. 1910. Registered trademark for mechanical doll. See **Sherwood, Katherine Mary.**

GODFREY, Emily Dorcas & Godfrey, Sarah & Godfrey, Catherine Maria. 1880 at 30 George Street, Croydon, Surrey. Doll manufacturers. Registered trademark 'S.G.' and a drawing of a wheat sheaf, no. 22, 346 on 3rd May, 1880 for dolls.

GOLBORNE DOLLS. See **N. G. Products & Co. Ltd.**

GOLDBERG, I.A. & Co. Livery Street, Birmingham. 1917. Toy Warehouse. Sold china-head dolls, toys of tin.

GOLDBERG, Louis, Ltd. 1935. Livery St, Birmingham. Manufacturing cheap soft toys and dolls including 6d. and 1s soft dolls with mask faces.

GOLDILOCKS. Introduced. 1968. 15″ Palitoy doll with hair that 'grows' and sleeping eyes. Dressed in an orange blouse under a blue denim pinafore dress. Retail price 51s 6d.

GOLDSMITH, Alfred. 55 Whitecross St, London EC. Advertised in 1925, clown doll and pierrot.

GOLLIWOGG. A black rag doll based on a character which first figured in a book by ·Miss Florence Upton published in 1895. She was born in New York in 1873 but her parents were English. Her mother Bertha Upton encouraged her to illustrate children's books and wrote the verses for "The Adventures of Two Dutch Dolls and a Golliwogg". Golliwogg was a pleasant, friendly fellow with red smiling mouth, shock of fuzzy black hair and staring white-rimmed eyes. Subsequent stories established him as a firm nursery favourite and the first dolls represented him faithfully, as in the book illustration, with pointed nose, stand-up collar, bow tie and bright jacket and trousers. The original doll on which Miss Upton founded her drawings came from her childhood in America and it now resides in Chequers (The Prime Minister of England's country house) where it was placed when the author sold it for charity during World War I, together with some of her drawings. The amount raised was enough to equip an ambulance, inscribed 'Florence Upton and the Golliwogg gave this ambulance'.

Later names were changed to Gollywog and Golliwog (one 'g') and many commercial and also hand-made replicas were produced. The actual derivation of the name is obscure. W.O.G. in Anglo-Indian parlance stood for Western Oriental Gentleman but this Golliwogg resembled more a fanciful Kentucky Minstrel—popular at that time. The Jam-manufacturing firm of Robertson (Paisley), who use the golliwog as a symbol for their products, advance an ingenious theory that the name could have originated from 'Polliwog', an old-fashioned term for a tadpole, with its large black head and tapered tail. See **Green Golliwog; Upton, Florence; Woolly Wally.**

GOLLYWOG. 1921. Dean's Rag Book Co. Woolly Wally, The Prince of Gollywogs.

GOOCH, Charles. Late 19th Century. Soho Bazaar. Distributed wax dolls by Charles Marsh.

GOODMAN, L. & A. L. 1926. At 53 Whitecross Street, London, EC1. Importer and agent for English and foreign lines. Registered 'Goody Goody' series, trademark no. 437896 for dolls and toys, 7th June, 1923. Registered 'Goody Goody' Doll was a baby doll.

GOODY GOODY SERIES. Registered trademark for dolls and toys. See **Goodman, L. & A. L.**

GOO-GOO. Trademark no. 399357 registered by Edward Hazell Jones for dolls, 9th January 1920.

GOO-GOO Doll. Boy and girl novelty dolls with goo-goo eyes made by Speights Ltd. c1920.

GOO-GOO PETLINGS. Doll range by Dean's Rag Book Co. Ltd.

GOO-GOO SERIES. c1912: See **Wiederseim, Grace.**

GOO-GOO SMILE. 1921. China character doll made by Dolls' Accessory Co.

GORLESTON TOY COMPANY. 1921. Factory at Gorleston-on-Sea, London showroom at Southampton House, 317 High Holborn, London WC. Doll and toy manufacturers. Dressed dolls, cheap dressed rag dolls with celluloid or material faces in 3 sizes.

GOSS, W. H. & Co. 1858-1944. Falcon Pottery, Stoke-on-Trent, Staffordshire. Made 'Parian' and 'Ivory' porcelain busts in the 19th century and bisque dolls' heads and limbs in the 20th century. After the outbreak of war in 1914 German dolls were no longer imported and Goss began making dolls' legs, arms and faces. In 1917 they were producing jointed and unjointed dolls from 11" to 30" with glass and painted eyes. They also made bisque heads for Potteries Toy Co. They were just beginning to capture the English toy market, despite their high price, when the war ended in November 1918. The factory was then forced to cease production of the dolls as the returning German dolls were cheaper and prettier.

In 1934 the firm was taken over by Cauldon Potteries and became Goss China Co. Ltd. In 1940 they were producing baby

Golliwog - black cotton body, fur wig; eyes made from white shirt buttons and black boot buttons; dressed in blue-tailed coat and red trousers (Bantock House Museum, Wolverhampton).

dolls with ring or socket necks and soft-bodied baby dolls with china heads. In 1941 the dolls were modelled by craftsmen from photos. Mr W. H. Goss was one of the committee formed in 1915 for the Potteries Toy Co., with Mrs G. H. Rittyer, Miss Deakin & Miss Green who took over British Toy Co., making up dolls with Goss parts.

GOSSET, James. London 1763. Carved portraits in wood and modelled them in wax.

GOTTSCHALK & DAVIES. 1915. At 5 Bunhill Rd, London EC. Sold calico printed stuffed rag dolls. Five different models were advertised at prices ranging from 1d to 6d. A larger doll 22″ long sold for 1/-

GRAHAM, Arthur. See **Peebo Doll.**

GRAHAM BROS. Beechwood House, 73 Endell Street, London WC2. Established 1887. Manufacturers' agents, exporters and importers of games and toys. Sold celluloid dolls in 1935. Trademark 'Fairylite'. By 1957 firm had changed its name to 'Fairylite Moulded Plastics Ltd'.

GRAY & NICHOLLS LTD. At 17 St. Anne Street, Liverpool. Wholesaler of games and toys; and of dolls, dressed and undressed, cheap and expensive. Sold mascot Eskimo dolls in 1916.

GRAY, W. Patent no. 27072, 28 November 1896. Dancing doll on platform worked by exterior crank handle.

GRECON. Registered trademark for dolls. See **Cohn, Margarete.**

GREEDY CHUGGY. Registered trademark for mechanical doll. See **Sherwood, Katherine Mary.**

GREEN, G. D. Obtained patent no. 109169 for applying coloured design of dolls' eyes on to heads made of china, earthenware or parian. 5th December 1916.

GREEN. S. A. Obtained patent no. 16067 for colouring dolls' heads made of parian, pottery etc., without firing. Nov. 15th 1915.

GREEN, Thomas. 93 Park Street, and 129 High Street, Camden Town, London, N1. 1855. Made dolls.

GREENAWAY, Kate. Dolls based on children drawn by K. G., author illustrator of children's books in 1880 and later. A 1977 'Pedigree' version has vinyl head and limbs. The Greenaway-style bonnet and smock was taken by the artist from late eighteenth and early nineteenth century children's fashions.

GRIFFITHS, Eric J. Sculptor and doll designer, worked for Chad Valley Ltd., Frido Ltd., Pedigree Ltd. Art Director for Sculpture with the Royal Doulton Group, 1970-81+. Designed a series of dolls with ceramic heads made by Royal Doulton Ltd. in conjunction with Peggy Nisbet Ltd.

GROSS & SCHILD. 4 Golden Lane, London EC1. Merchants. Registered trademark 'Marigold' no. 454,121 for dolls on 1st December, 1924.

GROVEWELL RUBBER CO. Established 1924. At 656 Forest Road, Walthamstow, London E17. Manufacturers of rubber toys and balloons. 1948 products include pliable plastic dolls. By 1952 the firm had changed its name to Grovewell Ltd.

GUILBERT, Pauline. 1912. A French artist who designed a series of dolls, tea cosies & bonbonnières for Dean's Rag Book Co. in 1912. The dolls were named Mignonne, Josephine, Eugenie and Marguerite, and were dressed in strong cotton, or silk satin in delicate colourings. Mignonne (12″ high), was reproduced in 1981 to raise funds and to mark the centenary of the Church of England's Children's Society.

GUM TRAGACANTH. Material used for making dolls. 17th to 19th century.

GUNNERSBURY PARK MUSEUM. Gunnersbury Park, London, W3. There are about 70 Dolls on display including one in Elizabethan fancy dress which may be a representation of Princess Alexandra of Wales as Queen Elizabeth, c1890.

China-headed doll marked Goss. Glass eyes; fabric body. c.1916.

H & L. See **Hewitt & Leadbeater.**

H RAG DOLL SERIES. See **Hughes & Son, Henry Jeffrey.**

HAAS, Albert F. London. Patent no. 1866 2nd August, 1860 for the body of a doll made with an enlarged seat to enable it to sit upright, and a joint at the knee to admit of a sitting position. Porcelain heads made by Fischer Naumann, Saxe Weimar, Germany were used.

HACHMEISTER, Hermann. 1908-11. At 48 Redcross Street, London, E.C. 1912-16:9 & 10 Redcross Street, London, EC. Doll-maker.

HAIR. For modern plastic dolls the hair used is usually nylon but in the Victorian period (and earlier) human hair was often used for wax, wooden and even china or papier mâché dolls. Lamb's wool was used for cheap dolls as it simulated curls. Other vegetable matters such as flax, and the coarse hair of goats and horses or the silky hair of the angora goat were imported from Turkey (mohair).

HAIR-DO DOLL. Introduced 1952. Fully jointed, plastic Rosebud doll with sleeping eyes and mama voice. Hair could be combed, shampooed, curled and set.

HALLETT, William. 1826-37. At 4 Field Place, Battle Bridge Gray's Inn, London. Dollmaker, composition and leather dolls.

HAMBURGER, A. & COSTON, H.E. London. Dover Street, Studios and Adart Ltd. Obtained patent no. 22825 on October 27th 1908 for stuffed dolls.

HAMER, William. c1848. 56 Shoe Lane, London, EC. Dollmaker.

HAMLEY BROS. c1760. Small toyshop called Noah's Ark in High Holborn, London, opened by Cornishman William Hamley. Sold tin soldiers and rag dolls. William Henry Hamley, born in 1843, established the world-wide reputation of his shop by adding an ever-expanding wholesale business to his retail shop, which eventually moved from 86 High Holborn to smart new premises in fashionable Regent Street, and became known as 'the European Toy Warehouse'. They imported dolls from Germany, France and America, and exported them to India, Australia and America. Nearly all the wax dolls made by the Pierotti family were sold by Hamley's.

John Green Hamley registered at least ten trademarks in Britain and one in France between 1904 and 1920. The British trademarks are as follows:
Buster Brown no. 265,091, 22nd July 1904
Ni-Ni no. 334,072, 1st June 1911.
Elfie No. 357,975, 20th January, 1914.
Pooksie no. 358,234, 30th January 1914.

Fumsup no. 359,090, 25th February 1914.
Lulu no. 374,013, 31st July 1916.
Wuwu no. 374,014, 31st July 1916.
Bluestocking dolls no. 379,471, 22nd August 1917.
Cilly Billy no. 397,855, 1st December 1919
Diddums no. 401,381, 2nd March 1920.

In 1931 the bulk of Hamley family's shares in the business were bought by Walter Lines of Lines Brothers (Triang-Toys). The store was run by him and then by his daughter Miss Peggy Lines until her retirement in 1977. In 1976 it was acquired by the Debenham Group of companies, who have opened a second shop devoted entirely to model making kits.

HAMLEY, John Green. See **Hamley Bros.**

HAMMOND MANUFACTURING CO LTD. Established by May 1915. Office and Works: Mosely Street, Burton-on-Trent. Doll, teddy bear and game manufacturers. One of the first of the many new firms started at the outbreak of war to develop the British Toy Industry. The manager, Mr Simmonds, before joining the company, was in business as a dollmaker in London, together with his wife. With the exception of the heads, all the dolls were produced throughout the premises—even the stuffing material for the bodies, wood and pine chips, was obtained from the firm's own mill. In 1916 Dolls had fixed and moving eyes, jointed or static bodies. In 1919 ranges included a variety of dolls jointed and unjointed in porcelain, composition and rag.

HAMMOND, Thomas Rundle. Took out a French Patent, 6th August 1858 for making dolls and animals from flesh-coloured rubber with invisible joints. Included because of the English-sounding name and the early invention of rubber. See **Rubber.**

'Wuwu', the Victoria Cross mascot doll; china with moving arms. Matching him, 'Lulu', the Red Cross doll. Hamley's catalogue, 1917.

HANCOCK, & SONS, S. Established 1857. 1891-1925+ at Cauldon, Staffordshire. 1892-1921 at Wolfe St (Gordon Works), Stoke-on-Trent. 1922-31 at Corona Works, Hanley, Stoke-on-Trent. 1932-7 at New St, Hanley.

The main products of this large pottery firm were table ware and a wide range of china ornaments and figures for the fancy goods trade. At the outbreak of the First World War in 1914 they promptly added to their decorative motifs the allied flags and other patriotic devices. Soon after, they were commissioned to produce the 'Fumsup' china mascot doll for Hamley's; then a series of rather similar dolls with moving arms, called 'Lulu', 'Wuwu' and 'Eyes Right'.

From there it was only a step to embarking, prompted by the Board of Trade, on the regular production of dolls' heads and limbs—a complex and highly specialised process requiring preliminary research and experiment.

By 1917, however, they were making over 70 varieties of heads, some with moulded hair, others with open pates. They were also making glass eyes, and were prepared to make special lines for individual doll assembly firms.

HANDY MANDY. 1976. 45cms high girl doll with long blonde rooted hair, sleeping eyes, jointed body, gripping hands that can hold things. Originally made in Italy for Lesney Products and Co. Ltd., and assembled in U.K., now made in East Germany.

HANSA. Dolls Trademark and brand name. See **B.U.T. Ltd.**

HANSEN, LAURIE & CO. LTD. 1915-21. At 9-15 Whitecross Street, London EC. Doll and toy manufacturers and wholesalers. Early days of firm concerned with importing and factoring, but by 1916 they were manufacturing pot-head dolls in over 100 different models both dressed and undressed. In 1917 large and varied selection. Baby dolls with real baby clothes. "Girl" series—River Girl,

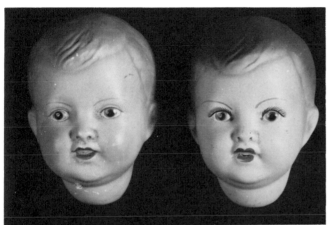

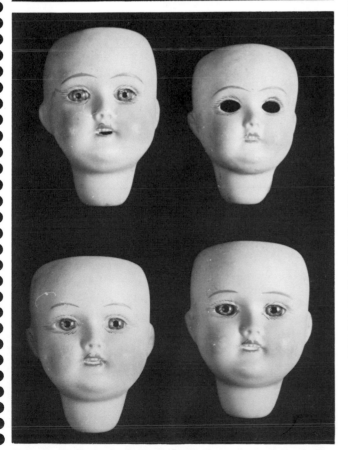

A workroom with dolls made by Hancock & Son, 1917.

Gaiety Girl, Skating Girl, Seaside Girl etc. The "Hilda Cowham" dolls with china or composition heads in all shades of velvet dresses and 'Dancing Girls'.

In 1918 Baby dolls with fully-jointed, unbreakable papier mâché bodies and china heads in fast colours.

HAPPY. 1939. A Mabel Lucie Attwell character doll, partner to 'Diddums' in assorted sizes and painted in pastel or bright colours. Made by Cascelloid Ltd. 'Palitoy' range.

HAPPY DAY TOY CO. LTD. c1918. Manufacturers of dolls, games, confectionery and novelties.

HARBER, William Francis. 1904. Chelsea London. Obtained a British Patent for a walking doll.

HARLEQUIN Series. 1929. Dolls in 3 sizes 19½″, 22″ and 27″ made by Dean's Rag Book Co. Ltd.

HAROLD LLOYD. 1928. See **Sant, J.S.**

HARPER & BELLAMY. 1950. At 2, Barnsbury Road, London N1. 'Makers of the perfect walking doll.'

HARPER, G. W. 1918. At 6, Comely Bank Road, Addison Road, Walthamstow, London E17. Manufacturers of dolls, teddy bears and wood toys.

HARRIS, A. C. Obtained patent no. 16012 5th July, 1909 for dolls with weighted lower parts and light upper parts and so balanced that if upset will right themselves.

HARRIS, John. 1858-60. At 54 York Road, London, SE. Made dolls.

HARRIS MUSEUM & ART GALLERY. Market Square, Preston, Lancashire. The Museum has a collection of about 130 dolls, including 3 wax dolls given in exchange for tea coupons in the 1880's. There is also a dolls' house of about 1820.

HARRISON, G. Obtained patent no. 19348 September 1903, for paper dolls and ornamental figures.

HARRISON, George. 1856-65. London. Made dolls.

HARWIN & CO LTD. 1915. The Eagle Works, Blackstock Road, Finsbury Park, London, N. Manufacturers and wholesalers

of dolls and soft toys. 1915 lines included Tipperary Tommy, Kittie, Sailor, French Soldier, Scout and Dixy Kid character dolls. 1916: Pyjama Baby, Red Riding Hood, Wee Willie Winkie. 1917: the 'Bluestocking Kid' doll, soft stuffed, dressed in linen hat, dress and petticoat; on each of these were printed different rhymes of an educational nature. The doll was sold by Hamley Bros. and its name was registered as a trademark by John Green Hamley. Also produced 'The Family' series of dolls and a range of natural jointed dolls, and sold 'Eyes Right' mascot dolls manufactured by Hancock & Sons. In 1919 Miss Dorothy Harwin designed a range of dolls called 'Dots Dolls' including Peggy Pimples, Pank, Tinkles, Wobbler, Bo-Peep, Snow Boy, Dutch Girl, Minnie Ha Ha, Rosebud, Zulu Chief, Zazz and Father Christmas.

HASSALL, John. 1914. England. Famous poster artist. Designed a series of dolls that were sent to the London Child's Welfare Exhibition. Did clever cartoons of sailors and fishermen for 'Punch'. Designed comic and caricature figures in 'Carlton china' made by Wiltshaw & Robinson Ltd, 6″ high, with movable heads.

HATCH, Mrs Sarah. 1884-1895. 303 Goswell Road, London. Dollmaker.

1918.

1916.

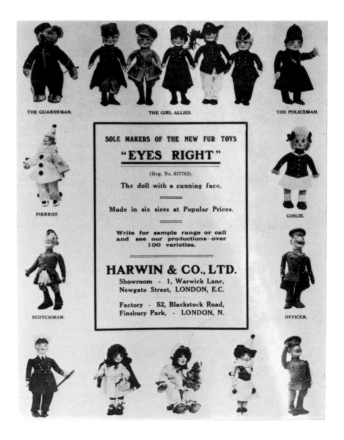

Two characters designed by John Hassall, 1915, and sold by A. Abrahams & Sons.

HATCH, Thomas. 1884-91. At 89 Long Lane, Smithfield, London. Made wax and composition dolls. Appears to have been succeeded by Mrs Sarah Hatch.

HAUGHTON, W. H. & GORDGE, J. Surrey. Obtained patent no. 488434 on January 14th 1937 for 'a face or head for dolls. . . .'

HAVOC, SECRET AGENT. 1974. Introduced. 9″ articulated girl doll dressed in zip-up black catsuit and boots with rifle, shoulder holster and pistol. Made by Model Toys Ltd.

HAWKSLEY & CO LTD. c1916. Dawson Street, Liverpool. Doll and toy manufacturers. Jointed dolls, dressed and undressed, baby character dolls, calico dolls, Eskimo dolls and plush animals.

HAWLEY, Horace. 1918-21. At 61 Hamilton Road, Grove Road, London E3. Manufactured dolls' limbs.

HAY, Will. 'Evripose Tru-to-Life' rag doll in the likeness of the famous English comic actor of the 1930's. The doll, introduced in 1938, has academic robe, plus cane and book.

HAYNES, Miss Rebecca. 1884-87. At 66 Paul Street, Finsbury, London EC. Made rag dolls.

HAZEL. 1927. A summer doll in finished silk with rosebud trimming. See manufacturer **Bland-Hawkes, Mabel.**

HAZEL, Henry John. 1891-1925+. At 2 Caversham Road, London, NW. and 228a-30 Kentish Town Road, London. Made dolls for the wholesale trade. 1909: New doll with roller skates on shoes. Made rag dolls,

dressed jointed dolls and juvenile fancy costumes.

HEATH ROBINSON, W. Cartoon artist. See **Tah-Toys Ltd**

HEATHER. c1925. See **Posy Buds.**

HEATHER BELLE. Registered trademark for toys and dolls. See manufacturers **Rees, Leon.**

HELEN'S BABIES. See **Frazer Rock, Helen.**

HELEN WHATELEY Dolls. Helen Whately Pratt. 13 High Street, Marlow, Bucks. The artist's interest in creating costume dolls arose from her career as dress designer and dressmaker. In 1969 she experimented with various substances and finally began using painted pottery heads, arms and legs with stuffed bodies for her hand-dressed models. They are approximately 12/13 inches high and are clearly marked with Helen Pratt signature and the year of firing at the back of the shoulder. Later, when the dolls are dressed, the artist adds HW, the design number and the limited edition number in Roman figures. Many of the dolls are exported to Japan and U.S.A. and a special collection is exhibited in the Historical and Cultural Museum in Cephalonia of the Ionian Isles, illustrating one of the early periods in the island's history. Dolls' house figures and child figures in parian are also made to special order.

HEMPIL, John. Made mechanical wooden toys for Edlin, 1818

HENRECK, S. c1917. At 59 West Ham Lane, Stratford, London E15. Manufacturer of Celluloid articles including dolls' faces.

HENRY. c1936. Boy doll, made by Dean's Rag Book Co. Ltd., wearing shorts and playshirt. Has oddly shaped bulbous head and long neck. He was based on a cartoon character popular at the time.

HEO TOYWORKS. See **Peskin, J.**

HERBIE BROWN ('erbie Brown). A jointed character doll made by Dean's, 1929.

HEREFORD & WORCESTER COUNTY MUSEUM. Hartlebury Castle, Kidderminster. There are over 200 dolls on display in this collection.

HERZOG, RAE. 11 Manor House Drive, London NW6. Doll manufacturers. Registered trademark 'Cinette' no. 694,463 for dolls 6th December 1950.

HETTY The Help Yourself Girl. October 1929. Dean's Rag Doll. Help Yourself Magazine was promoted by the London Stock Exchange with a view to raising funds for hospitals. Notable authors and artists contributed and there was a long list of donated prizes which were awarded lottery-fashion. The magazines each had a lucky number and 'Hetty' was the girl represented as giving out the prize.

HEWITT, Edwin. 180 Oxford Street, London W.1. A glover who made gloves for dolls.

HEWITT & LEADBEATER. (Hewitt Bros). Willow Pottery, Willow Street, Longton, Stoke-on-Trent, Staffordshire. From 1907-1919 the firm was known as the 'Willow Pottery' and from 1919-c1926 it was 'Hewitt Bros.' Manufacturers of porcelain, crest china and miniature art china; from 1914 made dolls' heads. According to a trade

Helen Whateley dolls: General Schuyler and his wife, made for the Saratoga Historical Museum, USA.

journal of the period, the firm was peculiarly well laid out for the manufacture of dolls' heads, and could, of all the pottery firms, most easily run the trade in with its ordinary business. They were also the first firm to take up the manufacture of dolls' heads after the outbreak of war. So great was the demand that they were compelled to take over another factory solely for the manufacture of dolls' heads and their component parts. By 1917 they were producing thousands of shoulder and socket heads with painted eyes or with apertures for glass eyes.

They registered the trademark 'Suner' no. 400,509 for dolls on 7th February, 1920, and used the marks 'H & L' and a willow tree symbol.

From 1920 onwards Leadbeater Co. owned a separate company concentrating on the manufacture of crest china and other china ornaments. Hewitt Brothers continued to make dolls' heads, and doll-like figurines similar to 'Where's Hubby?'.

HEYWOOD-ABEL & SONS LTD. 1832-1932. Manchester House, 47-61 Lever Street, Manchester. Doll and toy merchants. Sold English-made china dolls' heads with painted hair, wigs, china shoulder heads, hair-stuffed dolls with china heads, china heads with moulded hair and shoulder-and-socket heads with glass eyes and cut-out eyes. Also sold Tam O' Shanter china bonnet doll heads made by S. Hancock & Son and a 3½″ Baby head and New Darling Baby head.

HEYWOOD, Cecil K. c1918. At 24-25 Avenue Chambers, Southampton Row, WC1. Doll and toy merchant. Rag dolls, china head dolls, jigsaws and sundries.

HIBERNIAN NOVELTY CO. 1916. At 4 South William Street, Exchequer Street, Dublin, Southern Ireland. Doll and toy manufacturers. 1916 lines included dressed rag dolls with composition faces.

HI-DOLLS. 1976. Brand name of vinyl dolls made by Bambola Toys Ltd.

HIGGS, William. 1733. London. Made jointed wooden babies (dolls) turned on a lathe.

HIGHLAND DOLLS. c1957. Range of Pedigree unbreakable vinyl dolls with sleeping eyes and rooted Saran hair, dressed in authentic tartans. Girl and boy dolls from 7″ to 16″ high.

HILL, E. W. & CUSHING, E. C. 1914 London. Obtained patent no. 21607, October 27th 1914 for metal dolls' heads and limbs.

HINDE, John Lord. Trading as Hinde Bros. 1a City Road, Finsbury, London. Brush manufacturer. Registered trademark 'Dollie Dimple' no. 77,553, 21st June 1888.

HIPPY DOLL. 1967. Doll made by Almer Dolls.

Hewitt and Leadbeater 'Willow' dolls (Pollock's Toy Museum).

HISTORY OF LITTLE FANNY. See **Fuller, S. & J.** and **Paper Dolls.**

HOBBINS, John. 1856-65. At 47 Market Street, Borough Road. Made wax dolls.

HOCKLEY, J. See **Burnell & Hockley.**

HODGE. 1918. Doll designed by Elizabeth Ellen Houghton.

HODGSON, Ellen Sheraton Fortrose. Inverness, Scotland, wife of Major-General Hodgson, Bengal Army (retired). Patent 20116, 11th September 1896 for a clockwork swimming doll to be made of metal or rubber.

HOLDFAST. See **Cartwright, A. S. Ltd.**

HOLGATE, Margaret. Doll designer: See **Mfanwy Jones.**

HOLLADAY, A. J. & CO. LTD. 32 & 33 Aldermanbury, London EC2. Manufacturers of dolls, toys, games and fancy wares. Lines include in 1919, 'Master Givjoy' described as 'happiest spright, merry and bright' in 'Jacob-like coat'. Surprise Snowball containing dressed baby doll. Registered trademark "Givjoy" Toys no. B408,264, 29th September, 1920.

HOLLOWAY DOLLS ACCESSORIES LTD. 1950. At 7b, Byham Street, London, N.W.1. 1953 at 19 Westbourne Road, London N.17. Dollmakers. Registered trademark 'Holly Doll' no. 687,154, March 10th 1950.

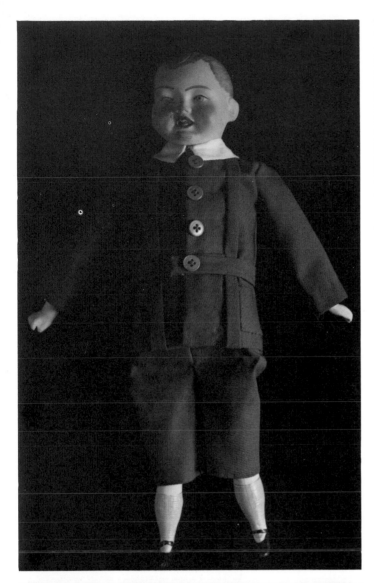

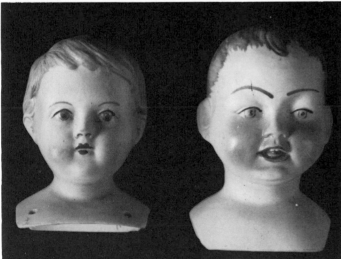

Hewitt and Leadbeater 'Willow' dolls.

HOLLY DOLL. Registered trademark: See **Holloway Dolls Accessories Ltd.**

HOME-MADE DOLLS. Families too poor to buy toys have often provided their children with some simple doll fashioned from any materials or domestic article close at hand: rags, wooden spoons, bed knobs, clothes pegs, even old shoes. Edward Lovett made a collection of 'emergent' or 'emergency' dolls as he called them; and it is said that when poor children realised this strange man was handing out new dolls or pennies for their old treasures there was a constant production of dolls by the children them-

selves. Beautiful hand-made dolls have also been fashioned by needlewomen as a pastime. See **Pedlar; Fortune-telling dolls.**
Many were made to sell at bazaars run for charity in the early 19th century when there was great distress caused by the economic problems of the Industrial Revolution. Amusing gift dolls include such models as "The Experienced General Doll" a novelty sold by Nell Foy & Co. 1918.

> "You stir your porridge with
>   my face
> And with my gown you dust
>   the place
> The dishes wash up with my shawl
> It is very strong and not
>   too small
> My skirt you see is not a hobble
> 'Twill clean your floor
>   without much trouble
> And if you want a mop,
>   'tis said
> You'll find it on my
>   wooden head."

The 'General' doll (Bantock House Museum, Wolverhampton).

HOOK & FRANKS LTD. 1964. At Grange Road, Walthamstow, London E17. Make 'Faerie Glen' dolls' clothing and accessories and playclothes for girls and boys. Also complete wardrobe for 'Tina', a 12" vinyl doll with rooted hair made in Singapore. The firm is run by Peggy Franks, former table tennis champion, now Mrs Hook, aided by her mother and a team of outworkers.

HOOPY LOU. Registered trademark for dolls: See **Mettoy Co. Ltd.**

HORNIMAN MUSEUM. At London Road, Forest Hill SE23. Ethnographical collections including dolls and puppets; Japanese Girls' Festival Set. Part of the Edward Lovett collection of folk dolls and toys.

Doll made from a weaving bobbin.

HOTWATER BABY. 1918. Soft doll designed by Elizabeth Ellen Houghton. Doll contained a small rubber bag which could be filled with hot water.

HOT WATER BOTTLE DOLLS.
> "Patty Comfort's a rubber-lined dolly,
> To buy any other were folly,
> When filled with air, she's
>   light and she's fair,
> And filled with hot water,
>   she's jolly."

A 1907 publicity jingle advertising the merits of the Patty Comfort, the new rubber hot water bottle. Another hot water bottle doll, made by Dunlop, was in the form of Little Red Riding Hood. See **Hotwater Baby; Rable, J. G.; Dunlop Products.**

HOUGHTON, Elizabeth Ellen. 13 St. Peter's Square, Hammersmith, London. Artist and doll designer. Registered trademark 'E.E. Houghton', no. 368,995, 31st August 1915 for dolls and like toys. During the 14-18 war, Mrs Houghton designed a series of stockinette dolls known as the 'Cuddley Ones' for The Three Arts Women's Employment Fund. She also designed dolls for the Shanklin Toy Industry, including Black Baby Doll, 'The Piccaninny', 'White Baby Doll', 'Baby Carrots' with red hair, and 'Bambino'. In the early 20s, Robert Bros of 'Glevum Toys' Gloucester took over the manufacture of her dolls. See **Hotwater Baby.**

HOUGHTON, James Albert. 1918-31. At 66 Penton Street, London N1. Made dolls.

Articulated home-made doll (Welsh Folk Museum, St Fagan's).

HOUGHTON, Mrs Edith. 1932. At 66 Penton Street, London N1. Repaired dolls. Took over from James Albert Houghton at same address.

HOUSE OF HENRIETTA. 1970. Brand name for rag dolls made by Gormla Moroney Ltd.

HOWARD, Henry (Harry). 1858-65. London 1859 at 10 Patriot Row, Cambridge Road, London NE. Made dolls.

HOWARD POTTERY CO LTD. Norfolk Street, Shelton, Stoke-on-Trent. London Showrooms: 44-50 Holborn Viaduct, London EC1. Earthenware manufacturers. Manufactured dolls from 1925 onwards. In 1940 the firm was making 'Brentleigh' dolls, dolls' heads; and toy tea sets, dressed and undressed dolls. Dolls' dresses in satin, taffeta; print frocks, white smocks.

HUCK, A. Obtained Patent no. 235032, 25th July, 1924 for improving the ball joints of dolls.

HUGHES & SONS, Henry Jeffrey. 1887-1925+. c1914 at 98 and 100 Tottenham Road, Kingsland, London, N. Doll, soft toy and rattle manufacturers. Established 1887. In 1909 made rag dolls and wood toys. 'Young England' series of character dolls including 'My Little Territorial'; 'Our Little Dreadnought' (boy & girl); Dutch Boy and Girl; "H" series of rag dolls. In 1914 new types introduced included "Leg Style" Eskimo Dolls, "Skirt Style" Eskimo Dolls, and Baby Bunting Eskimos, with celluloid faces and plush bodies, from 4d to 1s 6d each. Also a new range of fancy character dolls: Boy Scout, Dreadnought (doll dressed in sailor costume), Miss & Master Folly dressed as pierrotts, a nurse, a Dutch girl and several others. They had china heads and soft unbreakable bodies, and retailed at 1s 6d and 2s 6d. In 1924 New Folly dolls in Irish, Scottish and Welsh costume and velvet Jester dolls. In 1925 over 400 styles including Miss Crossword and entirely new reversible dolls.

HUGHES, Henry Richard. 1891-99. Agent for doll manufacturers. In 1899 at the same address as Henry Jeffrey Hughes.

HUGHES, Herbert Edward. 1895-1912. At 9 Long Lane, London 1921 at Toy Hall, Cheshunt, Hertfordshire. Doll and Toy importer and dealer. 1921 advertised 'Pinkie Doll'.

HUGMEE. Registered trademark for dolls and puppets etc. See manufacturers **Eisenmann & Co.**

HUME, A. E. At 7 Distaff Lane, London. Obtained patent no. 4042 on 15th March, 1915 for dolls' eyelids operated by wires or string from outside the dolls.

HUMPTY DUMPTY. Soft toys 1924. See **Worthing Toy Museum.**

HUNGARIAN DOLL. 1960. 20″ vinyl Pedigree doll with Saran hair in blonde, shoulder-length plaits. Authentic Hungarian National Costume with flower headdress trimmed with ribbons and lace, white satin blouse with red nylon lace edgings, black felt waistcoat with gold braid, white apron with silver lurex floral braid and red lace, turquoise blue taffeta skirt edged with floral braid in red and silver and red felt boots. Retail price £13 9s 6d.

HUNGRY GILES. Registered trademark for a mechnical doll: See **Sherwood, Katherine Mary.**

HUNTER TOY FACTORY. c1947. At 91 Foyle Street, Londonderry, N. Ireland. Doll and toy manufacturers.

Baby doll by H. Hughes & Son, 1919.

HUNTER, William Crosby & SIMS, Frederick Walter. Southampton. Obtained patent no. 196545, 19th October, 1922 for dolls' eyes that would close only after the doll had been rocked. Also obtained German patent for the same.

HUSH-A-BYE BABY. 1963. 20″ Pedigree doll that 'cries until she's picked up'. Complete with carry cot and non-spill battery.

HUSHEEN DOLLS. 1931. Furry dolls made from 'silkeen' plush for small children by Dean's Rag Book Co. Ltd.

HUVAN MANUFACTURING CO. 8 Ilford Lane, Ilford, Essex. Produced Novelty 'Dolliettes' series of cut-outs, children in 15 different attitudes, 6″ high. 10 per box. 3s 6d per box. 'The Latest Atrocity'—topical cut-out figures. 'Mad Kaiser, Clown Prince.' 'Charlie' (i.e. Charlie Chaplin). Trade mark 'Huvanco'.

HYACINTH. c1925. See **Posy Buds.**

HYATT, Joseph. 1891-1910. London. Imported dolls.

IBBETSON, Leonard. c1918. Manufacturer of rag dolls, bags, puzzles and wood toys.

IBBOTSON, C. W. P. See **Dol Toi Products (Stamford) Ltd.**

IDEAL DOLLS LTD. c1949. Aycliffe Trading Estate, South Shields. Doll manufacturers. Distributor: J. Cowan (Dolls) Ltd. In 1949 advertised American hard-body baby, with sleeping eyes and eyelashes, with or without voice, 14″, 16″ or 18″ high. Almost unbreakable.

IHLEE & HORNE. 31 Aldermanbury, London. 1879. Trademark for dolls and toys: Aladdin's Lamp and an acorn with leaf.

IKLE, JOHN JACOBY LTD. c1927. London. Registered trademark 'Ankidoodle', no. 478,714. 11th March, 1927 for dolls, games and toys.

ILFORD DOLL & TOY CO. December 19th 1918—April 1921. At 267 Ilford Lane, Ilford, Essex. Agents for dolls. In 1918 advertised hair-stuffed dolls, dressed and undressed baby dolls. In May, 1920, hair-stuffed dolls, pin-jointed dolls with compressed card bodies and sleeping eyes, 3 sizes, costing ½d, 1d and 2d.

IMANS, P. Obtained patent no. 165726, 2nd July, 1920 for a device for attaching wax arms to the shoulders of dolls etc.

I'MERE. 1921. Registered trademark for dolls. See **Polmar Perfumery Co.**

I MIT. c1919. See **Darenta Toy Works.**

IMPERIAL DOLL & TOY CO. c1916. Toyland Works, Ena Street, Hull. Manufacturers of dolls, soft toys and wood toys. Made character dolls of wood fibre, sizes

9½″, 12½″ and 18½″. In 1916 advertised Gladeye Doll and Esquimaux Dolls, and Whistling Boy, a china-headed doll with fur body. Proprietor R. Barkoff.

IMPY. 1916. A pantomime imp figure, wearing belted jacket and rag cap. Sold by Ellison Rees & Co. Also a simple soft rag doll sold by A. J. Holladay & Co. 1916.

INDIA RUBBER, GUTTA-PERCHA AND TELEGRAPH WORKS CO. LTD. Cannon Street, London. Manufacturers. 1908. Trademark Heart: See **Rubber; Gutta-percha.**

INFANT DOLLS. In the Collector's Encyclopedia of Dolls, Mrs D. Coleman defines Infant dolls as dolls dressed in long baby clothes, as opposed to babies in short clothes or rompers.

INFIELD, M. & DRIELSMA. 7-8 Albion Buildings, Aldersgate Street, London EC. Suppliers of squeakers, voices and glass eyes for dolls, toy animals and birds etc.

INFIELDS LTD. 1935. 174-5 Aldersgate St London EC1. Manufacturers of glass eyes, doll's masks, growlers and squeakers for soft toys. Company appears to be successor of M. Infield & Drielsma.

INGRAM, G. & CLARKE, T. Obtained patent no. 628883, 11th March, 1947, relating to dolls' eyes.

IRIS. c1925. See **Posy Buds.**

IRISH DOLLS. 1895-1925. Emily Florence Eaton started to make dolls in 1895; by 1903 there was also a doll-making industry in Stewartstown, County Tyrone. In 1919 Isobel Dodd of Dublin was making dolls. Before 1908 there was also the Orwell Art Industries Dublin. In the 1940s, Erris Toys had a factory at Elly Bay, County Mayo, and Crolly Toys a factory in County Donegal. Both firms made soft dolls and toys. Both were government-owned. Agents: William Girvan, Central Hotel Stockrooms, Dublin.

IRISH TOY CO. 1918. 162 N. Circular Road, Dublin, N. Ireland. See **Peskin, J.**

ISAACS, ABRAHAM & ISAACS, HENRY. 1881. London. 1884-87 Successor A. & J. Isaacs: 1891 Successor Isaac & Henry Isaacs. Made rag dolls. Imported and dressed dolls. Registered trademark 'The Cherub Doll' no. 56776 for dressed and undressed dolls on 15th September, 1886.

"I'SE ALL DICKY". 1919. See **Dolls' Accessory Co. Ltd.**

IVIMEY, Annie Alice. Manor Road, East Molesey, Surrey 1906. Registered name for dolls DOLLIT.

IVORINE MANUFACTURING CO. c1918. At 349 Euston Road, London NW1. Made celluloid dolls and celluloid dolls' masks and faces.

IVORY PORCELAIN. The name given by Goss to material of which they made some of their dolls' heads.

IVY. c1925. See **Posy Buds.**

IZZARD. 1814+. James Izzard had a turnery and toy warehouse in London from 1814-1860. From 1878, Frederick William Lee had a toy warehouse at 136 Regent Street, London W1. The label on a 3-wheeled walking doll reads: Izzard Importer & Manufacturer, 136 Regent Street.

Irish Paddy. 25cm; moulded and painted suede face on wire body; dressed in coloured suede and leather (Bantock House Museum, Wolverhampton).

J.F.J. PRODUCTS LTD. Obtained patent no. 754047, 1st July, 1954 for doll's eyes, and patent no. 846528, 15th April, 1958 for independently sleeping eyes.

JACK & JILL. See **East London (Federation Toy) Factory.**

JACKMAN, BARBARA (CRAFT) DOLLS LTD. 1970. Manufacturer of Yesterday Dollies: 17 different costume doll kits, each containing fully-jointed moulded plastic doll plus material and trimmings. Range includes historical and fairytale characters, national costume dolls and a special twin pack for Romeo and Juliet in Shakespearian dress.

JACK RAG DOLL. See **Wood, Maria.**

JACOB, Leopold Emil. London Wall, London EC. Toy Importer. Registered trademark 1893. Patent 1866, in 1874 for jointed construction doll on Crandall pattern.

JAMES, Arthur William. 29 Gloucester Terrace, Hyde Park, London. 1907. Trademark for dolls 'AABA'.

JANE. c1918. Doll made by British Toys.

JANE SPROGG. 1927. Wooden 'Dutch type' doll obtained from a Woman's Magazine plus cut-out fabric clothes to sew at home.

JAYCO Dolls. Series of dolls sold by J. Cowan (Dolls) Ltd.

JAYSANT. Trade name. See **Sant, J. S. Ltd.**

JAZZ DOLL MANUFACTURERS, THE. c1924. At 10/11 & 12 Eccleston Place, Victoria, London, SW. Manufacturers and wholesalers of the 'Jazz' doll.

JEANETTE. 1977. Dressing doll set made by H. Schelhorn Co.

JEANETTE. 1934. Excella range doll. See **Rees, Leon.**

JEDMUNDS. See **Edmunds, J. Henry.**

JEFFREYS, Edward Augustus. 1902-3 Moseley, near Birmingham. Obtained a German patent for a crying doll.

JELLY BABIES. Edible, human shaped sweets, made from gum tragacanth sweetened with honey or sugar, have been made in Europe since the Middle Ages. They were known in England until 1918 as "Unclaimed Babies", but were then rechristened "Peace Babies". One of the largest manufacturers of jelly babies in England states that "jelly babies are purchased in the main for children, although there is reason to believe that a significant number of adults buy them for their own consumption. Research indicates that some consumers of jelly babies bite off the heads

'Jernoid' doll mask, in a non-inflammable celluloid made by Jernoid Ltd., 1915.

first and others bite off the feet first. Whether or not there is a deep underlying psychological reason for this is unknown." (Letter from the sweet firm Bassett's to Pollock's Toy Museum, February 4th, 1974).

JERNOID LTD. c1915. Jernoid Works, Merton Abbey, Surrey. Manufacturers of a substance called 'Jernoid'. Began making dolls' masks in 1915.

JEWELLERY KIDDLES. 1968. See **World of Kiddles; Rosebud Mattel.**

Jane Sprogg, 1927.

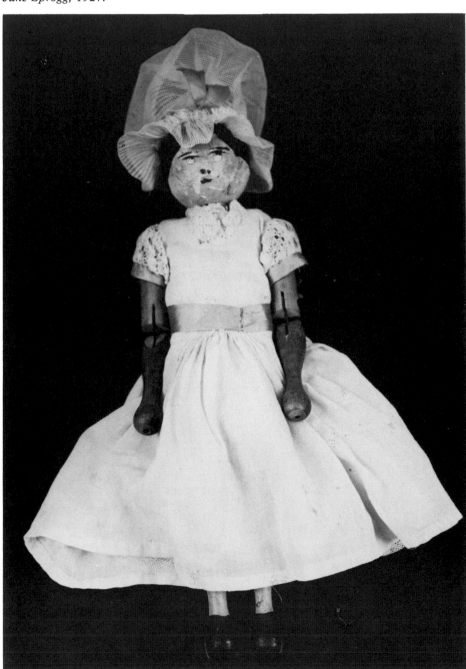

JEWITT, Henry. 141 Leighton Road, Kentish Town. Importer of toys from America. Agent for Crandall Toys.

JOAN 1936. Alpha 'Joy Day' doll made by J. K. Farnell & Co. Ltd.

JOAN. 1955. 13″ plastic 'Roddy' walking doll with vinyl ponytail head, glassene eyes and lock-rooted hair. Taffeta and organdie dress trimmed with lace and ribbon, shoes and socks. Made by D G. Todd & Co Ltd.

JOCKEY. 1922. See **Lawton Doll Co.**

JOHN BULL. 1914. A rag doll made by Dean's Rag Book Co. Ltd.

JOHNNIE. 1957. Registered trademark for dolls, toy animals and golliwogs. See **Randall & Wood Ltd.**

JOHNSON, A. J. See **Johnson Bros.**

JOHNSON BROS. 1860—before 1923. Birmingham. Successor 1923-25+ Chad Valley Co. Ltd. Cloth doll manufacturers. Trade mark 'La Petite Caresse' no. 433,592 registered by Chad Valley Co. Ltd, 25th January 1923, for dolls. In 1924, Chad Valley Co. Ltd, together with A. J. Johnson obtained patent no. 235424, 27th August, for a doll's head made partially or wholly of textile, stiffened with shellac and provided with openings in which glass eyes are inserted. Patents no. 237520, December 29th and no. 255184 on 14th May, 1925 for additions concerning methods of fixing the eyes.

JOHNSON, John Henry. c1855. Glasgow, Scotland. Obtained British patents for moulding India Rubber and gutta-percha to make dolls and other items. Set up as solicitor and attorney in the English Courts; and by 1857 was associated with William Johnson, consulting engineer and patent agent, as W. & J.H. Johnson, patentees.

JOHNSON & JOHNSON (GREAT BRITAIN) LTD. Fairlie Road, Slough, Buckinghamshire. Doll and toy manufacturers. Registered trademark 'Roostie', no. 512564, 1st May 1930 for Dolls and Toys.

JOHNNY. 1922. 'Evripose' cherub doll manufactured by Dean's Rag Book Co. Ltd.

JOHNNY WALKER. Paper doll made in connection with Johnny Walker Whisky; on display at Worthing Museum & Art Gallery, Chapel Road, Worthing, Sussex.

JOINTS. The evolution of the child's play doll is contingent on development in choice of materials and sophistication of jointing. The two are of course closely allied. Wooden dolls, skilfully fashioned with ball joints giving full articulation, were made as artist's lay figures in Europe certainly as early as the 16th century; and beautiful play dolls of a

'Peter Waggie', a folk-singer's dancing doll, made of wood with movable joints; attached to a stick and with feet touching one end of a board.

similar type have survived from Roman times. The rudimentary skittle-shaped English wooden dolls of 17th-18th century had leather arms nailed on the shoulder and wooden legs with a simple knee joint and at the hips a mortise and tenon joint. A further refinement sometimes found in these dolls is a turning head, severed from the body at the neck and fixed to a wire operated through the body.

When poured wax dolls became popular and composition heads were made in a mould, the heads and limbs were attached to the body through sew-holes or eyelets. They were assembled by hand with fabric-stuffed bodies. It was only with the industrialisation of the toy trade in the second half of the 19th century that more sophisticated body shapes, functional limbs and realistic features were invented and improved upon. Many patents referred to elastic string-jointing of parts. In modern times the introduction of synthetic materials and mass produced plastics revolutionised techniques of doll-making. Some of the very popular action dolls, such as Action Man, imitate the early pattern of ball-jointing.

JOINTS OF DOLLS. BRITISH PATENTS

1858 A. Benda. Elastic cord stringing.
1860 A. F. Haas, for knee joints enabling doll to assume sitting position.
1867 J. S. Clavell, for jointed doll with stringing and swivel neck.
1890 J. P. Bayly, Attaching limbs of dolls and animals etc.
1892 A. Kestner. Hooks for attaching head and limbs.
1901 H. Eckert. Ball and socket joints for dolls.

'Mr Jolliboy', a similar dancing doll advertised by Gamage's, 1910.

1902 H. Eckert. Ball and socket joints for dolls.

1907 G. Scherf. A knee joint made of wood paper, fabric etc.

1908 G. Scherf. A knee joint for leather and rag dolls.

1921 A. Bucherer. A frame for jointed dolls is provided with ball and socket joints.

1921 G. L. Nunn. Spring hinges at knee joint for walking doll.

1923 E. Pollard & Co. Ltd. A joint for rotating, connecting 2 members of a doll.

1924 A. Huck. Improvement of ball joints.

1927 Gems & French Bust Co. Ltd. Bayonet-joint devices.

1946 B. V. Bergstrom. Doll joint with intermediate member.

JOLLYBOY, Mr. c1919. Dancing doll manufactured by A. G. Owen.

JOLLY JACK. Sailor doll from Excella range. See **Rees, Leon.**

JOLLY & SON. 1831-1895. See **Lowther Arcade.**

JOLLY TODDLERS. Set of toddler dolls which first appeared in 1933. See **Wellings, Norah.**

JONES, Edward Hazell. 38 Warwick Road, Snaresbrook, Essex. Sale Organiser. Registered trademarks 'Goo-goo', no. 399,357 and 'Giggly', no. 399,358 for dolls and toys, 9th January 1920.

JONES, F. C. Chelsea, London. Obtained patent no. 432371, 15th February, 1934 for 'hollow rubber dolls. . . .'

JONES, Henry. 1852-55. At 23, Mitchell Street, St. Luke's London, EC. Wholesale wood doll and general toy manufacturer and warehouseman.

JONES, Richard William. 1851. Three Colt Lane, Bethnal Green, London. Made wooden dolls.

JONES, Robert. 1835-48. Made wooden dolls. Listed in two London Directories of the period as living at 21 and 23 Great Mitchell Street, St. Lukes, London EC., the latter address being the same as that of Henry Jones.

JONES, S. & CO. 1881. London. Made dolls.

JONES, William Henry. 1888-1954. 1910 at 3, Paper Street, London EC. Then 48, Red Cross Street, London EC. From August 1915 at 11 Charterhouse Buildings, London EC. 1928 at Great Arthur Street, London. Agent for German doll manufacturers. In September 1914, after the outbreak of war, he started to make soft toys and dolls, employing 6 girls. The following year he

'Bunnymum', made by W.H. Jones, 1927.

moved to Charterhouse Buildings and employed 46 girls. In March 1915 lines included various rag dolls, teddy bears and soft animal toys. In 1917: Baby doll with china head, 6d dressed dolls and rag dolls. Registered trademark 'Flopsie', no. 400,076 on 27th January, 1920, for dolls, toy animals, puppets and similar articles. In 1925 advertised strange round 'rabbit' doll called 'The Dinky Toy', which had a round body covered in fur fabric or plush material with rabbit ears and doll's face.

JOSEPH'S. c1850. Leadenhall Street, London EC. Porcelain-headed dolls were assembled at this address, prior to being hawked in London streets.

JOSYLIN. c1918. See **Daisy Dolls.**

JOYCE. c1918. See **Daisy Dolls.**

JOYCE. 1927. Velveteen and stockinette doll, dressed in velveteen. Kapok stuffed and hand-painted face. Made by S. & L. Manufacturing Co.

JOYDALE. 1948. Sleeping eye doll, 12/- plus tax, manufactured by Kensett Brothers.

JOY DAY. Registered trademark for dolls. See manufacturer, **Farnell, J.K. & Co. Ltd.**

JOY DAY SPECIALS. c1936. Doll Series manufactured by J. K. Farnell & Co. Ltd.

JOY DAY WOOLLIES. 1936. Dolls described as dressed in woolly suits, which correspond in every detail to the woolly suits then being sold for children. Manufactured by J. K. Farnell.

JOYSIE. 1918. Soft stuffed stockinette doll manufactured by Fretwell Manufacturing Co.

JULIE. 1955. 14" vinyl 'Roddy' doll with sleeping eyes and eyelashes, lock rooted hair, taffeta and organdie dress and shoes and socks. Made by D. G. Todd & Co. Ltd.

JULIE. Introduced 1975. 14" Matchbox doll with all-vinyl body, sleeping eyes and rooted blonde curly hair. Made in E. Germany for Lesney Products & Co Ltd.

JULIE & JON, THE DUTCH BOY AND GIRL. Introduced 1966. Make it yourself doll kit, containing wool and printed felt etc. Made by Trevor Toys Ltd. Retail price 10s 11d.

JULLIEN, H. J. & SON LTD. c1918. Doll and toy manufacturer, including: Esquimeaux dolls, dolls with celluloid faces, soft toys and wooden toys.

JUMPING JACK. 1916. Special doll portraying Miss Gertrude Miller, the well-known musical comedy star, as a pierrette with long flowing hair, in the revue 'Bric-a-Brac', c1916. Manufactured by Speights Ltd.

JUNE BABIES. See **Daisy Dolls.**

JUNGLE TOYS. c1915-1918+. At 82 Richmond Road, London, SW5. Director: Miss E. M. Daniels. Soft toys and rattles. Later made only jungle animal soft toys.

KAFFIR-KIDDY. 1916. See **Kingram Toys.**

KAMPAKAON. 1865. See **Longbottom, John.**

KALUTO. Registered trademark for dolls. See **Turner, Ernest.**

KAMLISH, J. & Co. c1916. At 68 Nelson Street, Commercial Road, London E. Doll manufacturers. In 1916 making Eskimo dolls, china dolls, caricatures and teddy bears.

K-AN-ESS. 1921. See **Kelty, E. & Sons.**

KAPOK. Stuffing used for soft toys and dolls etc.

KATIE KOPYCAT. 1971. 18" Palitoy doll which draws and writes and copies whatever is written. Complete with magic desk, pad and pen.

KAYE TOY & FANCY GOODS CO. c1916. 397, Lockner Road, Kingsland Road, London NE. Doll and toy wholesaler. In 1916 selling dressed and undressed dolls with

Jumping Jack, a doll made by Speight's Ltd. Based on a character played by Gertie Miller in 'Bric-a-brac', 1916.

The actress Gertie Miller.

celluloid and china faces, 4s to 12s 6d a dozen.

KEANE, Doris. See **Art Dolls.**

KEATS & CO. Wedgwood Toy Factory, Market Place, Burslem, Staffordshire. A cabinet-making firm which began making dolls in c1916. These had china heads treated with a special preparation which gave a 'velvety finish' like that of a wax doll. The dolls were produced in a variety of styles and sizes, prices from 5s 6d per dozen to 12s. Also made dolls' cots and beds, with bedding, in stained and polished wood, and white enamel finish.

KEEN & CO. c1912-18. At Milton Street, London EC. Doll manufacturing company started by Julius Kohnstam. Made 'Vera' jointed composition doll, also supplied parts separately. The doll's head was not originally made in England. After the outbreak of war Kohnstam was forced to cease trading and the business was taken over by the Lord Roberts Memorial Workshop. c1933 Kohnstam resumed business, trading under the name of 'Dollies Ltd.' and using a secret composition material. A German workforce was brought over to England to instruct.

In 1935 Dollies Ltd. amalgamated with Dean's Rag Book Co. Ltd. to form Dean's Dollies Ltd.

KEILLER, WM. & CO. c1918. At 11 Chichester Street, Belfast. Printed fabric for British manufactured rag dolls.

KELTY, E. & SONS. 1921. At 42 Stanley Street, Southport, Lancashire. Advertised dressed and undressed dolls and K-AN-ESS series of daintily dressed dolls with unbreakable bodies, fully jointed, and sleeping eyes.

KELVEDON VILLAGE INDUSTRY. c1918 Made dolls: Indian dolls, fairy dolls, character dolls and tumbling dolls.

KENSETT BROS. c1948. At 103 North Road, Brighton, Sussex (Head Office). Retailers of dolls, toys and games. Firm originally established 1881. In 1948 retailing 'Joydale' sleeping eye doll.

KENT TOY WORKS. c1920. Eridge Road, Tunbridge Wells, Kent. Made rocking horses, wooden spades etc. and 'Cannon' all-British Dolls. Except for wigs, dolls entirely made in the firm's factory.

KEWPIE. Trademark no. 355,194 registered for dolls on 3rd October 1913 by Geo. Borgfeldt & Co., Vienna, Austria. Doll originally designed by Rose O'Neill, an American. English versions of Kewpie dolls were manufactured by various companies, including Lord Roberts Memorial Workshops c1917 and Cascelloid Ltd.

KEY PRODUCTS. Trademark for dolls, no. 800,197 registered by Benjamin Frankel, manufacturer of 6 Cobb Street London E.1. on 9th January 1950.

KHAKI BOY. c1915. First World War boy doll, dressed in khaki uniform. 33″ high. Manufactured by Anglo-American Novelty Co.

KID. Bodies of dolls in Victorian times were often sewn from strong calico, especially for wax-headed or wax-over composition dolls. The arms on the other hand were often made from soft kid leather remnants from glove factories etc. From "Wonderland of Work" by C. L. Mateaux 1884 comes a first-hand witness: "The arms supply work for yet another distinct set of workers young and old, who have to provide themselves with all sorts of bits of coloured kid, pink and lilac and dove colour, and turn them into podgy,

A doll made entirely of kid, 1828. A label attached to it states; 'Made by the Ladies of Ashburnham for Louisa Powell' (Victoria and Albert Museum).

tight-looking arms, sewn on to calico tops. Awkward, troublesome work it must be to shape those few fingers, at any rate; and one that in England, where they are mostly made, is very badly paid, from three halfpence to sixpence halfpenny being given for a dozen pairs complete. A great many of these scraps of blue and red kid are also used in the manufacture of dolls' shoes and boots, of which one London firm, possessing a sewing machine for the purpose, turns out about a thousand pairs each week. They are made from odd pieces left by ladies' shoemakers. It takes three or five properly stamped out bits to shape one pair of wee boots. These, given out in grosses, are taken home by women and girls, who stitch the little soles to the uppers; binding them around neatly, fixing on absurdly high heels and embroidering the fronts, till they would do for a fairy Cinderella to dance at King Oberon's ball."

KID CORTEZ. 1976. Cowboy doll from the Matchbox Fighting Furies range. Manufactured in Hong Kong for Lesney Products and Co. Ltd.

KIDDICRAFT COMPANY. Purley, Surrey. Manufacturers of dolls and toys for babies and young children. In 1936 advertised an American 'Drinking Baby Doll, practically unbreakable, with patent socket for neck. Perfect face and features, and an unbreakable patent drinking bottle. The clothes are made in England: "nappy", bootees and vest, a long clothes frock, petticoat and bonnet in white organdie, trimmed with white lace and pale blue ribbons and with press fasteners.' Kiddicraft had the sole British rights of the doll until 1937. Range in 1936 also included rubber dolls, 'lifelike in appearance', and piccaninnies.

KIDDIELAND. Registered trademark for toys and dolls. See manufacturers **Eisenmann & Co.**

KIDDLUMS. 1917. Boy and girl dolls registered design no. 661017, made by Tah Toys Ltd. Registered trademark no. 378870.

KIDDYKIN. c1916. Brand name of baby doll. See **Perls, Charles, Manufacturing Co.**

KIDETTE. Trademark for dolls and toys no. 378,866 registered by Speights Ltd, 9th July 1917. The dolls had fully-jointed washable kidette bodies, hair-stuffed; English china heads; fixed or sleeping veined-glass eyes; composition forearms and lower limbs, and mohair wigs in various styles.

KIKI. Introduced 1975. 18″ fully-jointed Matchbox doll with long blonde hair, sleeping eyes, and jointed body. Made in Italy for Lesney Products & Co. Ltd.

KINGBABY. 1936. New Born Baby Doll with composition head and sleeping eyes. Non-inflammable by Dean's Dollies Ltd.

KING BROS. 1918-21. London. Made dolls.

KING GEORGE VI. Portrait model dolls dressed as Grenadier Guard at 15/-, Air Force Officer at 15/-, in Highland uniform at 15/- and in Coronation Robes at about £3. The dolls were exhibited at the British Industries Fair of 1937 (Coronation year) as a centrepiece, and received 'very flattering notices in the general Press.' See **Farnell, J.K. & Co. Ltd.**

KING, G. W. Obtained patent no. 323669 on 5th February 1929 for the design of a mechanical doll.

KINGRAM TOYS. c1915+. 21 Fitzwilliam Square, Dublin, Ireland. Manufacturers of soft toys and dolls and novelties. Registered trademark 'Kurly-Koon' no. 651188 for 'Coon dolls in 2 sizes, 18″ and 20″, at 72/- and 78/- per dozen'. Also 'Kaffir-Kiddy' a black baby doll in gala costume of coloured beads, silk frill and headdress and ornaments to match. Lady Louise Scudder Ryall King and Ethel Margaret Graham registered trademark Kingram Toys 21st January 1915, 365,517. Also mechanical toy, patent no 23,793 January 1915.

'Kiddykin', unbreakable composition head made by Charles Perls Manufacturing Co., 1918.

KIRBY, G. L. c1917. At 1-3 Golden Lane, London. An Australian who set up a toy and doll manufacturing company in England. Lines included Snow Baby, a goo-goo eyed doll in various colours of plush, and Sun Tan doll in Hawaiian costume. Also Clown doll and Jester doll.

KISMI. 1905. Registered trademark for toy dolls. See manufacturers **Stallard & Co.**

'Kurly-Koon' and 'Kaffir-Kiddy', made by Kingram Toys, 1916.

KITSON, Arthur. c1919. Leamington Spa, Warwickshire. Retailer and/or manufacturer. In the early part of 1919 he put on an exhibition of dressed and undressed dolls, kid-finished, with china heads and limbs and glass eyes, in 7 sizes from 15"-22". A special feature was the quality of the wigs and the charming modelling of the faces. A selection of fabric dolls was also shown; these were well stuffed and fitted with separate arms and legs, and cost 1s—1s 3d each. See **Speciality Toy Co.**

KITTIE. 1915. See **Harwin & Co. Ltd.**

KITTIES. c1900. Name given to dolls dressed in sailcloth made by ships' carpenters in Cumberland and in Yorkshire. In Yorkshire bread dolls baked light-brown and dressed in infants' robes. Also for Gingerbread dolls.

KLEENAGANE SERIES. 1925. Rag dolls with specially processed mask faces which could be wiped with moist soapy sponge or flannel, when dirty. Manufactured by Dean's Rag Book Co. Ltd.

KLEIN, P. See **Playlastic Toy Co. Ltd.**

KLEINER, J. & SONS LTD. c1900-1946+. 112-114 Houndsditch, London EC. & 1-7 Cutler Street, London EC3. Doll and toy wholesalers and exporters. 1946 range include Rag dolls from 18/- per dozen.

KLETZIN LTD. c1925. 9 & 10 Australia Avenue, London WC1. Made dolls.

KNEE BEND DOLLS. 1955. doll range with vinyl hands and lock-rooted hair. Dolls can kneel, sit and walk. Manufactured by D. G. Todd and Co. Ltd.

KNIGHT, A. B. 63 St. Charles Square, Notting Hill, London. Patent 19692, 19 October 1893 for a celluloid ball with two halves hinged, which open to reveal a doll.

KNIGHT BROS. & COOPER LTD. c1916-18+. Reliance Works, 152 Burton Road Derby. Doll manufacturers. 1916 range included: Bisque doll, "Reliance" doll series, character dolls—Welsh, Scottish, Irish, Dutch, Quaker Girl, Red Riding Hood, Shepherdess, Fairy, Pierrot and Peirrette, Soldier and Sailor. 1917: jointed doll in 2 sizes, with glass eyes, pretty wig and beautifully dressed. "Flapper Girls"—modern dolls, some dressed in smart sports coats in various colours. 1918: Stuffed, jointed, dressed and undressed composition and china dolls.

Knitted and crocheted dolls' clothes (Pollock's Toy Museum).

KNIGHT, E. G. & CO. 1894-95. At 45, Scrutton Street, London, E. Made dolls.

KNITTED AND CROCHETED DOLLS' CLOTHING AND KNITTED DOLLS. Towards the end of the 19th century it became more and more usual to dress children in hand-knitted or crocheted clothes. The mechanical production of knitting wool in balls and skeins added to the popularity of the knitting craze. It was still not considered healthy to wear wool next to the skin. but from 1890 onwards Weldon's Practical Needlework Books, and ladies' journals, published knitting patterns for vests, bootees, frocks, tam o'shanters, berets mittens and leggings. It was to be expected that dolls would follow suit, and they were soon equipped with smaller knitted versions of their owners' outfits. During the First and Second World Wars the general shortage of toys and materials led to the publication of numerous hints and instructions for making knitted dolls and toys from odds and ends of unravelled wool.

KNOCKABOUT TOYS. Series of rag dolls and toys made by Dean's Rag Book Co. Ltd.

KOHNSTAM, J. LTD. See **Kohnstam, M. & Co.**

KOHNSTAM, M. & CO. 1867-1914. Fuerth, Bavaria & 24 Milton Street, London, EC. Doll and toy manufacturers, originally established in 1867 by Moses Kohnstam, a German toy manufacturer. Registered trademark 'Cupid', no. 312,593, 28th April 1909 for dolls, and also registered trademark no. 322,248 (a picture of a baby's bottle with the words: 'Mother's Darling, quiet and good, requires no nursing, attention or food') on 2nd April 1910 for dolls and toys. Lines in 1909 included 'Cupid' dolls—in latest fashions for babies and children, designed by fashion publisher Weldon's Ltd.

Moses Kohnstam died in 1912 and was succeeded by Julius Kohnstam, a naturalized British subject. He set up a doll factory using the tradename Keen & Co. probably to conceal his German ancestry, but soon after the outbreak of World War I the company was forced to cease trading and its assets were taken over by Lord Robert's Memorial Workshops.

In 1920 Kohnstam established the doll and toy manufacturing company James Garfield and Co. which ran for 7 years. At the end of 1922 J. Kohnstam Ltd. was re-established, and in 1933 a doll manufacturing company, 'Dollies Ltd.', was established and Kohnstam brought a German work force to England to teach the art of composition doll making to the English workers. In 1936 the firm registered the trademark 'Mackenry' for dolls and toys and 'Moko'.

In 1981 a nephew of Julius, Richard Kohnstam, is managing director of R. Kohnstam Ltd., a toy importing firm.

KOVE, Nicholas. 1955. At 252 Finchley Road, London NW3. Toy and doll manufacturer. In 1939 Kove formed the company Airfix Products Ltd. for the manufacture of rubber toys filled with air. In 1948 the firm was producing plastic dolls with movable arms and legs. On 7th July, 1955 Kove registered the trademark 'Amandadoll' no. 744,165 for dolls. By 1957 the Kove family had no longer any connection with Airfix Productions Ltd.

KRAMER, Vera. See **Dolls in Wonderland.**

KUDDLEMEE DOLLS. c1923. Range of 'A1' dolls and toys manufactured by Dean's Rag Book Co. Ltd. 3 dolls in series, with 'Tru-to-Life' faces, down-stuffed bodies and dainty print shoes. 10½", 13" & 15".

KUM-ALONG KATIES. Introduced 1968. 15" Bluebell range walking doll with durable metal and plastic trainer. Manufactured by D.G. Todd & Co. Ltd.

KURLY-KOON. Registered trademark for black dolls. See manufacturer **Kingram Toys.**

KUTOY, MESSRS. c1936-May 1939. 54a High Street, South Norwood, London SE25. Soft toy manufacturers. 1936 range includes dolls, teddy bears, dogs; also novelty lines Peter Polony, Mother Goose and Humpty Dumpty.

KWACKY-WACK. Registered trademark for toys and dolls no. 348,262. See manufacturers, **Eisenmann & Co.**

KYDYTE. See **Dolls' Accessory Co.**

Wax doll dressed in long knitted jumper, 1880 (Victoria and Albert Museum).

L.S.D. DOLLS. 1960. See **Farnell, J.K. & Co. Ltd.**

LAAR, P. H. VAN. Obtained patent no. 236862, 25th March, 1925 for a stuffed doll which is converted to a pillow by folding the head on to the trunk, where it is retained by the legs being passed through loops formed by the arms.

LADY DI. c1921. Registered trademark for plush stuffed doll. Wears dress and hat with pom-pom in red and cream plushette. Artistic character doll. See manufacturers, **Wonderland Toymaking Co.**

LADY DOLL. To celebrate May Day on the 1st of the month, country people in England often made a flowery garland with a prettily dressed doll in the centre which would be carried in procession. The doll representing the "the Lady" probably had an early pagan significance as Mother Earth the Spirit of Spring.

LADY SNEERWELL. 18th century. See **School for Scandal Dolls.**

LADY TEAZLE. 18th century. See **School for Scandal Dolls.**

LAKE, W. R. Patent 2859. 16th September 1868 for dolls' heads made with buckram or fabric stiffened with starch. Patent 16354 April 1882 for singing doll (Webber doll with perforated sheet music invented in the U.S.A.) and Patent 11845 for an educational doll 1st September 1884 (patent of Cooper and Sibley U.S.A.). Lake was probably a patents agent, like A.V. Newton.

LAMBERT, CLARKE & CO. LTD. c1918. 115 & 117, Munster Road, , London, SW6. Showrooms: 12 Rose Street, Newgate Street, London EC4. Manufacturers of doll wigs.

LAMBETH WALKERS, The. 1938. Male and female character dolls associated with famous English song and dance 'The Lambeth Walk'. Made by Dean's Rag Book Co. Ltd.

LAMPLOUGH, Henry. 1916-25+. 44 Eleanor Road, Hackney, London E8. Obtained patent no. 108011, 17th July 1916 for dolls made of cardboard or similar material with a surface of cotton fabric coated with a celluloid varnish. Colour was applied to the dolls with a rubber stamp. In 1924 he advertised unbreakable dolls and dolls' heads.

LANDER, Hilda Gertrude. **See Cowham, Hilda.**

LANG & CO. c1860-69. At 26 Skinner Street, London, EC. 1868: 27 Houndsditch, London, NE. and Paris, France. 1869: 32 & 33 Cowcross Street, London EC. Made dolls and toys of India rubber and gutta-percha.

May Day 'Lady' doll.

LA PETITE CARESSE. Trademark no. 433,592 registered by The Chad Valley Co. Ltd. on 25th January 1923 for stuffed fabric dolls.

LATEST ATROCITY, The. 1916. See **Huvan Manufacturing Co.**

LATEX. Rubber. Became popular as dollmaking material in the 1950's.

LAWLEY & PAGE LTD. 1950. At 10 Newman Street, Oxford St, London W.1. January 1950 advertised the Singing and Speaking Doll. Says "Mummy, pick me up" and "I want my Mummy", sings a song, cries, laughs and gurgles. 26″ high. Open mouth, sleeping eyes. World patent pending.

LAWLEY SINGING DOLL. See **Lawley & Page Ltd.**

LAWRENCE, J. W. c1908-1915+. At 112 Houndsditch, London, EC. Manufacturer of dolls and dolls' parts, including squeakers, eyes etc. In 1908: Japanese type dolls, with squeakers, in cotton dresses. Different sizes. 1909: 'Boy Scout'. 1915: dolls with 'well modelled' wax and china faces, dressed and undressed.

LAWTON DOLL CO. Before 1922. At 38 & 40 Station Road, Blackpool, Lancashire. 63 Ardwick Green North, Manchester. c1922 57-59 Neal Street, Long Acre, London, WC2. 85-87 Graham Street, Long Acre, London, WC2. Doll manufacturers. 1921 lines include: 'Cupie' dolls—chemically hardened, unbreakable plaster dolls, hand-painted expressions, assorted colours, 'Cutie', 'Baby Vamp', 'Blackpool Belle' &

'Beauty' doll. In 1922: 'Miss Beauty Cupid', other love mascots or cupid dolls, 'The Flapper', 'Love Me', 'Belle', 'Jockey' and 'Princess'. In October 1922 the firm announced that its title would be changed to The Lawton Manufacturing Co. Ltd.

LAWTON MANUFACTURING CO. LTD. See **Lawton Doll Co.**

LAYFIELD, Joseph. 1917-1920+. 125a Hart Street, Southport, Lancashire. 22 Chapel Street, London, EC. 23 Paper Street, London EC. Doll manufacturer and wholesaler. In 1917 advertised semi-dressed doll with china head and limbs and with wig (3 different sizes) and Dutch costume dolls. In 1920: dolls dressed in proper Eskimo costume (five sizes). These were probably made by the South Wales Toy Manufacturing Co. for whom they acted as London Sales Agents.

LEADBEATER, Edwin. 1921. Commerce St. Longton, Staffs: Art China manufacturer, formerly associated with Hewitt & Leadbeater.

Two Cupie dolls made by the Lawton Doll Co., 1921.

Two dolls with china heads and rag bodies, sold by J.W. Lawrence, 1915.

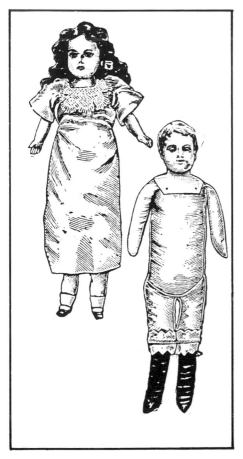

LEATHER. Arms of leather were used especially on dolls with cloth and/or leather bodies. In the 1870's hands were also made of china, and later of composition. By the start of World War I, leather hands were seldom used. Leather is an animal skin and so is pliable, and "breathes". It is therefore well suited for covering dolls' bodies. Kid in particular has been used for this purpose for many years. There are examples of all-leather dolls to be seen in Worthing Museum, Sussex and the Victoria & Albert Museum, London.

LEDA. 1917. Registered trademark for unbreakable, jointed, composition dolls with glass eyes. See **Salisbury, Thomas Charles; Spencer & Co.**

LEDA DOLLS LTD. 1919. At 109 Queen Street, Cardiff. 1920. at 20 City Road, Cardiff. Company registered 27th June 1919. See **Spencer & Co.**

LEE, ARTHUR H. & SONS LTD. c1915-18. At Stanley Road, Birkenhead. Manufacturer of celluloid dolls' faces.

LEE, David Thorpe. 1866. Birmingham. Obtained patent for a ball-jointed doll strung with either metal or rubber.

LEE, Thomas. 1857. London. Made dolls.

LEEDS CITY MUSEUM. Abbey House, Kirkstall, Yorkshire. Collection of dolls includes a wooden doll of the Stuart period, nearly two feet tall, with an elaborate stumpwork contemporary costume; and a Victorian doll with a 'wardrobe' of no less than eight dresses.

LEEWAY SCHOOL. Manor Works, Cray Avenue, St. Mary Cray, Kent. Toy and doll manufacturers. 1973 range included a long-haired doll in a two-coloured collapsible plastic cradle.

LEILA. 1960. Fully-jointed vinyl doll from De Luxe range by Pedigree. See **De Luxe Dolls.**

LEMON, D. M. & PAGE, S. V. French patent 417335 perfecting British patent 14922 (1910) for a doll crying real tears with a changing expression.

LESLEY. 1955. 11″ rubber doll made by Young & Fogg Rubber Co. Ltd.

Leather doll, shaped on a bottle (Worthing Museum).

'Clare' and 'Lisa', Lesney 'Matchbox' dolls, 1975.

LESNEY PRODUCTS & CO. LTD. Lee Conservancy Road, Hackney Wick, London E9. Toy manufacturers. Registered trademark 'Matchbox'. In 1972 they introduced dolls to their range with Miss Matchbox Disco Girls, 4 teenage dolls, Dee, Britt, Tia and Domino, a negro doll. These dolls are fully jointed with deep-rooted hair and real eyelashes, There are 24 different dress styles which are regularly updated. In 1975 Suky dolls were introduced; also the Fighting Furies series of male action dolls, 9½" high, with fully-jointed bodies and push-button action arms. All these dolls are made in Hong Kong. Numerous other dolls have subsequently been added to the firm's range.

LEWIS & OWEN. c1917. At 22 Colberg Place, Stamford Hill, London N. Manufacturers of composition and rag dolls, jointed and otherwise.

LIBERTY. Registered trademark. See **Liberty & Co. Ltd.**

'Disco Dolls', Lesney 'Matchbox' dolls, 1972.

LIBERTY & CO. LTD. 1906-80+. Regent Street, London W1. Makers of artistic fabrics and wares. Registered trademark 'Liberty' no. B 407,731 on 9th September, 1920 for dolls, toys, balls for games, puzzles, toy furniture, table games, bridge markers and Japanese paper lanterns.

LIDDLE MIDDLE MUFFET. 1968. See **World of Kiddles,** and **Rosebud Mattel.**

LIDO LADY. 1931. 21″ doll dressed in beach pyjamas, made by Dean's Rag Book Co. Ltd.

LIEBER BROS. c1949. Newark Street, Nottingham. Doll manufacturers. In April 1949 advertised baby boy dolls and sleeping dolls. Dolls are supplied 'in a box which forms a cot with colourful nursery characters.

LILAC. c1925. See **Posy Buds.**

Doll with magic hands, and lips which moved when it talked. Made by The Little People Toy Co., Whitechurch Lane, London, 1950.

LILLIPUT DOLL MUSEUM. High Street, Brading, Isle of Wight. A comprehensive collection of period dolls, including one, c1790, dressed in a remnant of Queen Caroline's wedding gown, an unusual bisque doll presented by Queen Victoria to an estate employee's daughter at Christmas 1885, and a wax portrait doll of Lily Langtry; also felt and fabric dolls by Lenci and Dean's Rag Book Co. Ltd. The collection includes a number of English-made dolls.

LILY LANGTRY. See **Lilliput Doll Museum.**

LINA WORKS. c1920. 407 West Green Road, Tottenham, London N. & 593 Green Lanes, Harringay, London N. Manufacturers of dolls' wigs and accessories. The wigs can be brushed and combed and are made of real hair and mohair. See **Roh.**

LINDA. 1976. Brand name of dolls and toys manufactured by Ceçil Coleman Ltd.

LINES BROTHERS LTD. See **Pedigree Soft Toys Ltd.**

LINDOP, W. c1916-c1919. At 38, Shudehill, Manchester. Doll and toy manufacturer. Made 'Alert' composition-headed doll with stuffed body.

LINDY. 1956. See **Petalskin Dolls** and **Pedigree.**

LION'S CLAW. 1914. Registered trademark for dolls, toys and games. See **McCubbin, Ethel Elizabeth Mary.**

LISA. 1975. 16″ Matchbox doll with sleeping eyes and rooted hair, dressed in red slacks and white striped top. Made in Italy for Lesney Products Co. Ltd.

LISA Rag Dolls. 1975. See **Dean, Mary.**

LITTLE BABY BURPS. 1978. Matchbox novelty baby doll. Drinks/wets and burps when patted on back. Doll is all-vinyl with rooted hair and is 39cms high. Made in Hong Kong for Lesney Products & Co. Ltd and assembled in U.K.

LITTLE BABY TEARS. Palitoy brand name of dolls and layette.

The 'Alert' doll, made by W. Lindop, 1916.

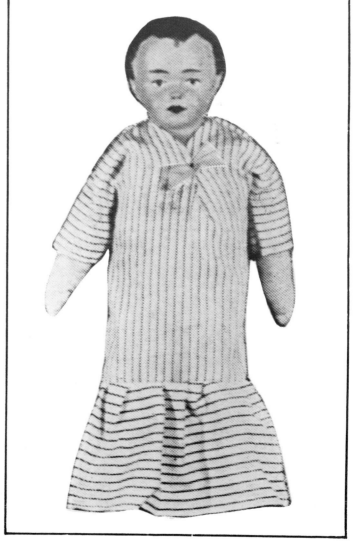

LITTLE BIG MAN. 1972. 6½" Palitoy adventure doll for boys.

LITTLE BLACK SAMBO. 1920. Doll made by The East London (Federation Toy) Factory.

LITTLE BO PEEP. c1935. See **Nursery Rhyme Character Dolls.**

LITTLE BO-PEEP c1948. Doll wearing bonnet and dress with chubby face, open mouth and short hair. Manufactured by Pedigree Soft Toys Ltd.

LITTLE BOY BLUE. c1935. See **Nursery Rhyme Character Dolls.**

LITTLE GRETEL. 1958. 11" doll supplied in a pack with enough wool for a playsuit, a simple pattern and needles to knit it with. Retail price 9s 11d. Manufactured by Lines Bros Ltd. Wool supplied by Copley Knitting Wools.

LITTLE HAPPY. c1939. Celluloid 1/- line doll. See manufacturers **Cascelloid.**

LITTLE JACK HORNER. c1935. See **Nursery Rhyme Character Dolls.**

LITTLE LADY ANNE. 1923. See **Bland-Hawkes, Mabel.**

LITTLE LIZZIE. 1963. Victorian style rag doll designed by Maria Wood for Pollock's Toy Museum.

LITTLE MISS FUSSY. 1968. Battery-operated baby doll which feeds, wets, kicks and cries. Retail price £7 4s 6d, manufactured by Palitoy.

LITTLE MISS MISCHIEF. c1932. Cuddly doll in plush, with fur-trimmed hat. 3 sizes and 4 pastel shades. See manufacturer, **Bland-Hawkes, Mabel.**

LITTLE MISS MUFFET. c1935. See **Nursery Rhyme Character Dolls.**

LITTLE MISS VOGUE. 1959. 10½" vinyl plastic Pedigree doll with Saran rooted hair. Comes in bra and panty girdle with nylon stockings, high heeled shoes and pearl earrings. Retail price 17s 6d. Outfits range from day dresses to evening wear including ballet dress and bridal dresses from 5s to 18s 6d.

LITTLE PEOPLE. c1939. Humorous soft doll series, designed by G. E. Studdy, artist, and creator of dog 'Bonzo'. See manufacturers: **Merrythought Ltd.**

LITTLE PET. 1908. Registered trademark for dolls. See manufacturers: **Eisenmann & Co.**

LITTLE SAMBO. c1913. Printed rag doll black with googly eyes, made by Dean's Rag Book Co. Ltd. "The Story of Little Black Sambo" published by Helen Bannermann 1899 established the book as a children's classic up to the present day

LITTLE TICH. 1903. Policeman doll 11½" high, based on well-known English Music Hall Character.

LITTMAN, L.J. c1916. 43 Dalston Lane, London, N. Manufacturer of rag dolls, dressed and undressed, 6d to 1/-

Portrait doll in wax of Lord Roberts, c. 1900. 18 inches high, with inserted hair, blue glass eyes, hair-filled body.

LIZA JANE. 1976. Brand name of dolls and toys. See manufacturer **Cornelius, W. H. Ltd.**

LLANDUDNO DOLL MUSEUM AND MODEL RAILWAY EXHIBITION. Llandudno. Wales. The collection consists of over 1000 dolls including a rare 'blue scarf' doll (with moulded headdress).

LLOYD, F. G. Patent 24378, 14th December 1894, walking doll worked by string, wire or elastic.

LLOYD GEORGE. 1915. Quaint toy or model showing Lloyd George, the Welsh politician, leaping over Government red tape to secure European liberty. It was purchased by Lloyd George at the 1915 Eisteddfod, and he assured the stallholder that it would be placed in his office, at the Ministry of Munitions. The model was made in the Vale of Clwyd.

LLOYD GEORGE. 1928. See **Sant, J. S. Ltd.**

LLOYD, MAYER & CO. c1919-c1925. At 2 & 3 Lillypot Lane, Noble Street, London EC2. & 34, Noble Street, London, EC2. Manufacturers of jointed composition dolls and toys. In 1920 advertised "Poppy" doll— jointed composition, with long wavy hair and lace-trimmed frock.

LOGAN, H. T. 25th February, 1913. A skating doll on castors.

LOLA BABIES. Baby dolls. See manufacturer **Kohnstam, J. Ltd.**

LO-LA DOLLS. c1940. A series of dressed or undressed dolls. See manufacturers, **Bailey Potteries Ltd.**

LONDON DOLL MARKET. German agents prior to World War I made this the largest doll market in the world. After the war the supremacy seems to have passed to New York City. Jumeau and other French firms also had agents in London.

LONDON RAG DOLLS. Especially popular in 1870s and 1880s. Clara L. Mateaux in 'The Wonderland of Work' (1884) describes them thus: 'Then comes that thoroughly English invention, the rag doll, with its soft, pinky-white face and wondering blue eyes. She comes to perfection from the London Maker's establishment.'

LONELY LISA. Introduced 1974. Pedigree rag doll with bendy joints.

LONGBOTTOM, John. Patent No. 1775 in 1865 for a composition for doll-making called Kampakeon.

LONG EXPOSURE. 1919. Brand name of china doll. See **Dolls' Accessory Co. Ltd.**

LORD KITCHENER. Before 1917: portrait doll in composition, with moulded moustache, dressed in British army uniform.

LORD ROBERTS. Wax portrait doll representing the British Commander-in-Chief during the Boer War. Made by the Pierotti family. Doll wears full uniform of Field Marshal with red felt jacket and white kid trousers.

LORD ROBERTS MEMORIAL WORKSHOPS. Headquarters at Fulham, London, S.W. c1915-1978+. A doll and toy manufacturing organisation set up after the outbreak of war to provide work for disabled soldiers and sailors. Various existing factories were taken over for this purpose, including the Novelty Construction Co. Ltd., Fulham, London. During the following years workshop branches were opened up all over the British Isles: Brighton, Birmingham, Colchester, Belfast, Bradford, Liverpool, Edinburgh, Leeds, Southampton, Plymouth and Cardiff. c1917 doll lines included the 'Vera' dolls. These were originally manufactured by Keen & Co. (see **Kohnstam M. & Co.**) but production was taken over by the workshops after the outbreak of war. Another popular line was the 'Kewpie' mascot doll, made with jointed arms, in composition. By the middle of 1916 other industries had been added to the toymaking: wooden household articles, cabinet making and leather work. The trademark for the Workshops was a picture of a soldier on horseback in sunlight, with the letter R (for Robert) in the top left hand corner. c1921 Head Office, at 122 Brompton Road, London, S.W.3. where it still exists, while a cabinet joinery manufacturing workshop is currently operating in Waterford Road, London, S.W.6.

'Vera' jointed composition dolls, with or without sleeping eyes. Made in the Lord Roberts Memorial Workshops, 1916.

LOUISE, Princess. c1853. Doll with wax head, bust and limbs and cloth body, representing one of Queen Victoria's daughters, and believed to have been made by Madame Montanari.

LOURETTA. 1960. See **Debutante Dolls.**

LOVE ME. 1922. See **Lawton Doll Co.**

LOVETT, Edward. A member of the Folk-Lore Society of Great Britain who spent many years in amassing a fine collection of dolls with the object of illustrating a scientific history from the standpoint of ethnography. See **Emergent Dolls.**

In 1916 he lent his collection of toys and dolls, which two years previously had been on show in Cardiff, for an exhibition at Whitechapel Art Gallery London. Many members of the Toy Trade were interested in this historical study of playthings. On exhibition also were examples from Lord Roberts Memorial Workshops for the disabled and a display from some of the other new wartime toy industries. See

Emergent Dolls—a term coined by Lovett for those made from simple materials readily obtainable: even a bone or old shoe. The Lovett collection is partly in the Museum of Childhood at Edinburgh. Some items are in the Horniman Museum, Forest Hill, others in the Cumin Museum, Walworth Rd., London. See also **Home-made Dolls.**

LOWE, Misses M. c1914-35. At 10 South Road, Handsworth, Birmingham. Dolls' clothing manufacturers. In 1918 making jerseys, sports coats, hats, velveteen coats and baby clothing. In 1923: All sizes and styles of Frocks, Hats, Coats, Undies etc. A large selection of knitted garments. 1935 Woollen Jersey suit in 10 sizes. Variety of dresses. Oilskin set and Jubilee sets in red, white and blue.

LOWE, RICHARD & CO. c1918. Manufacturer of toys and stuffed dolls.

LOWTHER ARCADE. 1831-1895+. The Strand, London. A series of small toyshops owned by Jolly & Son, selling expensive and

traditional penny toys. Some specialised in dolls, dressed or undressed with open or closing eyes; rag dolls; Dutch dolls (½"high to 18" high). Other shops specialized in toys.

LUCETTE. 1928. See **Dean & Son Ltd.**

LUCILLE. 1960. Teenage doll from L.S.D. range. See manufacturers, **Farnell, J. K. & Co. Ltd.**

LUCILLE DOLLS. c1926. Brand name of dolls' range. See **Rees, Leon.**

LUCKHAM, C. & CO. LTD. 1919-21+. January 1921 at 7 Manchester Avenue, Aldersgate Street, London, EC. Toy and doll importers. In 1921 it was reported that the firm 'has specialized in dolls and is financing and taking the entire output of three doll factories in Sonneberg. . . The dolls are dressed according to English styles and in the latest modes.'

Velvet coat and bonnet, 1916. Embroidered voile baby clothes and oilskin set made by M. Lowe, 1935.

LUCKY. Mark on doll's head in Pollock's Toy Museum collection. Made of plaster-resin composition, features painted in, metal sleeping eyes.

LUCKY LISA. Introduced 1971. Pedigree dice-throwing doll.

LUCKY PUCK. 1922. Series made by Dean's Rag Book Co Ltd, with patent design for a profile seam. Sold made-up or in fabric sheet form, with the slogan
> "You must certainly be struck
> By the looks of Mr Puck
> He may be an ugly duck
> But he will bring you luck."

LUCY. Introduced 1975. 11″ Matchbox baby girl doll with all-vinyl body, sleeping eyes and rooted hair. Originally made in Spain for Lesney Products & Co. Ltd. and now made in E. Germany.

LUCY LOCKET KIDDLES. 1968. Miniature doll. See **World of Kiddles.**

LULLABYE BABIES. c1926. A range of baby dolls. See **Rees, Leon.**

LULU. 1916. China doll figure with moving arms made by S. Hancock & Sons. John Green Hamley registered trademark no. 374,013 for the doll on 31st July 1916.

LULU. 1928. See **Dean & Son Ltd**

LU-LU. 1928. A dusky coloured baby doll with fuzzy hair, china head, balance eyes, composition body, jointed arms and legs. In 3 sizes, 6″, 8″ and 10″. Advertised by Whyte, Ridsdale and Co. Ltd. Houndsditch, London E1.

LULU. 1976. Palitoy 'pocket money doll'.

LUTON MUSEUM & ART GALLERY. Wardown Park, Luton, Bedfordshire. Has representative selection of dolls, including a group of straw dolls dating from the 19th century, made by the local straw plaiters. (Luton was formerly the chief centre of this craft).

LUVLY DOLLS. c1927. Range of dolls from 'A1' series. In 3 sizes 13″, 17″, 20″. See manufacturers, **Dean's Rag Book Co. Ltd.**

LUVMEE. c1935. Series of soft toys and dolls. See manufacturers, **S. & L. Manufacturing Co. Ltd.**

LUVY-DUVY. c1976. Brand name of doll series. See manufacturers, **Be-Be (Dolls) Ltd.**

LUXIDOLLY. 1949. Registered trademark for dolls and dolls' clothing. See manufacturers, **M.S.P. (Luxiproducts) Ltd.**

LYXHAYR. 1911. Stuffing for dolls, claimed to 'consist of vegetable fibre chemically treated by being boiled in alkali, and subsequently dyed, polished, curled,

English dressed baby and 'Lu-Lu', china-headed doll with sleeping eyes and composition body. Sold by Whyte, Ridsdale & Co. Ltd., 1928.

disinfected and rendered practically non-inflammable'. Manufactured by W. A. Dickinson & Lyxhayr Manufacturers Ltd.

M.S.P. (LUXIPRODUCTS) LTD. 1949. Altrincham, Cheshire. Registered trademark. 'Luxidolly' no. 679673 on 18th May 1949 for dolls and dolls' clothing.

MACKENRY. 1936. Registered trademark for dolls and toys. See **Kohnstam, J. Ltd.**

MACLEOD, A. I. 1949. London. Registered trademark 'Peter Pan', no. 678180, 24th March 1949, for dolls and dolls' garments.

MADELINE. 1936. Doll made by Dean's Rag Book Co. Ltd.

MADEN, James Henry. 1893-94. Manchester. Obtained two British patents, one with W. H. Nuttall no. 21052 on 6th November 1893 for celluloid dolls and masks, prepared in sheet form and moulded while hot. The other, no. 20186 on October 23rd 1894 for dolls' dresses with views, portraits or other pictures printed on them.

MADINGLAND. Trademark: See **South Wales Toy Manufacturing Co. Ltd.**

MAD KAISER. c1916. See **Huvan Mfg. Co.**

MAGIC FLESH. Dolls. 1956. All-vinyl doll range of 16 varying styles, dressed and undressed. Made by Pedigree.

MAGNETIC JOAN. 1954. Cut-out magnetised doll. See manufacturers, **Philmar Ltd.**

MAISIE. 1924. 17″ doll made by Dean's Rag Book Co. Ltd.

MALLY, JOSEPH ROBERT & CO. 1891-99. London. Fancy goods manufacturer. Obtained two British patents: no. 15678 on 16th September, 1891 for dolls' clothing, and no. 8937 on 28th April, 1896 relating to the operating of dolls' eyeballs.

MAMIE. 1927. Doll series made by S. & L. Manufacturing Co. Dolls had modelled faces, real mohair wigs and glass eyes, and were dressed in velveteen.

Straw work dolls, late 19th c. (Luton Museum).

MAM'SELLE BOUTIQUE. Dolls' Dresses 1959. Range of dolls' clothes for 'fashion-conscious dolls', made by Lines Bros.

MANDY LOU. 1952. See **Saucy Walkers.**

MANDY. 1956. Gaily-coloured soft negro doll made in plush with black rubber head and musical chime. 14″ high. made by Dean's Rag Book Co. Ltd.

MANN & MANN. c1923. Vale Road, London N4. Advertised large and miniature dressed dolls including a large doll called 'Doris'.

MANY MISFITZ FOLK. c1900. See **Faulkner, C. W. & Co.**

MARCHIONESS. 1920. Classic doll made by Speights Ltd.

MARCUSE, DAY & CO. LTD. 1916-22. In 1916, factory and offices in St. Albans, Hertfordshire and 8 South Street, Finsbury, London 1917: 19-21, Wilson Street, Finsbury, London. 1920: 55 Fann Street, London EC1. Manufacturer of dolls, toys and games. Trademark was 'Emdee'. In 1916 doll range included 'Pierrot', 'Pierrette' and 'Farmer's Boy'—china-headed dolls with stuffed bodies.

MARGARET, Princess. 1930. Baby doll dressed in a flowing white robe with fine lace insertions and wide silk ribbons. Lifelike unbreakable head, sleeping eyes, soft body and a natural crying voice. Marketed by Whyte, Ridsdale & Co.

MARGARET ROSE, Princess. c1938. Soft doll representing the younger daughter of King George VI. Manufactured by Chad Valley Co. Ltd. with the approval of Queen Elizabeth, the Princess's mother.

MARGOT THE MIDGET. 1921. A doll based on 'Daily Express' cartoon character, described as 'quaint little Quaker with circular hat, apron and satchel.'

MARIE DOLL. c1920. 'Classic' doll by Speights Ltd. Best china head with fixed or moving eyes. Hair-stuffed or jointed composition body. Real mohair wigs. 6 different styles. Removable clothes with hooks and eyes, and shoes and socks.

MARIE DOLL SERIES. c1948. Soft plastic dolls made by Mitchell Plastics Ltd. Described as 'the dolls of the future' which would give children great delight in bathing baby 'just as mother does.' Dolls' skin had 'soft flesh-like texture', limbs were removable and replaceable, with socket joints. All dolls had voices. Series included 'Marie-Lou', 'Marie-Valerie' and 'Marie-José'. See **Morris, Mitchell & Co.**

MARIE-LOU. 1946. See **Morris, Mitchell & Co.**

MARIGOLD. 1924. Registered trademark for dolls. See **Gross & Schild.**

MARINA. 1935. Nightdress case doll made in art silk taffeta by Dean's Rag Book Co. Ltd.

MARION & CO. 1916-17. 21 Camomile Street, London EC. Made dolls.

MARION, The. 1924. Registered trademark for dolls. See **Marn & Jondorf.**

MARKS, E.C.R. 1906 London. Obtained patent no. 19614 on 3rd September, 1906 for a phonographic doll.

MARLBOROUGH MANUFACTURING CO. c1918. At 338 Clapham Road, Stockwell, London SW9. Advertised Charlie Chaplin dolls and Red Cross Nurse Dolls in 1918.

MARN & JONDORF. 1924. At 86 & 87 Chiswell Street, London, EC1. Merchants. Registered trademark 'The Marion', no. 454,683 on 19th December 1924 for dolls.

MARSH, Charles and Mary Ann. Wax doll makers and restorers. 1878-95. Argyll St, London W1. Dolls guaranteed to withstand hot climate. From 1895-1901 Mrs Marsh ran a doll's hospital in 114 Fulham Road, London SW. An article in the Strand magazine about Dr. Marsh details the work and also shows large wax dolls for export to U.S.A. (Vol X 1895).

MARSH, Jessie. (daughter of Charles and Mary) carried on business at 114 Fulham Road until 1914. (As a child in the '20s I recall going to a doll-hospital in Fulham Road but I do not know how long it lasted or who ran it. I think it was mainly for china doll repairs.—Mary Hillier)

MARSH, William. Wax doll maker and probably the founder of the Marsh family business. He is recorded in 1865 as selling dolls at the Soho Bazaar.

MARTIN & RUNYON. 1862-5. In 1862 at 35 Florence Street, Cross Street, Islington, London. Made Autoperipatetikos (walking doll) patented in U.S.A. by an American, Enoch Rice Morrison on 15th July 1862, and in Europe on 20th December 1862. Alice Early possessed an 'Empress Eugenie' walking doll originally purchased at H. Martin in c1862.

MARTIN, S. F. 1900. Obtained Patent no. 5978 on 30th March, 1900 relating to mechanical walking dolls.

MARTY. 1959. Registered trademark for dolls and soft toys. See **Bartholomew, Marjorie Lilian.**

MARVO. 1946. Registered trademark for dolls. See **Silbertson, L. & Sons Ltd.**

MARY-ANN. 1960. 35" 'lifelike' Pedigree fully-jointed doll in lightweight plastic with vinyl head, long brunette rooted Saran hair with fringe, sleeping eyes and lashes. Doll is dressed in white non-iron cotton dress trimmed with nylon lace, a red and yellow waffle cotton all-over pinafore, stiffened nylon underskirt and panties, nylon socks and black patent shoes. Retail price £10 5s.

MARY BLIGH Dolls. 1938. A new range of character dolls from 21/-, made by Chad Valley Ltd.

MARY MAKE UP. 1967. Palitoy doll which can be made up with special cosmetics and whose hair can be changed from blonde to brunette or auburn.

MARY MARY. 1935. See **Nursery Rhyme Character Dolls.**

MASCOT DOLLS. Small dolls as souvenirs of some occasion or as lucky symbols carried for personal good fortune, or perhaps to bring victory to a sports team. E.g. celluloid dolls with dark blue or light blue fluffy topknots and ribbons and carrying miniature wooden oars for the annual Oxford and Cambridge Boatrace (1930s period). Some Norah Wellings dolls were adopted as mascots e.g. Harry Hawk, by the R.A.F. See also **Fumsup; Kewpie Dolls.**

MASK FACE DOLLS. These dolls usually have the back half of the head made of cloth or some material different from the more rigid face. The 'London Rag Dolls' had wax masks that were covered with muslin, and the back of the head was covered by a cap. Many of the celluloid dolls had mask faces. Celluloid doll masks were manufactured by Arthur Lee & Sons c1918, Milton Livesey & Co. Ltd. 1919, and Masks and Mouldings c1949.

MASKS LIMITED. 1942. Grove Street, Raunds, Northants. London Office: 2 Links Gardens, London SW16. Manufacturers of dolls' masks.

Masks Ltd., 1946.

MASKS & MOULDINGS LTD. Before 1949 at 22 Cross Street, London N1. From c1949 163 Edward Street, Brighton, Sussex. Manufacturers of dolls' masks and carnival masks. Trademark 'Plaztoy'.

MASON, C. G. FOSTER, F. A., ELMS J. C. and SPRAGUE, S. 27th October 1894 patent 20611 for dolls' clothing printed on fabric with outline for cutting.

MASTER GIVJOY. 1919. See **Holladay & Co. Ltd.**

MATCHBOX. See **Lesney Products & Co. Ltd.**

MATHEWS, T. & CO. LTD. 1918. Leicester. Little-Wide-Awake. Paper and card dressing doll with national flag dresses and hats, and moving eyes.

MATILDA. 1976. See **Moppits, The.**

MATTHEWS, L. 1918. Obtained patent no. 122100 on 22nd April, 1918 for dolls made of hanks of wool, tied so as to give required form. The features are formed by insertions of coloured wool and the like.

MAY BLOSSOM. 1922 Registered trademark for dolls, toys and games. See **Dennis Malley & Co. Ltd.**

MAY DAY DOLL. See **Lady Doll.**

MAYER & SHERRATT. 1906-47. Clifton Works, Longton, Staffordshire. Pottery firm manufacturing dolls' heads and limbs during the First World War. Used the mark 'Melba' and M & S England.

MAYHEW, Henry. 1812-1887. Dramatist, journalist, and author of one of the first outstanding sociological investigations to be published in England. ('London Labour and the London Poor', 1851). It included a long interview with a glass eye-maker (See **Eyes** for an extract from this). The volume was based on a series of letters which had first appeared in the Morning Chronicle in 1850: these contain many more details of other toy makers, and of how wooden dolls were made; also a harrowing account of how a sick man was trying to live by making wax dolls. A few days later the Morning Chronicle published a little note saying that several readers had been so moved that they had sent money to the newspaper offices to be passed on to the poor doll-maker. This is what Mayhew wrote:

"His whole appearance showed grinding poverty. His cheeks were sunken, and altogether he seemed, from grief and care, like a man half dead. His room was bare of anything to be called furniture, except only a very poor bed, a chair or two, and a table or bench at which he was at work with his paste and paper. In one corner was an oblong object, covered with an old quilt. It was a coffin containing the body of his child, a girl four years old, who had died of whooping cough. There were four living children in the room—all up, late as it was, and all looking feeble, worn and sickly. The man's manner was meek and subdued as he answered my questions.

"I make the composition heads for the dolls—nothing else. They are made of papier mâché (paper mashed, he called it). After they go out of my hands to the dollmakers, they are waxed. First, they are done over in 'flake' light (flesh colour), and then dipped in wax. I make a mould from a wax model, and in it work the paper—a peculiar kind of sugar paper.

"My little girl, fifteen years old, and myself can only make twelve or thirteen dozen a day of the smallest heads. For them I get 4s the gross, and the material, I reckon, costs me 1s 10d. If I make 2s 6d a day I reckon it is a good day's work—and what is half-a-crown for such a family as mine?

"My wife makes a few dolls' arms of stuffed sheepskin: sawdust is used. She only gets seven farthings a dozen for them, and has very little employment. My trade used to be far better: now they get the bodies stuffed with sawdust at 2s 6d a gross, and they used to pay 5s. It's starvation work, stuffing 144 bodies for half-a-crown. Ah sir, the children

of the people who will be happy with my dolls little think under what circumstances they are made, nor do their parents—I wish they did."

McCALMONT, R. 21st November 1895, patent for constructing paper dolls with gummed paper loops from fashion plate figures cut from magazines.

McCUBBIN, Ethel Elizabeth Mary. 1914. At 3 Boveney Road, Honor Oak Park, London SE. Registered trademark 'Lion's Claw' and picture, no. 363,437 on 11th September 1914, for dolls, toys and games.

Engraving by Arthur Boyd Houghton for Our Mutual Friend, by Charles Dickens, 1868. The drunken father and his crippled daughter.

McMILLAN, Adelaide. 1915. Workington, Cumberland. Obtained patent no. 10533 on 20th July 1915, for a cork-filled rag doll. The head and torso were made of 4 pieces, and the arms of 2 pieces each.

McSWEENY, Jane. 1970. Artist-modeller of the Princess Anne doll, produced and dressed in wedding regalia by Honor Wilson (1973).

MEECH, Herbert John & H. G. (Meech Bros). 1865-1891. 1870 at 50 Wilmington Road, London SE. By 1891 at Kennington Road, London, SE. Wax doll makers by Royal appointment.

MELANIE. 1975. 14″ soft-bodied doll with curly rooted hair, vinyl face and hands from the Matchbox doll range manufactured for Lesney Products & Co. Ltd. in Hong Kong & stuffed and assembled in the UK.

Dolls' heads by Mayer & Sherratt.

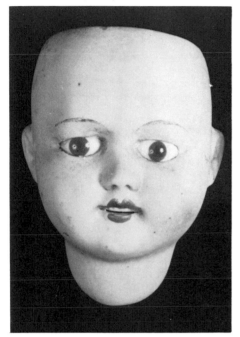

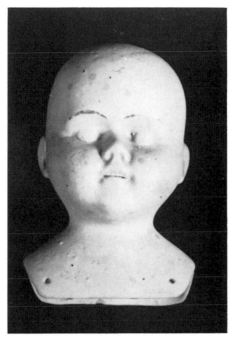

MELBA. 1915-20. Mark on dolls' heads made by Mayer & Sherratt. Used on bisque heads, some with wigs, others moulded. They were generally shoulder heads on rag or kid bodies.

MELUISH, Edwin. 1870. At 32 Goldsmith's Row, Hackney, London E. Made dolls.

MEMORIAL HALL MUSEUM. High Street, Dunster, Somerset. A collection of over 700 dolls, the earliest dating from the 18th century, collected by the late Molly Hardwick.

MERRYTHOUGHT LTD. Jan. 1930-1981+. 1932 at 113, Holborn, London EC1. Factory at Dale End, Iron Bridge, Telford, Salop. Manufacturers of dolls, toys and games. Original joint managers were H. C. Janisch & C. R. Randle, both of whom had previous experience in soft toys before establishing 'Merrythought'. In August, 1931 advertised range of dolls called 'Cuddly Coo'. On 8th March, 1932 the trademark 'Merrythought Movie-toys' no. 580,025 was registered for toys. 1933 lines included 'Silvia', a doll made in crushed silk plush, with glass eyes; 'Dixie Bebe', a black doll with scarlet frock; 'Patsie', in coloured velours with frock in contrasting shade. Both 'Dixie' and 'Patsie' had 'mama' voices and were kapok-stuffed.

In 1958 Merrythought appointed Dean & Son Ltd. their sole agents and now have a permanent showroom at 52-4 Southwark St, London E1.

Two hybrid dolls. The one on the left has a china head marked 'Melba'; the one on the right has a head marked 'Classic Cecily' on a body marked 'Jumeau'.

Mayer & Sherratt doll marked 'Melba'.

Merrythought A.R.P. mascot. 1940.

METROPOLITAN INDIA RUBBER & VULCANITE CO. 1870. At 32 & 33 Cowcross Street, London, EC. Made rubber dolls.

METTOY COMPANY LIMITED. 14 Harlestone Road, Northampton. Doll and toy manufacturers and merchants. The firm was established in England in 1933 by Philip Ullmann, a refugee from Germany, who had been a director of Bechmann & Ullmann, one of the leading toy manufacturers in Germany. The firm originally made only metal toys but they gradually extended their range to other materials, including plastic. In 1955 they were producing vinyl character dolls in brilliant colours, 8½" high, retailing at 10s 6d each. In 1958 they registered three trademarks for dolls: 'Nursery Rhyme' no. B774,249, 'Story Book' no. 774,627 and 'Hoppy Lou' no. 784,033.

'Simon' and 'Susan', Sunshine vinyl toys made by Mettoy Toy Co. Ltd., 1951. Fitted with safety squeakers.

Merrythought Golliwog, 1930.

MEWBURN, J. C. London 1871. Patent 3494 for a doll's head.

MEWMAN. 1906. Obtained patent no. 6220 for a talking doll.

MEYER, L. 1924-25. At 2 & 3 Lillypot Lane, Noble Street, London EC2. Doll importers. In 1924 advertised dressed and undressed 'Cupids'.

MEYERSTEIN, William. 6 Love Lane, Aldermanbury, London. Dealer in dolls 1876. Trademark: Elephant Head.

MFANWY JONES. 1969. Cut-out doll by Margaret Holgate, made as souvenir of the 1969 investiture of the Prince of Wales.

MICHAEL. 1936. Alpha 'Joy Day' doll made by J. K. Farnell & Co. Ltd.

MICHELE. Introduced 1966. 12" soft-bodied Pedigree baby doll, with deep-set sleeping eyes, vinyl limbs and head, and rooted washable hair. Initial wardrobe consisted of 7 different outfits.

MICHELE. Doll. 1959. 35" walking Palitoy doll in lightweight plastic with vinyl head, long rooted hair, sleeping eyes and a 'mama' voice. Retail price £10 14s.

MICHELLE. Introduced 1975. 14" fully jointed Matchbox doll with blonde hair and blue sleeping eyes. Made in Italy for Lesney Products & Co. Ltd.

MICHEL-LEVY, Fernande. 1947. At 783 Finchley Road, London NW11. Registered

'Chubee' unbreakable dolls made by J.P. Miller & Co., 1916.

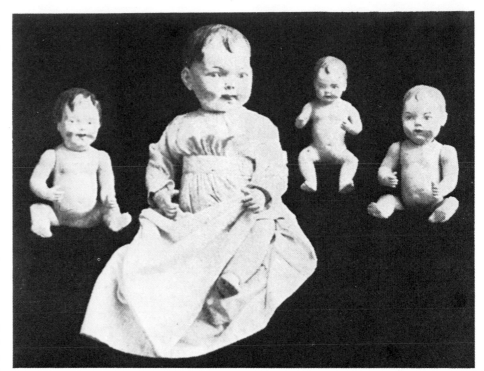

trademark 'Dolrite', no. 659953 on June 11th, 1947 for dolls and toys.

MIDDLESEX TOY INDUSTRIES LTD. 1952. Colne Road Works, Twickenham, Middlesex. Manufacturers of boxed games, novelties, squeakers and growlers and plastic mama voices.

MIGNON. See **Williams & Steer Mfg. Co. Ltd.**

MILITARY COSTUME. See **Farnell, J. K. & Co. Ltd.; P. Munster, F. J. & Co. Ltd.;** and **Nisbet, P.**

MILLER BROS. 1916. At 519 Cambridge Road, Hackney, London. Advertising dolls' limbs and Esquimaux & Dress dolls from 6d to 2/-.

MILLER, Gertrude. c1916. Jumping Jack character doll representing Miss Miller, the well known Musical Comedy actress, as she appeared in 'Bric-a-Brac', a revue, dressed as a 'pierrette' with long flowing hair. Made by Speights Ltd.

MILLER, J. P. & CO. 1916. At Roscoe Street, Liverpool with factory at Mount Vernon Road, Liverpool. 1917 at 24 Moorfields, Liverpool. Composition doll manufacturers. In 1917 advertised 'Chubee' 'Unbreakable Baby Dolls in three sizes, with movable arms and legs and head. Each doll tied in a box and dressed in shirt'.

In March 1918 the firm registered 2 trademarks, 'Compolite' no. 382,426 and 'Compolene' no. 382,427, for unbreakable composition materials for the manufacture of dolls.

MILLER, Leonard. 1919-1942. At 9-11 Christopher Street, Finsbury London EC2. 1942 at 344 Hackney Road, London E2. Manufacturer of dolls and doll parts. In 1919 doll limbs, white at 9/- per gross and painted at 12/- per gross. 1942 selling character dolls and soft-bodied unbreakable dolls; plaster heads for dolls, soft toys; and papier mâché unbreakable dolls' heads.

MILLIS, F.W. 15th December 1891. Patent 21887 for ventriloquist figure worked by compressed air and bellows.

MILLY. 1976. See **Moppits, The**

MILTON LIVESEY & CO LTD. 1919-20. Lion Works, Accrington & 173 Scotland Road, Liverpool. Doll manufacturers. In 1919 advertised dressed and undressed, fully-jointed compressed fibre dolls in 12 sizes, and celluloid masks. 1920: fully-jointed all-fibre dolls with leatherette bodies. Dolls supplied with either British or French made heads, sleeping or fixed eyes. Leatherette dolls with unbreakable fibre arms in 4 sizes.

'Miss Black Bottom' doll, regd. design 1926. by J. Sear Ltd.

131

MINDOL LTD. 1919. 190 Lavender Hill, London SW. Advertising miniature dolls and toys.

MINIATURE MODELS. c1924. Lifelike models in wax or plaster intended for the shop window, showcase or home. 'Priscilla', 'Spirit of Dance', 'Du Barry', 'an exquisite figure in the form of a tea cosy', and 'Salome' eastern dancer. Manufactured by J. S. Sant.

MINIKIDS. 1969. Turtle doll range, consisting of sixteen 11cm high dolls. See **Thernglade Ltd.**

MINNIE HA HA. c1920. Red Indian girl doll based on character in Longfellow's poem 'Hiawatha', with stuffed stockinette body. One of the series 'Dots Dolls' made by Harwin Ltd.

MINNIE MOPPIT. 1977. Soft-bodied Matchbox Character doll. 30cms high, with vinyl face and hands. Made in Hong Kong and stuffed and assembled in the U.K.

MIRANDA. 1958. 17″ Palitoy brown flexible vinyl doll, advertised as 'the first ever coloured vinyl doll'. Doll has curly rooted hair, fixed moulded eyes, a waffle dress with shoes and socks. Retail price 39s 11d.

MISS BEAUTY CUPID. 1922. See **Lawton Doll Co.**

MISS BLACK BOTTOM. 1926. Pierrot rag doll made by J. Sear Ltd., and inspired by the then current hit tune and dance, the 'Black Bottom'.

MISS CLEVERSTICKS. 1972. Bluebell range doll, made by Bluebell Dolls Ltd.

MISS CROSSWORD. 1925. See **Hughes & Son, Henry Jeffrey.**

MISS HAPPY HEART. 1971. Walking and sleeping doll with battery-operated beating heart. Manufactured by Bluebell Dolls Ltd.

MISSKA. Dolls. c1920. Stockinette dolls stuffed with kapok down and dressed in various shades of plush. 6 sizes. See manufacturers, **Art Toy Manufacturing Co.**

MISS LINDA. 1958. Registered trademark for dolls, toy animals and golliwogs. See manufacturers, **Randall & Wood.**

MISS MISCHIEF. 1932. Soft, cuddly mascot doll in furry pastel-shaded material, marketed by Bedington Liddiatt.

MISS MUFFET. c1920. 'Classic' doll. See **Speights Ltd.**

MISS MUFFET. 1926. Character doll made by J. K. Farnell & Co.

MISS NOBODY. 1973. See **Character Crafts Ltd.**

'Prince Charming' doll, by Mitchell & Hardy (Plastics) Ltd., 1949 (Pollock's Toy Museum).

MISS ROSEBUD BRIDE. Doll. 1959. Bride doll from 'teenager' range. 14½″ tall in unbreakable vinyl with rooted Saran hair, dressed in gown of white nylon net with overskirt of nylon figured lace. Many petticoats, a Coronet headdress, pearl necklace, nylon stockings and high-heeled shoes. Made by Rosebud Dolls Ltd.

MITCHELL & CO. 1917. At North Wing Mills, Bradford. Manufacturers of dolls' hair and accessories. In 1917 advertised doll cords and eyes and cardboard caps for socket heads. At the 1918 British Industries Fair displayed various wigs apparently much admired by Queen Mary, who is said to have remarked 'I have never seen anything more beautiful'. In 1919, after the death of Mr E.H. Mitchell, the company was renamed J. P. Mitchell & Co. Ltd. and had a factory at Victoria Works, Canal Road, Bradford. The directors were Mr. J. P. Mitchell, son of E. H. Mitchell, and Fred Jagger, a dyer of mohair, who had done all the dying of mohair for several firms in the trade.

MITCHELL & HARDY (PLASTICS) LTD. c1949. London Road, Bishop Stortford, Hertfordshire. Doll manu-

'Miss Mischief', sold by Bedington Liddiatt, 1932.

facturers. 1949 range included 'Prince Charming', a plastic boy doll, and a soft P.V.C. doll with sleeping eyes, 18½" high. Also 'Mormit' plastic dolls.

MITCHELL, J. D. 1947. Obtained patent no. 634266 on 1st December 1947 relating to a doll's eye.

MITCHELL PLASTICS. 1948. At 262 High Road, Wood Green, London N22. Make plastic dolls. See **Morris, Mitchell & Co. Ltd.**

MODELS (LEICESTER) LTD. c1919. Factory Street, Loughborough, Leicestershire. London Showroom: 11 Farringdon Avenue, London EC4. Doll and toy manufacturers. Registered trademark 'Bringlee' no. 390,954 on 7th May 1919 for dolls and toys, and 'Bringlee Unbreakable Doll' no. 391,750 on 29th May, 1919 for a doll. In August 1919 advertised jointed composition baby girl and boy dolls in four sizes, and fully-jointed composition dolls 18"-35" long with wigs and glass eyes.

MODEL TOYS LTD. Shotts, Lanarkshire, Scotland. Toy and doll manufacturers, a subsidiary of Berwick Timpo. In 1973 made 'Daisy' fashion dolls. See **Daisy.** 1974 Introduced 'Havoc, secret agent' girl doll and 'Daredevil' male adventure doll. See **Havoc** and **Daredevil.**

MODERN. Dolls. 1929. Range of dolls dressed in velvet and rich art silk plush with ribbon trimmings. Made by Dean's Rag Book Co. Ltd.

MOGRIDGE, W. H. & CO. 1918. Made dolls and doll masks.

MOKO trademark. See **Kohnstam, J. Ltd.**

MOLLY. 1933. Doll made by Dean's Rag Book Co. Ltd.

MOLLY POPPET. 1976. Doll made by Chad Valley Ltd.

MONICA. 1932. Doll dressed in striped pleated skirt, made by Chad Valley Co. Ltd.

MONICA. 1947. Registered trademark for dolls. See **Buckingham (London) Ltd.**

Wax doll 14 ins. high, marked in ink on body 'Montanari, Soho Bazaar'. Said to be a model of Princess Louise, Duchess of Argyll (Victoria and Albert Museum).

MONTANARI, Augusta. Wife of Napoleon Montanari and probably the most famous maker of wax dolls in London up to her death in 1864, aged 46, from T.B. The business was carried on by her son Richard, born in 1840. Madame Montanari was a specialist at dressing dolls and won medals at the Great Exhibition in 1851 when she showed models of the Royal Children. The dolls she made were often signed in brown ink across the base of the fabric torso. Her dressed dolls sometimes had little bracelets and necklets of seed pearls, and the best materials were used for costume and shoes and socks. At the 1851 exhibition the expensive wax dolls, costing between 10s and 105s, were accompanied by a case of "rag" dolls, made only of textile fabrics and

cheaply priced for the nursery at between 5s and 30s including dresses.

MONTANARI, Napoleon. First listed as an artist in waxwork 1849/50. At 13 Charles Street, Soho, 1862/64. He seems to have been a model-maker as well as probably designing the actual doll models for his wife. He exhibited a group of Indians at the Crystal Palace and it is thought he may originally have come from America. Later he vanished without trace; perhaps he went abroad, as his death is unrecorded in London.

MONTANARI, Richard Napoleon. The son of Augusta and Napoleon, he carried on the dollmaking at no. 3 Rathbone Place ((Oxford St, just opposite Soho Square). He perfected the London rag baby with a wax-over moulded fabric mask, backed with a bonnet in 1875. He married Fanny Fawley the daughter of an artist; they had a son, another Richard Napoleon, who died of pneumonia aged 26. A daughter of the family still lives but the wax doll craft seems to have died out during the 1880s, when wax dolls became less popular than imported china ones.

MOODY, E. c1870. Soho Bazaar, London. Name and address found on 1870 doll body label. Probably sold dolls at the Soho Bazaar.

MOPPET DOLL. See manufacturers **Cassidy Bros. Ltd.**

MOPPIETOP. c1914. Doll made by Dean's Rag Book. Co. Ltd.

MOPPITS, The. 1976. Soft bodied Matchbox Character doll range, vinyl face and hands, 35 cms high. Matilda and Milly. Made in Hong Kong and stuffed and assembled in the U.K.

MORITZ & CHAMBERS. 1927-1941. In 1927 at 3, Cotton Street, Barbican, London EC1. From January 1928 at 80 York Way, Kings Cross, London N1. Doll manufacturers, including celluloid dolls. In Jan. 1941 had full range of British-made dolls on display at the Victoria Hotel, Manchester.

MORGENTHALER, Sasha dolls. See **Trendon Toys.**

MORMIT. c1949. Brand name of plastic doll. See manufacturers, **Mitchell & Hardy (Plastics) Ltd.**

MORRELL, Horace W. & Charles and Mrs Jane Arundel ran famous London toy shops from 1870-1916—one in Burlington Arcade; and two in Oxford St. at no 164 and 368. They sold the wax dolls made by Marsh and also the mechanical dolls of Mrs. Sherwood together with a huge stock of English and foreign toys. The shop in Burlington arcade, which finally closed in 1951, was said to have been in business continuously since 1820, when it specialised in miniature goods of wood, ivory and silver for dolls' houses. In its last years it stocked some of the miniature military models made by craftsmen.

Montanari wax baby doll (Victoria and Albert Museum).

Montanari-type wax doll (Pollock's Toy Museum).

MORRELL, Frank & Richard. 1922. London. Distributed dolls.

MORRIS, MITCHELL & CO. c1946. At Welbury Street, London E.8 Doll manufacturers. In 1946 introduced 'Marie-Lou', the new All-Plastic doll. Described as 'Life-like in appearance with flesh-like texture. Soft-bodied doll made in fast colours'. Also made plastic doll masks. In 1948 the firm changed its name to Mitchell Plastics Ltd. and the address to 262 High Road, Wood Green, London, N22. The Company continued to produce the Marie doll series. See **Marie Doll Series.**

MORTYN, James Leicester. 1860-79. London. In 1868 at 13-14 Little Warner Street, Clerkenwell, London, EC. Made dolls.

MOTHER GOOSE. 1961. Soft toy and doll range by J. K. Farnell & Co. Ltd.

MRS CANDOUR. 18th century. See **School for Scandal Dolls.**

MRS & MASTER FOLLY. 1914. See **Hughes & Son, Henry Jeffrey.**

MULLER, H. 1905-1927. Obtained 3 patents: no. 21418, 1st October, 1905, for dolls' eyelashes; No. 234390, 8th December 1924, for an eye for a doll consisting of a cut glass 'diamond'; and no. 287727, 25th July 1927, for hollow figures forming containers for small objects.

MULLER, J. 1950. Obtained patent no. 680161, 23rd June, 1950, for a soft toy construction (doll or animal) in which a musical box is embodied.

MUNITION DOLL. 1915+. Doll. See manufacturers, **Bell & Francis.**

MUNN, J. A. 1863. Obtained patent no. 40 6th January 1863 for an automative walking doll.

MUNSTER F.J. & CO. LTD. 1967. 50-68 Hockley Street, Birmingham 18. Manufacturer of National costume dolls and regimental dolls in miniature. 1967 range included Boy and Girl pipers, Kettle Drummer and Officer with Regimental colour.

MUNYARD, A. R. 1923. London. Obtained patent no. 214722, 25th January 1923 for a doll which had a mechanism which produced changes of facial expression when rocked.

MUSEUM OF CHILDHOOD. Edinburgh. 34 High Street, Edinburgh, Scotland. The doll section has a special section devoted to ethnographical specimens such as fertility and magic dolls, votive figures, costume and boudoir dolls. There is also a doll made up by a slum child from a wrapped-up shoe. The collection is comprehensive and shows examples of most types of doll. It owes much of its original inspiration to Mr Patrick Murray who was the first Curator. See also **Lovett, Edward.**

MUSEUM OF COSTUME. Assembly Rooms, Bath, Avon. A fine display of dolls, and particularly good examples of dolls' clothing. Cut-out paper dolls for colouring and dressing are on sale.

MY BABY LOVE. 1977. Vinyl plastic doll made by H. Schelhorn & Co.

The 'Munition' doll, Bell & Francis, 1917.

MY DOLLIE'S NANNA. 1927. See **Bland-Hawkes, Mabel.**

MYERS, H. E. 1947. Obtained patent no. 644923 23rd September, 1947, for provision of a doll's eye in which the pictorial representation of the eye is protected against damage by rubbing or scratching. (Refers to specification 18089 of 1904 patented by E. Reinhardt.)

MYFANWY PRODUCTS LTD. 1963. Swansea, Glamorganshire, Wales. Manufacturers of Welsh costume dolls.

MY FIRST BABY. 1975. Carry around baby doll made by Pedigree.

MY KIDDIE. c1917. Brand name of soft stuffed dolls. See manufacturers, **Fretwell Toy Manufacturing Co.,** and wholesalers, **Abrahams, Hyman, A. & Sons.**

MY LITTLE TERRITORIAL. 1909. Character doll. See **Hughes & Son, Henry Jeffrey.**

MY SWEETIE. 1928. Registered trademark for dolls and toys. See **Fishman, S. Z.**

N. G. PRODUCTS & CO. LTD. 1952. At 59 Golborne Road, London W10. Doll manufacturers. Trade mark Golborne Dolls.

NANKEEN. (Nankin or Nanking). Dolls c1884-c1911. Dolls with commercially made cotton cloth bodies. O.E.D. definition: 'kind of cotton cloth originally made of naturally yellow cotton from Nankin(g) in China'. English manufacturers include: Stephen Erhard c1891 and British Novelty Company c1919.

NA-POO Series. 1920. China figurines made by Hewitt Bros. (formerly Hewitt & Leadbeater) with Willow tree pottery mark. See **Hewitt & Leadbeater.**

NATIONAL DOLL & GLASS EYE MANUFACTURING CO. February 1919-c1920. 13 Swan Street, Manchester. Made dolls, toys, glass eyes etc.

★ GLASS EYES
...FOR...
DOLLS, ANIMALS & BIRDS,
BLOWN OR SOLID.
ALSO
KID DOLLS,
FULLY JOINTED
WITH
MOVEABLE EYES,
in Two Sizes.

PROMPT DELIVERY.

Send your Enquiries to
Manufacturers—
National Doll & Glass Eye
Manufacturing Co., Ltd.,
13, Swan Street, MANCHESTER.

NATIONAL DOLL LEAGUE. c1915-c1917. 64 Regent Street, London W. Made dolls including exercising dolls. In October, 1915 an advertisement stated that revenue from sales went to the British Red Cross Society.

NAUTICAL NANCY. c1914. Rag doll made by Dean's Rag Book Co. Ltd.

NAYLOR, John. 1 Hoxton Market, London. Made dolls.

NEEDLEWORK DOLLS. Dolls have always been a stimulus to the practice of arts and crafts, and especially in Victorian times suggestions were continually made as to how ladies might use their time making doll miniatures for bazaars etc. The small wooden dolls dressed by Queen Victoria herself (Museum of London) are famous examples of a child being taught to use a needle and thread. The Girls' Own Book by Mrs Child (1842) and The Home Book by

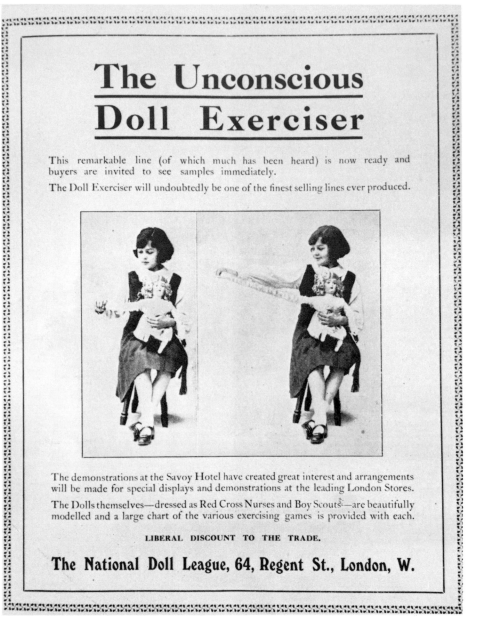

Mrs R. Valentine (1867) both contained detailed ideas for dressing dolls. The popular variations were for Fortune Lady, telling fortunes by paper slips hidden beneath her skirt; and for Pedlar dolls offering a tray or basket full of miniatures. Mrs Valentine suggested dolls of other countries, historical dolls, Watteau costume, rag dolls for babies and dancing dolls. Lady's companions and pin-cushion dolls came complete with needles and thimbles and reels of cotton. Special paper patterns were sold for children to use in making up doll clothes; for instance: Dolly's Dressmaker published about 1860 in London by A. N. Myers & Co. It was written by Frederike Lesser and translated into English by Mme de Chatelain. By the end of the century there were many others, e.g. The Little Mother, cheap packets of doll's paper patterns sold at 1d by Blackmore Fashion, Camden Town, London. Butterick patterns—American

publications—were also sold in London about this time.

NEGRO DOLLS (NIGGER). Very popular in the U.S.A. and Europe for many years, especially after the American Civil War; and again in the 1890's, when dolls of all races were being shown extensively. Some of the negro dolls were simply painted black; others had the black pigment mixed in the slip of the bisque and also had negroid features. English manufacturers include: Merrythought Ltd. 1933; Kingram Toys, 1916; Fairyland Toy Manufacturing Co. Ltd. 1920; J. Sear Ltd.; Chad Valley Co. Ltd.; Dean's Dollies Ltd. 1936; Frido Ltd. 1963.

NEIGHBOUR, R. C. & CO. 1921. London and Lewisham. Manufactured 'Livetoy' series of doll. Used 'Neto' as a trademark.

NELKE. 1920. Trademark. See **Weeks & Co. (London) Ltd.**

Nelke, soft dolls made by Weeks & Co., 1920.

NELLFOY. 1917. Registered trademark for dolls and dolls' dresses. See **Nell Foy & Co.**

NELL FOY & CO. 1915-21. At 55 Church Street, Chelsea, London, SW3. Doll and toy manufacturers. Company run by Jessica Borthwick who, on 29th October 1917 registered the trademark 'Nellfoy' no. 380,335 for dolls and dolls' dresses. In 1918 their range included wax statuettes advertised as 'the most beautifully modelled, tinted and dressed.' Two of them represented Doris Keane and Gaby Deslys, famous theatrical personalities of the period.

Manufacture of dolls followed. Wax-finished composition dolls with stuffed kid bodies; 'Fairy Queen' in 'gauzy white robes', and a range of character dolls including:- W.A.A.C., Scots girls, Irish girls, Red Cross Nurse and Old Mother Hubbards.

NENE PLASTICS. c1947. Raunds, Northamptonshire. Made 'Rosebud' plastic dolls. See **Smith, T. Eric.**

NEST, William. 1852. London. Made dolls.

NETO. 1921. Trademark used by Neighbour, R. C. & Co.

NEWARKE HOUSES MUSEUM. The Newarke, Leicester. Large and representative collection of Victorian dolls and toys. A lifelike wax portrait doll, representing a young girl with blue eyes and plaited hair c1870, is exceptional.

NEW BORN DOLLS' HEADS. c1920. 'Paradise' series, available in black or white china. Similar to Armand Marseille dolls of mid-20s.

NEW CENTURY DOLLS. c1917. Composition dolls, made by Nottingham Toy Industry.

NEW DARLING BABY. c1917. Doll head sold by Heywood-Abel & Sons Ltd.

NEW ECCLES RUBBER WORKS LTD. 1921-22. Morton Rd, Eccles, Lancashire. Made rubber dolls and toys. Trademark Flag at Mast marked N.E.R.W.

NEWFELD LTD. 1965. Ashford, Middlesex. Doll and toy manufacturers. Brand name Bendy Toys. 1965 introduced 18″ doll 'Bendykins' with vinyl head and hands, foam rubber bendy body, rooted hair, sleeping eyes and a romper suit. Retail price 45s. Manufactured some of the popular characters (e.g. Windy Miller) created for Children's TV programme Camberwick Green.

NEWMAN, Alexander Morris. 1906. Berlin, Germany. Obtained British patent no. 6620 on 14th March, 1906 for a phonographic doll that was supposed to be an improvement on the Edison doll.

NEWTON, A. V. 1871. Obtained patent no. 2942 2nd November, 1871, for a doll fitted with a clockwork mechanism which enabled it to imitate crawling, to move its head and produce inarticulate sounds.

NEW TREND. 1968. Doll series. See **Favourite Toys Ltd.**

NICKI. 1975. 14″ Matchbox vinyl drink/ wet doll with sleeping eyes and curly blonde rooted hair which can be combed and styled. Made in E. Germany for Lesney Products & Co. Ltd.

NIGGER PEGGY DOLL. 1935. See **Sear, J. Ltd.**

NIGHTY GIRL. 1920. Classic doll made by Speights Ltd.

NI-NI. 1911. Registered trademark for dolls. See **Hamley Bros.**

NIPPER. c1935. Soft character doll based on 'Daily Mirror' cartoon strip drawn by Brian White. Merrythought Ltd. was sole licensee of the doll.

NISBET, Alison. See **Tower Treasures.**

NISBET, PEGGY LTD. Old Mixon Crescent, Weston-super-Mare, Somerset. Started in a small way in 1953 when she designed a 7″ scale model of H. M. Queen Elizabeth II to commemorate the Coronation. This doll was made of fine quality bisque and dressed in full-length white brocade gown, with purple velvet robe lined in white erminatte fur with gold-thread embroidery and a rolled gold crown set with fine diamanté. Only 250 pieces were made, all sold exclusively to Harrods. Peggy Nisbet decided to make other miniature models, such as King Henry VIII and his six wives, Elizabeth I etc, but to use, for commercial purposes, polystyrene with steel moulds. A limited company was founded in 1956 and premises set up for making the dolls with the help of craftswomen outworkers. In 1970 that centre was destroyed by fire with all the original patterns etc. A new factory was eventually built and since then the firm's

Peggy Nisbet portrait doll, wearing bright pink outfit similar to that worn by Mrs Nisbet at her Silver Jubilee party in 1977; and a 'Harrod's' doorman, a jointed hard plastic doll made exclusively for this famous store, 1979.

Jointed, bone-china bisque doll 8½ ins. high, from the Peggy Nisbet Tower Treasure range, representing the King of Arms in Court dress. The traditional tabard is embroidered with the Royal Coat of Arms by special permission of the Lord Chamberlain, who limited its use solely to 1977, the year of the Queen's Jubilee.

range of models has increased and includes many authentic historical characters, American presidents and Hollywood film stars. A small model of Christopher Robin was one of Peggy Nisbet's designs but rather disappointingly it was based on the short-trousered Disney version rather than the original little son of A. A. Milne in his smock. During the '60s, after Norah Wellings retired, Peggy Nisbet, with the permission of their originator, made copies of the little sailor doll. In 1981, in conjunction with Royal Doulton Ltd., Peggy Nisbet Ltd. produced two series of Collector's Dolls in fine ivory bone china and dressed either as Kate Greenaway children or Victorian Birthday Dolls.

NOBODY'S DARLING. c1924. Soft doll. Name taken from popular song of 1923 'I Ain't Nobody's Darling'.

NODDY. Enid Blyton's children's book character, especially popular in the 1950's. Various dolls were made in Noddy's likeness.

NON-NYSA DOLLS. c1915. Fabric printed character dolls. See manufacturer **Turton, W. S.**

NONO. 1928. See **Dean & Son Ltd.**

NORENE. c1932. Series of soft dolls, see **Wellings, Norah.**

NORGATE, M. B. 1919. Obtained patent no. 157548, 17th October, 1919, for attaching a doll's head to a wooden block concealed in the upper portion of a stuffed body, to enable the head to turn easily.

NORTH OF ENGLAND OPEN AIR MUSEUM. Beamish Hall, Stanley, Co. Durham. Museum opened in 1971. Collection includes dolls and other Victorian and later toys.

NOTTINGHAM TOY INDUSTRY LTD. 1914-1920. The outbreak of war in 1914 led to a great deal of unemployment among women, who up to then had well-paid jobs in the lace making industry. Miss Wallis, a well-to-do young woman who played a leading part in the "Women's Emergency Corps", set up, in an annexe to her own home, a toy-making enterprise subsequently known as the Nottingham Toy Industry. At first only small rag dolls with composition masks were made. The enterprising Miss Wallis then asked a sculptor, Helen Frazer Rock, to design some china dolls' heads. Modelled from real children, these pioneer English china dolls were called 'Helen's Babies', and as the pottery firm that made them used an especially strong and solid material they were advertised as 'Rock China Dolls'. Miss Wallis next turned her attention to dolls' bodies, producing a featherweight 'Compolite' body. They were marketed under the name of 'Daisy' and 'Vogue' dolls. Slightly cheaper Rock china dolls were the twins 'Peter and Pauline' and 'Joyce & Josylin'. The Nottingham Toy Industry was represented in London by Miss Moller of British Toys Ltd., who was also the London agent for the Shanklin Toy Industry. Neither of these enterprises lasted very long after the cessation of hostilities.

NOW. 1920. Trademark of firm making jointed dolls, dressed and undressed. Trademark is a diamond shape with words 'NOW' and 'Trade mark' inside.

NOXID. c1919. Boy and girl dolls dressed in variety of costumes. See **Dixon, T. A.**

NOZO THE CLOWN. 1959. 19″ clown doll with vinyl head, hands and shoes, a painted face and fixed moulded eyes and rooted hair. Retail price 43s 6d. Made by Palitoy.

NUNN, George Lawrence Trading as NUNN & SMEED. August 1915-1927. At 55 Benledi Street, Liverpool. Doll manufacturer. Nunn and John Smeed, his partner, initially concentrated on producing two jointed dolls 20″ and 22″ high. They invented a new finish for dolls' bodies which did away with paint, resembled porcelain, and was non-poisonous and waterproof. From 1918 to 1920 they had a factory in Newbury, Berkshire to give work to returning soldiers in the post-war depression. Assembly work was carried out there.

Nunn obtained patent no. 1863232 on 26th August, 1921 for a walking doll made with spring hinges at the knee joints which are pivoted to the body without spring control so as to be able to move forward freely. c1920 the company was producing

John Smeed.

A Nunn & Smeed walking doll.

'Regina Dolls', advertised as 'life-like, washable perfect finish, porcelain heads, finest mohair wigs, all with sleepy eyes'. The range included two life-size Baby dolls retailing at 35/6 & 50/-, and a 17″ high jointed doll at 10/6. c1923 introduced the 'Nunsuch' walking doll, jointed, with composition head and papier mâché arms and legs. The doll was shown at the British Industries Fair and was proclaimed as 'a triumph for the British Doll Industry'. Queen Mary specially congratulated the manufacturers on the natural movement of the doll. On 1st October, 1924 Nunn registered the trade mark 'Colonel Bogey' no. 452,292 for dolls. In 1927 the company changed to furniture making, still under Mr Nunn's direction, and c1930 became 'Hygena Cabinet Co.'

Doll with china head coated in wax and composition body, marked 'Nunn & Smeed, Dolly Dimple No 1 Liverpool' (Pollock's Toy Museum).

NUNSUCH DOLL. c1923. Walking doll. See **Nunn, George Lawrence.**

NUNKEY. 1916. Stuffed rag doll, with high-clowned hat, made by Tah Toys Ltd.

NURSERY RHYME. 1958. Registered trademark for dolls no. B774,249. See **Mettoy Co.**

NURSERY RHYME CHARACTER DOLLS. c1935. Range of fabric dolls, representing nursery rhyme characters, made by Chad Valley Ltd. The dolls had fabric mask faces, and velveteen limbs, and were 14" high. Range included Little Miss Muffet, Mary Mary, Little Jack Horner, Little Boy Blue, Little Bo Peep and Simple Simon.

NURSERY RHYME DOLL CO. LTD. 1949. At 3 Oxford Street, London W1. Dealers in and manufacturers of dolls, toys and novelties.

NUTTALL, William Henry. 1893. Manchester, Lancashire. Together with James Henry Maden obtained patent no. 21052 on 6th November, 1893 for making celluloid dolls and masks moulded from hot sheets of celluloid.

OFFENBACHER, S. & CO. 1923-25. London. Handled dolls.

OGILWY, Robert. 1843-60. At 54 Tabernacle Walk, London. In 1852 Ogilwy was joined by George Teather to form the firm Ogilwy and Teather, but by 1856 each was working separately. Ogilwy made composition and waxed composition dolls.

OLD COTTAGE TOYS. 1948. Allangate, Rustington, Littlehampton, Sussex. Doll manufacturers, directors M. E. and S. Fleischmann. Firm's name registered as trademark no. 673861 on October 26th 1948.

Detail of Patent No 186232 for walking doll, Nunsuch, 1923.

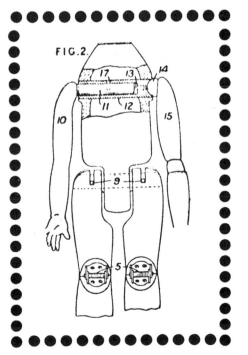

OLE BILL. 1915. 'Alpha' doll made by J.K. Farnell & Co. Reg. No. 662457. Stuffed cotton rag doll with pink velvet face, painted features and black tufted moustache, dressed as a First World War Soldier and based upon the character created by Captain Bruce Bairnsfather. His name appeared as

Old Bill in various war cartoons, the most famous of which was "Well, if you knows of a better 'ole, go to it" with Old Bill and his chum sharing a shell hole. The imperturbable, walrus-moustached Old Bill was warmly adopted as a symbol of the British Tommy, still preserving a sense of humour under the terrible conditions of the trenches on the Western Front. See **Farnell, J.K. & Co. Ltd.**

OLIDA DOLL & TOY MANUFACTURING CO. 1920. 46 St. James Place, Liverpool. Doll and toy manufacturers. In October, 1920 advertised baby dolls.

OMEGA. Trademark. See **British United Toy Manufacturing Co.**

ONAZOTE. Expanded ebonite compound used in toymaking. Manufactured by the Expanded Rubber Co. Ltd who also made Rubazote, a resilient rubber compound. Both products were proof against moisture, insects and bacteria.

OPPY. 1932. Registered trademark for dolls and toys. See **Dreyfus, Miriam.**

ORDENSTEIN, Richard. 1913. At 17 & 18 Basinghall Street, London, E.C. and 115 Fore Street, London E.C. Merchant. Registered trademark 'Ragtime Kids' no. 349,020 on 23rd January, 1913 for dolls.

ORGANDIE BEAUTY. c1948. Organdie dressed. See manufacturer **Toys (Components) Ltd.**

ORWELL ART INDUSTRIES. Before 1908. Dublin, Ireland. Made character dolls with unbreakable faces of a 'secret composition material'. The faces were painted and washable. Laura Starr had three of these dolls in her collection; one was an aged peasant woman and the others were young colleens.

OTTENBERG, I. & R. Rose Hill Street, Derby. Two artists who designed character dolls and historical figurines. Their models of Queen Elizabeth II and her maids in waiting, also dolls in Peeress robes (12"), were approved by the Board of Industrial Design as Coronation Souvenirs in 1953. The bisque parts were made by H. Schelhorn.

OUR BABY. See **Spear, J. W. & Sons.**

OUR LITTLE DREADNOUGHT. 1909. Character doll. See **Hughes & Son, Henry Jeffrey.**

OVERSEAS INDUSTRIAL AGENCY. 1917. At 36 Duke Street, London EC3. Factory in Richmond, Surrey. Made "Pep" dolls and toys. Unbreakable, jointed dolls.

OWEN, A. G. 1919. Doll and toy manufacturer.

'Ole Bill', 1915 (Bantock House Museum, Wolverhampton).

Trademark Overseas Industrial Agency.

OZOCERITE. 1884-1925+. A wax made from residue of petroleum and used for making dolls; tended to supplant beeswax, but was sometimes mixed with it.

Old Cottage toys, 1973.

'Mr Jolliboy', Gamage's catalogue, 1915.

Three 'Pep' dolls, 1917; cloth, unbreakable, jointed, washable.

145

'Pep' toys, 1917.

P. C. BLOGGS. 1934. English character doll from Excella range manufactured by L. Rees & Co. Ltd.

P.V.C. Plastic known as polyvinyl chloride which appeared in the 1930s. It can be produced in various forms, from a hard rigid material to a soft rubbery material for making dolls. P.V.C. pastes produced hollow dolls' heads by the technique of 'slush moulding'. Paste is poured into a mould which is then heated and cooled, thus forming a hard-wearing, warm-to-touch article.

PACHE & SON. 1852-1915. Lower Hurst St., Birmingham. Made artifical eyes for dolls, animals etc. including the 'Improved Artificial Eye'.

PACKERS (MANCHESTER) LTD. c1944. Sole distributor of dolls made by Webber's Dolls Ltd.

PALIGLIDE WALKING DOLLS. 1956. Palitoy doll range in various styles. The dolls have acetate bodies and limbs with flexible vinyl heads, sleeping eyes and rooted hair. Range includes: Sweet Sue and Penny, both 21″ tall, and Gillian and Sylvia, 20″ tall with 'mama' voices.

PALITOY. See **Cascelloid.**

PAL PETER. 1926. Doll made by J. K. Farnell & Co.

PANK. 1919. See **Harwin & Co. Ltd.**

PAPER DOLLS. Doll figures or miniature depictions of children, famous celebrities etc, accompanied by sheets of clothes for cutting out (or in some cases boxed sets of pre-cut clothes and models). The earliest, like

H.R.H. Princess Margaret and H.R.H. Princess Elizabeth, c. 1935.

the Juvenile Drama sets, were designed by artists and printed off copper plate engravings. Later, lithography was used. The figures were hand-coloured. Chromolithography was largely done in Germany before more modern colour printing techniques were adopted. See **Ackermann, Rudolph; Fuller S. & J.; Mathews, T & Co. Ltd; McCalmont Ltd.; Tuck, Raphael; Philmar Ltd.; Wallis J. & E. Mfg. Co.**

PAPER DOLLS (Crepe). A popular Edwardian pastime was making three-dimensional paper figures dressed in crepe paper. A booklet still published by Dryads of Leicester gives detailed instructions. Some of the dolls resemble those in the photograph of Aunt Gladys.

Several years ago a visitor to Pollock's Toy Museum handed over a cardboard box containing a number of figures made from crepe paper, saying 'My Aunt Gladys made these. Perhaps you will like them?'

Several years later the National Portrait Gallery sent us a photograph with a note saying 'Perhaps this is of interest to you?' On the back of the photograph is written 'My Aunt Gladys with some of her models in paper now in Leighton House Theatre Museum, Pollock's Toy Museum and the Australian War Museum, Canberra.'

PAPERWEIGHT EYES. Term used by some collectors for blown glass eyes with depth and detail similar to that found in fine paperweights.

Contemporary cut-out paper dolls with different paper outfits.

PAPIER MÂCHÉ DOLLS. Dolls made of type of composition defined (late 19c) as 'a tough plastic material made from paper pulp containing a mixture of size, paste, oil, resin or other substances; or from sheets of paper glued and pressed together'. Manufacturers of papier mâché dolls were the 'All British' Doll Manufacturing Co.' 1915.

PAPOOSKI, .The. 1916. Registered trade mark for dolls. See **Curling, Robert Sumner.**

PARADIS DES ENFANTS, LE. c1886. At 54 Oxford Street, London, W1. Toyshop owned by Parkins and Golto. Sold dolls, toys and games.

PARIAN. (Parian Bisque). A generic term referring to hard or soft paste porcelain. Defined in late 19c dictionary as 'hard, fine, half-vitreous porcelain resembling Carrara marble: used for objects of art and ornaments'. Invented during 1840s in England. In 1856 John Ridgeway at Cauldon Potteries advertised Parian products. In 1858 Goss & Co. were established in Staffordshire for the production of Parian and 'Ivory' porcelain busts. Parian dolls were popular in the 1870s.

Doll marked 'Paramount B.14301' (Pollock's Toy Museum).

PARKER, Ann. 67 Victoria Drive, Bognor Regis, Sussex. Since 1972 has designed and produced costume dolls made entirely by hand. She carves the original figure in plaster of Paris, then makes rubber moulds from which casts may be made in polyester resin. Outworkers assist after the original has been designed and dressed according to her patterns. Among some 25 models so far produced there are literary, historical and costume characters; the earliest being The Piccadilly Flower Girl, who has been called Eliza Dolittle, and one of the latest Beatrix Potter complete with rabbit. The artist researches very thoroughly both the aspect and background of her characters and brings them to life with a witty and sympathetic understanding. Her dolls are sold at Liberty's and Fortnum & Mason, London.

PARKINS & GOLTO. c1886. See **Paradis Des Enfants, Le.**

PASTE HEADS. Another name for composition heads.

PATCH. Introduced 1965 Pedigree doll, 'little sister' to Sindy, with her own wardrobe.

PATE. Term for the covering for the large hole found in the top of many dolls' heads. The wig is generally attached to the pate.

PATENTS. Dolls were probably not considered sufficiently important for their designs or improvements to them to be registered before the 19th century. The names occurring in the patents list are frequently the name of the 'patent' agent, especially when the design protected was registered from a foreign inventor. It is also apparent that patents were not always produced on a commercial scale, as a clever invention was not necessarily practical. Patents could exist for new materials, new methods, new designs and performance but Trademarks were registered for names of firms or brands. Patents were registered for a period of 15 years and then renewable.

PATRIOTIC DOLLS. Dolls produced during World Wars, intended to boost national feeling and morale. They were dressed in the First World War as Allies, Britannia, Victory, Tommy Atkins, Red Cross Nurse and during and after the Second World War as members of the various armed forces.

PATSIE. 1933. See **Merrythought Ltd.**

PATSY. c1949. See **Playlastic Toy Co. Ltd.**

PATSY. 1952. Trademark no. 707,767, registered on 3rd June, 1952 for dolls by Cascelloid Ltd.

PATSY DOLL. 1948. P.V.C. doll which drinks from its bottle and cries 'real' tears. Made by Cascelloid.

PATSY, THE WONDER DOLL. 1959. Palitoy doll patent no. 644965: 'She blows bubbles, says 'mama', cries real tears.' The doll also has sleeping eyes, drinks from her bottle and wets her nappy. Can be bathed and powdered.

PATTI PITTA PAT. 1967. Palitoy doll which walks with the aid of a concealed battery. She has rooted washable hair in blonde, brunette or auburn, and bright blue sleeping eyes, 54 cm high. She wears mini dress with lace-trimmed panties and buttoned shoes. Retail price £6 19s 11d.

PATTY COMFORT. c1907. See **Hot Water Bottle Dolls.**

PAUL. 1965. A teenage boy doll introduced as a boyfriend to 'Sindy' doll by Pedigree Dolls Ltd. He had vinyl head and limbs. Owing to lack of success, production of Paul was discontinued.

PAUL. 1975. 11″ soft cuddly Matchbox boy baby doll with all-vinyl body, sleeping eyes and rooted hair. The doll was originally manufactured for Lesney Products and Co. Ltd., in Spain, then later in East Germany.

PAWLEY. Fanny. See **Montanari, Richard Napoleon.**

PAYNE, John Edward. 1849. London. Obtained patent no. 12643 on 7th June, 1849, for moulding a doll out of gutta-percha combined with rubber.

PEACOCK. 1862. London. Exhibited wax and composition dolls in the London Exhibition. He advertised that he always had a stock of 1,000 dolls, both dressed and undressed. These included all kinds of composition dolls; among the latter were those made by the Pierottis. An Autoperipatetikos doll with untinted bisque head has been reported as marked 'J.

Patriotic Mascot dolls, 'Allies of the Great War' - advertisement in Hamley's catalogue, 1917.

Doll stamped 'Peacock' (Victoria and Albert Museum).

Peacock'. In 1889, he was established as a toyseller at the 'The Beaming Nurse', 525 New Oxford St, London.

PEACOCK, WILLIAM & SONS. 1903-11. London. Exported and distributed dolls.

PEARL POTTERY CO. 1894-1936. Brook Street, Hanley, Stoke-on-Trent. 1936-41 'New Pearl Pottery Co. Ltd.' Brook Street, Hanley. 1940 taken over by War Department. 1947 firm sold. See **Diamond Pottery Co. Ltd.**

PEBBLES FLINTSTONE. 1963. Rosebud doll based on the television cartoon character features in 'The Flintstones' with jointed arms and legs, and ponytail hairstyle. Retail price 49s 11d. Made by Rosebud Dolls Ltd.

PECK, Mrs Lucy Rebecca (née Brightman) born 22nd March, 1846, died 1930. 1894-1908. At 131 Regent Street, London, W1. 1908. 162 Shepherd's Bush Road, London. 1911. Kensington High Street, London. 1920. 306 Earl's Court Road, London, SW19. 1922-30. 279 King's Road, Kingston-upon-Thames, Surrey. She married Henry Peck, a pharmacist, 1876 and took up wax modelling from about 1894, producing both dolls for play and fashion models. She also ran a doll repair service from her shop in London, "The Dolls' Home". On retirement to Kingston in 1922 she took up clay modelling at Kingston Art School.

PECK, WILLIAM E. & CO. 1911. London Agent for Horseman, American doll manufacturer.

PEDIGREE AUTHENTIC PERIOD MINIATURES. 1959. Range of 7″ dolls dressed in period costume ranging from Tudor or Elizabethan to Late Hanover. Stuart period doll has a blue taffeta gown with white lace-edged neckline and sleeves, and white lace under sleeves. White apron, bodice trimmed with black ribbon bows.

PEDIGREE CHARACTER AND STORY BOOK DOLLS. 1955. Large range of 7″ dolls with moving eyes and jointed arms, representing typical 'characters' or story book personalities. Range includes: Bride, Mary had a little lamb, Little Bo Peep, P. C. 49, and Ride a Cock Horse.

A Lucy Peck-type doll (Pollock's Toy Museum).

PEDIGREE SOFT TOYS LTD. Before 1938-1977+. c1938 at Lines Bros. Factories Morden Road, Merton, London SW19. 1977: Canterbury, Kent. Doll and toy manufacturers. First firm in England to manufacture high-quality composition dolls by mass production methods. Every part could be produced in the factory. 1938: produced 'almost unbreakable composition dolls, 100% British'. All dolls have jointed arms and legs. Range includes 17″ high boy doll, with metal sleeping eyes, open mouth, teeth and tongue, dressed in romper suit and socks with ribbons. 17″ high girl doll with glass sleeping eyes and eyelashes, open mouth, teeth and tongue, dress and ribbon sash. Wig, hat, socks and shoes with buckles. 1942: registered trademark 'Pedigree' no, 620,731 for toys and dolls. 1948: Beauty Skin Dolls, Rubber Doll, the heads of which are injection-moulded with a light, but hard to break plastic material.

Woodflour composition baby doll, 20 ins., Pedigree 1938 (Pollock's Toy Museum).

Fitted with sleeping eyes and long lashes, the Beauty Skin doll was a realistic reproduction of a real baby. Her particularly attractive head was created by firm's own sculptor, who specializes in doll designs. The body and limbs have lightweight rubber skins, which feel just like human skin, and are filled with hygienic stuffing. The doll could be washed. Dresses were supplied in a variety of styles in the best quality materials available, e.g. embroidered art silk day dress and socks.

In 1955 a fully-jointed all-plastic walking doll was introduced, 21″ tall, able to kneel, talk, sleep and sit down, with Saran hair which could be brushed, combed and shampooed.

In 1963 Pedigree introduced the Sindy fashion doll, a 12″ teenage doll with free-moving arms and legs, hair which could be combed and styled, and many different outfits to wear. New up-to-date styles are introduced annually. The company also produce numerous accessories for Sindy

Plaster resin baby doll, 17 ins., Pedigree (Pollock's Toy Museum).

including a bed, wardrobe, bath and hairdryer etc.

In 1968 Pedigree was taken over by Rovex Industries Ltd., another Lines Bros. company, and doll production moved to Canterbury, and in 1972 after the collapse of the Lines Bros. Group, Rovex and Pedigree were taken over by the Dunbee Combex Marx Company.

c1974 introduced 'First Love'—a baby doll with jointed waist, that can be posed in almost any position. At the end of 1975 introduced 'My First Baby', a carry-around baby doll with sleeping eyes and turnable waist. The doll is made of polythene and P.V.C.

1977 range included 5 dolls modelled on Regency period characters of Kate Greenaway, two of them boy dolls. They are jointed at the arms, legs and waist. Also four Victorian-style dolls, 'Anna' and her horse 'Happytime' and 'Peter' with 'Sundancer'.

In 1980, after the collapse of the Dunbee Combex Marx Co., Pedigree Soft Toys Ltd. was taken over by Tamwade Ltd.

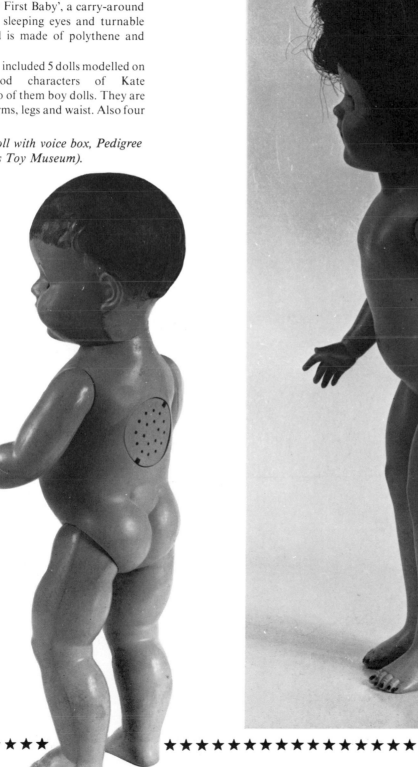

Hard plastic girl doll, Pedigree (Pollock's Toy Museum).

Hard plastic doll with voice box, Pedigree 1955 (Pollock's Toy Museum).

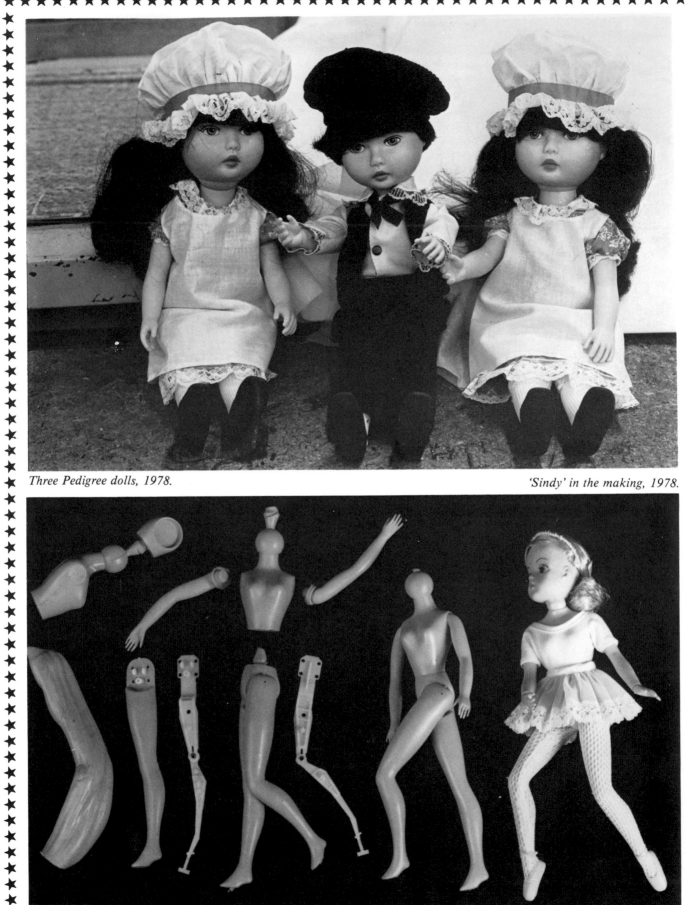

Three Pedigree dolls, 1978.

'Sindy' in the making, 1978.

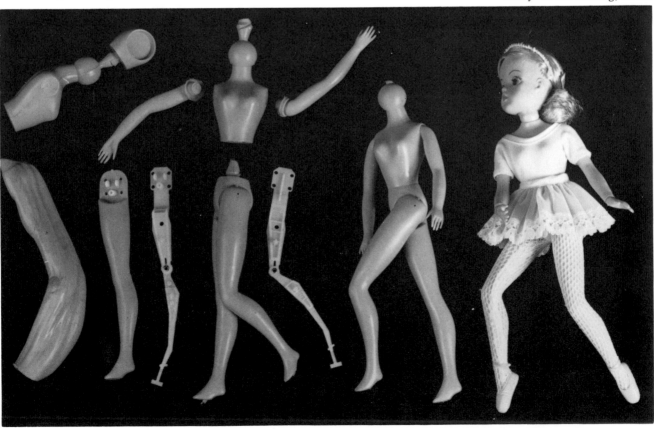

PEDLAR DOLLS. c1800-. Dolls representing street pedlars selling their wares. Mainly made for adult amusement. There is a typically English 12″ Pedlar Woman doll c1830, on display at Worthing Museum. She has a pickled apple head on a wood body; eyes of black and white glass, deep set; and open mouth carved out to leave a tongue. She wears a red-and-black striped flannel cloak and hood; and her tray of wares includes a tiny wood doll. C. & H. White of Milton, Portsmouth, Hampshire, made Pedlars, usually with heads of kid leather. See **Applehead Dolls** and **Salmon Pedlar Dolls.**

PEEBO DOLL. 1922. Trademark for dolls no. 422,184, registered on 9th January, 1922 by Arthur Graham, merchant, of 22 Highbury Place, London N5.

PEEK-A-BOO. 1911. Registered trade mark for dolls. See **Thompson, Bernard Home.**

PEEK-A-BOO. Introduced 1974. Fully articulated Pedigree doll. A pull of her string makes the doll's arms go up and down, either separately or together at random, so that she appears to hide behind her cot cover.

PEG DOLLS. See **Dryad Peg Dolls.**

PEGGIE. c1912. See **Wiederseim, Grace.**

PEGGY. c1923. Printed rag doll in a cloche hat and striped socks, made by Chad Valley.

PEGGY. c1927. 9½″ doll advertised by J. S. Sant Ltd.

PEGGY. 1937. See **Spear, J. W. & Sons.**

PELHAM PUPPETS. The firm established in 1947 by Bob Pelham at Marlborough, Wilts. The puppets, hand-made throughout, are meant for children, so are simple in manipulation and mostly 'tangle-free'. The idea first arose when Bob Pelham was in the Army in Germany in charge of a school with a hobbies workshop. Starting puppet-making in a small way he has created the interest, runs a puppet club 'Pelpups' and estimates his output at a million characters a year. Early examples: Bimbo the Clown; kilted, drunken MacBoozle; Fritzi and Mitzi; the witch; Mrs O'Blige, charwoman with mop and bucket. Today he makes more modern popular television puppets such as Muppets, Pink Panther, Snoopy, etc. Parana pine is used for bodies as it is suitable for holding screw eyes. The round wooden heads are of beech, sycamore or withy. Other heads are moulded from a traditional mixture of pumice powder and glue. (Photo shows Horse, Pinocchio, and Bimbo the Clown). Bob Pelham himself is the 'Pelpop'.

Wooden Pedlar doll, selling shellfish (Tunbridge Wells Museum).

PELICAN PRODUCTS. 1935. At 341 Kingsland Road, London E8. September, 1936, at River Street, Essex Road, London N.1. Made dolls' clothing and accessories and produced cuddly character dolls retailing at 1s 11d in 1936.

Take in in Galley 118 after Lesney Products

PENN, LETITIA. 20″ high. A famous wooden doll in the collection of the Pennsylvania Historical Society of U.S.A., dating from about 1699 and probably taken to America by a member of the William Penn family. There are many English wooden dolls in American collections, originally taken out by their pioneer owners and cherished as valuable heirlooms. Recently a little wooden torso was discovered behind the eaves of an old house in Salem, Mass. This relic has been restored as so little of the original fabric was left and the plaster nose completely gone.

PENNY. 1956. See **Paliglide Walking Dolls.**

PENNY. 1966. Rag doll: See manufacturers **Dean's Childsplay Toys Ltd.**

PENNY BRITE. 1964. See **De Luxe Toy Co. Ltd.**

PENNY PUPPYWALKER. Introduced 1971. A Palitoy doll who walks her own toy puppy dog.

PENNY, THE PERSONALITY DOLL. 1968. 17″ Pedigree teenage doll in 'up to the minute' fashions.

PENRHYN CASTLE. Bangor, Wales. A large collection of dolls from all parts of the world has gradually been built up since the early 1950's. A few date back to about 1820, and there are some mid 19c English wax dolls. There are portrait figures of First World War leaders, including Kitchener and French, and other uniformed dolls of c1940.

PENSHURST PLACE. Near Tonbridge, Kent. Collection of toys include a group of wax dolls in bridal costume.

PEP. 1917. Trade mark for 'unbreakable' jointed dolls made by the Overseas Industrial Agency.

PEPPER, John. 1866. Made gymnastic figures.

PERKS, E. S. A. 1916. Middlesex. Obtained two British patents: no. 104280 on 1st June 1916, for a doll with telescopic parts so that the size of the doll and its facial expression could be varied, and no. 105295 on 13th July 1916 for a doll provided with two pairs of eyes and different expressions which can be moved into position behind the eye sockets.

PERKS, R. M. 1924. Chislehurst, Kent. Registered trademark 'Dolfam' no. 448,814 on 29th May, 1924 for dolls.

Letitia Penn, taken to U.S.A. 1699. 20 ins. high, painted features on gesso over wood (Historical Association of Pennsylvania).

PERLS, CHARLES, MANUFACTURING CO. c1916-c1922. 18 Sussex Road, Holloway, London N. Made unbreakable composition doll heads which had the appearance of china; also celluloid headed dolls with composition bodies. In 1917 advertised 'Kiddykin' baby dolls' heads. Their trade mark was the initials of C. P. M. Co. In 1918, owing to the ill health of Charles Perls, the doll manufacturing side of the firm was put up for sale. In 1922 the firm was at 13 Paper Street, Cripplegate, London EC1. as importers and manufacturer's agents, advertising toys and fancy goods only.

PESKIN, J. (formerly Irish Toy Co.). c1918. 'Heo' Toy Works, N. Circular Road, Dublin, Ireland. Manufacturers of dolls and soft toys.

PESSY. 1932. Registered trademark for dolls and toys. See **Dreyfus, Miriam.**

PETALSKIN DOLLS. 1956. Palitoy flexible vinyl doll range in various styles including 'Lindy' with ponytail hair style, movable head, arms and legs, 13″ tall, dressed in waffle print design dress.

PETER. 1927. Soft doll in ribbed stockinette stuffed with kapok. Hand-painted face in washable colours. Manufactured by S. & L. Mfg Co.

PETER PAN. A fairy boy, the creation of James Barrie in a story called "The Little White Bird". Later adapted by the author as a play or children's pantomime, Christmas 1904, and has been acted in London each year since, the proceeds going, by Barrie's wish, to Great Ormond St. Hospital for Sick Children. Many character dolls of Peter and fairy Tinker Bell. See **Aerolite; Farnell, J.K. & Co. Ltd.**.

PETER PAN. Trademark used by Cecil Coleman Ltd.

PETER PAN. 1949. Registered trademark for dolls and dolls' garments. See **MacLeod, A. L.**

PETER PAN DOLL. Popular character doll based on hero of J. M. Barrie's children's stories 'Peter Pan' (1904); 'Peter Pan in Kensington Gardens' (1906); 'Peter Pan & Wendy' (1911). c1923 Peter Pan printed rag doll made by Chad Valley. 1926:

Peter Pan doll made by J. K. Farnell. c1936 Peter Pan soft doll dressed in green tunic and brown tights or vice versa, with fair wavy hair, made by J. K. Farnell. Registered design no. 816,525. This doll was made by arrangement with the Trustees of the J. M. Barrie 'Peter Pan' bequest. All royalties were paid to the Great Ormond Street Hospital for Sick Children, London. The ticket on the dolls showed Peter Pan entertaining a child in a hospital bed.

PETER & PATSY. 1933. Boy and girl dolls dressed in romper suits. Made by Dean's Rag Book Co. Ltd.

PETER & PAULINE. c1918. See **Daisy Dolls.**

PETER POLONY. 1936. See **Kutoy, Messrs.**

PETER & SUNDANCER. 1977. See **Pedigree Soft Toys Ltd.**

PETSEYMURPHY. 1919. Registered trademark for dolls and toys. See **Vincent, John.**

PHILIP TOY CO LTD. 1920. At 6 Philip Lane, Wood Street, London EC. Manufacturers, importers, exporters and dealers in dolls, toys and games, balls and books.

PHILMAR LTD. 62 Finsbury Pavement, London E.C.2. Toy manufacturers. 1954 lines included Fairy Princess cut-out doll with real hair and variety of dresses; Magnetic Joan, a cut-out doll with a concealed miniature magnet which holds in place a variety of dresses, each of which has a tiny piece of metal attached.

PHONOGRAPH DOLLS. 1889. (probable date of mass production of Edison's phonograph doll)-1925+
British patents for phonograph dolls include:
T. A. Edison no. 1644. 14th April 1878.
A. G. Brooks no. 616. 14th January 1888.
W. W. Jacques no. 5573. 2nd April 1889.
Thomas Bennett Lambert no. 9906. 1902.
A. M. Newman no. 6620. 14th March 1906.
E. C. R. Marks no. 19614. 3rd September 1906.
See also **Burgess, S. H.; Toitz, I.**

PHOTOGRAPHIC DOLLS. 1908. Adart Ltd. Dover St. Studios, London, Patent 22825, 1908 by H. E. Coston and A. Hamburger and Adart Ltd. Front and back of fabric doll bears photographs to be cut-out, sewn together and stuffed. The three-dimensional effect was obtained by photographing the original doll in a cylindrical mirror.

PICCANINNIES. 1929. 'Bonny Brown Babies' Soft stuffed, light and cuddly dolls Produced in a new soft material by Dean's Rag Book Co. for the A.1. series. Dressed in brightly-coloured frocks, they had jointed limbs and were made in three sizes, 14", 16" and 20".

PICCANINNY. See **Houghton, Elizabeth Ellen.**

PICKETT'S PHONO FIGURES. c1921. Elegant doll figures which fitted on to gramophone discs and danced to the melody, sold by S. H. Burgess.

PICKITOOP. 1935. Trademark no. 563,947 for dolls and soft toy animals registered by Dean's Rag Book Co. Ltd. on 19th October, 1935.

PICNIC PLAYSET. Introduced 1975. Doll and Play Environment, in a window display box. Manufactured by Lesney Products and Co.Ltd.

PIEROTTI. Family of wax-doll makers: According to family records they came from Volterra in Tuscany. Giovanni Pierotti (born 1730) owned vineyards and conducted a wine export trade. He married an Englishwoman (1750) and a son of the

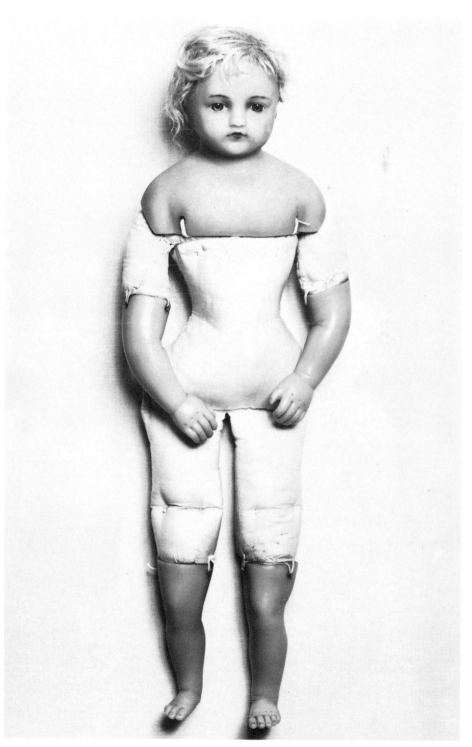

*Pierotti wax doll
(Victoria and Albert Museum).*

157

marriage, Domenico, came to England in 1770 when he was injured and needed medical treatment. Lodging with a Mrs Castelli, his mother's sister, at Portsmouth he learnt modelling and moulding with plaster, and wax-coated models and papier mâché dolls. He married an English girl in 1790, was naturalised in 1810 and founded a doll-making business in London. His ninth child, Anericho Cephas, born 1809 and known as Henry, later succeeded him in the wax doll business.

Henry was a fine craftsman and responsible for some of the best Pierotti models, with real hair, eyebrows and eyelashes. His shop at no. 108 Oxford St. was known as Crystal Palace after he had shown dolls at that Exhibition. (See advertisement printed in box). In 1828 Henry married Jane Gumbrell, and they too had a large family—four girls and five boys. Henry is said to have modelled some of his dolls on them: this could explain the Italianate look of certain Pierotti dolls and

Display of Pierotti tools and dolls' parts (Toy Museum, Rottingdean).

their quite beautiful Titian-shade hair. After the death of Henry (1871) the business was continued by his son Charles William, and when he in turn died of lead poisoning—a hazard of the industry—in 1892, his widow continued doll-making with her sons' help, marketing them through Hamley's and other West End shops. Mrs Pierotti dressed the dolls by hand with the help of her daughters; the two sons Henry and Charles Ernest having made the dolls in the traditional way, from molten wax heated over a kitchen range in a large cauldron and poured into plaster moulds. A selection of the moulds and the tools and accessories used by the Pierotti family is exhibited at Rottingdean Museum Sussex; it was given by one of the family after Charles retired in 1935.

PIERRETTE DOLLS. c1914-c1938. Dolls dressed in female version of Pierrot's costume. Publicised as 'Lucky Mascots'— 'Dainty little ladies dressed in beautiful shades of rich art silk, Stuffed with kapok. For the boudoir, motor, or as playthings.' English manufacturers include:
c1914 Dean's Rag Book Co. Ltd

c1916 Speights Ltd.
1916 Knight Bros. & Cooper Ltd.
1916 Marcuse, Day & Co. Ltd.
c1920 Fairyland Toy Manufacturing Co. Ltd.
PIERROT DOLLS. c1914-c1938. Boy dolls dressed in pierrot (clown) costumes. English manufacturers include:
1914 Henry Jeffrey Hughes & Son.
1916 Knight Bros. & Cooper Ltd.
1916 Marcuse, Day & Co. Ltd.
c1920 Fairyland Toy Manufacturing Co. Ltd.
1920 Art Toy Manufacturing Co. Ltd.

PILLAR DOLLS. See **Frozen Charlottes.**

PINCUSHION DOLLS. Ornamental dolls designed for use as pincushions. Making them was a popular pastime among 19th century women. They were made with manufactured head attached to the body, and with full or crinoline skirt, stuffed and sealed at the base to form a dense cushion. There is an example of an 1820 jointed pincushion doll at the London Museum, given by the late Queen Mary.

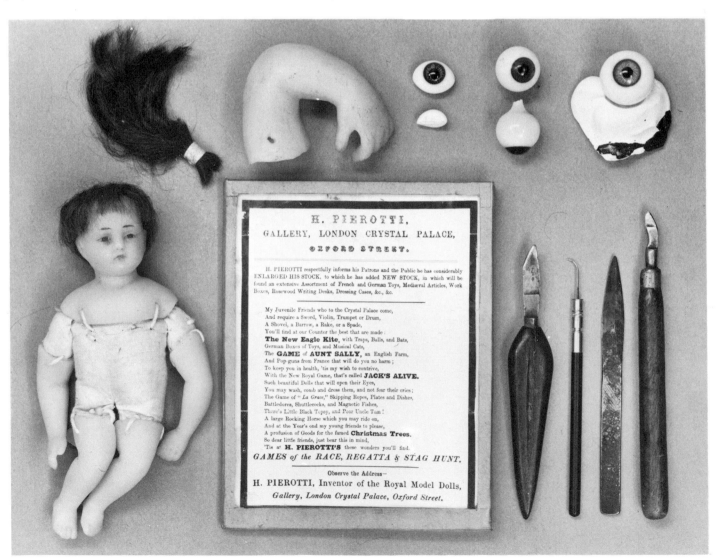

PINKA-BOO. 1921. Registered trademark for dolls, See **Polmar Perfumery Co.**

PINKIE DOLL. 1921. See **Hughes, Herbert Edward.**

PINOCCHIO. 1940. Rubber doll made in the likeness of the Disney film character by Chad Valley Co. Ltd.

PIN-UP DOLLS. 1952. Pedigree range of dolls with, according to their trade description, 'magic nylon hair which may be shampooed and play-waved with Pin-Up Play Perm outfit supplied.' Six models in teenage dresses; brunettes Alice, Brenda and Diana; and blondes Celia, Enid and Frances.

PIPPA. Introduced 1968. Pedigree standing baby doll with four different outfits. Retail price 47s 11d to 59s 11d according to style.

PIPPA. Introduced 1972. 6″ fashion doll by Palitoy with different outfits and accessories.

PIRATE TWIN, The, and PIRATE TWINS, The. 1929. Associated trademarks nos. 504,685 and 505,517 registered by Faber & Faber Ltd. on 22nd July, and 23rd August 1929, for dolls.

PITFIELD, William. 1868-94. At 17 de Beauvoir Crescent, London N. Made wax dolls.

PIXIE. c1923. Printed rag doll stuffed with down. Marketed under brand name 'Aerolite' made by Chad Valley.

PIXY AND DIXIE. 1935. Baby Bunting style soft dolls in plush with spotted trousers and spotted bow ties, rabbit ears and mask faces. Dixie was a black doll. Made by Merrythought Ltd.

PLASTER. (Plaster of Paris) 17th century-1925+. Used for making dolls and doll parts. Easily breakable.

PLASTER DOLL CO. c1923. Ribble Bank Mills, Preston, Lancashire. Made dolls. Company failed on 5th July, 1923 owing to shortness of capital.

PLASTEX. 1937. Trademark no. 581,099 registered on 4th November. 1937 by Cascelloid Ltd. for dolls, parts of dolls and toys.

PLASTIC DOLLS. Dolls made of natural or synthetic organic materials which can be moulded. A few dolls were called 'plastic' even in the 19th century.

In 1947 J. Cowan advertised 'The Type of Dolls to Come: New dolls in Art Plastics', and in 1948 'Sleeping Baby Doll, all plastic, injection-moulded, manufactured by Rodnoid, Art Plastics Ltd.' In 1952 specialist makers of injection-moulds advertised Nickel-Cobalt Carbon Alloy Die inserts or complete tools with electro-formed cavities: London and Scandinavian Metallurgical Co. Ltd.

British Manufacturers of plastic dolls include: S. Hanreck c1917; Cascelloid; Ivorine Mfg. Co.; Mitchell Plastics Ltd.; Mitchell & Hardy Plastics Ltd.; Moritz & Chambers; Nene Plastics; AA Products Ltd.; and D. G. Todd & Co. Ltd.

PLASTOLITE. 1917. A non-flammable plastic paste used for moulding dolls' heads and bodies. 'Plastolite' trademark registered in France by J. Roger Gault for the paste and for articles made with it. Plastolite dolls' heads were manufactured by Bedington Liddiat & Co. Ltd. in 1917.

PLAYCHARM. 1951. Registered trademark for dolls. See **Webber's Dolls Ltd.**

PLAYLASTIC TOY CO. LTD. 1947-49. London. Manufacturers of dolls and toys. On 19th September 1947, together with P. Klein they obtained patent no. 636968 for bendable sponge-rubber toys in human or animal likeness. July 1949 they introduced dolls 'Buster', 'Patsy', 'Trixie' and 'Tommy'.

PLAYSAFE DOLLS. 1955. See **Wendy Boston.**

PLAYTHINGS PAST MUSEUM. Beaconwood, Beacon Lane, near Bromsgrove, Worcestershire. Mrs Betty Cadbury's collection of Dolls and Toys may be visited by parties of between 20 and 35 persons by arrangement.

PLAYTIME DOLLS. 1925. Range of 4 small dolls 9½″ high. Retail price 6d made by Dean's Rag Book Co. Ltd.

PLAYWEAR MANUFACTURING CO. 1965. 5 St. Mary's Road, London N8. Dollswear manufacturer producing outfits to fit all dolls from 10″ to 24″, and a complete range for 12″ teenage dolls.

PLAZTOY. c1949. Trademark of Masks & Mouldings Ltd.

PLOPPY CHARACTER DOLLS. 1971. 12″ baby dolls with soft bodies filled with plastic and foam. 'Bedsie', 'Bitty' and 'Booful Baby Beans'. Manufactured by Mattel Ltd. In 1973 the range was increased to include 'Biffy', 'Cubby', 'Puppy' and 'Cry Baby Beans'.

PLUCKY. English pottery-head doll dressed in the blue uniform and red tie of a wounded soldier (1914-18 war). It carries a tag label entitled 'Plucky: The Big Boy Blue, Hero Souvenir Doll by E.B.B.S. Ltd.', also the trademark Ellarco of Ellison Rees & Co. Photo: courtesy of Mrs Kremer, Dolls in Wonderland.

PLUMB, Henry. 1865-68. 115a City Road, London & in 1868 at Change, East Road, London N.

PLUSH. A kind of silk cloth woven like velvet, but with longer and softer nap. The term was first introduced about 1629, which was probably the time when it was first manufactured. It was commonly used for all sorts of long-hair cloth especially suitable for soft cuddly toys, animals, teddy bears etc. See **Art Toy Manufacturing Co.; Burman Ltd; Cinders; Shirley Dolls.**

PODGIE DOLLS. 1935. Registered design no. 802,955. Plush dolls with mask faces, zip fastener inside pocket to hold child's nightwear etc. Made by J. K. Farnell & Co. Ltd.

POLLARD, E. & CO. LTD and ROBINS, F. E. 1923. Obtained patent no. 221280 on 8th June, 1923 for a rotating joint connecting two members of a doll.

POLLOCK, M. B. 1931. Obtained patent no. 388736 on 29th January, 1931 for a doll whose facial expression can be made to change by the use of a flexible distortable material, e.g. rubber.

POLLOCK'S TOY MUSEUM. 1 Scala St, London W.1. 01-636 3452. A small private museum in contiguous 18th and 19th century houses off Tottenham Court Road. The exhibits, for the most part gifts or loans from the museum's well-wishers, are mainly set in picture frames or antique showcases which enhance their evocative quality. The flavour is international throughout—from the optical, mechanical and street toys to the toy theatres, folk toys and dolls; but of special interest among the latter are a number of 19th century English wax dolls, several English dolls of the First World War period, and examples of early Dean's Rag Dolls and Norah Wellings dolls. On the ground floor is a museum shop with a wide range of old-fashioned toys and dolls for sale, including antique wooden 'Dutch' dolls and modern reproduction wax, bisque and rag dolls.

Founded in 1955 by Mrs Marguerite Fawdry, the museum was constituted a non-profit making Educational Trust in 1968. Entrance is by contribution of 30p for adults, 15p for children and students. The Museum takes its name from Benjamin Pollock, the last of the Victorian toy theatre printers, whose shop in East London was for 60 years a familiar haunt of Robert Louis Stevenson, Serge Diaghilev, Charlie Chaplin and other enthusiasts.

POLLYANNA. c1962. Rag doll drawn and hand-printed by Joy Wilcox.

POLMAR PERFUMERY CO. 1921. London. Manufacturing perfumers. Registered trademarks I'Mere no. 413,169 and 'Pinka-Boo' no. 413,170 on 8th March, 1921 for dolls.

159

POLYSTYRENE. Method of fashioning dolls in this plastic material is as follows. The model is first fashioned in clay or plasticine, then a resin prototype is placed in a vat which contains constantly moving water to which copper has been added. The model remains immersed for about six weeks, during which time a copper deposit builds up over the original. Then the mould is made in finely-tempered metal from which other mouldings can be made.

The dolls after moulding are cleaned and hand-painted after colour spraying. The material polystyrene is especially valuable for models as it is impervious to water and resistant to changes in temperature or attack by fungi.

POLYTHENE. The discovery of plastic revolutionised the toy business since it possessed many qualities making it especially suitable for their manufacture.

Polythene was first discovered in 1933 in the research laboratories of I.C.I. It was found that ethylene gas subjected to pressures above 15,000lb per square inch underwent a chemical change to form a white solid. The material had useful features in that it had electrical insulating properties and chemical resistance so its use for cables etc. was evident. By 1937 continuous testing was able to demonstrate its value and full-scale manufacture was undertaken in time for it to prove a vital help to the war effort in radar equipment. After the war its use was exploited in making toys as well as domestic articles. The outstanding property of polythene is its inherent flexibility. It is very tough and does not splinter or crack when dropped or trodden on. It is lightweight, floats in water, is easily moulded, and will take good impression of intricate detail. It is both waterproof and washable so is highly hygienic for children.

POMERANTZ, A. F. & SONS. 1925. London. Importers of dolls. Their brand name was 'Pomtoys'. Firm was succeeded by M. Pomerantz Ltd. in 1946.

POOKSIE, THE WAR BABY. 1914. Caricature baby doll, made of china, with moving arms and in 3 sizes. He was created by Mabel Lucie Attwell, and manufactured by Wiltshaw & Robinson Ltd. The doll is naked except for a soldier's cap and belt; it has goo-goo eyes and a heart on its chest. Retail prices 1/-, 1/6 & 2/-. John Green Hamley registered trademark 'Pooksie' no. 358,234 on 30th January, 1914.

POOLE, Edward. 1852-65. 14 Wellington Row, Bethnal Green, London. Made wax and composition dolls.

POOLE, John W. 1840-60. At 8 Twisters Alley, Bunhill Row, London. Made wooden dolls. L. Poole, his son, was listed at the same address from 1852-1855, also making wooden dolls.

POOLE, William. 1852-55. At 3 Commercial Street, Whitechapel, London. Made wax and composition dolls.

POP. 1930. Trademark no. 512,473 registered by the Daily Sketch and Sunday Graphic Ltd. for 'toys, dolls and sporting articles in the form of character reproductions.' The cartoon character 'Pop' was created by John Miller Watt and appeared in the 'Daily Sketch' from 1921-1964; he was 'balding, brow-beaten, walrus-moustached and bulging at the buttons'.

POPEYE. 1936. Doll based on American spinach-eating cartoon character of a sailor-man with pipe in mouth, Popeye the Sailor Man. Registered design no. 804,398. Manufactured by Dean's Rag Book Co. Ltd.

POPEYE. c1939. China doll representing the popular cartoon character 'Popeye, the Sailor Man'. The doll came in various sizes and was manufactured by Cecil Coleman Ltd.

POPPER, F. & POPPER, E. 1945. Obtained two patents no 589223 relating to eye mechanism in a dolls' head, and no. 589224 relating to eyes in a doll's head, on 20th March, 1945.

POPPET 23. 1976. Brand name of walking talking dolls, manufactured by Palitoy.

POPPETS or LITTLE BABIES. 18th century terms for 'dolls' as written in Richardson's Dictionary in 1720.

POPPY DOLLS. c1920. Jointed composition doll. See Lloyd, Mayer & Co.

POPSY POSY DOLL. 1970. Pedigree doll with jointed arms, legs, feet, neck and waist. 3 different outfits.

POPULAR. 1935. Doll series manufactured by Chad Valley Co. Ltd. Range includes 19" doll dressed in Tyrolean costume.

PORCELAIN. True porcelain is distinguished from pottery by being a vitreous, translucent substance coated with a hard, translucent glaze. It was widely used for doll-making in Germany and France from about the 1820s but it is doubtful whether there was ever a commercial output from the famous English factories. Chelsea 'toys' are sometimes mentioned, but this was a name given to small luxury figurines, decorative stoppers etc. See also Potteries.

PORCELITE CO, The. 1918. Portland Works, Newcastle Street, Burslem, Stoke-on-Trent. Manufacturers of dolls' limbs.

PORTER, Ralph. 1904-1905. 86 Tottenham Court Road, London W. Made dolls.

PORTRAIT DOLLS. Dolls portraying real people or fictional or fairytale characters. Royalty or theatrical personalities are especially popular. Often the similarity to the real person lies in the hair and clothing. English manufacturers who made these types of doll include Chad Valley Ltd. and J. K. Farnell.

POSY BUDS. c1925. Dolls made by Dean's Rag Book Co. Ltd. 12" high, dressed in felt: 'Lilac', 'Iris', 'Ivy', 'Heather', 'Hyacinth' and 'Rosebud'. Retail Price 7/6.

POSY DOLLS. c1925. Felt-dressed range of A1 dolls made by Dean's Rag Book Co. Ltd.

POTTERIES, The. There have been persistent rumours of early doll-making in the Staffordshire potteries (See Caughley and Cauldon), but it has yet to be proved as no attested examples have come to light. It is true that from the 1740s very attractive figurines were produced by the Astbury and Whieldon potters. These so-called 'image toys' were moulded in rather rustic patterns, sold cheaply and are now very well worth collecting. Cheap stoneware dolls for bazaar sale were made during the Victorian Period. The outstanding period for actual play-doll production was during the 1914-18 war, when the Staffordshire potters were instructed by the Board of Trade to make doll parts after their importation from Germany was forbidden. The industry died a natural death soon after the end of the war, when the superior German trade was resumed. See following entries.

Bailey and Baxter
Bailey Potteries
Beswick, J. W.
Blue John Pottery Ltd.
British Doll Mfg. Co.
Diamond Pottery Co.
Diamond Tile Co. Ltd.
Dodd, Thomas
Doll Pottery Co. Ltd.
Dolls' Accessory Co.
Doric China Co.
Dura Porcelain Co.
Elite Doll Co.
Empire Porcelain Co.
Goss, W. H.
Hancock & Sons
Hewitt & Leadbeater (Hewitt Bros)
Howard Pottery
Keats & Co.
Mayer & Sherratt
Pearl Pottery Co. Ltd.
Porcelite Co.
Potteries Doll Co.
Potteries Toy Co. (British Toy Co.)
Ridgeway, J. W.
Royal Crown Pottery
Silver Doll Series
Smith, W. H. & Son
Smith & Hoyle

Townsend, George
Wolstan Doll Co. Ltd.
Wiltshaw & Robinson Ltd.

POTTERIES DOLL CO. 1914- William Street, Stoke-on-Trent. Doll manufacturers. The company was established in November 1914 by several well-known ladies of Stoke. In July 1915, their range included a baby doll, a soldier, a sailor and a pierrot. Queen Mary was presented with a doll made by the firm.

Group of dolls made by The Potteries Doll Co., 1915.

The assembly room at the works of The Potteries Doll Co., 1915.

POTTERIES TOY CO. 1915. At 29 High Street, Stoke-on-Trent, Staffordshire. 1917: premises extended to include 25 and 27 High Street, Stoke-on-Trent. (The Wardol Works). The company was registered in July, 1915 and was established in order to take over the business of the British Toy Co. The company directors were G. H. Rittner, W. H. Goss, Miss Deakin and Miss W. Green. The firm assembled doll heads and parts made by Goss & Co. of which they had the monopoly. The dolls had cloth-stuffed bodies, jointed and unjointed limbs and bisque heads. In the 1917 British Industries Exhibition, the firm exhibited a group of dolls representing 'The Allies', the central figure being 'Britannia'.

POUTING PRETTY. 1967. 12″ Palitoy doll which can smile or pout. Retail price 34s 11d.

PRATT, Helen Whately. See **Helen Whately Dolls.**

PRECINCT TOY COLLECTION, The. 38 Harnet Street, Sandwich, Kent. A collection made by the museum's founder, Mrs Gandolfo. It includes a wide range of magnificent period dolls.

PRECIOUS. 1935. Doll made by Dean's Rag Book Co.

A 'Wardol', made by The Potteries Toy Co. Ltd., 1917.

PRECIOUS BABY DOLL. 1968. 17″ soft, moulded vinyl doll with moving eyes and bouffant hair. Comes with travelling car seat and accessories. Retail price 69s 11d. Manufactured by Favourite Toys Ltd.

PRESTON, A. M. London Patent 11434. 1910 for a dancing doll.

PRESTON, Chloe. c1925. Doll designer who worked for J. K. Farnell & Co. Ltd. Her designs included 'William & Mary' dolls and terra-cotta mascot figures.

PRETTY BABY. 1957. Palitoy baby doll series including 18″ doll with soft flexible head, body and limbs in petal skin vinyl and sleeping eyes; dressed in poke bonnet, smocked frock, nappie underskirt and socks.

PRETTY MISS KISS. 1967. Palitoy doll. 'Put her to your cheek, squeeze her arm and she'll give you a real kiss.' Washable hair, red, blonde or black; dressed in mini dress with toning pants.

PRETTY PEEPERS. 1956. 22″ Pedigree doll with fully jointed knees, she can walk, sit and kneel. She has golden Saran hair and her eyes can change colour, look all ways, and open and close whatever her position.

PRIEST HOUSE, The. West Hoathly, West Sussex. Collection includes about 35 Victorian and Edwardian dolls.

PRIEUR, Miss Marie. 1917-18. London. Made dolls.

PRIMROSE DOLLS. 1960. Doll range by Young & Fogg Rubber Co. Ltd. Range includes 13″ jointed doll with rooted Saran hair in blonde bubble cut, and with sleeping eyes. She is dressed in blue and white cotton dress, with white undies, socks and shoes.

PRIMROSE DOLLS AND BABIES. 1926. Doll range sold by L. Rees & Co. (Games and Toys January 1926 p.67)

PRIMROSE LEAGUE TOYMAKING INDUSTRY. c1918. At 64 Victoria Street, London SW1. Dealt in toys, games and dolls made by British children. The Primrose League was a political organisation championing the cause of the Conservative party.

PRINCE CHARMING. c1949. Plastic boy baby doll which feeds and wets and has sleeping eyes and voice. See manufacturers **Mitchell & Hardy (Plastics) Ltd.**

PRINCE EDWARD. 1938. Doll made in the likeness of Prince Edward of Kent. Made by Chad Valley.

PRINCE OF WALES & PRINCESS ROYAL. c1840+. Two small dolls 6 inches high representing the Prince of Wales and Princess Royal and originally belonging to them as children.

PRINCESS. 1920. Classic doll made by Speights Ltd.

PRINCESS. 1922: See **Lawton Doll Co.**

PRINCESS DOLLS. c1919. Unbreakable fully-jointed dolls. See manufacturers **Tattersall, J. Ltd.**

PRINCESS DOLLS. 1925. Series of fabric dolls made by Dean's Rag Book Co. Ltd. They were dressed in velveteen coats and bobble hats, trimmed with white 'bear plush'. They carried fur muffs and their facial expressions varied. Dressed in 6 different colours, sizes 12″ to 36″. Queen Mary bought one of these dolls at the 1925 British Industries Fair.

PRINCESS ELIZABETH. 1937: See **Spear, J. W. & Sons.**

PRINCESS PIPPA. Introduced 1974. De luxe dancing version of Palitoy's Pippa doll. Dressed in ball gown and with ankle-length hair.

PRISCILLA. 1920. Rag doll from A1 series dressed in a richly-coloured frock and sunbonnet of the Victorian era.

PRISCILLA. 1924. See **Art Dolls; Miniature Models;** and **Sant, J. S.**

PRISCILLA. 1938. Doll with plastex head made by Cascelloid. Registered design no. 824,206. Described as 'Our Miss Prim' in a 1938 advertisement.

PROFITEER. 1921. China character doll made by Dolls' Accessory Co.

PRUDENCE KITTEN Co. Ltd. 1950 at 11 The Grove, Highgate Village, London N.6. 1954 at 31 Clarges Street, London W.1. Doll and toy manufacturers and merchants. The company was run by Annette Mills, a popular television personality of the 1950s. She was well known for her children's programmes featuring the string puppet 'Muffin the Mule' and glove puppet 'Prudence Kitten'. Registered trademarks 'Prudence Kitten', no. 692,588 on 29th Sept. 1950 for dolls, and 'Puffer Dog', no. B728,711 on 2nd April 1954 for dolls, card games and board games.

PUCK. Fairy tale character of goblin or mischievous sprite, popular with doll manufacturers from c1880-1930. English manufacturers include Dean's Rag Book Co. Ltd. who produced 'Puck and his family' rag cut-out sheets and 'Puck', an A1 rag doll, in 1922. Dean's produced Baby Puck (small size); Master Puck (large size); and Silkeen Puck in plush in 1935.

PUCKANINNY. c1936. Puck-like soft character doll, wearing spotted outfit with bows. Has peaked head, goo-goo eyes and elephant ears, with brown or flesh-pink face. Made by Dean's Rag Book Co. Ltd.

PUNCH. A puppet with red face, hooked nose, projecting chin, humped back and protruding stomach, based on the Italian Polichinello and introduced to London about 1660 by travelling Italian showmen. The diarist Pepys recorded a performance in 1662 as 'very pretty'. Dolls seem soon to have been made in the Punch Image. A letter from Sir Thomas Browne (1682) mentions his grandson's having a Punch and his wife a straw King & Queen and ladies of honour. As puppet or doll it has remained popular ever since.

PUNCH. 1930. Stuffed rag jumping-Jack type puppet made by Dean's Rag Book Co. Ltd.

PUNFIELD, Frederick William. 1922-25+. London. Wholesale manufacturer of celluloid dolls. Sole British Agent for the Rhenische Gummi und Celluloid Fabrik Co.

PUSH-ALONG PIXIE. Introduced 1968. 18″ drink/wet with 24″ tubular steel push chair, from the Bluebell range by D. G. Todd & Co. Ltd.

PUSH-ALONG POPSIE. Introduced 1968. 16″ drink/wet doll with 23″ polystyrene pushchair. Dressed in red, removable coat and dress, turn-back bonnet, white mittens, nylon tights and white leatherette shoes. Retail price 82s 6d. Manufactured by Rosebud Mattel Ltd.

PYJAMA GIRL. 1920. Classic doll made by Speights Ltd.

QUANT, Mary. London fashion designer from 1950s to present day. She made her name during the era of 'boutiques and mini skirts'. The dolls 'Chelsea Girls' wore the sort of fashion promoted by Mary Quant at her King's Road, Chelsea boutique.

QUEEN VICTORIA DOLL. Portrait wax doll of Queen Victoria, on display at Bethnal Green Museum, London E.

QUEEN VICTORIA'S DOLLS. Her collection of Dutch dolls dressed to represent opera and theatre personalities and others. The dolls are in the Museum of London.

QUEEN VICTORIA TEACOSY DOLL. c1880. See **Teacosy** and **Telephone Dolls**.

QUINN, N. 1946. Together with A. & A. Merchandising Co. Ltd. obtained patent no. 626901 on 19th December, 1946 for a movable eyelid for doll's eye.

QUINTEX. c1949. Plastic dolls advertised as 'warm and soft to touch'; 'can be bathed in hot or cold water'. Manufactured by AA Products Ltd.

QUOSHIWOG. 1951. Registered trademark for soft toys, dolls and playthings. See manufacturers, **Carter, H. W. & Co. Ltd.**

Portrait doll of Queen Victoria (Bethnal Green Museum).

Part of a collection of 132 Dutch Dolls dressed by Princess Victoria at the age of 12.

R. A. C. SCOUT DOLL. 1930. See **Road Patrol Scouts.**

R. M. S. "QUEEN MARY" MASCOT. 1936 Saluting sailor mascot doll manufactured by J. K. Farnell & Co. Ltd.

RABLE, J. G. 1948. Obtained patent no. 652572 on 18th October, 1948, for a doll made in the shape of a hot-water bottle.

RADIO DOLL. 1949. 'Mignon', a large doll with a small loudspeaker in its body. When the doll is plugged into a radio it appears to be 'talking and singing'. See manufacturers, **Williams & Steer Manufacturing Co. Ltd.**

RAG DOLLS. One of the first mentions of commercial rag dolls was in connection with the prize-winning display by Madame Augusta Montanari at the 1851 Exhibition. Handmade textile dolls must date from very far back and the British Museum shows a Roman example discovered here. Strong calico was used for doll bodies for English wax and papier mâché dolls; but by the 1880s printed textile was sold for making dolls, first hand-printed (See Dean's Rag Book Co. Ltd.), then machine-printed in colour.

Many home-made rag dolls could be classed as "emergent" dolls, a term coined by Edward Lovett to describe dolls made of various accessible materials by folk too poor to buy toys, when toys were in short supply (wartime), or, of course, as a needlework or craftwork hobby—a labour of love.

The London Rag doll was a soft-bodied doll with wax mask face. See **Montanari, Richard Napoleon;** and **Rich, William.**

The growing interest in Victoriana which marked the post-war years in Great Britain was reflected in the reappearance of printed rag dolls to cut and sew. This initiative did not come however from within the established toy trade, but from talented young textile students, fresh from Art School. One of the first of these dolls was Polyanna, drawn and hand-printed by Joy Wilcox, followed closely in 1963 by Little Lizzie, designed by Maria Wood for Pollock's Toy Museum.

Over the years other cut-and-sew dolls have appeared, some only for quite short runs, while others, like those of Louise Elliott and Anne Wilkinson, have continued to sell steadily.

Rag doll manufacturers include:
All British Doll Mfg. Co.
Art Fabric Mfg. Co.
Art Toy Mfg. Co. Ltd.
Austin & Gray Ltd.
Bell & Francis.
Mabel Bland-Hawkes
British Novelty Co.
Cellaline Co.
Chad Valley

Dean's Rag Book Co. Ltd.
Dell & Co.
Dolphitch Mfg. Co. Ltd.
East London (Fed. Toy) Factory
Gorleston Toy Industry
Rebecca Haynes
Cecil K. Heywood
H. J. Hughes & Son
Leonard Ibbetson
Isaacs Family
J. Kleiner & Sons Ltd.
L. J. Littman
Nottingham Toy Industry

RAGS. c1938. Palitoy character boy doll with plastex head, described as 'the bad boy of a good family'. Registered design no. 824,207.

RAG TIME. c1914. Rag Doll series. See manufacturers, **Dean's Rag Book Co. Ltd.**

RAGTIME KIDS. 1913. Registered trademark for dolls. See **Ordenstein, Richard.**

RAINBOW. 1959. Registered trademark for dolls and puppets. See **Dagmar, Margot Ltd.**

RAINPROOF GIRL. c1946. Doll dressed in transparent raincoat and cap etc. Sold by J. Cowan (Dolls) Ltd.

Illustration from 'The Story of Two Dolls' by Mary Russell Mitford, showing two home-made rag dolls.

RALPH, H. S. c1923. At 2 Woodpecker Road, Clifton Hill, New Cross, London SE14. Importer and exporter of dressed and undressed dolls, dolls' heads, wigs, arms, bodies, hands and legs etc. Specialised in trade repairs.

RANDALL & WOOD LTD. 1954-1958. At 43 Caledonian Road, London N7. Doll manufacturers. Registered two trademarks for dolls: 'Johnnie', no. 772,591 on 30th December, 1957, and 'Miss Linda', no. 784,815 on 5th December, 1958.

RANSOM, Sidney. 1924. At 189 Bristol Road, Birmingham. Doll manufacturer. Registered trademark 'Sabo' no. 448,790 on 29th May, 1924, for dolls wholly or partly made of celluloid.

RATCLIFF, G. R. 1948. London. Obtained two British patents. No. 640217 on July 20th 1948, for 'sleeping eyes' which are actuated by a gravity arm, but move gradually in the closing direction only when the doll is rocked from side to side. No. 646308 on 22nd March, 1948, for dolls' heads with eyes made separately from main structure of the head; specially the 'sleeping eye' assemblage which secures the eye.

RATTLES. 1936. Doll made by East London (Federation Toy) Factory.

RAY OF SUNSHINE. c1916. Doll in Pollock's Toy Museum Collection: marked "Ray of Sunshine English make, 3½." Possibly made by Hancock and Sons.

A 'Rompa' stockinette doll made by Rayburn Townsend, 1924.

RAYBURN TOWNSEND CO. LTD. 1924-25. Regent House, 89 Kingsway, London W.C.2. Manufacturers of dolls and cuddly toys. Made the 'Rompa' series of dolls and toys, including the Rompa baby doll and the Rompa Policeman. The dolls are covered with stockinette and filled with non-absorbent kapok. The faces are hand-painted and can be washed with soap and water.

RED CROSS NURSE. A popular doll type especially during World War I. English manufacturers include:
Bell & Francis 1916
Stephen Erhard 1915
Marlborough Mfg. Co. c1918
Nell Foy & Co. 1918

RED HOUSE MUSEUM & ART GALLERY. Quay Road, Christchurch, Dorset. The collection includes a display of about 40 dolls, including one of the many parian portrait dolls made to represent Princess Alexandra at the time of her marriage to the then Prince of Wales in 1863.

RED RIDING HOOD Popular character doll based on the children's tale character. English manufacturers include:-
Three Arts Women's Employment Fund Toy Industry.
Speights Ltd.
Harwin & Co Ltd.

REES, Leon. Born in Bavaria, Rees came to England as a young man and entered the toy firm of Eisenmann & Co. In 1908 he married Miss Maud Eisenmann and soon became a partner in the company. Some time later he resigned his partnership and branched out on his own as a manufacturer and distributor. On 16th April, 1912 he obtained patent no. 8995 for dolls' eyes that can be turned from side to side, and remain in the selected position. On 4th April, 1914 he obtained patent no. 8608 for a doll's head that can be turned in various positions. At about this time it would appear that Rees was the director of the firm Ellison, Rees & Co. of 45 & 46 Basinghall Street, London EC. He acquired the 'Chiltern' Teddy Bear Factory at Chesham, and in partnership with Mr H. G. Stone opened another factory in North London to produce a range of 'Chiltern' plush animals. The Chesham factory was extended for the production of wooden toys and eventually became known as Amersham works.

They used the trademark 'Ellarco', and 'Dolleries' and 'Chesham' were brand names for dolls. In 1916 lines included 'Impey', a soft character doll, and 'Union Jack Baby' with balljoints. This was the first English doll with moving eyes. (The eyes were made in France). Before 1922 the firm became L. Rees & Co. and they had showrooms at 12 New Union Street, London EC2. In 1922 their Dollies' range included a 'Winter Sports Girl' dressed in a white fur-trimmed costume with hat to match; and a range of miniature dolls of the mascot variety dressed as Irish Colleens, Scottish and Welsh Girls. On 21st December, 1923 Leon Rees registered the trademark 'Heather Belle', no. 443,883 for dolls and toys. 1926 included stuffed dolls 'Cecille', 'Lucille' and 'Lullabye babies'. c1930 the company was producing 'Rosette' dolls with unbreakable faces and cloth bodies, arms and legs, and dressed in six different styles. In 1931 they introduced 'Babette', an unbreakable doll with head arms and legs made of felt and a handpainted face. In 1934 the firm advertised "Absolutely unbreakable hard-rubber dolls, natural flesh-coloured with noiseless movable joints. The dolls came in three types, one with sleeping eyes or eyes which 'go shy'; the second with a papier mâché body and a 'mama' voice; and the third a new born baby with a kapok-stuffed body, papier mâché limbs and sleeping or 'go shy' eyes". In the same year they produced Excella character, art and baby dolls. The range included P.C. Bloggs, a police constable doll in uniform with white gloves and patent leather boots. Also a Jolly Jack doll in sailor's outfit.

In 1941 the firm's showrooms were at Imperial House, Dominion Street, South Place, London, EC2. The 1941 range included a selection of art and baby dolls at popular prices and Excella novelty plush

'Dolleries' baby and character dolls, 1923.

dolls. By 1946 the firm's showrooms had moved to 31-35 Wilson Street, London E.C.2.

The company had also become the sole distributor of Rosebud miniatures and new-born babies, and remained as such until 31st December, 1958, when by mutual consent the association with Rosebud Dolls Ltd. was terminated. Rees, after a lifetime as one of the leading lights of the English toy trade, died on 23rd July, 1963, at 84 years of age.

REGINA DOLLS. c1920. Porcelain-headed dolls with sleeping eyes. See **Nunn, George Lawrence.**

REGINA DOLL. Manufacturing Co. 1920 York House, Newbury, Berks.

REID, J. A. 1900. Obtained patent no. 6176 in April 1900 for dolls and figures representing human beings or animals which are weighted at the feet so as to stand in an upright position and to regain a standing position when displaced. The figures may represent well-known characters or persons e.g. John Bull, and are formed of any light material (These were made at the time of the Boer War).

RELIABLE DOLLS. See **Gaeltarra Eireann** and **Canadian Dolls.**

RELIANCE. c1916. Doll series. See manufacturers, **Knight Bros. & Cooper Ltd.**

RENDLE, C. J. 1934. Obtained patent no. 438060 on 14th May for a doll whose interior is impervious to water.

RENNINGER, Charles. 1891. London. Imported and distributed dolls made by Metzler and Ortloff.

RETKIN, M. & RETKIN, R. 1948. Obtained patent no. 663954 on 31st December, for a sleeping eye mechanism for dolls.

REVILL, Edward Joseph. Traded under the name of Edwards and Pamflett. See entry.

REVILL, W. E. 1917. Obtained patent no. 116809 on 27th August for mounting dolls' eyes.

REYNOLDS, E. 1933. Obtained patent no. 425176 on 11th September, for a doll stuffed with sponge rubber and covered with leather. Its internal framework is made of wire, steel and wood.

RHYTHMBAR. 1953. Registered trademark for dolls, soft toys and card games. See **Bartley, Ena Marjorie.**

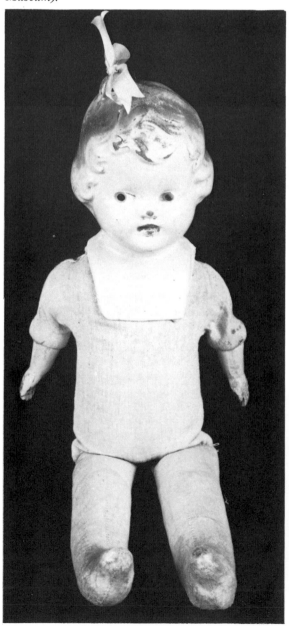

Doll marked 'Reliable' (Pollock's Toy Museum).

A similar doll, but unmarked.

RICH, William. 1853-81. At 14 Great Russell Street, Bloomsbury, London. Doll maker specialising in wax models and rag dolls. Displayed these types of doll at the 1862 London Exhibition.

RICHARDS, SON & ALLWIN LTD. 1924. At Sidway Works, Granville Street, Birmingham. 1936, at Great Bridge, Tipton, Staffordshire. Doll manufacturers. 1935 range consisted of over 100 models including mascots, cuddly dolls, character dolls, goo-goo-eyed dolls etc. They also produced the 'Rigmel' Green Golliwog based on a character in the children's book 'The Fairy's Password', and a doll representing Shirley Temple, the American child film star. The firm used the trademark 'Allwin'.

RIDGEWAY. c1800-1925+. Cauldon, Staffordshire. This pottery made dolls at some time not yet determined. Job Ridgeway founded the pottery at the end of the 18th century. His sons John & William Ridgeway carried it on. Their products were marked 'J Ridgeway' or 'J.R.' John Ridgeway was listed in the Birmingham Directory as a 'Parian Manufacturer'. He retired in 1859 and Messrs. Brown-Westhead and Moore took over the Company. This firm was known as Cauldon Potteries (see entry). When the factory was dismantled, a cache of porcelain dolls' heads and some skeins of hair were found, but the marks used on the heads have not been identified.

RIDGEWAY, J. W. c1917. Cauldon Works, Shelton, Staffordshire. Made dolls during World War I period—possibly those marked 'N.T.I.' and marketed in Canada and the United States by the Nottingham Toy Industry.

RIGMEL GREEN GOLLIWOG. See **Green Golliwog** and **Richards, Son & Allwin.**

RITCHIE, A.P.F. 1915. Obtained patent no. 14213 on 7th October, relating to the construction of joints for cubic dolls.

RIVER GIRL. 1920. Classic doll made by Speights Ltd.

ROAD PATROL SCOUTS. 1930. Automobile Association and Royal Automobile Club Scout mascot dolls manufactured by Chad Valley Co. Ltd. The dolls were wired so they could be moved into different positions. The AA doll had bulging eyes and a small black moustache; he was dressed in felt breeches and had one arm fixed in a saluting position. The R.A.C. doll was less impressive, with a milder face. The dolls were sold by Eisenmann & Co.

ROBB, W. R. 1899. Obtained patent no. 25341 for cardboard dolls with magnifying

An Allwin character doll with goo-goo eyes, made by Richards, Son and Allwin Ltd., 1935.

lenses behind the eyes, on which were advertisements.

ROBERTA. 1957. Registered trademark for dolls and dolls' clothing. See **Robertson, Jeanne Valerie.**

ROBERTS BROS. c1888-1956. Before 1902 at Llanthony Road and Upton Street, Gloucester. Late 1902 at Glevum Works, Gloucester. 1917 London Showroom: 7 Butler Street, Milton Street, London EC. Doll, toy and game manufacturers. The company was established c1888 by Harry Owen Roberts and John Owen Roberts. John Owen Roberts was an Alderman and was also Mayor and City High Sheriff several times. He died in 1929 in a house off Commercial Road in London. In 1903 a British Patent was obtained for a doll on wheels; and in 1921 the firm opened up a new department in their factory especially for the production of Houghton Stockinette dolls, which they took over from British Dolls Ltd of Greenwich. Trademark Glevum Toys.

In the early 1930s extensions to the factory enlarged it by a third and up to World War II 500 people were employed,

rising to 750 during the Christmas period. During the war the factory was requisitioned by the government until 1947; this lost the firm many skilled labourers and customers. They fought a constant battle to regain lost ground, but in 1954 the company was taken over by Chad Valley. In 1956 the old factory was closed and 33 of the 198 employees were offered jobs by Chad Valley. Production of Roberts Bros. lines was transferred to Birmingham and was updated and consolidated.

ROBERTSON, Jeanne Valerie. 1957. 23 Hamstead Road, Handsworth, Birmingham. Doll manufacturer and merchant. On 7th March, 1957 she registered the trademark 'Roberta', no. 763,227 for dolls and dolls' clothing.

ROBEY, George. c1925. Doll from 'Evripose' 'Tru-to-Life' range, representing the well-known English Music Hall comedian of that era. Made by Dean's Rag Book Co. Ltd.

ROBINS. From 1826-7 Joseph Robins, a composition doll maker, was listed in Pigot's Commercial Directory as living at Old Street, London, and in 1838 at 6 Tabernacle Walk, London. In 1852 he was at 6 Crown Street, Finsbury Square, London. From 1859-84 William Robins, who also made composition dolls, was listed at the same address as Joseph.

From 1887-1895 Mrs Harriet Robins made dolls at another London address, and from 1894-1901 Willie Robins made dolls at 31 Huntingdon Street, Hoxton, London N.

ROBINS, Madame E. c1916. At 57 Charnwood Road, South Norwood, London S.E. Made large quantities of stuffed doll bodies.

ROCHDALE DOLL CO. See **Emell Toy Manufacturing Co.**

ROCHDALE DOLL CO. Before 1918-1919 10 Suffolk Street, Rochdale, Lancashire. Doll manufacturers. The firm was taken over as the Rochdale Doll Manufacturing Co. on 28th December 1918. They made 'Eclipse' hair-stuffed dolls, dressed or undressed, with real hair or mohair wigs.

ROCHESTER MUSEUM. Eastgate House, Rochester, Kent. A small toy section includes an 'industrious housewife' doll loaded with pins, needles, buttons and other sewing necessities.

ROCK-A-BYE DOLLS. 1938. Baby dolls made of soft, light, unbreakable material which can be washed. Sold dressed and undressed. See manufacturers, **Farnell, J. K. & Co. Ltd.**

ROCK CHINA DOLLS. See **Frazer Rock, Helen.**

RODDY. Registered trademark for dolls. See **Todd, Daniel G.**

RODNO BABY DOLLS. See **Todd, Daniel G.**

RODNOID. 1948. Registered trademark for toys and games. See **Todd, Daniel G.**

ROH, Madame & ROH, W. c1921-23. In 1921 W. Roh, dolls' wig maker and supplier to dolls' hospitals, was at Lina Works, 407 West Green Road, Tottenham, London, N. In 1923 Madame Roh of Green Lanes, Harringay, London N. was advertising all types of dolls' wigs, dolls' heads, cord, eyes and limbs etc.

ROMEO & JULIET. 1970. See **Jackman, Barbara (Craft) Dolls Ltd.**

ROMPA. c1924. Doll series. See manufacturer, **Rayburn Townsend Co. Ltd.**

ROOSTIE. 1930. Registered trademark for dolls and toys. See **Johnson & Johnson (Gt. Britain) Ltd.**

ROSA. 1933. Doll made by Dean's Rag Book Co. Ltd.

ROSEBUD. 1919. See **Harwin & Co. Ltd.**

ROSEBUD. c1925. See **Posy Buds.**

ROSEBUD. 1947. Registered trademark for dolls. See **Smith, T. Eric.**

ROSEBUD BIG DOLLS. 1960. Lifesize doll range by Rosebud Dolls Ltd, which includes a 32″ vinyl walking doll.

ROSEBUD DOLLS LTD. See **Smith, T. Eric.**

ROSEBUD MATTEL LTD. Wellingborough, Northamptonshire. The company was formed in 1967 from a merger between Rosebud Dolls Ltd. and the American Company Mattel Inc. Rosebud dolls Ltd. became a wholly-owned subsidiary of Mattel with its English management, directed by T. Eric Smith, still continuing in active direction of its operation. The first dolls produced by the company included 'Baby First Step' and 'Cheerful Tearful', a baby doll whose face can be made to alter from a smile to a pout to crying 'real' tears. 1968 range included a dressed doll baby of durable plastic, 14″ high with movable limbs, sleeping eyes and rooted bubblecut hair and with six different dresses. In November 1968 T. Eric Smith resigned as managing director and as a member of the board and by 1971 Rosebud had been dropped from the company's name, which became Mattel Ltd.

ROSEBUD TEENAGE DOLLS. 1958. Doll range designed for the slightly older girl, in various styles, from a doll in sweater and tailored jeans to a doll in evening dress of taffeta and organdie. The dolls are 20″ tall

with fully-jointed vinyl limbs and vinyl head, sleeping eyes and rooted Saran hair. Made by Rosebud Dolls Ltd.

ROSEBUD WALKING DOLL. 1956. A lightweight plastic, non-inflammable, almost indestructible doll, with fully-jointed knees enabling her to sit, kneel and walk. Has sleeping eyes and a variety of hairstyles and outfits. Two sizes: 13″ and 16″. Made by Rosebud Dolls Ltd.

ROSEBUD ASSOCIATED MANU-FACTURERS LTD. 11 Upper Grosvenor Street, London W.1.. Doll and toy manufacturers. 1955 lines include 'Dolly's Bath Set', comprising a 6″ doll with sleeping eyes and movable limbs; with a polythene bath, real soap, a brush and bath-tidy set.

ROSETTE. c1930. Cloth doll with unbreakable face. See manufacturer, **Rees, Leon.**

ROSINE. 1928. See **Dean & Sons Ltd.**

ROSS & CO. c1921. At 80 Sydney Avenue, Moor Lane, London EC. Made miniature dolls.

ROSS Dolls. c1916. Range of daintily dressed dolls. See manufacturers, **Wholesale Toy Co.**

ROTTINGDEAN TOY MUSEUM. The Grange, Rottingdean, Sussex. The dolls and toys now housed in the Public Library will eventually be moved to one of the outbuildings of the Royal Pavilion, at Brighton.

ROYAL ALBERT MEMORIAL MUS-EUM & ART GALLERY. Exeter, Devonshire. The collection includes several 18th century and early 19th century dolls and a number of attractive dolls' accessories, including gloves, fans and parasols, a fur muff, an unusual chatelaine with pince-nez, scissors and crochet hook, and a crinoline frame with watch-spring stiffeners c1862.

ROYAL CROWN POTTERY. c1918. 24 Liverpool Road, Burslem, Stoke-on-Trent, Staffordshire. Made dressed dolls and dolls' tea sets.

ROYAL DOLLS. Several famous wax-doll makers during the Victorian era claimed to have made the 'Royal Baby', by which was understood a model of one of Queen Victoria's numerous progeny. See **Montanari, Augusta; Pierotti; Edwards, John; Meech Bros.** Mrs Peck modelled Queen Victoria as a young woman (though probably from an engraved portrait). Small dolls were often dressed as members of the Royal Family and this occurred especially at the time of some special event, birth, marriage, death—as a commemorative. English manufacturers include:
1930 Chad Valley, Princess Elizabeth

c1933 Chad Valley, Princess Margaret Rose
1935 Liberty & Co. issued Queen Mary
1937 J. K. Farnell, King George VI doll
1938 Chad Valley, Princess Elizabeth
1938 Chad Valley, Princess Margaret Rose
1938 Chad Valley, Prince Edward of Kent
c1949 Simpsons of Surrey, Prince Charles
1952 Chelsea Art Dollmakers, Princess Anne
1952 Chelsea Art Dollmakers, Her Majesty Queen Elizabeth II
1952 Chelsea Art Dollmakers, Prince Philip

ROYAL PUMP ROOM MUSEUM. Harrogate North Yorkshire. This interesting collection of dolls and toys includes a Montanari wax fashion doll.

ROYAL TUNBRIDGE WELLS MUS-EUM & ART GALLERY. Civic Centre, Tunbridge Wells, Kent. An outstanding toy collection with well over 100 dolls of all kinds including some well-laden pedlar dolls.

ROYTOYS. See **Sieki, Masa Roy.**

RUBBADUBDUB. 1920. Trademark for rubber dolls. See manufacturers, **Franklin, J. G. & Sons.**

RUBBER. Dolls made of rubber or gutta-percha have the great disadvantage to the collector that they deteriorate with age. Early examples are rarely in good condition. The two materials are obtained from different sources and the process of manufacture differs. Both materials come from vegetable sources: rubber from the sap of the Hevea Brasiliensis (originally supplies all came from South America), gutta-percha from that of the Palaquium in the Malay Archipelago. Natives in these areas have used the products for centuries.

Commercial use of rubber was enormously increased when the process of vulcanisation was discovered independently by the Englishman T. Hancock and the American C. Goodyear (1842-3). Whereas the rubber substance had to be cooked in iron moulds in a vulcanising bath containing sulphur etc. the gutta-percha paste could be rolled in sheets, pressed into warm moulds to shape, and then dipped into cold water to release ready for a surface of paint. See **Atlantic Rubber Co. Ltd.; Beauty Skin Doll; Bierer, F.L.; Chad Valley; Gatter, Edward; Hammond, T.R.; Lang & Co.; North's Rubber Co.**

RYE MUSEUM. Ypres Tower, Rye, Sussex. A small museum which includes in its collection a few Victorian dolls.

S. & L. MANUFACTURING CO. LTD.
1926. At 362a Wandsworth Bridge Road, Fulham, London SW6. 1934 at 3 High Street, Putney, London SW15. Doll and soft toy manufacturers. 1926 range included stockinette dolls dressed in velveteen. 1934 range included the Luvmee series of soft toys and dolls. 1941 range included long-and short-clothed baby dolls.

SABO. 1924. Registered trademark for dolls. See **Ransom, Sidney.**

SABU, THE ELEPHANT BOY. 1937. Doll based on the film character played by Sabu, the Indian boy film star of the era. Made by J. K. Farnell & Co. Ltd.

SAFFRON WALDEN MUSEUM. Saffron Walden, Essex. The collection includes an early 19th century doll in Quaker dress, and others dating from 1825 onwards. There are also some good examples of dolls' clothes.

SAILOR. A popular type of military costume doll in the 19th century. Many tiny bisque soldiers and sailors can still be found today. The popularity of the sailor suit for children grew steadily from 1840-1910, especially as Queen Victoria dressed her children, both boys and girls, in this style.

SALFORD MUSEUM & ART GALLERY. Peel Park, Salford, Manchester. The collection includes some dolls, mainly 19th century.

SALISBURY & SOUTH WILTSHIRE MUSEUM. St. Ann Street, Salisbury, Wiltshire. A few dolls and toys are included in the collection.

SALISBURY, Thomas Charles. 1917. 160 Richmond Road, Cardiff, Wales. On 21st February, he registered the trademark 'Leda' no 376,950 for dolls. He was possibly a director of Spencer & Co., a doll manufacturing company which made Leda dolls at the same address. See **Spencer & Co.**

SALLY HAPPYTALK. Introduced 1968. Pedigree talking doll.

SALLY SAYS. Introduced 1970. Palitoy walking talking doll, which recites 10 phrases and nursery rhymes, and sings Christmas carols. Battery-operated.

SALMON PEDLAR DOLLS. c1840. Stratford-upon-Avon. A pair of 16½" Pedlar dolls made by Mr & Mrs Salmon. The dolls have painted papier mâché heads and are dressed in beautifully worked linen smocks, with sheepskin wraps. Their trays have various Shakespearian mementos including miniature commemorative mugs, prints of Stratford, a Shakespearian broadsheet and a perfect miniature in china of Shakespeare's birthplace. The dolls are on show at the Leeds Museum.

SALME. 1924. See **Miniature Models.**

SAM. c1936. A 'Tru-to-Life' rag doll with 'Evripose' joints made by Dean's Rag Book Co. Ltd. The doll was based on the character in a dramatic recitative called 'Sam pick oop tha musket' popularized by the well-known comedy actor of the period, Stanley Holloway.

SAMBO. Negró doll made by Dean's Rag Book Co. Ltd.

SAMBO THE TURK. 1937. Black character doll dressed in velveteen and felt, trimmed with silk and gold braid. Made by J. K. Farnell.

SAMMIE. c1920. Character doll made by Fairyland Toy Manufacturing Co. Ltd.

SANDOW, Eugene. 1912-14. Obtained patent no. 26113 on 14th November, 1912 for a wall exercise to induce young children to take exercise. Concealed within the body and limbs of a doll are elastic cords, hand grips and stirrups. The cords are connected to a device which discharges a sweetmeat after the handles have been pulled a predetermined number of times. He also obtained patent no. 16772 on 14th July, 1914 for a variation on his original patent.

In 1915 the National Doll League were producing exerciser dolls based on Sandow's design and in 1917 the All British Doll Manufacturing Co. became sole owners of the patent. In 1919 Whitely Exerciser Ltd. were producing an exerciser doll using Sandow's principle.

SANDY. 1928. Stuffed fabric Scots boy doll made by John Sear Ltd.

SANDY. Introduced 1975. 14" fully jointed Matchbox Doll with sleeping eyes and long rooted hair. Dressed in floral dress with detachable lace apron. Made in Italy for Lesney Products & Co. Ltd.

SANT, J. S. LTD. 1924. At 25 Bartlett's Buildings, Holborn Circus, London EC4. Manufacturers and importers of dolls and fancy goods. 1924 lines included wax or plaster miniature models. 1925: the Fly Doll. 1927: Peggy, a girl doll holding some toys and a parasol. In July 1928 the firm advertised mechanical tumbling toys which turned head over heels. Models included Lloyd George, Harold Lloyd, Winston Churchill, Charlie Chaplin, Policeman, Parson and a Scotsman. The firm used the trade name 'Jaysant'. See **Fly Doll; Miniature Models.**

SANTY. 1850-60. 340 Long Room, Soho Bazaar, London. Made wax dolls, with real hair curls and stuffed bodies, which were sold in Soho Bazaar, London.

SARAH STARER. 1914. Girl rag doll made by Dean's Rag Book Co. Ltd.

SAROLD MANUFACTURING CO LTD.
1950 London and Kirkby Trading Estate

Santy wax doll, c. 1850 (Victoria and Albert Museum).

near Liverpool. Doll manufacturers. Registered trademark 'Sarold' no. 689831 on 14th June, 1950 for dolls. 1952 range included dressed and undressed plastic dolls, 19″ and 25″, with moving eyes and mama voices. The company are believed to have sold quantities of plastic dolls to Woolworths.

SASHA DOLLS. See **Trendon Toys Ltd.**

SAUCY JOYCE. 1936. Doll made by Austin Gray Ltd.

SAUCY WALKERS. 1952. Pedigree walking doll range. Dolls say 'Ma-ma'. Range included negro twins Mandy Lou and Dixie.

SCHELHORN, H. & Co. Cobden House, Cobden Street, Leicestershire.

Manufacturers of Telitoy range. The family came to England from Sonneberg early in 1935 as refugees. Heinrich Schelhorn was born in Sonneberg in 1897, and the present director of the firm, his son Karl, in 1923. They were a doll-making family who transferred their skills to

'School for Scandal' dolls (Bethnal Green Museum).

England and started in a small way manufacturing glass eyes and supplying a firm in Leicester (Palitoy). Later, after internment, H. Schelhorn made pottery dolls with clay obtained in "pug" form (ready for potting) from the Stoke-on-Trent area. On 16th October 1945 he obtained patent no. 602522 for an artificial eye for dolls. He assisted the Ottenbergs of Derby in producing their doll models by making the artistic heads. Schelhorn now produce vinyl plastic 'My Baby Love', Baby Jonathan, and Jeanette, a doll dressing set. Mrs Judy Brereton, daughter of H. Schelhorn, assists in the management.

SCHMIDT, Richard. 1895-1911. London. Importer and distributor of dolls.

SCHOOL FOR SCANDAL DOLLS. Three supposedly 18th century wooden dolls said to represent characters in Sheridan's comedy of manners 'The School for Scandal'. (The dolls have been identified as Lady Teazle, Mrs Candour and Lady Sneerwell. All have hair fashionably dressed. Mrs Candour, as an elderly lady, wears a dress in an older fashion, with panniers; Teazle and Sneerwell wear up-to-date dresses.) The dolls are in Bethnal Green Museum and were made in the 20th century.

SCOTT, J. Fred. 1915. Lund St, Colnbrook, Manchester. Made hand-coloured sateen dolls' masks and Penny Bazaar novelties.

SCOTT, William. 1856. 10 Kossuth Terrace, Hackney Wick, London. Made gutta-percha dolls.

SCOTTISH DOLLS. Popular type of national costume doll. Many doll manufacturers have made dolls dressed in Highland dress, Scottish soldiers, guards, peasants etc. Scottish souvenir dolls are also popular with tourists, though many of them are very cheaply made.
English manufacturers:-
1916 Knight Bros & Cooper Ltd
1924 Henry Jeffrey Hughes & Son.
c1939 Chad Valley
c1920 Speight's Ltd.

SEA BABY. 1915. Registered trademark for dolls. See **Tarpey, Jessie Toler Kingsley.**

SEAR, J. LTD. 1933. Showrooms at 75-77 Golden Lane, London EC1. 1941 at 61a Fortress Road, Kentish Town, London, NW5. 1952 at 18 Charlotte Road, London

EC2. Soft toy and doll manufacturers. 1928 lines include 'Miss Black Bottom' a pierrot rag doll and Sandy, a stuffed fabric Scots boy doll. 1935 lines include unbreakable dolls at 6d and 1s and 'Nigger Peggy' doll with black velvet face.

SEASIDE GIRL. 1920. Classic doll made by Speights Ltd.

SEELIG, William. 1925. 23 White Street, Moorfields, London, EC2. Merchant. On 19th March, 1925 he registered the trademark 'Everrest' no, 457,374 for dolls, dolls' furniture, indoor games and outdoor games, mechanical and construction toys, soft toys, wooden toys and papier mâché toys.

SEGMENTED DOLL. The name used in the trade for dolls with many separate segments joined together, such as ball-jointed dolls.

SEMCO LTD. Before 1962-1967. Crystal Palace, London. Doll manufacturers. In 1962 the firm was taken over by Airfix Industries. Semco made 12″ baby dolls, all of which were sold through Woolworths. The firm closed down in 1967, but the name was retained in Airfix.

SERVICE DOLLS. 1939. Set of four service dolls: a sailor, soldier, airman and marine, manufactured by Chad Valley. Production of these and other dolls was soon halted when the factory was used for the war effort.

SEYFARTH, H. 1926. Obtained patent no. 279785 on 27th October, 1926 (Convention date), for an artificial eye for dolls.

SHANKLIN TOY INDUSTRY LTD. 1915-19. Shanklin, Isle of Wight. Doll Manufacturers. In 1916 they were producing stockinette dolls designed by Mrs Elizabeth Ellen Houghton; including 'The Piccaninny' black baby doll, and 'Baby Carrots', a white baby doll with red hair. This company and the Nottingham Toy Industry amalgamated their products, which were marketed by British Toys Ltd. (from 1920 British Dolls Ltd). under the directorship of Miss M. Moller. Other lines included New Century composition dolls, Vogue rag dolls and Frazer Rock indestructible dolls.

SHEENA. c1974. Palitoy doll with hair that 'grows'.

SHERWOOD, Katherine Mary. 1910. At 8 Seaside Road, Eastbourne, Sussex. Married name: Mrs Cochrane. From June to August 1910 she registered trademarks for mechanical dolls, all with a variation on the same principle. As a child she loved the 'greedy beasts' her father made from paper with gaping mouths. She took out patents for similar 'beasts' that could swallow sweets operated by a string at the back. They were

Shirley Temple, the American film star

sold in London shops and were promoted by a nursery story 'The Goblin Gobblers', written by H. Lockyer Sherratt, illustrated by Chas E. Crombie and printed by Frederick Warne. See photo: From left to right the models are Bhankawala (greedy figure in Indian parlance), Dadoowala (frog-faced one), Greedy Chuggy (pig-faced), Festive Froggy and Hungry Giles. The golly completes the group. The book lent by Mrs Cochrane, now in her 80's.

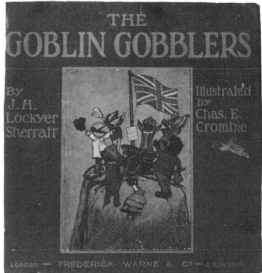

'Allwin' unbreakable doll, 1936, dressed as Shirley Temple in various film roles.

SHIELDS, John & Mrs M. 1852. At 11 Mount Street, Lambeth, London. Made composition dolls.

SHIRLEY DOLLS. 1955. Silk plush dolls in pink, blue and gold. 14½" tall with buckram faces, hygienic stuffing and with wool muff and trimmings. Wholesale price 78s per dozen. Made by Castle Toy Co. Ltd.

SHIRLEY TEMPLE DOLL. c1936. Doll representing American child film star of the 1930's. See manufacturers, **Richards, Son & Allwin.**

SHIRLY. 1918. Soft doll designed by Elizabeth Ellen Houghton.

SHOOLBRED & CO. Established 1882. Tottenham House, 152-155 Tottenham Road, London. Shop selling toys, dolls and games.

Wood and plaster mechanical dolls made by John Hempil in 1820 and sold at Edlin's, Bond Street London.

SHOPS. In the 18th century dolls were sold at shops selling all sorts of millinery or luxury goods, while the cheaper sort were probably hawked around by pedlars. In London there were bazaars selling toys among other things: The Old Pantheon Bazaar at Oxford St. where Marks & Spencer's now stands, the Soho Bazaar which opened in 1816, the Burlington Arcade in 1819, the Lowther Arcade 1831. The early specialist toy shops were: Toy and

Fancy Repository, Kensington High St. (1854) opened by Joseph Toms and later becoming the store of Derry & Toms; Edlin's Rational Repository of Amusement and Instruction, 37 New Bond St (where Sotheby's auctions are now held), later to become Spurin E. C. Toy Warehouse, which was the London representative for the German firm of Fleischmann in 1851.

Edlin was a turner and silversmith and was listed since 1811. See **Hempil, John.** The famous shop of W. H. Cremer was at 210 Regent St. and the owner wrote small books about the toy trade, undertook conjuring and magic shows and travelled extensively on the continent, acquiring all sorts of novelties.

The famous Hamley's was at 35 New Oxford St, 512 Oxford St and then 64 Regent St, where it still stands. It originated in the 18th Century with a toy warehouse called the Noah's Ark, in High Holborn.

SHORT, S. & A. LTD. Established 1915. At 15 Albion Buildings, Bartholomew Close, London EC. Doll and toy manufacturers.

SHORTER, E. A. 1938. Hertfordshire. Obtained patent no. 512722 for a doll constructed on a unit system of separate parts which can be assembled together as required. The head is manipulated by pressure of the fingers from without, to give the desired facial contortion. The eyeballs are mounted with hinges, or by means of ball-and-socket joints to the ends of rods, which in turn slide into holes behind the eye sockets, providing a means of projecting the eyeballs forward from the head.

SHORTLAND, J. W. 1918. Obtained British Patent no. 116866 on 19th February, 1918 for a doll's eye mechanism which permits the eyes to move in any direction in stationary sockets, and has movable eyelids.

SHRIEKING SUSAN. c1914. Rag doll made by Dean's Rag Book Co. Ltd.

SHYNALL RAG DOLL CO. 1913+. London. Doll manufacturers.

SIEKI, Masa Roy. 1959. At 50 Crescent Road, Plumstead, London SE18. Doll and puppet manufacturer trading as 'Roytoys'. Registered trademark 'Dizzy Whizz', no. 789,232 on 6th April, 1959 for puppets and dolls.

SILBERTSON, L. & SONS LTD. 1946. London. Registered trademark 'Marvo', no. 654031 on 27th November, 1946 for dolls.

SILVER SERIES. c1918. Series of dolls with china heads and limbs, cloth-stuffed bodies and sleeping, fixed or painted eyes. The Egyptian cotton used to cover the dolls' bodies had a lustre to it, hence the name 'Silver'. The Elite Doll Company was one of

the first firms to introduce the sleeping-eye doll to England. See **Elite Doll Co.**

SILVIE DOLLS. 1930. Dolls dressed in velveteen trimmed with silkeen plush. 9 sizes. Made by Dean's Rag Book Co Ltd.

SIMON & SUSAN. 1956. 'Sunshine' vinyl dolls in permanent colours, washable, fitted with safety squeakers. Made by The Mettoy Co. Ltd.

SIMPLE SIMON. 1935. See **Nursery Rhyme Character Dolls.**

SIMPSON FAWCETT & CO. LTD. 1915. At Hunslett, Leeds. 1952 at 268 Kingsland Road, London E8. 1958 at 11 Old Jewry London EC2. Toy and doll manufacturers. In 1952 a new company was founded, with headquarters in Kingsland Road, to manufacture, wholesale and retail dolls and plastic products of all kinds. In January 1958 they registered the trademark 'Cygnet' no. 772,947 for dolls, dolls' prams, toy motor cars and children's pedal cars.

Wax baby, 4½ ins., made by Myrtle Smith, 1975. The asymmetrical limbs are attached with knotted elastic.

SIMPSON, Jessie. 1880s. Worthing. Made up dolls of Nursery Rhyme characters as dolls, pincushions etc from hand-painted fabric. They sold successfully in London stores.

SIMPSON, W. S. 1887. Obtained patent no. 15754 for dolls on musical wheeled toy.

SINDY DOLLS. Introduced 1963. 12″ teenage fashion doll produced by Pedigree Dolls Ltd. Designed by Dennis Arkinstall and Eric Griffiths who took over the Sindy doll project. Sindy was the first British doll to be promoted by an extensive TV campaign. The doll has many different outfits in up-to-date styles

which are renewed annually and also many specially designed accessories. In 1975 a fully articulated Active Sindy Doll was introduced. See **Active Sindy; Pedigree Soft Toys Ltd.**

SISSONS BROS & CO. LTD. c1917. Hull, Yorkshire. Manufacturers of 'Dolac' a preparation used in the manufacture of dolls, which gave them a wax-like finish.

SKINTEX. 1947. Registered trademark for dolls. See **British National Dolls Ltd.**

SKIPPING DOLL. See **Wonder Toys Ltd.** and **Wonder Toy Co.**

SLATER, M. H. 1924. Obtained patent no. 229960 on 24th September, 1924 for a doll which is made of semi-transparent sheet rubber, and has eyes which move as doll is tipped from side to side.

SLEEPA DOLL CO. 1950. London. Doll manufacturers. Registered trademark 'Wendy Wonder Doll' no. 692487 on September 26th 1950 for dolls.

SLEEPING EYES. See **Eyes, Dolls'**

SLIPSY SLIDDLE. 1968. See **World of Kiddles.**

SLOAN & CO. 1916-18. At 2 King Street, Liverpool. Made dressed felt dolls and toy animals.

SLYMPHS. 1921. See **Burgess, S. H.**

SMART SET DOLLS. 1928-38. Range of 'Boudoir' dolls made by Dean's Rag Book Co. Ltd.

SMEED, John. See **Nunn, George Lawrence.**

SMILERS. 1939. Doll series made by J. K. Farnell.

SMITH, Edward. c1880. 8 Cheapside, London EC. Handled wax dolls.

SMITH, Joachim. 1763. London. Modelled wax portraits in miniature.

SMITH & HOYLE. c1915. Clarendon Works, Longton, Stoke-on-Trent, Staffordshire. Produced dressed and undressed dolls with porcelain heads and stuffed bodies.

SMITH, Myrtle. Bromley Road, Colchester, Essex. Designs wax dolls made in the traditional poured wax manner and dressed by hand. In 1981 Myrtle Smith remarried and is now known as Naomi Laight.

SMITH, F. H. 1917-1981+. Attifer Works, Gainsborough, Yorkshire. Makes dolls' wigs.

SMITH, T. Eric. c1947-1968. At Raunds, Northamptonshire. In 1934, on the death of his father, Smith took over the family business of manufacturing wooden toys, specialising in beech horses, dolls' houses

Dolls, 34 ins. and 11 ins., made by Myrtle Smith. Poured wax heads and limbs, cloth bodies, inserted human hair.

Wax doll stamped 'Edward Smith,
The City Toy Shop' (Victoria and Albert
Museum).

and forts. In the late 1940's he began a doll-making business, first using various compositions based on sawdust and glues, and later working with plastics.

The company was known as Nene Plastics. On 20th March, 1947, he registered the trademark 'Rosebud' no. 657461 for dolls. The name Rosebud came about when a little girl who had visited the factory was presented with a doll, and when asked what she most liked about it, replied 'What lovely rosebud lips the doll has'. c1949 the concessionaires for Rosebud dolls were L. Rees & Co. Ltd. and this association continued until the end of 1958 when by mutual consent it was terminated. In 1950 Smith obtained two patents, no. 667091 for a doll moulded in sections by the injection process and secured together, forming the wall of the body internally with a flanged projection or recess in which a 'mama' or other sound-producing device could be secured; and patent no. 667906 for a body, head or limb of a doll moulded in plastic in two parts, secured together with a hook (for attachment) which is incorporated in the moulding. In 1960 a new factory was purchased at Wellingborough to take over the complete dollmaking process. In 1967 Smith agreed a merger with the American Company Mattel Inc., as a result of which Rosebud Dolls Ltd. became a wholly-owned subsidiary of Mattel, with its English Management led by Smith who still continued in active direction of its operations. In November 1968 Smith resigned both as managing director and as member of the Board.

SMITH, W. H. 1792-Present day. In 1792 Henry Walton Smith and his wife opened a tiny newsagent's shop in Little Grosvenor Street, London. When he and then his wife died the sons carried on the business as H. & W. Smith, moving their shop to Duke Street, Mayfair in 1818. The elder brother was less interested in the business and by 1828 it became known as W. H. Smith, after the younger brother. William Henry Smith set about providing the fastest and most efficient newspaper delivery in the country. In 1846 his 21-year-old son was taken into partnership and the firm became W. H. Smith & Son. The company went on from strength to strength until they had hundreds of station bookstalls and shops all over England.

In 1916 a doll and toy factory was established in Norfolk Street, Shelton, Stoke-on-Trent, Staffordshire under the direction of George Henry Buckmaster, manager of Shelton Branch.

Initially the firm produced cheap dressed and undressed dolls, mainly for the overseas and colonial market, but in 1917 they began specialising in better-quality dolls. By May 1917 they were manufacturing 20 series of composition jointed dolls, each with six designs, and in October 1917 were producing dark and light leatherette dolls. The brand name for the firm's dolls and toys was 'Toyland'.

SNOW BABY. c1917. See **Kirby, G. L.**

SNOWBALL, Mrs S. 1855, London. Made wax dolls.

SNOW BOY. 1919. See **Harwin & Co. Ltd.**

SNOWSHILL MANOR. Near Broadway, Gloucestershire. A Cotswold manor-house full of innumerable treasures including some dolls and dolls' houses.

SNOW WHITE. 1938. 16″ fabric doll made by Chad Valley Co., based on the Disney animated film.

SOFA DOLLS. See **Alpha Sofa Dolls.**

SOFA DOLLS. 1935. Gaily dressed lady dolls made by Chad Valley Company. The dolls were 21″ high and made with pressed felt faces; the costumes were made of floral crepes, art silk and velveteen. Their faces are typical of the period, with tiny rosebud mouths and sideways glancing eyes. See **Boudoir Dolls.**

SOFTANLITE. Trademark for dolls and toys. See **Teddy Toy Co. Ltd.**

SOLDIER BOY IN KHAKI. 1914. A sixpenny doll sold by Whyte, Ridsdale & Co.

SOLDIER'S BABY, THE. 1914. Registered trademark for dolls. See **Boase, Elizabeth.**

SOMERSET COUNTY MUSEUM. The Castle, Taunton, Somerset. The toy section consists of about 20 dolls, an 18th century dolls' four-poster bed and a group of miniature dolls.

SONIA. c1923. Printed rag doll in German or Swiss Costume, made by Chad Valley Company.

SONNY BOY. 1929. Registered trademark for dolls. See **Cowan de Groot & Co.**

SOUTHPORT MANUFACTURING CO. c1919. At 27 King Street, Southport, Lancashire. Manufacturers of dolls and doll parts, producing dressed and undressed dolls from 8″ to 36″ high, and 'unbreakable' composition pasteboard heads with wigs. Other lines included 6 sizes of doll masks and 10 sizes of composition legs.

Workroom of the Shelton branch of W.H. Smith, 1916.

W.H. Smith 'Toyland' doll, 1918.

SOUTH WALES TOY MANU-FACTURING CO. LTD. 1916-22. At 47 Salisbury Road, Cardiff. 1918-22. 2 & 6 Miskin Street, Cardiff. Works at 39 Salisbury Road, Cardiff. Soft toy and doll manufacturers. Lines included dressed dolls, Eskimo dolls and teddy bears. Their Trademark was 'Madingland'. The company went out of business in 1922. Joseph Layfield, Whitecross St, London EC1. were their London Sales Agents.

SPANIARD. 1937. Fabric character doll made by J. K. Farnell. The stuffed body was made in brightly-coloured felt and the doll was dressed in black velveteen with a white satin blouse.

Magic Dressing Doll, J.W. Spear & Sons, 1937.

SPEAR, J. W. & SONS. 1878. Eldon Street, London. Firm was founded in 1878 by J. W. Spear who lived in Nuremberg. It is chiefly renowned for finely printed boxed games but as it was one of the earliest firms involving in chromolithography some interesting dressing doll sets were also produced. Spear had six sons, one of whom was taken into partnership. Another son, Carl, built a large modern factory in Nuremberg in 1899, where goods for London were manufactured. In 1932 a factory was opened at Green Street, Enfield, in Middlesex, after free trade was discontinued and duty introduced on imported games. The present chairman, Richard Spear, is grandson of the founder. Early dressing doll sets included a character doll with changeable heads, Dorothy and

her dresses and Our Baby. 1937 lines included Magic Dressing Doll series comprising cardboard dolls dressed in real material which clung without the aid of tabs or paste. Series included Princess Elizabeth, Peggy and Baby.

SPECIALITY TOY CO. c1919. Leamington Spa, Warwickshire. Doll manufacturers for wholesale and export only. Lines included dressed and undressed dolls, kid-finished, from 15″ to 22″ high. The dolls had china heads and limbs and hair-stuffed bodies with glass eyes and 'luxuriant' wigs. Also made fabric dolls. The firm's sole agent was Arthur Kitson.

SPEIGHTS LTD. 1913-16. At 16 Bradford Road, Dewsbury, Yorkshire. 1916-18 at Oates Street, Dewsbury & Classic Works, Union Street, Dewsbury, London Showrooms at Finsbury Court, Finsbury Pavement, London EC. Before the First World War the firm produced dolls' hair and wigs and crepe hair for real and theatrical purposes. They were so successful with dolls' hair that they were even selling it to German and Austrian manufacturers, who were considered the top producers of doll's hair. Soon after war broke out they were asked by the Board of Trade to set themselves up for large-scale manufacture of dolls' wigs in order to capture the German trade.

In October 1915 they were pressed to take up doll-body making, and in 1916 they took over the premises of S. Crawshaw & Sons in Oates Street, Dewsbury and set up a factory to manufacture complete dolls, employing 400 workers. One of their 1916

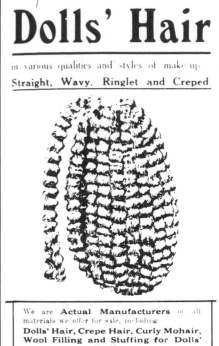

lines was a 'Jumping Jack' doll, portraying the well-known English musical comedy actress Miss Gertie Miller, as she appeared in the stage revue 'Bric-a-Brac', dressed as a pierrette. By 1917 their range comprised over 1000 designs including the 'Classic' range of dolls, and in the same year they registered the trademark 'Kidette', no. 378,866 on 9th July for dolls and toys. In March 1919 jointed 'Kidette' dolls were advertised as having fully-jointed, washable, hair-stuffed kid bodies; English china heads; fixed or sleeping veined glass eyes; composition forearms and lower limbs, and mohair wigs in various styles.

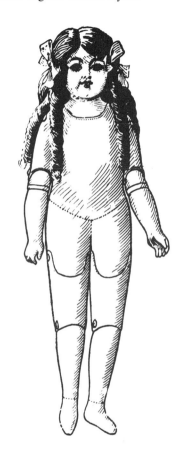

'Kidette' fully jointed doll with china head made by Speights Ltd.

In May 1920 the firm's 'Classic' doll catalogue included the 'Marie' doll with hair-stuffed body at about 10s, and in jointed composition at about 1 guinea; the Little Red Riding Hood doll, fully-jointed composition in three sizes or hair-stuffed in four sizes, with china head and fixed or moving eyes, and dressed in a flower-print frock with white apron and red cloak with ribbon tie: the 'Georgette' doll with bisque china head, composition limbs, moving eyes and mohair wig and cluster curls and ribbons, dressed in blue, rose or pink georgette draped with white net: Dutch boy and girl, Viscountess, Princess, Marchioness, Duchess, Countess, Flossy, Fairy

doll, Seaside girl, Storm girl, Country girl, Nighty girl, River girl and Pyjama girl etc.

Speights gradually abandoned the doll-making business and used their skilled work force for the more profitable occupation of making lampshades, which they still do today, although the factory has now moved from the centre to the outskirts of Dewsbury, Yorkshire.

SPENCER & CO. c1916-1919. At 160 Richmond Road, Cardiff, Wales. Doll manufacturers. Made 'Leda' dolls which were fully-jointed and made of pratically unbreakable composition, washable and painted with non-poisonous paint. They also made dressed and undressed china dolls. In 1919 their range consisted of 15 doll varieties, including a baby doll in jointed composition dressed in long or short clothes, complete with comforter; a pierrot doll, and soft-bodied china-headed dolls dressed in silk or muslin. The trademark 'Leda', no. 376,950 was registered for dolls on 21st February 1917 by Thomas Charles Salisbury of the same address as Spencer & Co.

In 1919 a new company was registered called Leda Dolls Ltd. at 109 Queen Street, Cardiff.

SPICER, GILBERT & CO. 1916. Leamington. Advertised well-made china and composition-headed dolls with glass eyes.

SPRATT, Miss H. 1881. At 130 St. Johns Road, Hoxton, London N. Made dolls at the same address as Thomas Betts.

SPRAYTEX. c1949. Brand name of plastic moulded-in hair made by Britoy Ltd.

STAFFORDSHIRE COUNTY MUSEUM & MANSION HOUSE. Shugborough, Staffordshire. The collection includes a small group of dolls.

STAFFORDSHIRE DOLL CO. c1916. At 308 King Street, Fenton, Stoke-on-Trent, Staffordshire. Made undressed stuffed dolls.

STALLARD & CO. 1905. London. Registered the trademark 'Kismi', no. 274917 on 11th August, 1905 for dolls.

STAMFORD DOLL CO. c1946-1949+. Alliance Works, Belfast Road, London N16. Director: Mr W. Retkin, formerly managing director of Britannia Toy Co. Made composition doll heads and limbs. In 1949 introduced the Stamford walking and talking doll.

STAR MANUFACTURING CO. 1887-1925+ Davis Street, Cubitt Town, London E. Manufacturers and exporters of dolls and toys. Made composition dolls and stuffed dolls, including baby dolls with porcelain heads and 'cry' voices. Their trademark was a six-pointed star with the word 'Star' in it.

STATHAM, Samuel Edmond. 1893. Manchester. Manufacturer. Obtained patent no. 23342 on 5th December, 1893 for seamless vulcanised rubber dolls.

STEEVANS MANUFACTURING CO. LTD. c1918. Ghosall, Staffordshire. Doll and toy manufacturers.

STEINMAN-BEYENCENET, Maurice. 1923. At 13 Well Street, London EC1. Merchant. Registered trademark 'Wob-li-gob' no. 437,490 on 25th May, 1923 for dolls, toys and marionettes.

STEVENS, LANHER, PARRY & ROLLINSON. Obtained patent no. 532157 on 3rd September, 1938. 'Relates to rubber, the germane purpose of the present invention being to provide an improved doll, and particularly to provide in such a doll structural appendages which will not be displaced from the doll.'

STEVENS SALES CO LTD. 1950. At 7 Noel Street, London W1. January 1950 advertised unbreakable dolls with life-like skin texture, flirting eyes and natural hair wig.

STIFF, Walter. 1881-97. 1894-5. At 181 Goswell Road, London EC. Made and exported wax dolls and wax figures.

STOCKINETTE. A close-knit material suitable for hose. The term and perhaps the material itself dates from 1837. Stockings were originally hand-knitted but with the industrial revolution came mechanical knitting looms which superseded the old methods for cheap clothing and caused great economic hardship to home industries. See Manufacturers of stockinette dolls: **American Kiddie; Bland-Hawkes, Mabel; Chad Valley; Fretwell Co. Ltd.; Nottingham Toy Industry; Rayburn-Townsend; Roberts Bros; Shanklin Toy Industry; Three Arts Women; Toddler Doll.**

STOKE-ON-TRENT DOLLS SUPPLIES CO. 1896. From 1896 it was a printing firm, but c1918 the company was producing dolls' limbs at their premises at 5 Glebe Street, Stoke-on-Trent, Staffordshire.

STORM GIRL. 1920. Classic doll made by Speights Ltd.

STORY BOOK. 1958. Registered trademark for dolls. See **Mettoy Co. Ltd.**

STORY BOOK KIDDLES. 1968. See **World of Kiddles.**

STOTEN, Pat. See **Tricia Dolls.**

STRANDERS, W. & PERRY, J. J. 1889. Obtained patent no. 14356 on September 11th, 1889 for dolls and figures constructed to imitate crawling, rowing and swimming movements.

Miniature wax doll, 1700 (In the Ann Sharp Baby House at Strangers' Hall, Norwich).

STRANGER'S HALL. Charing Cross, Norwich, Norfolk. A fine collection of dolls and toys including some well-furnished dolls' houses.

STRATTON DOLL. In 1917 the Countess of Northbrook founded a village industry of doll-making at Stratton in Hampshire. A central depot was opened at Winchester and the dolls were successfully sold at London and provincial stores. The designs for doll patterns were provided by the Countess herself for the Stratton Doll Industry.

STROLL WITH ME DOLL. 1969. Durable plastic doll with strong action: walking legs, movable arms, sleeping eyes and rooted hair. Manufactured by Rosebud Mattel Ltd.

STROME & CO. Established 1892. 1952: at 92 Victoria Street, London SW1. Manufacturers and merchants of dolls, games and toys.

STUFFING, DOLLS'. Numerous materials have been used to stuff dolls from ancient times to present day. Cloth-and kid-bodied dolls were at first stuffed with sawdust, later with horsehair. Other stuffings include hay, straw, bracken, wood chippings, wood wool, down and kapok.

Modern standards require hygienic stuffing, so a synthetic material e.g. plastic sponge is often used which enables the doll to be put in a washing machine. See **Wendy Boston.**

SUFFRAGETTE DOLL. Doll dressed in 1890s costume and said to represent the 'New Woman' later manifested in the Suffragette movement. The doll is a shoulder bisque with fabric body stuffed with sawdust. It is on display at Tunbridge Wells Museum.

SUKY DOLLS. Introduced 1975. 15cm Matchbox dress-up doll with jointed body, rooted hair and hands that can hold accessories. Range comprises Ballerina, Nurse, Tennis Player, Horse Rider, Skater, Shopper. In 1976 a Bedtime doll and Swimmer were introduced. The dolls are manufactured in Hong Kong and the clothes are regularly updated. Suky Playsets, comprising a Suky doll and various play environments in a window display box, were introduced in 1975. Range consists of Picnic Playset, Home Cleaning, Camping, Wedding, Cinderella and Cooking Playset.

SUMMERTIME GIRLS. 1977. See **Airfix Products Ltd.**

SUNBONNET BABY. c1923. Baby doll dressed in check rompers and bonnet. 1923 advert reads 'they WALK and TALK. The 'liveliest' thing imaginable in dolls.' Manufactured by Dean's Rag Book Co. Ltd. Sunbonnet Babies were based on the kindergarten books 'Sunbonnet Babies' and 'Overall Boys' published in 1905 and written by Mrs Eulalie Osgood Grover.

SUNDAY BEST DOLLS. 1957. Doll series by Cascelloid.

SUNER. 1920. Registered trademark for dolls. See manufacturers, **Hewitt & Leadbeater.**

SUNLIGHT, SIEVE & CO. c1915-c1919. Crescent Works, Chapel Street, Salford, Manchester. Wholesale and export doll and toy manufacturers. 1915 lines included printed fabric stuffed dolls, Soldier and Sailor Dolls from 1d to 6d. In 1917 produced dolls with celluloid faces, composition heads and china heads, and unbreakable jointed dolls. In 1918: 'very high-class lines of dressed and undressed dolls.' In 1919: medium-priced dolls with glass eyes and loose-jointed limbs, a doll with 'bobbed' hair, and a Baby doll with comforter.

SUNNY JIM. A rag doll introduced as a mascot advertising the breakfast food Force (malted and toasted wheat flakes introduced from the U.S.A.). Originally the characters were Jim Dumps, a morose fellow who never had breakfast of Force, and Sunny Jim full of verve and vim, who did. Gradually Jim Dumps dropped out and the first Sunny Jim Doll was made in the 1920s, when production of the food began in England. It was discontinued in 1940 on outbreak of war and reintroduced in 1955 when all the ingredients were again obtainable. Force was produced in the U.S.A. from 1890 but the doll was a U.K. creation and never sold in the States.

SUNSHINE. 1956. Brand name for vinyl dolls made by Mettoy Co. Ltd.

SUNSHINE BABS. 1934. Baby doll made by British National Dolls Ltd.

SUNSHINE GIRL. 1912. Registered trade mark for dolls and toys. See **Bings Ltd.**

SUNSHINE KID. 1912. Registered trade mark for dolls and toys. See **Bings Ltd.**

SUN TAN DOLL. c1917. See **Kirby, G. L.**

SUPERIOR. 1935. Doll series manufactured by Chad Valley Co. Ltd. Range included 14″ girl doll dressed in crepe and felt 16″ girl doll with smiling face dressed in crepe and felt; and a boy doll with velveteen limbs dressed in pyjamas and dressing gown.

SUSIE. c1920. Character doll made by Fairyland Toy Manufacturing Co. Ltd.

SUTHERLAND DOLL CO. c1918. The Potteries, Stoke-on-Trent, Staffordshire. Manufactured dressed dolls with china heads. The heads were produced by a pottery firm.

SUZIE SING-A-SONG. Introduced 1969. Pedigree singing doll.

SUZY SMART. 1963. See **De Luxe Toy Co. Ltd.**

SWEET DREAMS. 1976. See **Airfix Products Ltd.**

THE BEST VARIETY OF

DRESSED DOLLS

ON THE MARKET.

Extensive Range - Beautifully Dressed

Exclusive Designs.

Also Printed Fabric Dolls from 1d. to 6d. lines.

Buyers will do well to pay a visit to our SHOW at the

Board of Trade Fair Exhibition,

Imperial Institute, South Kensington, February 26th—March 9th.

STAND No. C21. West Gallery.

SUNLIGHT, SIEVE & Co., Crescent Works, Salford, Manchester

Advertisement, 1915.

'Sunny Jim'.

SWEETHEART DOLL. 1949. Registered trademark for dolls. See **Drial, William, Products Ltd.**

SWEET SUE. 1956. See **Paliglide Walking Dolls.**

SWINGING SWEETIE. Introduced 1968. 15″ Bluebell range doll, drinks and wets, complete with 20″ tubular steel swing. Manufactured by D G. Todd & Co. Ltd.

SYER, Ernest. 1919-22. London. Doll importer.

SYLVIA. 1956. See **Paliglide Walking Dolls.**

TAH TOYS LTD. 1916. At 97 St Johns Hill, London SW11. Directors: James Caulfield Goff and Walter John Surman. Toy and doll manufacturers. 1916 lines included long or short-haired rabbit fur doll called 'Baby Bunny' and 'Babes in the Wood' felt dolls. 'Kiddlums' trade mark no. 378,870 was registered on 9th July, 1917 for boy and girl dolls, and in the same year their doll range included 'Dilly Dick', a character doll. In 1918 they advertised 'Brer Rabbit', a baby

'Kiddlums', Tah Toys Ltd, 1917. Trade Mark 378870; reg. design 661077. Flesh-coloured stockinette body, removable clothes.

'Softanlite' new-born baby doll, Teddy Toy Co.

bunting type plush doll with long rabbit ears. Heath Robinson, the well-known 1930s cartoonist, designed some of their toys.

TALKATIVE JANE. 1962. 22″ talking Pedigree doll. Phrases include 'Please brush my hair' and 'My name is Jane'. Retail price £5 17s 6d.

TALKING DOLLS. As a follow-on from the doll which could say 'Mama, Papa' by means of bellows-worked voice box with squeeze action, or manipulated by string or leverage, dolls were equipped with phonograph mechanical voices, miniature gramophones, radio and recorded tapes. The modern child expects her doll to have a repertoire of phrases spoken or sung. See **Alice in Wonderland; Babbling Baby; Bazzoni; Chatty Kathy; Clever Kerry; De Luxe Toy Co; Edison, T. (Appendix 1); Lawley and Page; Sally Happitalk; Sally Says; Stamford doll; Stroll with me; Sunbonnet Baby; Suzie Sing-a-Song; Tippy Tumbles; Tip-tap; Talkative Jane; Toddle Talks; Topsy.**

TAMMIE. c1974. Articulated Palitoy doll.

TAM O'SHANTER. c1917. Bonnet doll, head made by S. Hancock & Son.

TARPEY, Jessie Toler Kingsley. 3 Buckingham Mansions, West Hampstead, London NW. Registered trademark, 'Sea Baby' no. 365653 January 29th, 1915 for dolls.

TA-TA DOLLS. 1917. A range of cheap character dolls (five designs) made by Dean's Rag Book Co. Ltd.

TATTERSALL, J. LTD. 50 Stanley Street, Southport, Lancashire. Co. registered 12th September, 1919. Wholesale and retail dealers and manufacturers of dolls, dolls' houses, dolls' clothing, sports equipment; also printers. Specialists in the manufacture of body parts and limbs, jointed dolls, also dolls' celluloid masks. Makers of "Princess" unbreakable jointed dolls, and a doll-walking appliance which, fitted to any doll, teddy bear or similar toy, converts it into a walking toy.

TEACOSY and TELEPHONE DOLLS. c1855-1925+. Decorative dolls designed to conceal telephone or teapots. In December

1922 the Toy and Fancy Goods Trader reported the arrival of 'very tall creatures with powdered heads and bouffant skirts' designed for this purpose. Worthing Museum has a Queen Victoria tea cosy doll on display, c1880. The head is in stockinette moulded over papier mâché to portray Her Majesty's 'We are not amused' expression. The doll is believed to have been made by a lace-mender in the Queen's Household.

TEARFUL TAMMY. 1967. Drink/Wet baby doll from Bluebell range manufactured by D. G. Todd & Co. Ltd.

TEATHER, George. 1856. London. Wax doll maker.

TEDDIE c1912: See **Wiederseim, Grace.**

TEDDY TOY CO. 1914. At 1 Nicoll's Buildings, Playhouse Yard, London EC1. c1941 at Fenton, Stoke-on-Trent, Staffordshire. Soft toy and doll manufacturers. Trademark 'Softanlite'. 1934 lines included a range of soft dolls with composition heads, incorporating dolls dressed in attractive English styles and New Born baby dolls in long and short clothes. 1935 range included soft velvet dolls from 1s to 21s each.

TEEN-AGE DOLLS. See **Doll Industries Ltd; Lesney Products & Co. Ltd.; Pedigree Soft Toys Ltd.**

TEENY TINY TEARS. 1966. 12″ version of 'Tiny Tears' plus accessories, made by Palitoy.

TELITOY. See **Schelhorn, H. & Co.**

TELMA MANUFACTURING CO. 1917. Telma House, Red Lion Street, Clerkenwell Road, London EC. Manufacturers of woollen dolls, dressed and undressed china *Advertisement, 1920.*

'Softanlite' new-born baby doll, Teddy Toy Co.

and composition dolls, china and composition heads and limbs. Also made woollen toys, rattles, balls etc. and bath toys.

TENNANT, W. J. Doll maker. Obtained patent no. 436264 1st December, 1934, for dolls' head and eye mechanism.

TERRITORIAL. 1915. Soldier Doll. See **Fall In.**

TERRY, William J. 1890. At Welbury Works, 96 Lavender Grove, Hackney, London NE. Manufacturer of soft toys and dolls, including Eskimo dolls.

TESSTED TOYS. Trademark of Bedington Liddiatt & Co. Ltd.

TEXTILE NOVELTY CO. The. 29 Brad Street, London EC. See **Art Manufacturing Co. Ltd.** Taken over by latter in 1913.

THEDA 1960. See **Debutante Dolls.**

THERNGLADE LTD. Wrexham, Denbighshire. Toy manufacturers. In 1969 they commenced assembling dolls manufactured in W. Germany by Schildkrot AG. A new factory was later built to enable the dolls to be wholly manufactured in Britain. Brand name Turtle: dolls, made of plastic called Tortuflex, a soft, flexible material. Range includes talking, walking and wetting dolls, white and coloured dolls from 8″ to 28″. 50 different clothes styles. In 1970 they began marketing 'Bella dolls', manufactured by the French subsidiary of Schildkrot.

THOMAS, Garrie. Caerffynnon Hotel, Talsarnau, Merioneth, North Wales. Doll manufacturer. Registered trademark 'Cariad' no. 783521 3rd November, 1958 for dolls.

THOMAS INDUSTRIES (LONDON) LTD. c1945. Doll and toy manufacturers. Under the name 'Adora Toys Ltd.' they registered trademark 'Adora' no. 642199 for dolls and toy animals, 22nd November, 1945. They exhibited the Adora series of dolls at the Manchester Toy Fair in 1945, and their unbreakable 'Tocoly' dolls in 1946.

THOMASON, Henry. 1870. 10 & 11 Burlington Arcade, London W. Made dolls.

Advertisement for stuffed rag stockinette dolls, 1920.

THE

Three Arts Women's Employment Fund,

126 Belgrave Rd. S.W. 1

Phone : Victoria 7311

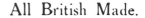

THE ORIGINAL CUDDLEY ONE

"Bonnie Babs"

All British Made.

THOMPSON, R.A. and FREEMAN, W.S. Patent 25883 for mechanical sports dolls (cricket, hockey, golf, etc) 7th December 1898. Operated by cylinder and piston using a compressed air ball bellows action, these were the forerunners of the amusement arcade games of the 'penny in the slot' type.

THOMSON, Bernard Home. 44 Queen's Gate, London SW. Civil servant. Registered trademark 'Peek-a-boo' no. 337690 on 13th November, 1911 for dolls.

THORNE BROS. 1915. At 1 Essex Street, Strand, London WC. Doll and toy manufacturers. Made 'Tumble-It' grotesque tumbling dolls dressed in khaki with carved wooden faces.

THORPE, Joseph. London. 1856. Made wax dolls.

THREE ARTS WOMEN'S EMPLOYMENT FUND TOY INDUSTRY, 1917. At 32 Wigmore Street, London W. Soft toy and doll manufacturers. 1917 lines included 'Cuddley Ones' stockinette dolls designed by Elizabeth Ellen Houghton. 1919 lines included dressed and undressed dolls, some in long clothes with muslin robe trimmed with lace and sash, others with cloaks and bonnets. Other doll types included Red Riding Hood, boy doll in romper suit, nigger doll with coloured turban and shirt, baby doll in embroidered frock and matinée coat, and Baby Boy and Baby Girl in muslin frocks.

TIA. 1972. See **Lesney Products & Co. Ltd.**

TICH. 1932. Urchin boy doll made by Cartoon Novelties, Albion House, New Oxford St., London. Based on the cartoon strip then running in the Daily Mirror and Sunday Pictorial.

TICKLES. Introduced 1972. Soft Pedigree baby doll which laughs when tickled or hugged. Dressed in knitted nylon romper suit.

TILSON, William. 1867. At 16 Mile Street, Mile End, London. Doll maker.

TIMES REMEMBERED DOLL & TOY MUSEUM. The Coach House, Syon Park, Brentford, Middlesex. The museum closed in 1981. The collection is now on show, March to October, at Sudeley Castle, Winchcombe, Glos.

TINY TEARS. Introduced 1965. Palitoy doll with 'true-movement' limbs which adopt the realistic poses of a real-life baby. She drinks from her bottle, cries real tears, wets her nappy and blows bubbles. Voted Girl's Toy of the Year by the National Association of Toy Retailers in 1966.

TINY TOT TOY CO. LTD. Nottingham. Manufacturers of dolls and soft toys. Registered trade mark 'Chummy' no. 694024 on 21st November, 1950.

TIPPERARY TOMMY. 1915. See **Harwin & Co. Ltd.**

TIPPY TOES. 1968. Palitoy toddling baby doll, with battery-operated walking mechanism. 21″ tall with sleeping eyes, blonde urchin hair style and wearing a lace-trimmed smock with matching pants.

'TIMPO TOYS'. See **Toy Importers Ltd.**

TINA. 1965. See **Hook & Franks Ltd.**

TINA. 1975. Doll from Disco Girl doll range, made by Lesney Products & Co. Ltd.

TING-A-LING TRUDY. 1972. Palitoy doll which talks on toy telephone.

'TINKERBILL'. c1915-20. Stuffed toy sprite with devilish expression in white plush and dressed in red with red cap. Advertised by Messrs Laurie Hansen & Co. Ltd.

TINKLES. 1919. See **Harwin & Co. Ltd.**

TINY BELLE. 1948. Doll made by Toys (Components) Ltd.

TINY TALKER. 1962. 20″ Pedigree talking doll, sister to 'talkative Jane'. Retail price £5 9s 6d.

TIPPY TUMBLES. Introduced 1969. Palitoy doll which does press-ups, handstands, front and back flips, operated by remote control.

TIP TAP. Introduced 1969. Toddler doll which can pedal its tricycle, shuffle along on a toy pony, or take tiny steps on tip-toe holding a child's hand. Battery-operated. Made by Rosebud Mattel Ltd.

TOCOLY DOLLS. 1946. See **Thomas Industries (London) Ltd.**

TODD, Daniel G. c1937. Todd was managing director of Toy Time Toys Ltd., a doll and toy manufacturing company at 46-50 Stanley Street, Southport, Lancashire with factories in Southport and Birkdale. The firm produced various dolls including a range of soft and 'continental' type character dolls which were shown by J. Ailion & Co., wholesalers and agents, at the 1937 British Industries Fair. The firm's 1940 range included British Baby dolls of almost unbreakable composition with sleeping and painted eyes, also Dolls' Hospital sundries. 1941 range included soft and hard-bodied negro dolls. The firm's trademark was 'Toy Time Toys'.

By 1947 Todd had formed a new company, D. G. Todd & Co. Ltd, with a factory at Grosvenor Works, Tulketh Street, Southport and offices at 82a, Shakespeare Street, Southport. The company specialized in the manufacture of plastic dolls and toys,

'Tich', 1932.

which were distributed solely by J. Cowan (Dolls) Ltd. 1947 lines included Rodno Baby Dolls, black and white, with painted or sleeping eyes. In September 1948 Todd registered the trademark 'Rodnoid' no. 660719 for toys and games and in the same year produced an all-plastic, injection-moulded sleeping baby doll 9″ high. At about this time the firm was using the trademark 'Roddy' for its dolls.

In March 1949, Todd together with J. Robinson obtained patent no. 663405 for providing a specialised 'sleeping eye' element for dolls, and in October 1953 they obtained a further patent for dolls' eyes, no. 744823. By 1955 the company was producing costume models, sitting and standing dolls, and walking dolls led by hand or self-propelled. Toy Time Toys Ltd. was at this time specialising in the production of small plastic dolls 2″-4″ high. In 1969 Todd's company became 'Bluebell Dolls Ltd.'. In 1974 it was announced that owing to the rising cost of materials the doll making side of the business would have to be shut down, but Denys Fisher Toys stepped in and continued to manufacture the Bluebell, Gaiety and Roddy Doll range in Southport.

In 1971 Bluebell Dolls marketed Miss Happy Heart with an electronically controlled beating heart beneath her navel, and Katie Kopycat who could copy all her owner drew on the opposite side of her magic desk. The marketing manager Mr Norman Stephens had also tried an experimental batch of boy dolls (See **Genital Dolls),** Negroid featured dolls aimed at the immigrant market, and white-faced golliwogs exported to South Africa, but without success. Taste in sophisticated dolls usually reflects the opinions of adults who buy them and not the children who play with them.

TODDLER, The. c1915. Stockinette doll made by the Shanklin Toy Industry.

TODDLES. Trade mark for toys no. 341939 registered 17th April, 1912. See **Eisenmann & Co.**

TODDLE TALKS. 1970. Pedigree doll which walks and talks by remote control.

TODHUNTER, M. E. England. Doll maker. Obtained patent no. 281791 on 17th September, 1926 for doll which has skeleton of flexible copper wire, and head with features modelled in clay and covered with soft leather and coloured with oil paints.

TOITZ, I. 1934. At 38 Windmill Street, Stratford, London E15. Doll manufacturer. Obtained patent no. 433006 on December 27th 1934 for a stuffed doll incorporating a miniature gramophone provided with means for re-setting the reproducer on the record and for retaining the reproducer on the

recorded date while playing. In 1941 Toitz advertised 'high class soft body baby dolls with unbreakable heads'.

TOMMY. c1949. See **Playlastic Toy Co. Ltd.**

TOMMY ATKINS. Dressed soldier made of cloth with movable head and velvet face. He wears a badge which reads 'Our Tommy / Are we downhearted / NO / Made in England'. In two sizes. Wholesaler: Whyte, Ridsdale & Co. 1914.

Movable head, velvet face, made in two sizes. 1914.

'TOMMY' DOLLS. Dolls made during World War I. O. E. D. definition of Tommy: 'Private in Army; derived from Tommy Atkins, a name often used as an example on forms etc.'

TOMMY FUZBUZ. 1914. Set of Rag doll ninepins and rag doll soldiers with fur busbies plus two soft balls covered with wool net, made by Dean's. Accompanied by a booklet 'All about Tommy Fuzbuz' recounting the history of the little soldier ninepins.

TOMMY GUNN. Introduced 1966. British fighting soldier doll with several outfits and accessories made by Pedigree. Retail price 37s 6d.

TONY. Introduced 1972. Boy 'Matchbox' doll, designed as boyfriend to Disco Girls. 23 cm high with gripping hands; fully movable limbs, waist and head; and deep-rooted, pop-style hair. Made for Lesney Products Co. Ltd. in Hong Kong.

TOOTS. 1927. Soft doll dressed in silk trimmed with marabout, in 5 sizes. Made by Mabel Bland-Hawkes.

TOOTS. 1965. 9″ Paul doll, 'sister' to 'Tressy'. Has hair that 'grows', legs which bend at the knee and ankle, and a range of 10 outfits.

TOPPER TOYS. 1964. At 133 Blyth Road, Hayes, Middlesex. Doll and toy manufacturers, division of the De Luxe Toy Co. Ltd. Producing 'Penny Brite' doll and accessories and 'Suzy Smart'. See **De Luxe Toy Co. Ltd.**

TOPSY. 1957. 20″ black Paliglide walking doll with curly wig and hoop earrings. Made by Palitoy.

TORQUAY MUSEUM. Babbacombe Road, Torquay, Devon. Dolls and dollhouses.

TORRINGTON, W.J. Obtained patent no. 21654 on 28th October, 1914. 'A sunshade or umbrella is adapted for use as a doll'.

TOWER TREASURES. A company directed by Alison Nisbet (daughter of Peggy Nisbet) for marketing limited editions of collector's model dolls: Queen Elizabeth I, Queen Victoria, H. M. Queen Elizabeth II; Arabella Stuart; and others.

TOWNSEND, George. c1850-1928. St. Gregory's Pottery, Longton, Staffordshire. Made china toys and figures.

TOY IMPORTERS LTD. 1941. At 26, Westbourne Grove, London W2. Doll and toy manufacturers. 1941 range comprised over 200 different kinds and models, including dressed and undressed dolls with composition and 'pot' heads, and soft-bodied dolls. 1943 lines included a negro doll and 1946 an Eskimo. Trademark 'Timpo Toys'.

TOYLAND TOYS. See **Smith, W.H. & Sons.**

TOYS (COMPONENTS) LTD. 1948. At 157 Portobello Road, London W11. Doll manufacturers, wholesalers and exporters. Dolls included "Tiny Belle" and "Organdie Beauty".

TOY TIME TOYS LTD. See **Todd, Daniel G.**

TRACY. Introduced 1972. Palitoy doll fully articulated, battery-operated. Her blue eyes glance up and down as she pours tea. Complete with table and tea set.

TRADEMARKS. The register of legal trademarks exists since 1875 when the Trademarks Registrations Act was passed on 13th August. This was to prevent piracy and make it possible to prosecute a firm who imitated the recognised trademark of some other firm. Up to this date there are fewer named products. For her wax dolls made in London, for instance, Augusta Montanari had a personal signature which she scrawled across a doll's linen torso. Charles Marsh used an ink stamp.

TRAVELLING TRACY. Introduced 1968. 18″ drink/wet doll plus washable travel chair, from Bluebell range made by D. G. Todd & Co. Ltd.

TRAVEL TOTS. 1928. A1 doll series made by Dean's Rag Book Co. Ltd. Hand-painted faces, glass eyes and velvet bodies. Three styles and three sizes, fully dressed and equipped for travel with a little suitcase containing modern night attire, and an umbrella.

TRENDON TOYS LTD. Houldsworth Street, Reddish, Stockport. Together with their associate company Frido Ltd. they began manufacturing Sasha dolls in 1965 but by 1970 were responsible solely for the output. They had made other more orthodox dolls but were especially attracted to the Sasha dolls designed by Sasha Morgenthaler when they saw some photographed in Graphis. Sasha Morgenthaler was born 30th November, 1893 in Bern. Her gift was recognised by the artist Paul Klee who made it possible for her to leave school and enroll in Geneva Art School. She took up sculpture after her move to Munich 1915. After her marriage to the painter Ernst Morgenthaler she lived in Switzerland and began making toys and dolls after 1924 and the birth of three children. By the early 1940 period she was making her 'Sasha' type dolls but also very involved in the transport of refugee Jewish children from Germany. Her models became famous and by 1963 there was an attempt to mass-produce them so they might be provided to children at a reasonable price. Her dream was to create internationally acceptable dolls and also to alter the conventional pretty smiling featured doll. Trendon cooperated with Mrs Morgenthaler in translating this idea and produced a very high quality range. Boys

Sasha dolls.

and girls, babies, fair or dark-skinned, they all possess a sort of wistful innocence which appeals very much to children.

Sasha Morgenthaler died 1975 and there is a museum of her work in Zürich, 20-22 Bärengasse. Trendon Co. make the Sasha dolls and outfits.

TRESSY. Introduced 1964. 12″ Palitoy doll whose waist-length hair can be shortened or lengthened by inserting a key in the doll's back.

TREVOR TOYS LTD. 1966. At 446 Hoe Street, Leyton, London E17. Toy and doll manufacturers. Lines include 'Make Yourself' doll kits, Julie and Jon, the Dutch boy and girl.

TRIANG TOYS. See **Pedigree Soft Toys Ltd.**

TRICIA DOLLS. 1975. Victorian rag doll. Designed by Pat Stoten, 12 de Burgh Place, Clare, Suffolk. Also one pottery-headed doll made locally: "Charlotte".

TRIKE TOYS. 1929. Figures mounted on miniature bicycles which pedal in a most natural way when the cycle is drawn along by means of a trailing cord. Series included Buster Brown, Cot Cat, Dismal Desmond, Princess Doll, Frilly Doll, Bedtime Bunnikins and Jacko. All the figures except Jacko were also made in the Safety First line (with many heads: look right, look left). Mask by Dean's Rag Book Co.

TRIXIE. 1925. 13½″ doll, short hair with fringe, dressed in patterned frock, white socks and shoes. Made by Dean's Rag Book Co. Ltd.

TRIXIE. c1949. See **Playlastic Toy Co. Ltd.**

TRIXIE RIDE A TRIKE. 1969. Doll with tricycle from Bluebell range by D. G. Todd & Co. Ltd.

TRUE LIFE DOLLS. 1955. Palitoy soft doll range. Dolls had plush bodies with flexible neck, hands and feet. Some had moulded flexible plastic heads with painted or sleeping eyes.

TRUFANT, Bertha. Patent 2002, 29th July 1895 for cardboard toys, dolls and baby carriages.

TRU-TO-LIFE DOLLS. Introduced 1913. Series of 30 rag dolls made by Dean's Rag Book Co. Ltd. The doll was described as 'almost indestructible, with a natural face comparable to that of a breakable china doll. Guaranteed hygienically stuffed.' The dolls were dressed in 'artistically designed costumes,' some of which could be taken off. Prices ranged from 2s 6d to 25s. Series included Betty Blue and Big Baby Doll.

Advertisement, 1895.

TUCHER, C. 1916. At 5 Russell Street, London Road, Manchester. Wax figure and doll's head maker.

TUCHMANN & CO., VICTOR. Invicta Works, Chapel Road, Stamford Hill, London. Doll and toy manufacturers. Registered trademark (a picture of boy and girl with dolls and toy boat) no. 154326 on 24th February 1891. 'Specialities, rag and fur dolls'.

TUCK, Raphael. Established in 1866 by a Prussian business man who set himself up as "Fine Art Publisher and Picture Frame Manufacturer". Later he specialised in oleographs (a type of chromolithograph made to imitate oil paintings and then mounted on canvas and varnished) which were printed in Saxony. The firm was continued by his two sons Adolf and Herman and exists today. They produced

also coloured scraps and cards and took out patents for dressed paper dolls for children: 1893 patent 11367 for a baby model dressed in tissue paper cape; 30th November 1894 no. 23003 for dolls in colour with changeable dresses, including a technique for fitting on dresses under a slit at the neck. A competition was set for the public with a substantial prize for suitable designs for such dolls. The sets, pretty and usually well boxed, are a useful guide to the fashions of the day, as every type of character was used including Nursery Rhyme characters in Fancy Dress for small children, and noted actresses of the day such as Miss Maude Adams, Mrs Lesley Carter and Mrs Ada Rehan. Tuck's had many imitators: their printing techniques, at that period, were impressive.

TUFTEX. Name for unbreakable composition used for the making of dolls' heads, bodies, legs and arms. Manufactured by Art Statue Co.

TUMBLE-IT DOLLS. 1915. See **Thorne Bros.**

TUMBLING DOLL. 1920. Doll made by East London (Federation) Toy Factory.

TURNBULL & CO., Charles Edward. 1903-1925+. At 45 and 47 Clerkenwell Road, London EC1. Made dolls, golliwogs, trenches and forts, sandbricks and 'Forestry Archery' sets.

TURNER, Ernest. 7 Manchester Avenue, Aldersgate Street, London EC1. Toy and doll merchant. Registered trademark 'Kalutu', no. 508077, 22nd November, 1929 for dolls.

TURTLEDOLLS. See **Thernglade Ltd.**

TURTON, W.S. 1915. At 1 Moreton Street, Manchester. Doll and toy manufacturer. 1915 lines included 'Non-Nysa' dolls from Rainbow Series. These were 1d line dolls, fabric-printed with hygienic fillings and divided legs. Range comprised six different

dolls including Drummer Boy, Boy Scout, Territorial and Red Cross Nurse.

TUSSAUD, Marie. This famous wax modeller was left an orphan at 6 years old (1766) and adopted by an uncle, Johann Creutz, a Swiss German who established a wax modelling studio in Paris in 1780. Here Marie learnt all the art of modelling and met many famous people. She taught the art to King Louis XVI's sister. After the Revolution she came to England with her two small sons and brought the famous waxworks museum of her uncle with her. She reputedly modelled some infants, and the one pictured here is said to represent Caroline Harris, born November 1798. It is made as a doll with shutting eyes worked by a wire. The Harris family were Quakers and Caroline's father was a corn factor said to have had dealings with France and perhaps with émigrés. The modelling is exceptionally fine and the doll is still in the family, handed down from Caroline Harris who died in 1874. Marie Tussaud founded the famous wax show which is still exhibited in London though few of her originals remain after the disastrous fire of 1925. Nantucket Historical Association, Mass. possess another fine infant model, said to represent the French Dauphin and perhaps to be Tussaud work.

TWINS. 1939. A celluloid boy and girl doll boxed together. 2/6. Made by Cascelloid Ltd.

TYNESIDE TOYS LTD. 1918 at Swan's Building, St. James Street, Newcastle-upon-Tyne. Doll manufacturers. 1918: dressed and undressed dolls with china and unbreakable heads. 1919: dressed nigger doll and boy and girl doll. Agents: J. A. Brothers.

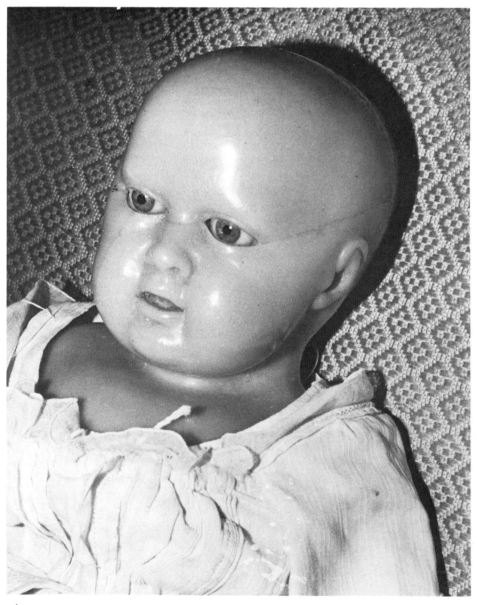

Baby doll, 1789, reputedly made by Madame Tussaud. Wax head and limbs.

UNCONSCIOUS DOLL EXERCISER. See **National Doll League; Sandow, Eugene; Whitely Exerciser Ltd.**

UNION JACK BABY. 1916. See **Rees, Leon.**

UNITY PACK CO. 1946. At Unity Works, Southport, Lancashire. Doll manufacturers. 1946 lines included 'Anita'.

UPPERTON. Patricia Gwendoline Elisabeth. 69a Windmill Hill, Enfield, Middlesex. Manufacturer. Registered trademark 'Giddikids' no. 783,095 on October 22nd, 1958 for dolls, games and playthings. Traded as Fantasc.

UPTON, Florence. 76 Fellows Road, Hampstead, London NW. Illustrator of children's books. Born in New York of English parents. At the age of 16, after her father's death, she started working as a designer and illustrator. She and her mother, Bertha Upton, returned to England in 1893 and Florence began working on the illustrations of the children's book 'The Adventures of Two Dutch Dolls and a Golliwogg', the verses of which were written by her mother. The book was published by Longman's Green & Co. and was a great success.

VELVET. Velvet fabric originated in the East, probably in China as it is made purely from silk. Its characteristic is a short, thick pile, formed by a second set of warp threads woven over already woven silk cloth. The threads are passed over wires and cut before the wires are removed. The material used in doll manufacture was more often velveteen: this was made by the same process but with cotton backing. Now the term is indiscriminately used for man-made fabrics: nylon velvet etc. See **Dixie Dolls.**

VELVETEEN. First mentioned in 1863, when it was probably originally manufactured. See **Velvet.**

VERA DOLLS. c1913+. The first British-made jointed composition dolls, originally manufactured by J. Kohnstam and Keen & Co. After the outbreak of the 14-18 war production of the dolls was taken over by Lord Roberts Memorial Workshops. A 1917 Workshops advertisement reads: 'Vera' doll with stocked or china heads, real hair wigs, blonde or brunette, double-jointed legs and arms, fitted with our patent ball and socket. 'Vera' Baby doll; character doll with single-jointed limbs and strong composition head. See **Keen & Co.** and **Kohnstam, J. Ltd.**

VICTORIA & ALBERT MUSEUM. South Kensington, London SW7. Collection includes some very well-preserved 18th century dolls and the celebrated 'Lord and Lady Clapham', bought for the museum for £16,000.

VICTORIA TOY WORKS. See **Wellings, Norah.**

VICTORY. 1917. Registered trademark no. 380831 for dolls. See **Benjamin, Henry Solomon.**

VICTORY BABE. c1914-20. Baby doll made by Nottingham Toy Industry.

VINCENT, John. 1919. At 86 St. Mary Street, Weymouth, Dorset. Jeweller and watch and clock maker. Registered trademark 'Petseymurphy' no. 387,493 on 10th January, 1919 for dolls and toys.

VOGUE DOLLS. c1918. Fashionable dolls with china head and limbs and leatherette bodies, made by the Nottingham Toy Industry Ltd. One doll in the range was dressed in a silk frock of rose, blue and lavender with cap to match and a 'saucy outcrop of curls.'

VOGUE RAG DOLLS. c1914-20. Rag dolls made by the Nottingham Toy Industry Ltd.

WALKAWAY. Chad Valley Registered trademark no. 566,438 for dolls, toys, indoor games and puzzles, 14th February, 1936.

WALKIE TALKIE DOLLS. 1949. Walking talking dolls manufactured by Dolls Industries Ltd.

WALKING BABY LOVES YOU. 1976. 19" walking doll made in Hong Kong for Airfix Products Ltd. Constructed of composite rigid and flexible plastics. The walking

'Baby Loves You', walking doll, 1976.

action is activated by pressing the doll's hands. Movable head with rooted blonde hair. Dressed in one-piece jumpsuit and matching red-trimmed pinafore.

WALKING DOLLS. Mechanical walking dolls were exhibited in England during the 18th century and were a matter of wonder, but they were usually introduced by foreign showmen and were certainly made on the continent by German or Swiss masters. The earliest record of London-made models seems to be of those of Charles Brugier (from Geneva) who made "a little doll who walked like a real person, putting one foot after another and turning her head. The mechanism which worked her was entirely hidden in the body, which was left unclothed to demonstrate the fact. This little figure could walk on any table and she carried a rake which gave her the necessary balance." Most walking dolls cheated by moving on a small wheeled chassis with a wound-up clockwork spring. The Autoperipatetikos was a famous American invention: a doll on a crinoline type base (concealing the clockwork) which actually worked on two feet. In 1888 W. Britain took out a patent no. 17258 for fly-wheel drive which he incorporated in some moving toys such as a walking elephant, a walking race for little men, the General riding his hobby-horse etc.

The twentieth century inaugurated the walking and performing doll worked by electric battery and mass-produced in plastic.

See also **Adlon; Airfix; Brohead, S. Baby First Step; Baby Walk Alone; Charstone, W.J.; Clark, W.; Cornelius, W.; Desdemona; Edmunds, J. H.; Gans, O.; Harber, W. F.; Harper & Bellamy; Hethersay, E.S.; Kum-along-Katie; Lloyd, F. G.; Martin & Runyon; Nunn, G. L.; Saucy Walkers; Stamford Doll; Stroll-with-me Doll; Sunbonnet Baby; Thompson, W. P.; Tippy Toes; Walking Princess.**

WALKING PRINCESS. 1955. Walking doll made by D. G. Todd & Co. Ltd.

WALKING AND TALKING LIZA. 1976. Vinyl doll with rooted washable hair, dressed in long Victorian-style dress or corduroy trouser suit. Battery-operated walking mechanism and voice, operated separately. Double-sided voice record, 8 phrases on one, a song on the other; press-button action. Retails at about £18.95 Manufactured by W. H. Cornelius Ltd.

WALLIS, J. & E. 1812. Manufacturers of paper dolls. Made 'St. Julien, the Emigrant' paper doll set, which consisted of 7 cut-out paper figures in costume. The doll is similar to the one featured in 'The History of Little Fanny'.

WALLINGTON HALL. Cambo, Morpeth, Northumberland. The nursery at Wallington has been arranged to look as if a family of children had just left it. Among the toys on display are some Victorian dolls and some remarkable dolls' houses, one of which, dated 1882, has 36 rooms, running water and a lift, about 1000 pieces of furniture and 50 dolls.

WARD, Samuel Henry. See **Forget-me-not.**

WARDOL WORKS. See **Potteries Toy Co., The**

WARWICK DOLL MUSEUM. Oken's House, Castle Street, Warwick. Fine collection of high-quality dolls and toys.

WASHEY DOLLY. 1920. Doll. See manufacturers **East London (Federation Toy) Factory.**

WATSON, K. E. K. 1936. 16th November. Obtained patent no. 473317 for material for making dolls' eyes.

Wax over papier mâché dolls, glass eyes (Pollock's Toy Museum).

WATTS BROS. 1918-19. At 70 Cannon Street, Manchester. Doll wig manufacturers. The hair used was human and mohair. The wigs were woven and stitched on to a canvas shape. There were a number of styles available; some dressed frizzy, others wavy, and some in ringlets. Colours were auburn, blonde, light brown, mid-brown, dark brown, flaxen and golden.

WAX DOLLS. Wax modelling for funeral effigies, portrait reliefs, various maquettes for china, plaster work, medals etc was established as an art in England from mediaeval times; and it would be reasonable to suppose that little wax dolls were also made equally early. Certainly by the 18th century there were toymakers selling dolls with moving eyes and wax faces, as these are mentioned in letters and literature of the period. One of the first historical references to a toymaker is to Mrs Salmon, who ran a famous waxworks and also taught the art in Fleet St. See "A Biographical Dictionary of

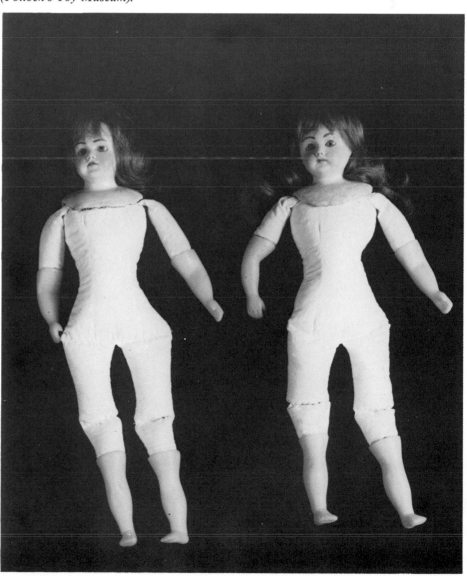

*Portrait of Queen Anne in wax and
rolled paper. (Victoria & Albert Museum).*

Wax Modellers" by E. J. Pyke, O.U.P. 1973.

By the 19th century London wax dolls were famous. The best of them were very luxurious and expensive, beautifully constructed and dressed. They were made by pouring liquid wax into moulds fashioned for the purpose from the original sculpted head and shoulder, and limbs. The resulting shells were hand-worked, holes were cut for eyes and sometimes eyelet holes added for stringing to a fabric body. See **Edwards, John; Marsh, Charles; Meech; Montanari; Pierotti; Peck, Mrs Lucy; Tussaud, Marie.** In 1893 it was reported that there were in England forty manufacturers of high-class wax dolls; and there were many more who produced cheaper dolls, some of them wax-dipped over a papier mâché frame or small 'penny' dolls.

Modern artist-craftsmen, such as Margaret Glover, have produced fine work using early methods.

English wax dollmakers include:
James Gosset 1763
Joachim Smith 1763
Pierotti Family 1780-1925
Douglas & Hamer 1843-1847
Robert Ogilwy 1843-60
Lucy Rebecca Peck 1894-1922
George Teather 1850
Thomas Bluett 1850
Montanari Family 1851-84
Edward Poole 1852-65
P. Bianchi 1855
Mrs S. Snowball 1855
John Edwards 1856-85
Joseph Thorpe 1856
John Hobbins 1856-65

Joseph Evans & Sons 1868-81
Horace W. Morrell 1870
Charles Marsh 1878-1894
Mrs Helena Elwick 1879
Thomas Hatch 1884-91
James and William Wheelhouse 1911-1920
C. Tucher 1916.
Meech, Herbert John 1865-91

WAX FINISH. For china. A process of making rough china-headed dolls look softer and giving them a better complexion. See **Bailey, Doris Sylvia; Baxter, Sarah Jane.** Also **Sissons Bros. & Co. Ltd.**

Wax doll, possibly by Lucy Peck.
Blue glass eyes, inserted hair, hair-stuffed
rag body (Pollock's Toy Museum).

The large wax doll in the centre and the smaller doll wearing a bonnet were made by Madame Montanari in 1863. The third doll, by Lucy Peck, dates from 1870. All three are in their original dresses.

Collection of dolls and dolls' furniture, English, 18th and 19th centuries (Victoria & Albert Museum, gift of H. J. Powell).

Wax over papier mâché doll, c. 1840. Kid arms, rag body (Pollock's Toy Museum).

Wax doll with pumpkin head, rag body, and wooden limbs, dressed in Welsh traditional costume. The shirt is made from striped Welsh flannel.

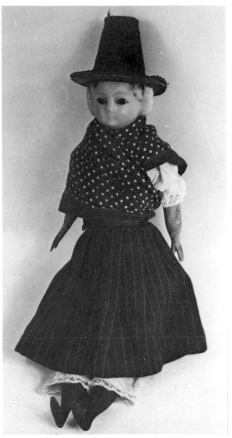

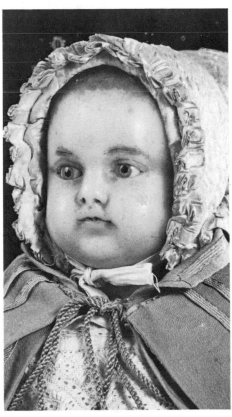

This doll belonged to a family of 19 children. It was bought in 1851, along with several others made by Madame Montanari as likenesses of the Royal Family. The original gown is embroidered with a design of oak leaves.

Wax doll with wooden voice box in body; original clothes. Possibly made by Edward Smith, The City Toy Shop.

Wax headed doll, 20 ins., composition limbs coated with wax, rag body.

WEBB, Florence. 1916. Obtained patent no. 104075 for a doll head, hands and feet made of mock kid leather. The head was moulded over a buckram form and stuffed with cotton wool. The fingers, thumbs and toes were made flexible by means of a wire framework.

WEBBER'S DOLLS LTD. 1944-51. Hayfield Mills, Percy Street, Pendleton, Salford 6. Lancashire. Doll manufacturers and merchants. Designer, Mrs Donner: Producer, Mr Donner. The firm had factories in London and Manchester and their sole agents were Packers (Manchester) Ltd.

WEBER, W. & WEBER, H. 1894. Obtained patent no. 9811 on 19th May, 1894, for a device to produce a to-and-fro movement of a doll's head about a vertical axis.

WEEKS & CO. (LONDON) LTD. 1920. At 2 Ramillies Street, London W1. Soft toy and doll manufacturers. Dolls had no pins or buttons, were claimed to be unbreakable and were very lightweight. They had hand-painted faces. Firm used the trademark Nelke.

WEE WILLIE WINKIE. 1916. See **Harwin & Co. Ltd.**

WEIGEL, A. 1899. Obtained patent no. 24044 for hopping dolls.

WEISSBECK, Henry. 1893. Llandudno, Wales. Obtained patent no. 22622 on 25th November, 1893 for dolls' eyes that rotated vertically; these eyes were used in wax or china heads.

WELLINGS, Norah. 1919-59. From 1926 at Victoria Toy Works, Wellington, Shropshire. From 1919 Norah Wellings worked as a designer at Chad Valley for seven years. In 1926 she established her own soft toy factory in Wellington, the business side of which was managed by her brother Leonard, while Miss Wellings concentrated on design and manufacture. On November 24th 1926, she obtained a patent no. 282955 relating to a doll's head formed of fabric or felt and backed with buckram. The inner surface was to be coated with plastic wood. Fixed or movable eyes were attached to the inner surface, and a waterproof coating was applied finally, so as to make the face washable. Miss Wellings made pressed-felt and velveteen-faced dolls with painted features and with eyes sometimes of inset glass. She claimed that all her dolls were fully marked with a sewn-on label, either on the wrist or under the foot of the doll. She made mainly character dolls, which included the Britannia doll with a quilted plumed fabric helmet and coat of mail; Little Bo Peep; a Maori boy with velvet face, inset glass eyes, smiling mouth and swivel head; a

South Sea Islander Doll, Sailor dolls, Mountie dolls and Cowboy dolls. Many of her dolls were made as mascots to be sold on board the great Atlantic ocean liners. 'Harry the Hawk', the Royal Air Force mascot doll, was sold during the Second World War in aid of Royal Air Force comforts. Another of Miss Wellings' dolls, 'Cora', was presented to Her Majesty Queen Mary when she visited the Victoria Toy Works in 1927. In 1932 the 'Norene' range including Dutch,

Spanish and Chinese dolls, was introduced and in 1933 a set of toddler dolls, the 'Jolly Toddlers'.

In 'Norah Wellings—A Personal Recollection' Peggy Nisbet says 'Her dolls were her life, into which she put much of herself, and she felt they were her family. This may be why her own creations seemed to have more character than other not dissimilar dolls produced by larger manufacturers of the same period.'

Felt soldier dolls: Norah Wellings label on foot (Faith Eaton).

Felt doll, swivel neck (Faith Eaton).

'Harry the Hawk', RAF airman doll.
A percentage of the manufacturers' sales of
these mascots went to the RAF
Comforts Fund.

'Japanese Doll by Norah Wellings.

'Zuzu', 1933 (Pollock's Toy Museum).

Norah Wellings with some of her dolls at
the British Industries Fair, 1935.

WELSH DOLLS. Dolls in Welsh National costume are produced in large numbers for the tourist trade. The girl dolls usually wear the traditional high black hats. A Welsh cut-out doll called 'Mfanwy Jones' was made by Margaret Holgate as a souvenir of the 1969 Investiture of His Royal Highness the Prince of Wales. Welsh doll manufacturers include: Welsh Toy Industries of Cardiff, c1919; South Wales Toy Manufacturing Co. of Cardiff, 1916-22.

WELSH FOLK MUSEUM. St. Fagans, Cardiff, Wales. This museum has a miscellany of Victorian dolls and toys, including two simple dolls carved out of solid timber.

WELSH TOY INDUSTRIES. c1919. Crwys Bridge, Cardiff. London Showroom: Buchanan Buildings, 24 Holborn, London EC1. Manufacturers of composition and china dolls, soft and wood toys and teddy bears. The firm's proprietors were Gibbon & Sons Ltd, of the London address. The firm used the trademark 'WE-TO' toys. In 1919 they advertised a range of 30 dolls from 15/9 per dozen to 158/- per dozen including jointed dolls with fixed or sleeping eyes, baby dolls, dressed and character dolls.

WEMBLEY WILLIE. c1924. Stuffed rag doll made by Dean's Rag Book Co. Ltd. to commemorate the Wembley Exhibition held in 1924 and 1925. The doll was patented in Great Britain, Germany and France. It had flesh-coloured painted features and wore a purple felt suit, white waistcoat, purple hat with black band, shoes and spats.

WENDY. 1924. 17″ Tru-to-Life doll by Dean's Rag Book Co. Ltd.

WENDY. 1959. 17″ Palitoy petalskin doll with sleeping eyes, a mama crier and rooted hair that can be washed, waved and set.

WENDY. 1969. Bluebell range walking and talking doll manufactured by D. G. Todd & Co. Ltd.

WENDY AND HER WARDROBE. c1923. An 'A1' doll sheet to cut out, make up and stuff, made by Dean's Rag Book Co. The completed and dressed 'Wendy' rag doll could also be purchased.

WENDY BOSTON. Queen Street, Abergavenny, Monmouthshire. Doll and toy manufacturers. Since 1955 'Playsafe' dolls and soft toys were made with fillings of washable plastic sponge and could be put through an automatic washing machine. By 1965 the firm had changed its name to Wendy Playsafe Toys Ltd. 1965 range included a 15″ soft doll with body made of peach-coloured courtelle jersey, filled with polyether crumb, and hair of nylon plush. She wore white velvet shoes, and the eyes and nose were plastic screws with nylon nuts,

guaranteed never to pull out. In 1968 the firm was taken over by Denys Fisher Toys Ltd.

WENDY WONDER DOLL. 1950. Registered trademark for dolls. See **Sleepa Doll Co.**

WESTON, Samuel & William James. 1922. London. They obtained a German patent for dolls' eyeballs.

Early 20th century flat wooden Welsh doll, made at the Vale of Olwyn Works (Bantock House Museum, Wolverhampton).

WESTWOOD. Baby Doll. 1844. All-wax nativity figure with painted eyes and mouth. Given by Thomas Westwood to his wife Eliza on 2nd January 1844, fearing she was going to bear him no children; subsequently she had seventeen. The doll is on display at Worthing Museum.

WE-TO TOYS. c1919. Trademark for dolls and toys. See **Welsh Toy Industries.**

WHEELDON, Arthur Leonard. 1913-18. London. Together with Dean's Rag Book Co. Ltd obtained patent no. 100469 on 17th March, 1916 and no. 105888 on 14th February, 1917. The earlier patent was in connection with the manufacture of stuffed dolls and animals; the sheet material

forming the front and back of the foot has extension pieces, so that by sewing the two sheets together and drawing in a central portion a complete foot is formed. The second patent was for shaping the material for making a stuffed doll, so as to form a skirt or other garment in one therewith.

WHEELER, John. 1879. 15 New Gate Street, London. Manufacturer of dolls and dolls' dresses. Used a picture of a crown as a trademark.

WHEELHOUSE, James & William. London. 1911-1920. Made dolls, including wax dolls.

WHEELHOUSE, Miss M. 1925. Listed in a London Directory as a dollmaker.

WHEELHOUSE, William & Charles. 1857-1865. Made dolls.

WHISTLING BOY. 1916. See **Imperial Toy Co.**

WHITE'S. c1850. Houndsditch, London. Dolls were assembled here prior to being hawked in the London streets.

WHITING, O. K. 1942. British subject temporarily residing in New York, U.S.A. Obtained British patent no. 544661 on April 22nd, 1942, for a doll fitted with one or more magnets for the purpose of attracting and supporting other toy articles, which in turn are fitted with metallic parts. The dolls can thus be made to 'carry' articles such as umbrellas, baskets, etc.

WHITE, C. & H. Early 19th century. Milton, Portsmouth. Made pedlar dolls. Most of their dolls had heads made of kid leather; and some had faces of chicken skin. A pair of C. and H. White pedlar dolls is in the Bethnal Green Museum, London.

WHITELY EXERCISER LTD. 1919. 35 Southwark Bridge Road, London SE. Manufacturers of doll cord and rubber springs for toys. The firm also produced an exerciser doll designed to encourage children to exercise their arm and leg muscles. The doll was made along the lines of the exerciser toy patented by E. Sandow in 1914.

WHOLESALE TOY CO. c1916. 52a Blackstock Road, Finsbury Park, London N. Doll manufacturers. 'The Ross Dolls' was the brand name of the company's doll range; they were made in a variety of styles and particularly notable for their 'dainty' dresses. Every part of the dolls was made in their factory.

WHYTE, RIDSDALE & CO. c1876-1923. 73-76 Houndsditch, Bishopsgate, London E. Doll and soft toy wholesalers. In 1914 they were selling 'Dolly Dimple', a china-headed doll, and 'Tommy Atkins', a British-made rag soldier doll with movable head.

199

WICKS, Henry (Harry). 1852-65. At 27 City Terrace, City Road, London EC. Made composition dolls.

WICKS, James. 1852-54. At 15 Whitmore Road, Hoxton, London. Made composition dolls.

WIEDERSEIM, Grace. Grace Wiederseim was born in Philadelphia, U.S.A. in 1877. Her maiden name was Gerbie and all her early work is signed G. G. Wiederseim. In 1911 she divorced her husband Theodore E. Wiederseim and married W. Heyward Drayton. Until her death in 1936 she used the name, by which she is best known in America, Grace G. Drayton. Her drawings of chubby little children with roguish goo-goo eyes are said to resemble herself. The Campbell Kids, designed to advertise a soup company were perhaps her most popular creations. In 1912 she designed some dolls for Dean's Rag Book Co. Ltd., Teddie and Peggie. They were originally sold as Wiederseim series but name later changed to Goo-Goo Series. These dolls were reissued by Dean's in 1979.

'Playsafe' soft dolls by Wendy Boston

WIGS. The earliest wooden or wax dolls were made up with human hair or perhaps a scrap of lambskin representing curls. The fine poured-wax dolls of the Victorian period in England had human hair inserted by needle or slitted in tufts: by the mid-century there were professional doll-wig makers. Human hair was woven upon a thread, the threads being sewn to a cap-shaped frame which could be stuck to a doll's pate. The firms using human hair obtained much of it from convents, where the novices had their hair cut short. A curious report in Games and Toys 1917 states that a great deal of hair for dolls' wigs came from China. Though coarse in quality and black it could be refined, bleached and dyed to beautiful shades suitable for dolls. It was considered much superior to mohair. In 1913, 3,667,867 pounds of hair was reported to have been exported from China. After the downfall of the Manchu dynasty the Chinese man's queue was abolished and the edict was followed by wholesale cutting (and selling) of the traditional queue of long hair. Mohair, manufactured from the long hair of the Angora goat, was practically the monopoly of English firms and after the 1914/18 war Germany was so short of materials for their dolls' wigs they had to make a substitute. See:

All British Doll Manufacturing Co. 1915-19
Be-Be (Dolls) Ltd. c1941
British Jointed Doll Co. c1920
Dolgar Manufacturing Co. 1939
Dolphitch Manufacturing Co. Ltd. 1915-16
Lambert, Clarke & Co. c1918
Lina Works. c1920.
Mitchell & Co. 1917-19
Speights Ltd. Before 1913-1928
Ralph, H. S. 1923
Roh, Madame 1921
Smith, F. H. 1917
Watts Bros. 1918-19
Wig World 1972

WIG WORLD. 1972. At 154 New Cavendish Street, London W.1. Wig manufacturers. In 1972 they were manufacturing 'Dolly-Locks' doll wigs. Made of fireproof washable Dynel, they can be brushed, combed and restyled. 4 colour shades, black, brown, blonde and red, and 3 sizes.

WILCOX, Joy. See **Pollyanna.**

WILD, Lewis. 1884-1925. London. Importer and agent for foreign doll manufacturers. From 1884-91 he imported wax, composition and china dolls. From 1921-25 he was agent for Canadian and German dolls.

WILKINS, F. 1915. Obtained patent no. 11064 on 30th July, 1915 for a doll provided with articulated limbs which are retained in their sockets by elastic springs. See **Doll Supplies Ltd.**

WILKINSON, Anne. Contemporary designer of rag dolls.

WILLIAM AND MARY. 1925. See **Preston, Chloe.**

WILLIAMS, S. F. LTD 1941. 2-5 Dingley Road, City Road, London EC1. Manufacturers of accessories for the doll trade, specializing in unbreakable heads and limbs.

WILLIAMS & STEER MANU-FACTURING CO. LTD. 1949. At 25 Dingley Place, City Road, London EC1.

1952 Factory at 21, Pickering Street, Essex Road, London N1. and Office and Showroom at 20 Story Street, Caledonian Road, London.

Obtained patent no. 646668 on 9th September 1948, for a doll containing a loudspeaker which in connection with a wireless receiver makes the sound appear to proceed from the doll. In 1949 the doll was advertised in a trade paper, it was named 'Mignon' and was large and well-dressed. The company appears to have been connected with S. F. Williams Ltd.

WILLOW PATTERN DOLLS. 1927. Doll range made by Dean's Rag Book Co. Ltd. Three sizes, three colours. Frocks and bobbed wigs.

WILLOW POTTERY. See **Hewitt & Leadbeater.**

WILLSHUR, Charles. 1891-99. At 32

Pedlar dolls made by C. & H. White, Milton, Portsmouth, 1820/30.

Norman's Buildings, London (1894-5). Made dolls' bodies. In 1899 he was succeeded by Mrs Henrietta Willshur.

WILSON BROS LTD. 1923-c1930. At 80 Great Eastern Street, London EC2. Wholesalers for dolls and soft toys, including dressed and undressed dolls, character dolls, baby dolls, art dolls. They were also agents for 'Gloria' and 'Gloria Princess' dolls, made in Sonneberg, Germany.

WILSON, G. L. 1894. Obtained patent no. 14984 for a hot-water bottle in the shape of a doll.

WILSON, Honor. At 1 Dentdale Drive, Knaresborough, Yorkshire. A modern craftsman dollmaker who began making hand-dressed costume dolls in 1974. These were plastic dolls; but 18 months later, with ceramic parts made for her in limited editions of 100, she produced costume figures to order. The first in her Royal series was Princess Anne in her wedding dress. This elaborate doll with handmade leather body had a limited edition of 50. She wore a dress of pure Swiss silk trimmed with hundreds of pearls and mirror stones and a shoulder train hand-embroidered and set with over 1000 pearls; and her tiara was of hallmarked silver set with mirror stone. A suitably equivalent Captain Mark Phillips followed with fabrics and trimmings all 100% authentic and a miniature replica of his sword commissioned from Wilkinson's. Currently the artist is working on Children's Classics in ceramic, the first two being Alice and the Mad Hatter. A permanent exhibition may be seen of her work at Sudeley Castle, Gloucestershire.

WILSON, Thomas Francis. 1854-95. At 22 Abbey Street, Bethnal Green, London. (1894-95). Made dolls of wax. From 1856-65 George Isaac Wilson also made wax dolls at the same address.

WILSTSHAW & ROBINSON LTD. 1915-23. Carlton Works, Stoke-on-Trent, Staffordshire. Manufacturers of earthenware and porcelain. They made 'Carlton China' novelties, and in 1915 were manufacturing John Hassall's comic and caricature figures in Carlton Ware, 6 inches high with movable heads, and 'Pooksie', the war baby, a military caricature baby doll with moving arms, designed by Mabel Lucie Attwell. In 1916 they were producing porcelain dolls' heads and china dolls' heads and limbs.

WINDSOR CASTLE. Windsor, Berkshire. On display at the castle, near Queen Mary's famous dolls' house designed by Sir Edwin Lutyens in the 1920s, is a selection of the small dolls dressed by Queen Victoria, and also dolls presented to members of the royal family in the course of their travels.

WINKY BLINKY MOPPIT. 1977. Soft-bodied character doll with vinyl face and hands. Squeeze one hand she winks, squeeze the other she blinks. Size 40 cms. Made in Hong Kong for Lesney Products & Co. Ltd. and stuffed and assembled in the U.K.

WINSTON CHURCHILL. 1928. See **Sant, J. S. Ltd**

WINTER SPORTS GIRL. 1922. Dolleries range doll. See **Rees, Leon.**

WITCHCRAFT DOLLS. The use of a doll made of wax, clay, lead or other material, to kill, injure or seduce a person represented by the doll, is known to have existed the world over, and indeed still exists in some places even to-day. It is said to have its roots in childhood experiences, when a child believes that a doll is a real person and can be cosseted or hurt. A likeness of the victim is made in the shape of a doll, then pins or thorns are thrust into various parts of the body in order to bring pain or even death to its human counterpart. In 1964 the figure of a naked woman, 6 inches long and of modelling clay, with a sliver of hawthorn piercing its heart, was found in Norfolk. It may have been meant to kill its victim or to seduce her by piercing her heart with love.

WITTON, T. F. 1855. At 10 Abbey Street, Bethnal Green, London. Made dolls.

WOBBLER. 1919. See **Harwin & Co. Ltd.**

WOLLHEIM, H. 1899. Obtained patent no. 12246 on 12th June, 1899 for hollow dolls and toys made from cardboard or millboard, stamped in relief.

WOOLLY WALLY. 1921. Golliwog with plush wig and brightly-coloured clothes made by Dean's Rag Book Co. Ltd.

WOLSTAN DOLL CO. LTD. 1919-1928. Park House, Pit Green Lane, Wolstanton, Stoke-on-Trent, Staffordshire. Manufacturers and dealers in dolls, toys and fancy goods. Director: Mrs Shaw. In 1920 lines included 'Dorothy' dolls in a variety of styles both dressed and undressed. In 1923 a toy trade periodical reported that 'a year earlier the British doll industry seemed dead, or at least doomed, but Mrs Shaw, the dominating spirit of the British Doll Industry, continued with her plans for developing doll-making in England, and subsequent results have justified her confidence. It is interesting to note that the manufacture of dolls' heads had again been resumed in the Potteries, owing to the insistence and encouragement given by the Wolstan Doll Co.' The firm's lines in 1923 included a range of mascot dolls in many attractive styles. 1926: Dorothea, fully-jointed sleeping dolls.

WOMEN'S EMERGENCY CORPS. York Place, Baker St. A voluntary body during World War I which among other things organised toy-making. Baby dolls, 'Boy in Khaki', Alsatian Peasants, Boulogne Fishwives, Soldier dolls, Dolls' Houses.

WOMEN'S VOLUNTARY SERVICES. See **W.V.S**

WONDERLAND TOYMAKING CO. 1921-23. At 43 Old Gloucester Street, Southampton Row, London WC. Doll and toy manufacturers. Their range included 'artistic character doll' in plushette and satin etc., peasant doll, waterproof bathing dolls, cossacks, negro dolls and 'Lady Di', a stuffed doll dressed in a cream and red plushette outfit, with a pom-pom hat and a painted face.

WONDERLIFE BABY DOLL. 1962. 20" baby doll in blue and white knitted romper suit. When wound up she will move 'naturally and automatically like a new born baby. She will also hold her toes and put her thumb into her mouth'. Made by Rosebud Dolls Ltd.

WONDER TOY CO. 1927. Silver Works, Goodman Street, Birmingham. Doll and Toy manufacturers, 1927 producing a skipping doll with celluloid head and metal body. A skipping rope made of wire is held in each hand and when wound up the doll goes through a series of skipping motions. Supplied with assorted coloured dresses. The firm appears to have a connection with Wonder Toys Limited.

WONDER TOYS LTD. c1923. At 9 St. Martins, Leicester. Doll and toy manufacturers. In 1923 they advertised a 'world-startling invention'—a self-balancing skipping doll.

WOODEN DOLLS. There are curiously few details available about wooden doll-making and few examples extant earlier than the end of the 17th century. Some simple form of turned wooden doll was probably sold in mediaeval times, and certainly reports show that the Bartholomew Fair Babies were famous by the 16th century.

A legal case report of April 1733 quoted in English Dolls, by Mrs Alice Early, (1955) mentioned William Higgs, a turner, whose chief business was making babies or wooden dolls dressed by his wife. It is clear he also made chairs and that his dolls were jointed and painted, hand-dressed and then sold to shops: those mentioned are one in St. Catharine's Lane and the other Mr Robottom's in Whitechapel. The dolls were sold for 2½d each whilst a chair cost 14d.

Higgs was proud of his dolls and declared "Never a man in England makes such babies besides me".

By the end of the 17th century some very splendid wooden dolls were made: witness the example of Lord and Lady Clapham. See **Clapham Dolls.**

The workmanship deteriorated and the cheaper types brought out by the 19th century give evidence both of the struggle to compete with very cheap imported German wooden dolls and the lessening demand when different varieties of dolls became popular, such as wax and china. See **Body Construction.**

English wooden dolls, 1720-1790, from Christiane Hermelink's collection.

In 1850 Mayhew wrote of an interview with an old toyman who said his best years had been between 1809-1816, and he cast light on the rather pitiful conditions. "I make the wooden jointed dolls. The turned work (the body) is the work of the turner's lathe, I do it myself, and the faces of the commoner dolls are a composition put on afterwards. I go in for beauty as much as I can, even in the lower-priced dolls. These dolls now are carved, after having been turned out of wood. The 'carving' and 'drawing'—making the eyes, eye-brows, and lips in colours with a fine brush—are the fine touches of the trade. Nice lips and eyes set the article off. The lower-priced dolls have wooden joints at the middle by which the legs are fastened to the body. We don't go in for symmetry in the commoner sorts of legs; nor, indeed, for any

calves at all to them. They are just whitened over. The better ones have nicer calves, and flesh-coloured calves too. They are more like nature. The joints of the two sorts are made on the same principles. I buy their ringlets—it's generally ringlets, but, sometimes, braids or plaits, ready made—and have only to fit them on. That's not very different from human nature, I take it. The arms are stuffed leather, made by others. The best time for my trade was from 1809 to 1816. In every one year that I have named, I made 35 gross of dolls a week: but they were little creatures, some of them 4 inches long, dwarfs of dolls. I don't deal with the little creatures now. I'm in the larger line, as you see. A namesake of mine at that time made 100 gross a week. That's 1,960,880 dolls a year, is it? Look at that, now, for us two only. The little things I spoke of used to fetch a penny, now it's a farthing. I make now, I believe, two gross of dolls one week and one another. The larger dolls require more time, which accounts, independent of the demand, for the difference. My dolls are sold to the public at 3s and 1s: that's the retail price, mind, and small are my profits. Wooden doll making is generally confined to families, so we can't speak of journeymen's wages. There are eight other doll makers, and perhaps each may make twice as many as I do, but as they make so many more of the smaller sort, the cost (to the public) wouldn't be more than mine, perhaps about the same—but I can only guess, I have felt a great falling off in the demand since the last tariff—at least one quarter less is now made. When the duty was highest I knew a gentleman who now and then would venture £1,000 in buying foreign toys. It was, he said, a speculation, but he generally got £2,000 for his £1,000, and the toy trade was benefited, for variety and new fashions were seen, and there was better demand for toys."

WOOD, Maria. Contemporary designer of rag dolls and toys including 'Little Lizzie' and 'Jack' rag dolls.

WOOD-WOOL. Advertised for the stuffing of dolls and toys. See **Bell and Francis.**

WOOLAM, SAMUEL, MANUFACTURING CO. c1920. Longford, Gloucester. Doll and toy manufacturers. Used trademark 'Cathedral' toys. In 1920 their range included dolls dressed in costumes of all nations. The firm specialised in good underclothing for their dolls.

WOOLLEY, A. G. LTD. 1951. At 11 Mill Lane, Wimborne, Dorset. Doll manufacturers. On 14th June, 1951 they registered the trademark 'Dolly-Doc' no. B699,021 for dolls, doll parts and fittings.

WOOMBO. Black dolls. 1936. Negro dolls with earrings and three tufts of hair standing up on top of the head. Manufactured by Dean's Dollies Ltd.

WORCESTER ALL-BRITISH DOLL FACTORY. Before 1920. Worcester. Doll manufacturers. Firm closed down in December 1920 due to inability to compete with German goods.

WORCESTER CITY MUSEUM AND ART GALLERY. Tudor House, Museum, Friar Street, Worcester. The collection includes a group of 1930s German bisque dolls from the Worcester Dolls' Hospital, some interesting dolls' house items, and a small English wax doll, c1840, with black boots. The doll is still in mint condition in its original box.

WORCESTER, I. D. 1904. Obtained patent no. 13775 on 18th August, 1904 for a 'window tapping' doll. A 'tick-tack' device is secured to a window pane, and by pulling a string and releasing it, a tapping noise is produced.

WORLD OF KIDDLES. Introduced 1968. Miniature doll range by Rosebud Mattel Ltd. Some of the dolls are thimble size with life-like hair, and some can walk. The smallest dolls can be tucked in a brooch or ring. Liddle & Story Book Kiddles Series includes 3½" dolls with bendable bodies and rooted hair. The costumes are removable and dolls come with a 24-page story book. 'Liddle Middle Muffet' and 'Slipsy Sliddle' are included. 'Jewelry Kiddles' are ⅞" tall and come encased in jewellery specially designed for children.

WORTHING MUSEUM AND ART GALLERY. Chapel Road, Worthing, West Sussex. An outstanding collection, with most toys dating from about 1750-1910. Includes 'The History of Little Fanny' (1810), a rare cut-out paper doll combined with a story book, and some Pierotti wax dolls. The extensive doll collection is admirably described and photographed in the museum's doll catalogue.

WORTHING TOY FACTORY. 1924. Worthing, Sussex. Doll and toy manufacturers. Made 'Humpty Dumpty' soft toys. In 1924 introduced Cry Baby and Baby Bunting dolls.

WORTHITT & CO. 1916. At 265 Amaby Road, Hull, Yorkshire. Manufacturers of soft dolls and dressed dolls.

WU-WU. 1916. Registered trademark for dolls. See **Hamley Bros.; Hancock & Sons, S.**

W. V. S. During the Second World War the Women's Voluntary Service helped in various ways with the war effort and a pattern was published to teach people how they could provide economical stuffed toys for their little children. A satisfactory "skin" was suggested from old stockings as near as possible to flesh tint and there were hints for sewing on hair and making their clothes. The charming design was put out by Winifred Ackroyd from Girlington Hospital Supplies Depot. It would still make a very useful fundamental pattern for a "first" toy or for an older girl's hand-work. Sometimes amateur doll-makers found that they had such an aptitude for designing that it led them to set up a small business commercially. See **Rag Doll.**

WYNJOY. 1941. Registered trademark for soft dolls and toys for export. See **Colonial & Overseas Export Co. Ltd.**

WYNNE, William Richard. 1895-97. London. Obtained a German patent for a feeding doll, and British patent no. 24679, on 25th October, 1897 for a bubble-blowing doll.

XYLOLITH. 1882. Material for making dolls' heads, mentioned in a German patent.

YARN DOLLS. 1890-1925+. Dolls which were especially popular in the 1920s when there were numerous design patents that used yarn for making dolls.

YAWNIE. Introduced 1975. Palitoy doll that yawns and closes her eyes when her left hand is squeezed. Dressed in pink romper suit and bonnet trimmed with white Broderie Anglaise.

YESTERDAY DOLLIES. See **Jackman, Barbara (Crafts) Dolls Ltd.**

YOUNG ENGLAND. Series 1909. Character doll series. See manufacturer, **Hughes, Henry Jeffrey & Son.**

YOUNG & FOGG RUBBER CO. LTD. 1955. Wimbledon, London SW19. Manufacturers of rubber dolls, toys and balloons. Brand name 'Gartex'. Lines included 'Biddy' and 'Butch', comic rubber dolls, and 'Lesley', 11" rubber doll. In December 1958 firm became member of the Lines Bros. Group of companies.

YVONNE. 1955. Flexible Palitoy doll 21" tall. Movable arms and legs; delicate features and sleeping eyes, plastic rooted hair that can be washed, combed, waved and set.

ZAZZ. 1919. See **Harwin & Co. Ltd.**

ZOBEIDE. 1921. Cut-out card figure 5" high, one of a series produced by Aldon Studios of 27 Princes Street, Hanover Square, London W.1.

ZULU or ZUZU and DUDU 1930. Soft negro dolls made by Norah Wellings.

APPENDIX 1

APPENDIX INCORPORATING FOREIGN INVENTORS AND MANUFACTURERS WHO OBTAINED BRITISH PATENTS AND REGISTERED TRADEMARKS IN ENGLAND.

As an appendix, a list of some of these foreign patents is added here in alphabetical order though it is not always proof that a specific doll was sold in England. Before World War I the trade with French and German doll makers was immense and a limited number of French dolls were still imported from France during the War, and later on from Canada and America. The U.S. involvement in the toy trade continued to grow and today large British firms are owned by U.S. concerns and the financial direction is very complex.

When the German doll output competed again after the World War I, there was so much patriotic feeling that often the makers were at pains to register a doll under an English name, e.g. Kammer & Reinhardt's "My Darling". The maker's name and country of origin had to appear but were stamped in a less prominent position.

BABY DIMPLES. 1932. Trademark for dolls registered by Bedington Liddiatt & Co. on behalf of American firm Horsman.

BERTRAN, CHARLES. 1878. 4 Rue des Archives, Paris, France. Registered trademark 'Ondine' no. 15,333 for a swimming doll on 28th September, 1878.

BOLLAG, LEON. 1923. Zurich, Switzerland. Registered trademark 'Goolagool', no. 438716 for dolls and balls on 4th July, 1923.

BROONAN, RICHARD ARCHIBALD. 1848-58. American who obtained British patent no. 2639 on 20th November, 1858 for making dolls' heads from gutta-percha by moulding, stamping or embossing.

COHN, G. Obtained British patent no. 4356 on 28th February, 1899 for dolls cut out of sheet metal or card with movable joints.

ECKERT, HEINRICH. 1901-5. Munich, Bavaria. Obtained British patents no. 23650 21st November, 1901 and no. 8798 15th April, 1902 for ball and socket joints for dolls.

EDISON, THOMAS ALVA. American inventor of the phonograph obtained British patent no. 1644 on 24th April, 1878 for a phonograph doll with moving lips. This crude prototype was later improved upon by W.W. Jaques and the doll was commercially produced in 1890 with a bisque-headed doll of Simon & Halbig the German makers.

GANS, OTTO. Waltershausen, Thuringen, Germany. Obtained two British patents for walking dolls in 1923; patent no. 232982 relating to voice-producing devices in dolls in 1924 and patent no. 283881 for the design of dolls' glass eyes in 1927.

GOLDMAN, ISAAC. 1918. New York, U.S.A. Obtained British patent no. 134532 on 16th October, 1918 for attaching hair to a doll's head by using fluid adhesive for single strands or small bunches.

GOOLAGOOL. See **Bollag, Leon.**

GUICHARD, EDWARD AUGUSTE DESIREE. Obtained British patent no. 1455 in 1854 for flocked ornamentation of dolls by powdered material added to an adhesive surface.

HADDON, HERBERT. 1896-1920. Agent for dolls of Kammer & Reinhardt (missing out the Great War years).

HEITHERSAY, E.S. Malvern, Australia. Engineer. Obtained British patent no. 169753 on 1st June, 1920 for a mechanical walking doll.

HENDRICKS & SCHRUM, P.J. Obtained British patent no. 1298 on 18th January, 1904 for a doll made of wire mesh in the form of a bag.

HENKELMANN, A.C.H. 1943. Husum, Sweden. Obtained British patent no. 556163 on 22nd September, 1943 for a doll whose lips are movable as a result of the motion of the arms.

HENSTES, B.L. (Assignee of L. Shafer). Obtained British patent no. 250898 on 15th April, 1925 (Convention date) for a stuffed doll.

HERTWIG & CO. 1864-1925+, Thuringen, Germany. 1881-84, London. Doll and porcelain steam factory specializing in making bisque dolls, china dolls and nankeen dolls.

HEUBACH, HUGO. 1894-1925+, Sonneberg, Thuringen, Germany. c1900 at 29 Barbican, London E.C. Doll manufacturer and exporter.

HEYNE, FRANZ 1911. Blummerstrasse, Leipzig-Schleussig, Germany. Obtained British patent no. 16771 on 21st July, 1911 for improvements in or relating to talking or singing dolls.

HUNGARIAN RUBBER GOODS FACTORY LTD. Obtained British patent no. 484556 on 18th October, 1937 for inflatable rubber dolls with movable limbs connected to the trunk.

INSAM & PRINOTH. 1820-1925+. St. Ulrich Grödnertal, and Nuremberg, Bavaria. Exported and distributed wooden dolls made as cottage type industry in the Austrian Tyrol. ('Dutch' Dolls). Their London agent continued into the 20th century.

KAMMER & REINHARDT. 1886-1925+. Waltershausen, Thuringen, Germany. Agent in England: G.F. Redfern & Co. 15 South Street, Finsbury, London, EC2. Doll manufacturers. Registered two trademarks in Britain: a shield with 'Jointed doll/My Darling/K (star) R' on it. no. 284,259 on 30th June, 1906 for dolls and dolls' parts, and 'Naughty' no. 407,094 on 19th August, 1920 for dolls and dolls' parts. Obtained British patent no. 303104 on 28th December, 1927 (Convention date) for a coloured hollow doll's head, and British patent no. 389993 on 29th March, 1932 for reinforced soft rubber dolls.

KLEPSCH, W. Obtained patent no. 12883 on 16th June, 1908 for a balancing doll.

KUNDY, FRANZ. c1923. Catterfelder Puppenfabrik, Catterfeld, Germany. Doll manufacturer. Registered trademark 'Little Sunshine' no. 442,345 for dolls on 6th November, 1923. U.K. agent was J.E.S. Lockwood of 3 New Street, Birmingham.

LAMBERT, THOMAS BENNET. An American who obtained British patent no. 9906 in 1902 for a Phonograph doll.

LEHMANN, ERNST PAUL. 1881-1925+. Brandenburg, Prussia; later Nürnberg, Bavaria. Doll manufacturer. In 1904 he obtained a British patent for a walking doll with oscillating movement.

LENCI. See **Scavini, Enrico.**

LINDNER, JOHN CHRISTOPHER (Johannes Christoph). c1875-c1894 at 19 and 20 Hamsell Street, London, EC. Dollmaker. Appeared in German directories as a dollmaker from 1863-1902.

LITTLE SUNSHINE. See **Kundy, Franz**

LOWENSTEIN, O. Obtained British patent no. 361298 on 12th May, 1930 for a speaking doll.

MARIQUITA PEREZ SOCIEDAD ANONIMA. 1948 Madrid, Spain. Registered trademark 'Mariquita Perez', no. 672536 on 9th September, 1948 for dolls and dolls' clothes.

METSAPURO, J. Obtained patent no. 621083 on 23rd December, 1946 for a toy figure, doll etc. with readily detachable members.

MORA, ANTONIO LUIGI. Obtained patent no. 3739 for one or more dolls jumping as for a skipping motion.

MY DARLING. See **Kammer & Reinhardt.**

MY PEARL. See **Steiner, Hermann.**

NAUGHTY. See **Kammer & Reinhardt.**

OHLENSCHLAGER, K. Obtained patent no. 5320 on 27th February, 1897 for a jointed arobatic doll worked by string.

OHLHAVER, G. Hamburg, Germany. Obtained British patent no. 295259 on 5th August, 1927 (Convention date) for dolls' heads and other parts cast from papier-mâché soaked in varnish.

OVERHOLT, M. Los Angeles, California, U.S.A. Obtained British patent no. 196865 on 9th October, 1922 for detachable limbs for dolls.

REDFERN, G.F. & CO. 1910-20. London agents for Société Française de Fabrication de Bébés et Jouets, Sussfeld & Cie, and Kammer & Reinhardt.

REINHARDT, E. Obtained patent no. 18089 on 20th August, 1904 for closing eyes for dolls made from celluloid.

RHENISH RUBBER & CELLULOID CO. LTD. 1873-1925+, Germany. c1914 at 58 Basinghall Street, London EC. Manufacturers of rubber and celluloid dolls. On 2nd July, 1914 they registered the trademark no. 362,245 which was a picture of a turtle, representing the long life and durability of their products. In 1922 Frederick Punfield was their sole British agent. In December 1935 they obtained patent no. 460158 for a celluloid doll with movable limbs, and in April, 1937 patent no. 474510 for a hollow moulded doll's head of celluloid or rubber. In September, 1937, together with H. Fromm and A. Angermayer they obtained patent no. 491117 for a coloured celluloid doll or doll's head.

ROBERT, ANDRE FRANCOIS EMILE. 1858. Paris, France. Obtained British patent for moulding vulcanized rubber dolls. Articulated wooden or metal limbs were inserted so the doll could bend. A belt covered the junction of torso and limbs.

ROGERS, F.H. English agent for German company Eckardt Ges., Geb. Obtained on their behalf on 12th December, 1928 patent no. 323622 for dolls and other toy figures made of wood, porcelain or like material.

ROSE, WILLIAM W. 1866-74. New York U.S.A. In 1866 he obtained a British patent for metal and wooden dolls which could assume different poses if the pieces were re-arranged. In 1874 he obtained another British patent for improvements over the first one.

ROUSSY DE SALES, GEORGES DE. 1917-20. Belleville and Paris, France. Obtained three British patents for moving dolls' eyes in any direction by manipulating a device on the outside of the doll.

SAMHAMMER, PHILIPP., & CO. 1878-1915. Germany and London. Obtained patent no. 17702 on 4th December, 1878 for a method of applying movable eyes to the cheaper kind of rag doll. The doll was to contain bellows or squeaker for a voice; the legs of the doll were covered with knitted hose and the feet had buckled shoes. In 1905 the firm was listed in London as handling dolls of every description, dressed and undressed.

SCAVINI, ENRICO. 1922. 5 Via Marco Polo, Turin, Italy. Doll manufacturer. In 1922 registered trademark 'Lenci' for art dolls for grown ups. Lenci was the pet name of his wife Elena.

SCHAEFFER, E.G. 1935. Obtained patent no. 448596 for a doll whose face can assume various expressions by relative rotation between the head and torso.

SCHERF, G. 1908. Sonneberg, Germany. Obtained patent no. 13104 on 8th June, 1908 for a knee joint for a doll, made of wood, paper, fabric etc.

SCHIMANSKY, HERMANN. 1878. Obtained patent no. 5530 on 13th April, 1878 for constructing dolls' heads and limbs of cast metal in a special manner.

SCHMETZER, LOUIS. 1875-76. Chicago, Illinois, U.S.A. residing in Bavaria. Obtained British patent for a jointed wooden doll and a patent for clothing for the doll made so that it would hide joints.

SCHMIDT & CO., FRANZ. 1890-1925+. Georgenthal, Germany. Obtained patent no. 1218 on 23rd January, 1891 for sleeping eyes in dolls, made so that the upper lids moved further and faster than the lower lids.

SCHMIDT, OSCAR JULIUS. 1887-1909. Sonneberg, Germany. Doll manufacturer. In 1887 he obtained British patent for dolls made of glazed pasteboard.

SCHNEEGASS & CO., LOUIS. 1909-23. Waltershausen, Germany. Doll manufacturers. In 1910 they obtained a British patent for stamping out at the same time the eye sockets, the mouth, and the hole in the skull for the wig, as the halves of the hollow dolls' heads were moulded. Likewise, ball-and-socket jointed bodies were to be made in two halves with stamped out lugs and pressed sockets. Coloured paper was to be used to obviate the use of surface colour, which would destroy the sharp outlines obtained by stamping out the items. Finally an acid bath was to be used to harden and make the members rigid.

SCHOEN, M, 1921. New York, U.S.A. Obtained British patent no. 173454 on 31st March, for a bust for stuffed dolls.

SCHOENHUT & CO., A. 1872-1925+. In 1903 obtained patent no. 24185 for jointed circus clown dolls.

SCHWAB, SAMUEL MICHAEL. 1893. New York, U.S.A. Obtained British patent no. 17143 on 12th September, 1893 for a stuffed fabric doll or animal.

SCHWARZHART, D. Obtained patent no. 675120 on 14th December, 1949 for a doll or teddy bear etc. whose jaw and squeaker can be moved simultaneously.

SENF (born SCHULDT). Obtained patent no. 449053 on 14th June, 1935 for dolls or parts of dolls made of cottonwool and/or celluloid.

S.F.B.J. Registered trademark. See **Société Française de Fabrication de Bébés et Jouets.**

SHIRLEY TEMPLE. Trademark no. 564,231 for dolls, dolls' costumes and dolls' wigs. Registered on 8th November, 1935 by the Ideal Novelty & Toy Co. New York, U.S.A.

SMITH, CHARITY. 1893. U.S.A. An American artist who obtained two British patents, nos. 1222 and 20870 on 19th January, 1893 for rag doll and animal designs.

SOCIÉTÉ FRANÇAISE DE FABRICATION DE BÉBÉS ET JOUETS. 1910. 8 Rue Pastourelle, Paris, France. Doll and toy manufacturers. Registered trademark no. 325,541, their initials S.F.B.J. in a circle, for dolls and toys on 21st July, 1910. English agents: G.F. Redfern & Co.

SOCIÉTÉ INDUSTRIELLE DE CELLULOID. 1910. Rue St. Martin, Paris, France. Obtained British patent no. 16732 on 20th July, 1910. for a floating doll of hollow celluloid.

STEINER, HERMANN. 1921-25+. Neustadt and Sonneberg, Germany. Made dolls, dressed and undressed. Registered trademark 'My Pearl' no. 416,122 on 14th June, 1921 for dolls, dressed and undressed. London agents were Boult, Wade and Tennant. Obtained British patents no. 263432 on 3rd June, 1926 (Convention date) for improvement of dolls' eyes, and no. 265872 on 1st September, 1926, for movable eyeballs and pupils movable within the eyeballs.

STEINER, RUDOLPH. 1889, Sonneberg, Germany. Obtained British patent no. 14534 on 14th September, 1889 for a doll which imitated a child sucking from a bottle. The liquid was siphoned from a bottle through the doll's mouth and into a hidden receptacle under the doll.

STEINMAN-BEYENCENET, MAURICE. 1923. 13 Well Street, London, EC1. Merchant. Registered trademark 'Wob-li-Gob' no. 437,490 on 25th May, 1923 for dolls, toys and marionettes.

SUESSENGUTH, C. 1898. Obtained patent no. 18871 on 3rd September, 1898 for a jointed doll formed of paper, cardboard, straw or leather, with head and forearms of porcelain, wood, wax or other composition.

SZPRING, T.G. 1949. Obtained patent no. 666357 on 17th August, 1949 relating to the design of a sleeping eye.

THOMPSON, W.P. Obtained patent no. 9941 on 15th July, 1887 for dolls manufactured from leatherboard (a sort of glazed pasteboard.) Patent no. 23958 on 28th December, 1892 for walking dolls turning their heads from side to side. (This was for the German firm of Fleischmann and Bloedel.) Patent no. 4282 on 20th February, 1904 for acrobatic dolls which are suspended from a support and revolve.

UHRIG, R.U. 1903. Obtained patent no. 3071 on 9th February, 1903 for a jumping doll.

VANHEEMS & WHEELER. Early 20th century. London. Distributed dolls made by the Société Française de Fabrication de Bébés et Jouets.

VAN RAALTE, H. & A. 1891. London. Imported dolls.

WALSS, WALTER COURT. 1950-56. Obtained three British patents; no. 680388 on 2nd November, 1950, for a moving eye and eyelid mechanism in a doll; nos. 826626 and 826627 in 1956 for a walking doll whose head moves from side to side as it walks, and a doll which blinks.

WEBBER, WILLIAM AUGUSTUS. 1882-84. Medford, Massachusetts, U.S.A. Together with three others. Obtained British patent no. 1645 on 4th April, 1882 for a 'singing' doll.

WERNICKE R. 1931, Waltershausen, Germany. Obtained British patent no. 389172 in October 1931 for a doll's head produced by an inflation moulding process.

WITTMAN, M. 1934-37. New York, U.S.A. Obtained three British patents. No. 438982 on 24th July, 1934 for an air and liquid tight limb joint, for a doll such as is used for teaching mothercraft. No. 443406 on 24th July, 1934 for a feeding doll, and no. 495564 on 15th February, 1937 relating to movable dolls' eyes.

WOB-LI-GOB. See **Steinman-Beyencenet, Maurice.**

WOLKOFF, V. 1920. Obtained patent no. 155121 on 2nd January, 1920 for soft cloth dolls with flexible wire skeletons: the wires were not rigidly connected and were inserted in each finger and thumb.

WURZ, HENRY & NEWTON, EDWARD. 1865-66. New York, U.S.A. Obtained British patent for artificial material to be used in moulding dolls and other toys, for which vulcanized rubber, horn, ivory, bone, shell or papier-mâché had previously been used.

APPENDIX 2

With the aim of making this dictionary as helpful as possible the following lists have been compiled from the archives of Pollock's Toy Museum.

The list consists of eight sections. Each section covers three consecutive letters of the alphabet, and within each section the arrangement is chronological. Some facts may be incorrect, and there is a tantalising lack of information where only a name and date has been discovered in some old directory or shop record. Readers may perhaps contribute to the list or use it in conjunction with the main text. Interesting trends in doll-making may be traced: phases covering different materials, fashions in doll naming and in doll types. As a perhaps slightly random guide to the evolution of dolls we hope it may prove useful.

ABC

AD50	Clay figurines from children's graves (Roman): Colchester Museum.
1585	Babes and Puppets: Gifts to American Indians: Walter Raleigh.
1614	Bartholomew Babies: Ben Johnson: Bartholomew Fair.
1638	Bartholomew Babies.
1683	Bartholomew Babies: Witt & Drollery.
1754	Bride doll: Laetitia Clark: Doll: V. & A.
1764	Ackerman, Rudolph: Paper dressing dolls.
1777	Alabaster doll of Dorothea Herbert: Bought in Bristol.
pre 1799	Caughley Pottery: Dolls foot discovered.
1815	Bruguier, C. A.: Mechanical dolls.
1824	Crying dolls: Maelzel English patent.
1826	Bazzoni, A.: Wax, composition and speaking dolls.
	Butler, C.: Made dolls.
1835	Brogden, J.: Composition dolls.
	Brooks, J.: Made dolls.
1840	Buckland, Edmund: Made dolls.
1843	Colombo, John: Doll maker.
1847	Barton, John: Wax doll maker.
1850	Crying dolls: Bazzoni: Mayhew ref.
1852	Cannon, James: Doll maker.
	Churchill, James: Composition dolls.
1855	Bianchi, P.: Made wax dolls.
1856	Bluett, Thos.: Wax and composition dolls.
	Columbo, William: Doll maker.
1858	Benda, A.: Doll stringing patent.
1862	Burley, G.: Exhibited dolls.
	Clark, W.: Doll patent.
	Cremer: Sold Pierotti wax dolls.
1865	Alice in Wonderland dolls: After publication of ditto with Tenniel drawings.
	Clark, W.: Patent composition for dolls' heads.
	Coxeter, Clara: Made dolls.
1866	Clavell, J.: Patent dancing doll.
1867	Clarkson, T. C.: Doll patents.
	Clavell, J.: Articulated doll.
1870	Britain, William: Mechanical dolls and toys.
1871	Crawling doll patent: A. V. Newton.
1876	Clarkson, T. C.: Patent corkwood doll.
1878	Aldis, Frederick: Doll maker and importer: sold Pierotti wax dolls.
1879	Betts, Thos.: Wax and/or composition dolls.
1881	Aldred, Thos.: Doll maker and importer, used Pierotti heads.
1883	Batt, John & Co.: Doll maker.
1886	Brierley, W.: Patent doll and puppet heads.
	Cherub doll: Abraham Isaacs.
1887	Boult, A. K.: Patent hair fixing.
1888	Brooke, A. G.: Patent phonograph doll.
1889	Crawling doll patent: Stranders & Perry.
1890	Alderson, M.: Dolls hand patent.
	Bayley, J. P.: Doll limb patent.
1893	Boult, A. J. & Clay, W. A.: Patent musical doll.
	Cox, Palmer: Brownie rag dolls printed America.
1897	Biddle, C: Patent smoking doll.
1898	Bowden, J: Patent dancing doll.
1899	Browne, Thomas: Rag dolls.
1900	Bauman, Victor: Composition doll maker and wholesaler.
1902	Brohead, S.: Walking toy patent.
	Charstone, W. J.: Moving doll patent.
	Cryer & Naylor.
1903	Bergman, Fritz & Co.: Doll maker.
	Consterdine, Herbert: Acrobat patent.
1904	Arnold, M. O.: Mechanical dolls on wheels.
	Atkinson, A. & Conway, M: Bicycle doll.
	Berger, C.: Doll patent.
	Buster Brown: Hamley Bros.
1905	Barker, F.A.: Fabric aromatic dolls.
	Coleman, Cecil Ltd.: Fabric dolls.
1906	Bell and Francis: Rag dolls.
	Burrell & Hookley, J.: Rag doll patent.
	Chapman, Constance Mary: Wallypug doll regd.
1907	Aaba: A. W. James.
	Angelo Doll: C. K. Gibbons.
	Betts, Marion: Wax and composition dolls.
	Christie, W. G.: Trademark.
1908	Arnold, M. O.: Phonograph doll bodies.
	Bierer, F. L.: Rubber toys trademark.
	Big Baby Doll: Dean's Rag Book Co.
	Butterfly Series: Eisenmann & Co.
	Cook, H., & Solomon, J.: Fluff Fluff etc.
1910	Bhankawala dolls: K. M. Sherwood.
1911	Bedington Liddiatt & Co Ltd.: Manufacturers games and toys.

1912   Beaky Ba: Eisenmann & Co.
        Bergman Kleeman & Co.: Doll manufacturers.
        Bings Ltd.: Sunshine Girl etc.
1913   Abrahams, Hyman A. & Sons: My Kiddie etc.: Agents
            for Leda dolls.
        Art Fabric Mfg. Co.: Took over Art Fabric Mills etc.
        Betty Blue: Dean's Rag Book Co.
        Bradley & Galzenati: Dolls' heads manufacturers.
        British Rag Doll Co.: Taken over by Art Fabric Man.
            Co.
        British Textile Novelty Co.: Taken over by Art Fabric
            Man. Co.
        Bunny Hug: Trademark Eisenmann & Co.
1914   Attwell, Mabel L.: Postcards produced by Valentine.
        Boase, Eliz.: The Soldier's Baby.
        Boy Sprout: Dean's Rag Book Co.
        British Doll Mfg. Co.: Character dolls.
        British United Toy Mfg. Co.: Variety of dolls etc.
        Cecily: Doll Pottery Co.
        Chunky: Lord Roberts Memorial Workshops.
        Cowan, S. D.: Cheap dolls.
1915   Allbrit: All Brit. Mfg. Co.
        Batgers: Wax and composition dolls.
        Bell & Francis: Munition doll etc.
        Beswick, J. W.: Dealer in pot heads.
        Borough British Dolls.
        Britannia Toy Co.: Doll and toy manufacturer.
        British Novelty Works: Toy and doll manufacturer.
        Cowham, Hilda: Dean & Son: Kiddies.
1916   Alert doll: Lindop, W.
        Amersham Works Ltd.: Impey, Union Jack Baby etc.
            Leon Rees.
        Babes in the Wood: Tah Toys.
        Baby Bunny: Tah Toys.
        Baby Carrots: E. E. Houghton.
        Bailey, D. S. & Baxter, S. J.: Wax-dipped pot dolls.
        Baxter, Chas.W.: China heads, wigs, games and toys.
        Bambino: E. E. Houghton.
        Bedington Liddiatt & Co. Ltd.: Plastolite.
        British Doll & Novelty Co.: Doll manufacturers.
        British Novelty Co.: Rag, china and character dolls
            etc.
        Buckmaster, G. H.: W. H. Smith & Sons.
        Charlie Chaplin: Huvan Mfg. Co.
        Chesham Brand Doll: Ellison, Rees & Co.
        Clown Prince: Huvan Mfg. Co.
        Collins & Robins: Doll makers.
        Compolite & Compolene: J. P. Miller & Co.
        Curling, R. S.: Papooski reg.
1917   Airman: Dean's Rag Book Co.
        Bell, W.: Dolls eye mechanism.
        Bluestocking Dolls: J. Green Hamley.
        Bluestocking Kid: Harwin & Co.
        Boy Scout: All Brit. Mfg. Co.
        British Babies: Shanklin Toy Ind. E. E. Houghton.
        Classic regd.: Speights.
        Colonial Dolls: Dean's Rag Book Co.
        Cooper, Frederick & Sons: Bonnedol Works.
        Crabat Shape Co.: Rag dolls.
        Cuddley Ones: Three Arts Women's Employment Fund
            Toy Ind.
1918   American Kiddie: Fretwell Mfg. Co.
        Angel, L. V. & Nunn G. L.: Patent for composition
            dolls or toys.

        Art Dolls: Nell Foy & Co.: Famous actresses: Wax
            over composition.
        Art Statue Co.: Tuftex composition and baby dolls.
        Blake Bros.: Doll makers.
        Mabel Bland-Hawkes: Designer and manufacturer.
        Bonnedol: Frederick Cooper & Sons Ltd.
        Braxted Doll Ind.: Original dolls.
        Brer Rabbit: Tah Toys Ltd.
        British Products Mfg. Co.: Composition and other
            type dolls.
        Bubbly Kiddie: Fretwell Toy Mfg.
        Cecily Doll: Edwards & Pamflett.
        Christopher: E. E. Houghton.
        Conchie Doll: Toy Trader reg.
        Cornelius, W. H. Ltd.: Manufacturers and importers.
        Crown Pottery: Dolls and tea services.
        Cuthbert: Poy Toy Co.
1919   Albany Toy Co.: Soft toys and dolls.
        Art Toy Mfg. Co.: Misska dolls.
        Assael, G. M.: Wholesaler French and English dolls.:
            Manufacturer of dolls.
        Baby Boy: Three Arts Women's Employment Fund.
        Baby Girl: Three Arts Women's Employment Fund.
        Bathing Jeff: Art Toy Mfg. Co.
        Bo-Peep: Harwin & Co.
        Bringlee Unbreakable Doll: Models: Leicester Ltd.
        Britannia dolls: Cowan de Groot.
        Bronyx: Dolls Supplies Ltd.
        Burman Ltd. J. & A. J.: Doll and toy manufacturer.
        Canada's Victory Dolls: C. Britton.
        Cellalaine Co.: Soft toys and dolls.
        Charlie Chaplin: Dean's Rag Book Co.
        Cilly Billy: Hamley Bros.
        Cowan de Groot: Britannia doll.
        Crown Staffordshire Porcelain Co. Ltd.: Jointed dolls.
1920   Baby: Speights Ltd.
        Bell & Francis: Unbreakable baby dolls.
        Bow Belle: Dean's Rag Book Co.
        Brinsley W. H. & F. R.: Dolls joint patent.
        British Jointed Doll Co.: Composition dolls.
        British Toys Ltd.: Became British Dolls Ltd.
        Charlie Chaplin: Foster, Blackett & Wilson Ltd.
        C.Q. Dolls Industry.
        Cannon Dolls: Kent Toy Works.
        Compressed Card bodies: Ilford Toy Co.
        Countess: Speights Ltd.
        Country Girl: Speights Ltd.
1921   Aldon Studios: Zobeide.
        Baby Vamp: Lawton Doll Co.
        Beauty Doll: Lawton Doll Co.
        Blackpool Belle: Lawton Doll Co.
        British & Colonial Novelty Co.: Stuffed and celluloid
            dolls.
        Bucherer, A.: Patent ball and socket joints.
        Burgess, S. H.: Slymphs: Mascots.
        Camoufrage: Dolls' Accessory Co.
        Coogan Kid: British Novelty Works.
        Cupid Dolls: Lawton Doll Co.
        Cutie: Lawton Doll Co.
1922   A1 dolls and toys: Dean's Rag Book Co.
        Beach, M. P.: Towelling and sponge doll.
        Belle: Lawton Doll Co.
        Cabbagerino: M. A. Dakin
        Christmas Tree Dolls: Mabel Bland-Hawkes.
        Chu Chin Chow: S. Hancock.

1923
Confectionery Containers: Mabel Bland-Hawkes.
Adlon walking doll: Whyte, Ridsdale.: Wholesaler.
Aerolite rag dolls: Chad Valley.
Atlantic Rubber Co.: Toggy.
Baby Bunting: Dean's Rag Book Co.
Baby Royal: Mabel Bland-Hawkes.
Bercovitch, L. W. & S. & Annison J. H.: Bersonian dolls.
Braxted Doll Ind.: All-leather and carved wood dolls.
Buster Brown: Dean's Rag Book Co.
Cherub Doll Jenny: Dean's Rag Book Co.
Curly Locks: Dean's Rag Book Co.

1924
Art Dolls: Sant: Walking Felix: Nell Foy & Co.
Baby Peggy: Dean's Rag Book Co.
Chinn, H. T.: Patent moving doll.
Colonel Bogey doll: George Lawrence Nunn.
Cry Baby: Worthing Toy Factory.

1925
Armitage, H. K.: Diving doll patent.
Bobiche: Dean's Rag Book Co.
Clown doll: Alfred Goldsmith.

1926
Babette: Dean & Son Ltd.
Billie Bimbo: J. K. Farnell & Co.
Cecille: Leon Rees.
Christiansen, B. K.: Patent.
Clown: A. S. Holladay & Co.

1927
Ankidoodle: Reg. trademark of J. J. Ikle.
Babs: Mabel Bland-Hawkes.
Babymine: Norah Wellings.
Colwell, W. E.: Walking mechanism patent.
Cora: Norah Wellings.

1928
Baby Betty: Dean's Rag Book Co.
Baby Dolls: Dean's Rag Book Co.
Bedtime Baby Dolls: Dean's Rag Book Co.
Boudoir Dolls: Dean's Rag Book Co.
Bunnymum: W. H. Jones Ltd.
Charlie Chaplin: J. S. Sant, Ltd.

1929
Bell Boy: Dean's Rag Book Co.
Cinders: Norah Wellings.

1930
A.A. Scout: Road Patrol Scouts.
Colleen dolls: Lines Bros.

1931
Babette: Leon Rees & Co.
Cuddley Coo: Merrythought.

1932
Altschulers: patent loudspeaker doll.
Baby Toddles: G. & T. reg.
Bambina Dolls: Chad Valley.
Barber, V. S.: Patent adjustable doll.
Beach Baby: Dean's Rag Book Co.

1933
Babs: J. K. Farnell & Co.
Barrett, L.: Patent voice.
British National Dolls: China head dolls.
Colleen: Mabel Lucie Attwell: Chad Valley.
Cropper, B.: Patent.

1934
Austin Gray Ltd.: Soft dolls, etc.
Baby Mary: Leon Rees & Co.
Baby Norene: Norah Wellings.
Beach Belle: Austin Gray Ltd.
Cabaret: Austin Gray Ltd.
Chubby: The Wonder Doll: B.N.O. Ltd.

1935
Allwin: Trademark of Richards, Son & Allwin.
Alpha Cherub: Dolls trademark: J. K. Farnell & Co.
Alpha Joy Day dolls: J. K. Farnell & Co.
Alpha Smilers: J. K. Farnell & Co.
Belisha Bea Coney: Dean's Rag Book Co.
Bexoid Cherub: Cascelloid.
Binkie Babs: Ken Donald Mfg. Co. Ltd.

Bonny: Dean's Rag Book Co.
Bowers, C. E.: Doll voice patent.
Cami dolls: Dean's Rag Book Co.
Cookman, Winifred: Dolls' accessories.

1936
Ailion, J. & Co.: Costume dolls.
Alpha Piccaninnies: J. K. Farnell & Co.
Alpha Soft Dolls: J. K. Farnell & Co.
B.U.T. Ltd.: Mfg. export and wholesale.
Ba Ba series: Dean's Rag Book Co.
Babs: East London (Federation) Toy Factory.
Bambetta: Chad Valley.
Betty Oxo: Dean's Rag Book Co.
Bubbles: Dean's Rag Book Co.
Buddy: Merrythought Ltd.
Caresse: Chad Valley.
Carina: Chad Valley.
Cherub: East London (Federation) Toy Factory.
Coney Kid: Dean's Rag Book Co.

1937
Baby: J. W. Spear & Sons.
Cherub doll series: Palitoy.
Cupid dolls: Palitoy: Cascelloid.
Chuckles: Cascelloid.
Chuckles: Pedigree Soft Toys Ltd.
Coronation Dolls: J. K. Farnell & Co.

1938
Bubbles: Cascelloid
Chamberlain, Neville: J. K. Farnell & Co.

1939
Airfix Products Ltd.
Allam, Ruth: Doll repairer.
Bill the Sailor: Cascelloid.

1940
Baileys Potteries Ltd.: Lo-la dolls etc.
Blue John Pottery Ltd.: Dolls.
Brentleigh Dolls: Howard Pottery Co. Ltd.
Cohn, Margarete: Grecon dolls.

1941
A.A. Merchandising Co.: Jointed dolls etc.
Allen, F. H. Ltd.: Wholesaler, dolls and toys.
Be Be dolls Ltd. Manufacturers, soft toys and dolls.
British Artware Ltd.: Dolls and toy manufacturers.
Colonial & Overseas Export Co. Ltd.: Wynjoy.

1942
Arthur Askey doll: Dean's Rag Book Co.
Bell (Toys & Games Ltd.): Bell trademark.
Brothers & Babington Ltd.: Manufacturers.

1943
Crowther, C., Whiteley & Burton: Patent dolls eyes.

1944
The Acorn Toy Co.: Dolls and toys.
Biltoys: Lewis Bonnan.
Bonnan, W.: Trademark, Biltoys.

1945
Adona Toys Ltd.: Dolls and animals.

1946
Anita: Unity Pack Co.
Artistic Dolls Ltd.: Doll manufacturers.
Bailey's Agencies Ltd.: Wholesaler.
Canadian Unbreakable Dolls: Gaeltarra Eireann.
Crolly Dolls: Gaeltarra Eireann.

1947
British Indoor Pastimes Ltd.: Mormit dolls.
Britoy Ltd.: Composition dolls.
Buckingham (London) Ltd.: Monica trademark.

1948
Anne: Airfix Products Ltd.
Beauty Skin doll: Pedigree Soft Toys Ltd.
Belloid Co. Ltd.: Hard dolls.
Bisto Kids: Cerebos Ltd.

1949
Amalgamated Impex: Distributors for Simpsons' Prince Charles dolls.
Aston & Co.: Wool crinoline dolls.
Baby Doll Co. Ltd.: Manufacturers and dealers.
Belinda: North's Rubber Co. Ltd.
Brandt, R. & Co. (Mfg) Ltd.: Dolls' eyelashes.
Buster: Playplastic Toy Co. Ltd.

Cesar, C. F.: Doll limb patent.

Charles, Prince: Amalgamated Impex (London) Ltd.

1950 Art Plastics Ltd.: Unbreakable dolls: J. Cowan (Dolls) Ltd.

Blue Ribbon Playthings: Be Be (Dolls) Ltd.

Burtoys Mfg. Co.: Doll makers.

Chummy: Tiny Tot Toy Co.

Cinette: Rae Hertzog.

1951 Carter, H. W. & Co. Ltd.: Quoshiwog.

1952 Alice: Pin-Up Dolls.

Amanda Jane Ltd.: Conrad & Elsin Rawnsley: Dolls accessories.

Brenda: Pin-Up Dolls.

Briteyes Dolls: Britannia Toy Co. Ltd.

Celia: Pedigree: see Pin-Up Dolls.

Cesar, S. S.: Dolls' hair manufacturer.

Chelsea Art Doll Makers.

1953 Bartley, Ena Marjorie: Rhythmbar trademark.

Beefeater doll: Deans Rag Book Co.

Bumbly: Michael Bentine Enterprises Ltd.

1955 Amanda Doll: Trademark N. Kove.

Anne Bathtime set: Palitoy.

Babs: Roddy: D. G. Todd & Co. Ltd.

Bathtime Baby Sets: Palitoy.

Belles of Brighton: Pedigree Soft Toys Ltd.

Biddy & Butch: Young & Fogg Rubber Co. Ltd.

Bubbles: Roddy: D. G. Todd & Co. Ltd.

Bunty Doll: Palitoy.

Castle Toy Co. Ltd.: Shirley Dolls.

Cowan, J. (Dolls) Ltd.: Jayco & Roddy Distributors.

1956 Comfy Glow: Be Be Dolls Ltd.

1958 Cariad: Trademark, Thomas Garrie Falconer.

Carry-me-case doll set: Lines Bros.

Clements, R. A.: Dolls eye patent.

Cygnet: Simpson, Fawcett & Co. Ltd.

1959 Bartholomew, Marjorie L.: Marty Trademark.

1960 Belinda: Palitoy.

1961 Alice: Palitoy.

1962 Babykins: Chiltern.

Chatty Cathy: Rosebud Dolls Ltd.

Chiltern Dolls: Ballerina doll and Lullaby soft-bodied baby doll.

1964 Almar Dolls Ltd.: Costume dolls.

1965 Bendykins: Newfelt Ltd.

1966 Action Man: Palitoy.

Beck Bright: Dean's Childsplay Ltd.

1967 Baby Angel: Rosebud Mattel Ltd

Baby First Step: Rosebud Mattel Ltd.

Baby Maybe: Palitoy.

Baby Walk Alone: Pedigree.

1967 Betsy: Pedigree.

Captain Scarlett: Pedigree Dolls Ltd.

Cheerful Fearful: Rosebud Mattel Ltd.

Choosy Susie: D. G. Todd & Co. Ltd.

1968 Carnaby Kate: Rosebud Mattel Ltd.

Chubby girl doll, white or negro.

1969 Bluebell dolls: D. G. Todd & Co. Ltd.

1970 Babbling Baby: Palitoy.

1971 Action Girl: Palitoy.

Bedsie: see Ploppy Character Dolls.

Bitty: see Ploppy Character Dolls.

Booful Baby Beans: Ploppy Character Dolls.

Bradgate: Palitoy.

Casden dolls: Cassidy Bros.

1972 Avrils Bathtime: Palitoy.

Baby Love: Palitoy.

Baby Tender Love: Mattel Ltd.

Carrie in her carrycot: Palitoy.

Cuckoobird: Lavender Dolls.

1973 Alice in Wonderland: Palitoy.

Biffy: see Ploppy Character Dolls.

Blythe: Palitoy.

Character Crafts Ltd.: Miss Nobody etc.

Clever Kerry: Palitoy.

Cry Baby Beans: Ploppy Character Dolls.

Cubby: Ploppy Character Dolls.

1974 Baby First Love: Pedigree Dolls Ltd.

Bennett, J. & Erland, S.: Individual dolls.

Britt: Palitoy.

1975 Active Sindy: Pedigree.

Amara Designs: Souvenir rag doll.

Art Master of Chelsea Ltd.: Costume doll kits.

Bubbles & Squeak: Model Toys Ltd.

Captain Hook: Fighting Furies, Lesney Products & Co. Ltd.

Captain Peg Leg: Fighting Furies, Lesney Products & Co Ltd.

Charlotte: Tricia Dolls.

Claire: Lesney Products & Co. Ltd.

1976 Air Hostess: Lesney Products & Co. Ltd.

Black McCoy: Lesney Products & Co. Ltd.

Crazy Horse: Lesney Products & Co. Ltd.

1977 Abrahams (Toys) L. D. Ltd.: Wholesaler and importer.

Anna and Happytime: Pedigree Dolls & Toys Ltd.

Baby Jonathon: H. Schelhorn & Co.

Champions: Pedigree Dolls & Toys Ltd.

1978 Abba Dolls: Lesney Products & Co. Ltd.

Anna: Abba Dolls.

Bennie: Abba Dolls.

Bjorn: Abba Dolls.

Brigitte: Lesney Products & Co. Ltd.

Country Miss rag dolls: Burbank Toys.

DEF

1811 Dixon, Elizabeth: Made dolls.

1843 Douglas & Hamer: Made wax and composition dolls.

1844 Forster, Thos.: Patent rubber composition.

1850 Davis, Alfred: Assembled china dolls.

1852 Edwards, Charles: Wax over composition manufacturer.

1856 Edwards, John: Wax dolls.

1868 Evans, J. & Sons: Manufacturers and importers wax dolls.

1879 Elwick, Mrs. Helena: Wax dolls.

1881 Eisenmann & Co.: Manufacturers and distributors of dolls.

1887 Erhard, Stephen: Doll and toy manufacturer and importer.

Foskett & Edler: Manufacturers and agents for foreign dolls.

1893 Dallimore, W. H.: Patent doll movement.

1894 Douglas, Anna Marie: Patent upside down doll.

Eates, Henry: Manufacturing dolls.

Fell, J. C.: Patent paper garments for dolls.

1895 Eaton, Florence Emily: Erin Doll Industry composition dolls.
1900 Faulkner, C. W. & Co.: Paper people toys.
1901 Dunn, W.: Patent dancing doll.
1904 Dancing dolls: H. P. Rugg: regd.
1906 Dollit Dolls: A. A. Ivimey.
1908 Dean H. S. Ltd.: Dean's Rag Book Co. Ltd., Deans: Dean's Rag Book Co. Ltd.
Fluff-Fluff: Henry Cookman.
Fluffy-Ruffles: Henry Cookman.
1909 Eskimo dolls: Popularity: Discovery of North Pole.
Fitch, Darrell Austin: Dolphitch Mfg. Co.
1910 Dadoowala: K. M. Sherwood.
1911 Dickinsen, W. A. & Lyxhayr Mfg. Ltd.: Patent stuffing.
Dum Tweedle: Dean's Rag Book Co. Ltd.
Eckart, Hans Englebert: Toy and doll importer: Trademark.
1913 Dolly Dear: Textile Novelty Co.
Edwards, T. W.: Patent limb fastening.
Fuzbuz: Trademark Dean's Rag Book Co. Ltd.
1914 Dolleries: Leon Rees.
Dolly Dimple: Whyte, Ridsdale & Co.
Elfie: Trademark: Hamley Bros.
Floatolly: Trademark Eisenmann & Co.
Fry, Roger: Child's Welfare Exhibition.
Fumsup: John Green Hamley, Patent.
1915 Daniels, Miss F. M.: Jungle Toys.
Doll Pottery Co. Ltd.: China heads and limbs.
Dolls Supplies Ltd.: Manufacturer.
Dolphitch Mfg. Co. Ltd.: Composition and wax.
Drummer Boy: W. S. Turton.
Dura Porcelain Co.: Manufacturer dolls heads and limbs.
Ealon Toys: East London (Federation) Toy Factory.
East London (Federation) Toy Factory: Wax and china dolls and soft toys.
Eleanor Works: Dolls' masks.
Elite Doll Co.: Manufacturers.
Erhard, S.: Red Cross nurse.
Evans A. E.: Patent moving doll.
Fryer Thos.: Repaired and distributed dolls.
1916 Ellanco: Ellison, Rees & Co.
Ellison, Rees & Co.: Doll manufacturers.
Emdee: Trademark: Marcuse, Day & Co. Ltd.
Empire Porcelain Pottery: China dolls heads.
English Doll Mfg. Co.: Manufacturers.
Esquimaux dolls: Miller Bros.
Farmer's Boy: Marcuse, Day & Co. Ltd.
1916 Finburch, Samuel & Co.: Printed rag dolls.
Frazer Rock, Helen: Nottingham Toy Industry Ltd.
1917 Dell & Co.: Rag and china dolls.
Dilly Dick: Tah Toys Ltd.
Dolac: Sissons Bros. & Co. Ltd.
Dolls' Accessory Co.: Dolls and china figures.
Dolls, Messrs.: Manufacturers.
Dolly Dimple: All Brit Doll Mfg. Co.
Dolly Dips: Dean's Rag Book Co. Ltd.
Emell Toy Mfg. Co.: Doll manufacturers.
Family, The: Harwin & Co. Ltd.
Flesho: Dolls' Accessory Co. Ltd.
Fretwell Toy Mfg. Co.: Doll and soft toy manufacturers.
1918 Daisy Dolls or June Babies: Nottingham Toy Industry Ltd.

Dixon, T. A.: Noxid dolls.
Eclipse Dolls: Rochdale Doll Co.
Edwardes & Pamflett, Mesdames: Papier mâché dolls.
English Doll & Toy Co. Ltd.: Doll and toy manufacturers.
Fleet Dolls: Nottingham Toy Industry Ltd.
Forget-me-not: Trademark S. H. Ward.
1919 Darenta Toy Works: Doll and toy manufacturers.
Dazzle Dazzle Doll: Speights Ltd.
Dinkie: Speights Ltd.
Dodd, I.: Durax trademark.
Dots' dolls: Harwin & Co. Ltd.
Durax: Dodd, I.
1920 Diddums: Hamley Bros.
Dietrich, T. G.: Patent metal doll limbs.
Dolly Dimple: East London (Federation) Toy Factory.
Dolly Doll Co.: Made dolls.
Dorothy Dolls: Wolstan Doll Co.
Duchess: Speights Ltd.
Dutch boys and girls: Speights Ltd.
Eckart, Walker & Ronald: Made dolls.
Erhard, S.: Kewpie.
Fairyland Toy Mfg. Co.: Hand painted dolls.
Fifi: Speights Ltd.
Flopsie: Trademark W. H. Jones.
Flossie: Speights Ltd.
Franklin, J. G.: Rubber dolls.
Frolix: Darenta Toy Works.
1921 Dennis Malley & Co. Ltd.: Import and export, German manufacturer.
Dew, S. T. & Trautmann, F. O.: Skipping doll patent.
Evripoze: Patent joints Dean's Rag Book Co. Ltd.
Farnell, J. K. & Co. Ltd.: Toy and doll manufacturers.
Fluff: Mabel Bland-Hawkes.
1922 Dainty May: Dennis Malley & Co. Ltd.
Dakin, M. A.: Cabbagerino.
Delmacol: Dennis Malley & Co. Ltd.
Flapper, The: Lawton Doll Co.
1923 Doris: Mann & Mann.
Dorris & Co. Ltd.: Manufactured dressed dolls.
Fantasy Dolls: Factor.
1924 Diamant, L.: Cheap doll and teddy bear manufacturer.
Dolfam: R. M. Perks.
Dora: Dean's Rag Book Co.
Doric China Co.: Manufacturers.
Folly Dolls.: H. J. Hughes, & Son.
1925 Dinky Toy.: W. A. Jones.
Everest: W. Seelig.
Fly Doll: J. S. Sant Ltd.
1926 Dean & Son Ltd.: Doll shaped books.
Dinkie Dolls: Dean's Rag Book Co. Ltd.
Dorothea: Wolstan Doll Co.
Elegant dolls: Dean's Rag Book Co. Ltd.
1927 Dulcie: Mabel Bland-Hawkes.
Frilly Dolls: Dean's Rag Book Co. Ltd.
1928 Dickins, H. M.: Patent stuffed toy figure.
Doll (Jointed) Books: Dean & Son Ltd.
Dolly: Dean's Rag Book Co. Ltd.
Fishman, S. Z.: My Sweetie trademark.
1929 Dinah: Dean's Rag Book Co. Ltd.
Domestic Utility dolls: Dean's Rag Book Co. Ltd.
Erbie Brown: Dean's Rag Book Co.
Faber & Faber Ltd.: The Pirate Twin.
1930 Daily Sketch & Sunday Graphic: Pop.
Dellco dolls: Dell & Co.

Dudu or Zuzu or Zulu: Norah Wellings.
Elizabeth, Princess: Chad Valley.
1931 Doreen Dolls: Dean's Rag Book Co. Ltd.
1932 Dreyfus, Miriam: Various trademarks.
1933 Diamond Tile Co. Ltd.: Earthenware dolls.
Dixie style dolls: Merrythought Ltd.
Dollies Ltd: J. Kohnstam Ltd.
Duckie dolls: Dollies Ltd.
Flo: Dean's Rag Book Co. Ltd.
1934 Duchess Doll: Dean's Rag Book Co. Ltd.
Dunlop Products: Red Riding Hood hot water bottles.
Excella dolls: Leon Rees.
1935 Dean's Dollies Ltd.: Dean's Rag Book Co. Ltd.
Dimple: Dean's Rag Book Co. Ltd.
Donald, Ian Mfg. Co. Ltd.: Soft dolls and toys.
Dora: Dean's Rag Book Co. Ltd.
Dorrie: Dean's Rag Book Co. Ltd.
Edna: Dean's Rag Book Co. Ltd.
Fairylite trademark: Graham Bros.
1936 Darling: East London (Federation) Toy Factory.
Dolly Dimple: J. Sear Ltd.
1937 Diddums & Happy: Cascelloid Ltd.
Dinky Baby dolls: Cascelloid Ltd.
1938 Daisycroft Studios: Dolls mask manufacture.
1939 Diddums: Cecil Coleman Ltd.
Dolgar Mfg. Co.: Dolls wigs and clothes.
1941 Diamond dolls: Diamond Tile Co. Ltd.
1947 Dolrite: Michel-Levy, Fernande.
Doma Doll Ltd.
Emlu Doll & Toy Co.
Eskimo Interlining Co. Ltd.: Promotional eskimo doll.
Eskimo Tot: Eskimo Interlining Ltd.
1948 Doll in Doll: Doll Industries Ltd.
Doll Industries Ltd.: Manufacture.
Fleischmann, M. G. & S.: Old Cottage toys.
1949 Delite Dolls: Pedigree.
Drial, William, Products Ltd.: Sweetheart doll.
Ellisdons: Dolls eyelashes and voices.
1950 Edmunds, J. H.: Walking dolls.
Frankel, Benjamin: Key Products trademark.
1951 Dollys-Doc: Trademark A. G. Woolley Ltd.
1952 Diana: Pin-Up Dolls.
Dixie: Pedigree Soft Toys Ltd.
Doll Repair Services: Repairs and renewals.
Dolls Masks (London) Ltd.: Manufacture dolls' masks.
Enid: Pedigree Soft Toys Ltd.
Firth, Harry Ltd.: Dolls' hair manufacturers.
Frances: Pedigree Soft Toys Ltd.
1955 Edna: D. G. Todd, & Co. Ltd.
Fifi: D. G. Todd, & Co. Ltd.
1956 Fairy Princess: Philmar Ltd.
Fondle: Burman Ltd.
1959 Dagman, Mangot Ltd.: Rainbow patent dolls and puppets.
Dizzy Whizz: Masa Roy Sieki
1960 Deans Childsplay Toy Ltd.: Dean's Rag Book Co. Ltd.
Debbie: Palitoy.
Debutante dolls: Pedigree Dolls Ltd.
De Luxe Dolls: Pedigree Dolls Ltd.
Dolls of all Nations: Doltoi Ltd.
1962 Frido Ltd: P.V.C. Dolls.
1963 De Luxe Toy Co. Ltd.: Lines Bros.
1964 Franks, Peggy: Hook & Franks.

1967 Destiny Angel: Pedigree Dolls Ltd.
Florence.
1968 Falconer, Thos. G.: Cariad.
Favourite Dolls Ltd.: Vinyl dolls.
1969 Desdemona: Palitoy.
1972 Daisy: Model Toys Ltd.
Dee: Lesney Products & Co. Ltd.
Disco Girls: Lesney Products & Co. Ltd.
Dolly-locks: Wig World.
Domino: Lesney Products & Co. Ltd.
1974 Daredevil: Model Toys Ltd.
Emma and her Pony: Palitoy.
Erland, Susan: Bennett & Erland.
1975 Danny: Lesney Products & Co. Ltd.
Dashing Daisy: Model Toys Ltd.
Dean, Mary: Rag dolls.
Fighting Furies: Lesney Products & Co. Ltd.
Flair Toys Ltd.: Berwick Timpo Ltd.
1976 Dolly Denim: Chad Valley.
Don Bricks Ltd.: Importers.
Flexi: Dean's Rag Book Co. Ltd.
1977 Farrah: Airfix Products Ltd.
1978 Frida: Abba dolls.

GHI

1733 Higgs, William: Painted wooden dolls, babies.
1760 Hamley Bros.: Rag dolls.
1763 Graham, A.: Peebo doll.
1826 Hallett, William: Composition and leather dolls.
1836 Gay, Benjamin: Made dolls.
1848 Hamer, William: Doll maker.
1855 Green, Thos.: Made dolls.
1856 Harrison, George: Made dolls.
Hobbins, John: Made wax dolls.
1858 Hammond, Thos. Rundle: Patent rubber dolls.
Harris, John: Made dolls.
Howard, Henry (Harry): Made dolls.
1860 Haas Albert F.: Patent jointed,sitting doll.
1879 Ihlee & Horne: Trademark Aladdin's lamp, acorn and leaf.
1880 Godfrey, E. D., S. & C. M.: Trademark S. G. and wheatsheaf.
1881 Isaacs, A. & H.: Rag dolls, imported and dressed dolls.
1884 Gatter, Edward: Gutta-percha.
Hatch, Mrs. Sarah: Doll maker.
Hayes, Miss Rebecca: Rag dolls.
1886 Isaac, A. H.: Trademark The Cherub doll.
1888 Hinde, John, Lord: Hinde Bros.: Trademark Dolly Dimple.
1891 Hazel, Henry John: Made dolls.
Hughes, Henry Richard: Doll manufacturers' agent.
Hyatt, Joseph: Imported dolls.
1894 George, John: Made dolls.
1895 Gibson, G. T.: Patent paper garments.
Golliwog: Florence Upton.
Hughes, Herbert Edward: Dolls.
Irish Dolls, Emily Florence Eaton: Doll maker.

213

1896 Gray, W.: Patent dancing doll.
Hodgson, Ellen Sheraton: Patent swimming doll.
1898 Gilbert W. V.: Cardboard cut-out dolls.
1903 Harrison, G.: Patent paper dolls.
1904 Harber, W. F.: Patent walking doll.
1906 Gifford, S. D.: Dolls' eye patent.
Hockley, J.: Burnell & Hockley.
Ivimey: Regd. Dollit.
1907 Gibsons, Chas. K.: Trademark Angelo doll.
Hot water bottle dolls: Patty Comfort.
1908 Gems, G. F. & Nicks, W. F.: Patent collapsible doll bodies.
Hachmeister, Herman: Doll maker.
Hamburger, A. & Coston, H. E.: Patent stuffed dolls.
India Rubber, Gutta-Percha and Telegraph Works Co. Ltd.: Manufacturers.
1909 H Rag doll series: Hughes & Son.
Harris, A. C.: Patent weighted doll.
1910 Gamages: Trademark Chantecleer soft toy.
Goblin Gobblers: Trademark K. M. Sherwood.
Greedy Chuggy: K. M. Sherwood.
Hungry Giles: Patent K. M. Sherwood.
1912 Goo-Goo series: Grace Wiederseim.
Hugmee trademark: Eisenmann & Co.
1914 Hassall, John: Designed dolls.
Hewitt & Leadbeater: China dolls' heads.
Hill, E. W. & Cushing, E. C.: Patent metal heads and limbs.
1915 Green, S. A.: Doll colouring patent.
Hammond Mfg. Co. Ltd.: Doll, teddy bear and game manufacture.
Hansen, Laurie & Co. Ltd.: Importing and factors.
Harwen & Co. Ltd.: Manufacture and wholesale dolls and toys.
Houghton, Elizabeth Ellen: Trademark.
Hume, A. E.: Patent eyelids.
1916 Gladeye Doll: Imperial Doll & Toy Co.
Gray & Nicholls Ltd.: Mascot eskimo dolls.
Green, G. D.: Doll eye patent.
Hammond Mfg. Co. Ltd.: Dolls.
Hansen, Laurie & Co.: Pot head dolls.
Hawkesley & Co. Ltd.: Doll and toy manufacture.
Hibernian Novelty Co.: Composition doll and toy manufacture.
Huvan Mfg. Co.: Cut out dolls.
Imperial Doll & Toy Co.: Manufacture toys and dolls.
Impy: Sold by Ellison, Rees & Co.
1917 Girl series: Laurie Hansen.
Goldberg, J. A. & Co.: Sold china dolls.
Hanreck, S.: Celluloid faces.
Heywood, Abel & Sons: Doll and toy merchants.
1918 Happy Day Toy Co. Ltd.: Manufactured dolls etc.
Harper, G. W.: Manufactured dolls, teddy bears and wood toys.
Hawley, Horace: Manufactured dolls limbs.
Heywood, Cecil K.: Doll and toy merchant.
Hodge: E. E. Houghton.
Hot Water Baby: E. E. Houghton.
Houghton, James Albert: Made dolls.
Ibbetson, Leonard: Manufacture rag dolls and wood toys etc.
Ilford Doll & Toy Co.: Agents for dolls.
Irish Toy Co.: J. Peskin Heo Toyworks.
Ivorine Mfg. Co.: Celluloid dolls faces.

1919 Hammond Mfg. Co. Ltd.: Bisque, composition and rag dolls.
Holladay & Co. Ltd.: Master Givjoy.
I Mit: Darenta Toy Works.
I'se All Dicky: Dolls' Accessory Co. Ltd.
1920 Garfield, James & Co.: Doll and toy manufacture.
Georgette: Speights Ltd.
Giggly: Trademark Edward Hazell Jones.
Goo-Goo: Trademark for dolls Edward Hazell Jones.
Imans, P.: Patent arm fixing (wax) dolls.
1921 Gilbert the Filbert: Dean's Rag Book Co. Ltd.
Goo Goo Smile: Dolls' Accessory Co.
Gorleston Toy Co.: Rag, celluloid and dressed dolls.
I'mere: Trademark dolls Polmar Perfumery Co.
1922 Graham, Arthur: Peebo Doll.
1923 Goody Goody series: Baby Doll.
Heather Belle: Leon Rees.
1924 Gross & Schild: Marigold.
Grovewell Rubber Co.: Rubber toys and balloons.
Huck, A.: Patent joint improvement.
Humpty Dumpty soft toys: Worthing Toy Factory.
1925 Goldsmith, A.: Clown doll and pierrot.
Heather: Posy Buds.
Howard Pottery Co.: Made dolls.
Hyacinth: Posy Buds.
Iris: Posy Buds.
Ivy: Posy Buds.
1926 Goodman, L. & A. L.: Importer and agent English and Foreign.
1927 Garden: Mabel Bland-Hawkes.
Hazel: Mabel Bland-Hawkes.
Ickle, J. J.: Ankidoodle: trademark dolls, games and toys.
1928 Girly: Dean's Rag Book Co. Ltd.
Harold Lloyd: J. S. Sant Ltd.
1929 Harlequin Series: Dean's Rag Book Co. Ltd.
Herbie Brown: ('erbie Brown) Dean's Rag Book Co. Ltd.
Hetty: Dean's Rag Book Co. Ltd.
1931 Husheen dolls: Dean's Rag Book Co. Ltd.
1932 G. & G. Art Dolls: Manufacturing.
Gem Dolls: Dean's Rag Book Co. Ltd.
Houghton, Mrs. Edith: Doll repairs.
1935 Goldberg, Louis: Cheap soft dolls and toys.
Graham Bros.: Celluloid dolls.
Infields Ltd.: Manufacturer, eyes, masks, noses.
1936 Green Golliwog: Richards, Son & Allwin.
Henry: Dean's Rag Book Co. Ltd.
1937 Haughton, W. H.: Gordge, J.: Patent face or head.
1938 Hay, Will: Evripose Tru-to-Life Rag doll.
1939 Happy: Cascelloid, Palitoy.
1940 Grecon: Margarete Cohn.
Howard Pottery Co. Ltd.: Brentleigh dolls.
1944 Gaeltarra Eireann: Doll manufacture.
1946 Ginsberg & Smith: Hard bodied dolls.
1947 Hunter Toy Factory: Doll and toy manufacturer.
Ingram, G. & Clarke T.: Patent dolls eyes.
1949 Ibotson, C. W. P.: Dol-Toi Products.
Ideal Toys Ltd.: Doll manufacture.
1950 Herzog, Rae: Trademark Cinette.
Holloway Dolls Accessories Ltd.: Trademark Holly doll.
1952 Hair-Do doll: Rosebud.
1956 Gillian: Paliglide walking dolls.
1957 Graham Bros: Fairylite trademark.

	Highland dolls: Pedigree Soft Toys Ltd.
1958	Garrie, Thomas: Cariad.
	Giddikids: Upperton P. G. E.
	Hoopy Lou: Trademark Mettoy Co. Ltd.
1960	Hungarian doll: Pedigree Soft Toys Ltd.
1963	Hush-a-Bye Baby: Pedigree.
1964	Hook & Franks Ltd.: Faerie Glen dolls' clothes.
1966	Gloria and Gloria Princess: Wilson Bros. Ltd.
1967	Hippy Doll: Almar Dolls.
1968	Goldilocks: Palitoy.
1969	Gaiety: Bluebell Dolls Ltd.
1970	Gay Gadabout: Palitoy.
	House of Henrietta: Gormla Morony Ltd.
1971	Genital dolls: Bibi.
1974	Havoc Secret Agent: Modd Toys Ltd.
1976	Ghost of Captain Kidd: Lesney Products & Co. Ltd.
	Handy Mandy: Lesney Products & Co. Ltd.
	Hi dolls: Bambola Toys.
1977	Greenaway, Kate: Pedigree Dolls & Toys Ltd.
1978	Ginny Baby: Lesney Products & Co. Ltd.

JKL

1831	Jolly & Son: Owned Lowther Arcade.
1835	Jones, Robert: Made wooden dolls.
1850	Joseph's: Assembled porcelain dolls.
1852	Jones, Henry: Wooden doll and toy manufacturer.
	Jones, Richard William: Wooden dolls.
1855	Johnson, John Henry: Patent rubber and gutta-percha dolls.
1857	Lee, Thomas: Made dolls.
1860	Johnson Bros.: Later became Chad Valley.
	Lang & Co.: Made dolls and toys, India rubber and gutta-percha.
1865	Longbottom, John: Patent doll composition.
1866	Lee, David Thorpe: Doll patent.
1867	Kohnstam, M. & Co.: German-owned doll and toy manufacturers.
1868	Lake, W. R.: Patent rag doll.
1874	Jacob, Leopold Emil: Patent.
1881	Jones, S. & Co.: Made dolls.
1893	Jacob, Leopold Emil: Toy importer.
	Knight, A. B.: Doll patent.
1894	Knights R. G. & Co.: Made dolls.
	Lloyd, F. G.: Patent walking doll.
1900	Kitties: Yorkshire Sailcloth dolls.
	Kleiner J. & Sons Ltd.: Wholesaler and exporter.
1902	Jeffreys, Edward Augustus: German patent crying doll.
1903	Little Tich: Music hall character doll.
1905	Kismi: Trademark Stallard & Co.
1907	James, Arthur William: Trademark Aaba.
1908	Lawrence, J. W.: Doll manufacture.
	Little Pet: Eisenmann & Co.
1910	Jones, William Henry: Agent for German doll manufacturers.
	Lemon D. M. & Page: Patent crying doll.
1911	Kiddieland: Trademark Eisenmann & Co.
	Lyxhayr: Dickinson W. A. & Lyxhayr Mfg. Ltd.

1912	Keen & Co.: Vera doll.
	Kohnstam J. Ltd.: Importer and merchant.
	Kwacky-Wack: Eisenmann & Co.
1913	Kohnstam, J. Ltd.: Patent doll's body.
	Little Sambo: Dean's Rag Book Co. Ltd.
	Logan, H. T.: Skating doll.
	Lowe, Misses M.: Dolls' clothes manufacturer.
1914	John Bull: Dean's Rag Book Co. Ltd.
	Jones, William Henry: Doll and toy mfg.
	Lions Claw: Trademark E. E. M. McCubbin.
1915	Jernoid Ltd.: Dolls' masks.
	Jungle Toys: Doll manufacture.
	Khaki Boy: Anglo-American Novelty Co.
	Kingdom Toys: Soft toys, dolls and novelties.
	Kittie: Harwin & Co. Ltd.
	Knockabout Toys: Dean's Rag Book Co. Ltd.
	Kurly-Koon: Kingram Toys.
	Lawrence, J. W.: Wax and china dolls.
	Lee, Arthur H. & Sons Ltd.: Manufactured celluloid doll faces.
	Lloyd George: Welsh Industry.
	Lord Roberts Memorial Workshops: Doll and toy manufacture.
1916	Jumping Jack: Speights Ltd.
	Kaffir-Kiddy: Kingram Toys.
	Kamlish J. & Co.: Eskimo, china, caricature dolls manufacture.
	Kaye Toy & Fancy Goods Co.: Doll and toy wholesaler.
	Keats & Co.: Wax over china dolls.
	Kiddikin: Perls Chas. Mfg. Co.
	Knight Bros: & Cooper: Doll manufacture
	Lamplough, Henry: Patent cardboard doll.
	Lindop, W.: Alert doll.
	Littman: L. J.: Rag dolls manufacture.
	Lulu; S. Hancock & Sons, Hamley trademark.
1917	Kewpie: see Lord Roberts, and Cascelloid.
	Kiddlums: Trademark Tah Toys Ltd.
	Kidette: Speights Ltd.
	Kirby, G. L.: Made dolls.
	Layfield, Joseph: Doll manufacturer and wholesaler.
	Leda: Spencer & Co.
	Lewis & Owen: Manufacturer, composition and rag dolls.
	Lord Kitchener.
1918	Jane: British Toys.
	Josylin: Daisy Dolls.
	Joyce: Daisy Dolls.
	Joysie: Fretwell Mfg. Co.
	Jullien, H. J. & Son Ltd.: Doll and toy manufacture.
	June Babies: Daisy Dolls.
	Keane, Doris: Art dolls.
	Keiller, Wm. & Co.: Printed rag dolls.
	Kelvedon Village Industry: Made dolls.
	King Bros.: Made dolls.
	Lambert Clarke & Co.: Dolls' wigs manufacture.
	Lowe Richard & Co.: Stuffed dolls manufacture.
1919	Jollyboy, Mr.: A. G. Owen.
	Kitson, Arthur: Doll manufacture.
	Leda Dolls Ltd.: Spencer & Co.
	Lloyd Mayer & Co.: Composition dolls manufacture.
	Long Exposure: Dolls' Accessory Co.
	Luckham, C. & Co. Ltd.: Toy and doll importers.
1920	Jack & Jill: East London (Federation) Toy Factory.

Jones, Edward Hazell: Trademark Goo Goo and Giggly.

Kent Toy Works: Cannon dolls.

Liberty & Co. Ltd.: Liberty trademark.

Linda: Cecil Coleman Ltd.

Little Black Sambo: East London (Federation) Toy Factory.

1921 K-An-Ess: E. Kelty, & Sons.

Kelty, E. & Sons: K-An-Ess dolls.

Kydyte: Dolls' Accessory Co.

Lady Di: Wonderland Toymaking Co.

Luckham, C. & Co. Ltd.: Doll importer.

1922 Jockey: Lawton Doll Co.

Johnny: Dean's Rag Book Co. Ltd.

Lawton Doll Co.: Doll manufacturer.

Love Me: Lawton Doll Co.

Lucky Puck: Dean's Rag Book Co. Ltd.

1923 Kuddlemee Dolls: Dean's Rag Book Co. Ltd.

La Petite Caresse: Chad Valley Co. Ltd.

Little Lady Anne: Mabel Bland-Hawkes.

1924 Jaysant: Sant, J. S. Ltd.

Jazz Doll Manufacturers, The: The Jazz doll man; and wholesale.

Lamplough, Henry: Unbreakable dolls and heads.

Little Miss Vogue: Mabel Bland-Hawkes.

Johnson, A. J.: Johnson Bros.

1925 Kletzin Ltd.: Made dolls.

Laar, P. H. van: Patent pillow doll.

Lilac: Posy Buds.

1926 Lucille Dolls: Leon Rees.

Lullabye Babies: Leon Rees.

1927 Jane Sprogg: Women's Magazine.

Joyce: S. & L. Mfg. Co.

Luvly Dolls: Dean's Rag Book Co. Ltd.

1928 Lloyd George: Sant, J. S. Ltd.

Lucette: Dean & Son Ltd.

Lulu: Dean & Son Ltd.

Lu-Lu: Whyte, Ridsdale & Co. Ltd.

1929 Kaluto: Trademark Ernest Turner.

King, G. W.: Patent mechanical doll.

1930 Johnson & Johnson (G. B.) Ltd.: Roostie trademark.

1931 Jolly & Son: Lowther Arcade.

Lido Lady: Dean's Rag Book Co. Ltd.

1932 Little Miss Mischief: Mabel Bland-Hawkes.

1933 Jolly Toddlers: Norah Wellings.

1934 Jeanette: Leon Rees.

Jol Jack: Leon Rees.

Jones, F. C.: Patent rubber doll.

1935 Jones, Robert: Made wooden dolls.

Joy Day: J. K. Farnell & Co. Ltd.

Little Bo Peep: Nursery Rhyme Character Dolls.

Little Boy Blue: Nursery Rhyme Character Dolls.

Little Jack Horner: Nursery Rhyme Character Dolls.

Little Miss Muffet: Nursery Rhyme Character Dolls.

Luvmee: S. & L. Mfg. Co. Ltd.

1936 Joan: J. K. Farnell & Co. Ltd.

Joy Day Specials: J. K. Farnell & Co. Ltd.

Joy Day Woolies: J. K. Farnell & Co. Ltd.

Kiddiecraft Company: Doll and toy manufacture.

Kingbaby: Dean's Dollies Ltd.

Kutoy, Messrs.: Doll and toy manufacture.

1937 King George VI: British Industries Fair.

1938 Lambeth Walkers, The: Dean's Rag Book Co. Ltd.

1939 Little Happy: Cascelloid Ltd.

Little People: Merrythought Ltd.

1940 Lo-La dolls: Bailey Potteries Ltd.

1947 Klein, P.: Playplastic Toy Co. Ltd.

1948 Kensett Bros: Joydale doll.

Little Bo Peep: Pedigree Soft Toys Ltd.

1949 Leiber Bros.: Doll manufacture.

Luxidolly: M. S. P. (Luxiproducts) Ltd.

1950 Jedmunds: J. Henry Edmunds.

Key Products: Benjamin Frankel.

Lawley & Page Ltd.: Singing doll.

1954 J.R.J. Products Ltd.: Patent dolls eyes.

1955 Jayco dolls: J. Cowan (Dolls) Ltd.

Joan: Todd, D. G. & Co. Ltd.

Julie: D. G. Todd & Co. Ltd.

Knee Bend dolls: D. G. Todd & Co. Ltd.

Kove, Nicholas: Amandadoll.

Lesley: Young & Fogg Rubber Co. Ltd.

1956 Lindy: Petalskin dolls.

1957 Johnnie: Randall & Wood Ltd.

1958 Little Gretel: Lines Bros. Ltd.

1959 Little Miss Vogue: Pedigree Soft Toys Ltd.

1960 L.S.D. Dolls: J. K. Farnell & Co. Ltd.

Leila: De Luxe Dolls.

Louretta: Debutante Dolls.

Lucille: J. K. Farnell, & Co. Ltd.

1963 Little Lizzie: Maria Wood.

1966 Julie & Jon The Dutch Boy and Girl: Trevor Toys.

1967 Katie: Pedigree

1968 Jewellery Kiddles: Rosebud Mattel.

Kum-Along Katie: D. G. Todd & Co. Ltd.

Liddle Middle Muffet: Rosebud Mattel.

Little Miss Fussy: Palitoy.

Lucy Locket Kiddles: World of Kiddles.

1969 Jones, Mfanwy: Margaret Holgate.

1970 Jackman, Barbara (Craft) Dolls Ltd: Yesterday Dollies.

1971 Katie Kopycat: Palitoy.

Lucy Lisa: Pedigree.

1972 Lesney Products & Co. Ltd.: Matchbox dolls.

Lisa's Trousseau: Palitoy.

Little Big Man: Palitoy.

1973 Leeway Selcol: Doll and toy manufacture.

1974 Lovely Liza: Pedigree.

1975 Julie: Lesney Products & Co. Ltd.

Kiki: Lesney Products & Co. Ltd.

Lisa: Lesney Products & Co. Ltd.

Lisa: Dean, Mary.

Lucy: Lesney Products & Co. Ltd.

1976 Kid Cortez: Lesney Products & Co. Ltd.

Linda: Cecil Coleman Ltd.

Liza Jane: W. H. Cornelius, Ltd.

Lulu: Palitoy.

Luvy-Duvy: Be Be Dolls Ltd.

1977 Jeanette: H. Schelhorn & Co.

MNO

1843 Ogilwy, R.: Wax and wax over composition dolls.

1849 Montanari, Napoleon: Wax dolls.

1852 Nest, William: Made dolls.

1860 Martyn, J. L. Made Dolls.

1862 Martin & Runyon: Autoperipatikos.

1863   Munn, J. A.: Patent walking doll.
1864   Montanari, R. N.: Wax dolls.
1865   Marsh, William: Wax dolls.
      Meech Bros.: Wax dolls.
1870   Melhuish, Edwin: Made dolls.
      Metropolitan India Rubber & Vulcanite Co.: Rubber dolls.
      Moody, G.: Sold dolls.
      Morrell, H. W. & C. & Mrs. J. Arundel: Sold wax dolls.
1871   Mewburn, J. G.: Dolls' head patent.
      Newton, A. V.: Crawling doll patent.
1876   Meyerstein, W.: Dealer in dolls.
1878   Marsh, Charles & Mary Anne: Wax dolls.
1884   Nankeen dolls: Stephen Erhard.
      Ozocerite: Wax used in doll making.
1891   Mally, J. R.: Two doll patents.
      Millis, F. W.: Ventriloquist figure patent.
1893   Maden, J. H.: Patent celluloid masks.
      Nuttall, W. H.: Patent celluloid masks.
1894   Mason, C. G, Foster, F. A, Elms, J. C. & Sprague: Printed rag doll patent.
1895   McCalmont, R.: Paper doll patent.
1900   Many Misfitz Folk: C. W. Faulkner, & Co.
      Martin, S. F.: Walking doll patent.
1905   Muller, H.: Doll Patent.
1906   Marks, E. C. R. Phonographic doll patent.
      Mayer & Sherratt: Pottery doll manufacturers.
      Mewman: Patent talking doll.
      Newman, A. Morris: Patent phonographic doll.
1908   Orwell Art Industries: Unbreakable character doll manufacturer.
1909   My Little Territorial: H. J. Hughes & Son.
      Our Little Dreadnought: H. J. Hughes & Son.
1913   Ordenstein, Richard: Merchant, Ragtime Kids trademark.
1914   McCubbin, E. E. M.: Lion's Claw trademark.
      Moppietop: Dean's Rag Book Co. Ltd.
      Mrs. & Master Folly: H. J. Hughes & Son.
      Nautical Nancy: Dean's Rag Book Co. Ltd.
      Nottingham Toy Industry: China and composition dolls.
      Omega: British United Toy Mfg. Co. trademark.
1915   McMillan, Adelaide: Patent rag doll.
      Melba: Mayer & Sherratt.
      National Doll League: Made dolls.
      Nell Foy & Co.: Doll and toy manufacture.
      Non-Nysa dolls: W. S. Turton.
      Nunn & Smeed: Pottery dolls.
1916   Mad Kaiser: Huvan Mfg. Co.
      Marcuse, Day & Co. Ltd.: Doll and toy manufacture.
      Marion & Co.: Made dolls.
      Miller Bros.: Esquimaux and dolls.
      Miller, Gertrude: Speights Ltd.
      Miller, J. P. & Co.: Composition doll manufacture.
      Munition doll: Bell & Francis.
1917   Mitchell & Co.: Dolls' hair and accessories.
      My Kiddie: Fretwell Toy Mfg. Co.
      Nellfoy: Nell Foy & Co. trademark.
      New Century Dolls: Nottingham Toy Industry Ltd.
      New Darling Baby: Heywood-Abel & Sons Ltd.
1918   Marlborough Mfg. Co.: Charlie Chaplin & Red Cross dolls.
1922   May Blossom: Dennis Malley & Co. Ltd.
      Miss Beauty Cupid: Lawton Doll Co.

      Morrell, Frank & Richard: Distributed dolls.
1923   Mann & Mann: Dolls.
      Munyard, A. R.: Doll patent.
      Nunsuch doll: George Lawrence Nunn.
      Offenbacher, S. & Co.: Handled dolls.
1924   Maisie: Dean's Rag Book Co. Ltd.
      Marigold: Gross & Schild trademark.
      The Marion: Marn & Jondorf.
      Mayer, L.: Cupids.
      Miniature Models: Figurines.
      Nobody's Darling.
1925   Miss Crossword: A. J. Hughes & Son.
1926   Miss Muffet: J. K. Farnell & Co. Ltd.
1927   Mamie: S. & L. Mfg. Co.
      Moritz & Chambers: Celluloid doll manufacture.
      My Dollie's Nanna: Mabel Bland-Hawkes.
1928   Miss Black Bottom: J. Sear Ltd.
      My Sweetie: S. Z. Fishman.
      Nono: Dean & Son Ltd.
1929   Modern dolls: Dean's Rag Book Co. Ltd.
1930   Margaret, Princess: Whyte, Ridsdale & Co.
1932   Merrythought Ltd.: Made dolls.
      Miss Mischief: Bedington Liddiatt.
      Monica: Chad Valley.
      Norene: Norah Wellings.
      Oppy: Miriam Dreyfus.
      Our Baby: J. W. Spear & Sons.
1933   Molly: Dean's Rag Book Co. Ltd.
1935   Marina: Dean's Rag Book Co. Ltd.
      Mary Mary: Chad Valley.
      Nigger Peggy doll: J. Sear Ltd.
      Nipper: Merrythought Ltd.
      Nursery Rhyme Character dolls: Chad Valley.
1936   Mackenry: Trademark for J. Kohnstam, Ltd.
      Madeline: Dean's Rag Book Co. Ltd.
      Michael: J. K. Farnell & Co. Ltd.
1938   Margaret Rose, Princess: Chad Valley.
      Mary Bligh: Chad Valley.
1946   Marvo: L. Silberston & Sons Ltd.
      Morris, Mitchell & Co.: All plastic doll.
1947   Michel-Levy: Dolrite trademark.
      Mitchell, J. D.: Eye patent.
      Monica: Buckingham (London) Ltd., trademark.
      Myers, H. R.: Dolls' eye patent.
      Nene Plastics: Eric Smith.
      Mathews, T. & Co.: Paper dressing doll.
      Matthews, L.: Doll patent.
      Mogridge, W. H. & Co.: Doll manufacture.
1919   Master Givjoy: Holladay & Co. Ltd.
      Miller, Leonard: Doll manufacture.
      Milton Livesey & Co. Ltd.: Doll manufacture.
      Mindol Ltd.: Miniature dolls and toys.
      Models (Leicester) Ltd.: Doll and toy manufacture.
      National Doll & Glass Eye Mfg. Co.: Dolls' eyes etc.
      Norgate, M. B.: Patent dolls' head.
      Noxid: T. A. Dixon.
      Owen, A. G.: Doll and toy manufacture.
1920   Marchioness: Speights Ltd.
      Marie: Speights Ltd.
      Minnie Ha Ha: Harwin Ltd.
      Misska Dolls: Art Toy Mfg. Co.
      Miss Muffet: Speights Ltd.
      Nelke: Weeks & Co. (London) Ltd. trademark.
      New Born: Dolls heads.
      Nighty Girl: Speights Ltd.

Now: Trademark.

Olida Doll & Toy Mfg. Co.: Baby dolls.

1921 Margot The Midget: Daily Express cartoon character doll.

Neighbour, R. C. & Co.: Manufacturer Livetoy series.

Nero: Neighbour, R. C. & Co. trademark.

New Eccles Rubber Works: Doll and toy manufacture.

1922 May Blossom: Dennis Malley & Co. Ltd.

Miss Beauty Cupid: Lawton Doll Co.

Morrell, Frank & Richard: Distributed dolls.

1923 Mann & Mann: Dolls.

Munyard, A. R.: Doll patent.

Nunsuch doll: George Lawrence Nunn.

Offenbacher, S. & Co.: Handled dolls.

1924 Maisie: Dean's Rag Book Co. Ltd.

Marigold: Gross & Schild trademark.

The Marion: Marn & Jondorf.

Mayer, L.: Cupids.

Miniature Models: Figurines.

Nobody's Darling.

1925 Miss Crossword: A. J. Hughes & Son.

1926 Miss Muffet: J. K. Farnell & Co. Ltd.

1927 Mamie: S. & L. Mfg. Co.

Moritz & Chambers: Celluloid doll manufacture.

My Dollie's Nanna: Mabel Bland-Hawkes.

1928 Miss Black Bottom: J. Sear Ltd.

My Sweetie: S. Z. Fishman.

Nono: Dean & Son Ltd.

1929 Modern dolls: Dean's Rag Book Co. Ltd.

1930 Margaret, Princess: Whyte, Ridsdale & Co.

1932 Merrythought Ltd.: Made dolls.

Miss Mischief: Bedington Liddiatt.

Monica: Chad Valley.

Norene: Norah Wellings.

Oppy: Miriam Dreyfus.

Our Baby: J. W. Spear & Sons.

1933 Molly: Dean's Rag Book Co. Ltd.

1935 Marina: Dean's Rag Book Co. Ltd.

Mary Mary: Chad Valley.

Nigger Peggy doll: J. Sear Ltd.

Nipper: Merrythought Ltd.

Nursery Rhyme Character dolls: Chad Valley.

1936 Mackenry: Trademark for J. Kohnstam, Ltd.

Madeline: Dean's Rag Book Co. Ltd.

Michael: J. K. Farnell & Co. Ltd.

1938 Margaret Rose, Princess: Chad Valley.

Mary Bligh: Chad Valley.

1946 Marvo: L. Silberston & Sons Ltd.

Morris, Mitchell & Co.: All plastic doll.

1947 Michel-Levy: Dolrite trademark.

Mitchell, J. D.: Eye patent.

Monica: Buckingham (London) Ltd., trademark.

Myers, H. R.: Dolls' eye patent.

Nene Plastics: Eric Smith.

1948 Marie series: Morris, Mitchell & Co.

Mitchell Plastics: Plastic dolls.

Old Cottage Toys: Doll manufacture.

Organdie Beauty: Toys (Components) Ltd.

1949 M.S.P. (Luxiproducts) Ltd.: Luxifolly trademark.

Macleod, A. L.: Peter Pan trademark.

Masks & Mouldings Ltd.: Dolls' masks.

Mignon: Williams & Steer Mfg. Co. Ltd.

Mitchell & Hardy (Plastics) Ltd.: Prince Charming and Mormit.

Nursery Rhyme Doll Co. Ltd.: Made dolls.

1950 Miller, J.: Soft doll patent.

Nozo the Clown: Palitoy.

1952 Mandy Lou: Pedigree Soft Toys Ltd.

Masks Ltd.: Dolls masks.

Middlesex Toy Industries Ltd.: Mama voices.

N.G. Products & Co. Ltd.: Golborne trademark.

1953 Nisbet, Peggy: Makes dolls.

Ottenburg, I. & R.: Coronation dolls.

1955 Magnetic Joan: Philmar Ltd.

Mettoy Co. Ltd.: Vinyl dolls.

1956 Magic Flesh dolls: Pedigree Soft Toys Ltd.

Mandy: Dean's Rag Book Co. Ltd.

1958 Mettoy Co. Ltd.: Doll patents.

Miranda: Palitoy.

Miss Linda: Randall & Wood.

Nursery Rhyme: The Mettoy Co.

1959 Mam'selle Boutique dolls' dresses: Lines Bros.

Marty: Trademark for M. L. Bartholomew.

Michell doll: Palitoy.

Miss Rosebud Bride doll: Rosebud Dolls Ltd.

1960 Mary Ann: Pedigree Soft Toys Ltd.

1961 Mother Goose: J. K. Farnell & Co. Ltd.

1963 Myfanwy Products Ltd.: Welsh costume dolls.

1965 Newfield Ltd.: Bendy toys.

1966 Michele: Pedigree Soft Toys Ltd.

1967 Mary Make Up: Palitoy.

Minikids: Thernglade Ltd.

Munster, F. J. & Co. Ltd.: Costume dolls.

1968 New Trend: Favourite Toys Ltd.

1969 Mfanwy Jones: Margaret Holgate.

1971 Miss Happy Heart: Bluebell Dolls Ltd.

Moppet doll: Cassidy Bros. Ltd.

1972 Matchbox Ltd.: Dolls.

Miss Cleversticks: Bluebell Dolls Ltd.

1973 Miss Nobody: Character Crafts Ltd.

Model Toys Ltd.: Daisy.

1975 Melanie: Lesney Products & Co. Ltd.

Michelle: Lesney Products & Co. Ltd.

My First Baby: Pedigree.

Nicki: Lesney Products & Co. Ltd.

1976 Matilda: The Moppits.

Milly: The Moppits.

Molly Poppet: Chad Valley.

1977 Minnie: The Moppits.

My Baby Love: H. Schelhorn & Co.

PQR

1699	Penn, Letitia: A wooden doll.
1800	Pedlar dolls.
1810	Pierotti, Giovanni: Wax dolls.
1826	Robins, Joseph: Composition dolls.
1840	Poole, John R.: Wooden dolls.
1848	Peck, Mrs. Lucy Rebecca: Wax dolls.
1852	Pache & Son: Artificial eyes.
	Poole, Edward: Wax and composition dolls.
	Poole, William: Wax and composition dolls.
1853	Rich, William: Wax and rag dolls.
1862	Peacock: Wax and composition dolls.
1865	Plumb, Henry: Dolls.
1866	Pepper, John: Made gymnastic figures.

1868   Pitfield, William: Wax dolls.
1871   Pierotti, Chas. W.: Wax dolls.
1878   Phonograph doll patent: T. A. Edison.
1886   Paradis des Enfants, Le: Sold dolls.
       Parkins & Co. Ltd.: Paradis des Enfants.
1888   Phonograph doll: A. G. Brooks, patent.
       Robert Bros.: Made dolls.
1889   Phonograph doll: W. W. Jaques patent.
1891   Retkin, M. & R.: Dolls' eye patent.
1899   Robb, W. R.: Cardboard doll patent.
1900   Reid, J. A.: Doll patent.
1903   Peacock, William: Exported and distributed dolls.
1904   Porter, Ralph: Made dolls.
1905   Peter Pan trademark: Cecil Coleman.
1907   Patty Comfort: Hot water bottle doll.
1910   Preston, A. M.: Dancing doll patent.
1911   Peck, William, G. & Co.: Agent for Horseman, American doll manufacturer.
       Peek-a-Boo: Trademark of B. H. Thompson.
1912   Peggie: Grace Wiederseim.
       Rees, Leon: Dolls' eye patent.
1913   Ragtime Kids trademark: Richard Ordenstein.
1914   Papier Mâché dolls: All British Doll Mfg. Co.
       Pierette dolls: Dean's Rag Book Co. Ltd.
       Plucky: Ellison, Rees & Co.
       Pooksie: Trademark of J. G. Hamley.
       Potteries Doll Co.: Doll Manufacturer.
       Rag Time: Dean's Rag Book Co. Ltd.
       Rees, Leon: Dolls' head patent.
1915   Potteries Toy Co.: Assembled dolls.
       Red Cross Nurse: Stephen Erhard.
       Ritchie, A. P. F.: Doll joint patent.
1916   Papooski, The: R. S. Curling.
       Perks, E. S. A.: Doll patents.
       Perls, Charles: Unbreakable composition dolls.
       Pierrette dolls: Speights Ltd.: Knight Bros. & Cooper Ltd.: Marcuse, Day & Co. Ltd.
       Red Cross Nurse: Bell & Francis.
       Red Riding Hood: Harwin & Co. Ltd.
       Reliance: Knights Bros. & Cooper Ltd.
       Robins, Madame, G.: Stuffed doll bodies.
       Rock China dolls: Nottingham Toy Industry Ltd.
       Rose Dolls: Wholesale Toy Co.
1917   Plastic dolls: S. Hanreck.
       Plastolite:Bedington Liddiatt.
       Prieur, Miss Marie: Made dolls.
       Revill, W. E.: Dolls' eye patent.
       Rochdale doll: Emell Toy Mfg. Co.
1918   Peskin, J.: Doll manufacturer.
       Peter & Pauline: Nottingham Toy Industry Ltd.
       Porcelite Co., The: Dolls' limb manufacturing.
       Primrose League Toymaking Industry: Dealt in dolls.
       Red Cross Nurse: Marlborough Mfg. Co.: Nell Foy & Co.
       Rochdale Doll Co.: Doll Manufacture: Eclipse.
       Royal Crown Pottery: Doll manufacturing.
1919   Pank: Harwin & Co. Ltd.
       Petsey Murphy: J. Vincent.
       Princess dolls: J. Tattersall Ltd.
       Red Riding Hood: Three Arts Women's Employment Fund.
       Rosebud: Dean's Rag Book Co. Ltd.
1920   Philip Toy Co. Ltd.: Manufacturers and dealers in dolls.
       Pierrette dolls: Fairyland Toy Mfg. Co.

       Poppy Dolls: Lloyd, Mayer & Co.
       Princess: Speights Ltd.
       Pyjama Girl: Speights Ltd.
       Red Riding Hood: Speights Ltd.
       Regina Dolls: G. L. Nunn.
       River Girl: Speights Ltd.
       Rubbadubdub: J. G. Franklin & Sons.
1921   Pickett's Phono figures: Gramophone dolls.
       Pinka-Boo: Trademark: Polmar Perfumery Co. Ltd.
       Pinkie Doll: H. E. Hughes.
       Priscilla: Dean's Rag Book Co. Ltd.
       Profiteer: Dolls' Accessory Co.
       Roh, Madame & Roh, W.: Dolls' wig manufacturers.
       Ross & Co.: Miniature dolls.
1922   Peebo Doll: Trademark of Arthur Graham.
       Princess: Lawton Doll Co.
       Puck: Dean's Rag Book Co. Ltd.
       Punfield: F. W.: Celluloid doll manufacturer.
1923   Peggy: Chad Valley.
       Pixie: Chad Valley.
       Plaster Doll Co.: Made dolls.
       Pollard, E. & Co. Ltd. & Robins, F. E.: Patent doll joints.
       Ralph, H. S.: Imported and exported dolls.
1924   Perks, R. M.:Trademark Dolfam.
       Priscilla: J. S. Sant.
       Ransom, S.: Celluloid dolls.
1925   Playtime dolls: Dean's Rag Book Co. Ltd.
       Pomerantz, A. F. & Sons: Pomtoys.
       Posy Buds: Dean's Rag Book Co. Ltd.
       Posy Dolls: Dean's Rag Book Co. Ltd.
       Preston, Chloe: J. K. Farnell & Co. Ltd.
       Princess Dolls: Dean's Rag Book Co. Ltd.
       Rayburn Townsend Co. Ltd.: Soft dolls.
       Rompa series: Rayburn Townsend Co. Ltd.
1926   Pal Peter: J. K. Farnell & Co. Ltd.
       Peter Pan: Chad Valley.
       Princess Dolls & Babies: L. Rees & Co.
1927   Peggy: J. S. Sant Ltd.
       Peter: S. & L. Mfg. Co.
1928   Rosine: Dean & Son.
1929   Piccaninnies: Dean's Rag Book Co. Ltd.
       Pirate Twin, The & The Pirate Twins: Trademark of Faber & Faber.
1930   Pop trademark: Daily Sketch & Sunday Graphic.
       Punch: Dean's Rag Book Co. Ltd.
       R. A. C. Scout doll: Chad Valley.
       Roostie: Johnson & Johnson (G. B.) Ltd.
       Rosette: Leon Rees.
1931   Pollock, M. B.: Doll patent.
1932   Pessy: Miriam Dreyfus.
1933   Patsie: Merrythought Ltd.
       Peter & Patsy: Dean's Rag Book Co. Ltd.
       Reynolds, E.: Doll patent.
       Rosa: Dean's Rag Book Co. Ltd.
1934   P. C. Bloggs: L. Rees & Co.
       Rendle, C. J.: Doll patent.
1935   Pelican Products: Made dolls and accessories.
       Pickitoop: Dean's Rag Book Co. Ltd.
       Pixie & Dixie: Merrythought Ltd.
       Podgie dolls: J. K. Farnell & Co. Ltd.
       Popular: Chad Valley.
       Precious: Dean's Rag Book Co. Ltd.
       Richards, Son & Allwin Ltd.: Allwin trademark.

1936   Peter Pan: J. K. Farnell & Co. Ltd.
      Peter Polony: Messrs. Kutoy.
      Popeye: Dean's Rag Book Co. Ltd.
      Puckaninny: Dean's Rag Book Co. Ltd.
      R.M.S. Queen Mary Mascot: J. K. Farnell & Co. Ltd.
      Rattles: East London (Federation) Toy Factory.

1937   Palitoy: Cascelloid Ltd.
      Peggy: Spear, J. W. & Sons.
      Plastex: Cascelloid Ltd. & Rednoid.
      Princess Elizabeth: J. W. Spear & Sons.

1938   Pedigree Soft Toys Ltd.: Composition dolls.
      Prince Edward: Chad Valley.
      Priscilla: Cascelloid Ltd.
      Rags: Palitoy.
      Rock-a-Bye Dolls: J. K. Farnell & Co. Ltd.

1939   Popeye: Cecil Coleman.

1940   Pinocchio: Chad Valley.

1944   Packers (Manchester) Ltd.: Webbers Dolls Ltd.

1945   Popper, F. & E.: Doll patents.

1946   Quinn, N.: Patent dolls eye.
      Rainproof Girl: J. Cowan (Dolls) Ltd.

1947   Pelham Puppets: Wooden marionettes.
      Plastic dolls: J. Cowan (Dolls) Ltd.
      Rodno Baby Dolls: D. G. Todd & Co. Ltd.
      Rosebud: T. Eric Smith trademark.

1948   Patsy doll: Cascelloid.
      Rable, J. C.: Hot water bottle doll patent.
      Ratcliff, G. R.: Dolls' eye patents.
      Retkin, M. & R.: Dolls' eye patent.
      Roddy trademark: D. G. Todd & Co. Ltd.
      Rodnoid: D. G. Todd & Co. Ltd.

1949   Patsy: Playplastic Toy Co.
      Peter Pan trademark: A. L. Macleod.
      Plaztoy trademark: Masks & Mouldings Ltd.
      Prince Charming: Mitchell & Hardy (Plastics) Ltd.
      Quintex: A. A. Products Ltd.
      Radio doll: Williams & Steer Mfg. Co. Ltd.

1950   Prudence Kitten Co. Ltd: Annette Mills.

1952   Patsy: Cascelloid Ltd. trademark.
      Pin-Up dolls: Pedigree Soft Toys Ltd.
      Plastic dolls: D. G. Todd.

1953   Rhythmbar: E. M. Bartley.

1954   Philmar Ltd.: Paper dolls.
      Randall & Wood Ltd.: Doll manufacturers.

1955   Pedigree Character and Storybook dolls: Pedigree Soft
        Toys Ltd.
      Playsafe dolls: Wendy Boston.
      Rosedale Associated Manufacturers Ltd.: Doll
        manufacturers.

1956   Paliglide Walking dolls: Palitoy.
      Penny: Palitoy.
      Petalskin dolls: Palitoy.
      Pretty Peepers: Pedigree.
      Rosebud walking doll: Rosebud Dolls Ltd.

1957   Playcharm: Webber's Dolls Ltd.
      Pretty Baby: Palitoy.
      Quoshiwog: H. W. Carter & Co. Ltd.
      Roberts: J. V. Robertson.
      Robertson, J. V. Dolls and clothes.

1958   Rosebud Teenage dolls: Rosebud Dolls Ltd.

1959   Patsy the Wonder Doll: Palitoy.
      Pedigree Authentic Period Miniatures: Pedigree.
      Rainbow: Margot Dagmar Ltd.
      Roytoys: Masa Roy Sieki.

1960   Primrose dolls: Young & Fogg Rubber Co. Ltd.

      Rosebud Big dolls: Rosebud Ltd.

1962   Pollyanna: Joy Wilcox.

1963   Pebbles Flintstone: Rosebud Dolls Ltd.

1964   Penny Brite: De Luxe Toy Co. Ltd.

1965   Patch: Pedigree.
      Paul: Pedigree.
      Playwear Mfg. Co.: Doll's clothes.

1966   Penny: Dean's Childsplay Toys Ltd.

1967   Patti Pitta Pat: Palitoy.
      Pouting Pretty: Palitoy.
      Pretty Miss Kiss: Palitoy.
      Rosebud Mattel Ltd.: Plastic dolls.

1968   Penny The Personality Doll: Pedigree.
      Pippa: Pedigree.
      Precious Baby Doll: Favourite Toys Ltd.
      Push-along-Pixie: D. G. Todd & Co. Ltd.
      Push Along Popsie: Rosebud Mattel Ltd.

1970   Popsy Posy doll: Pedigree.
      Romeo and Juliet: B. Jackman (Craft) Dolls Ltd.

1971   Penny Puppywalker: Palitoy.
      Ploppy Character dolls: Mattel Ltd.

1972   Parker, Ann: Costume dolls.
      Pippa: Palitoy.

1974   Peek-a-Boo: Pedigree.
      Princess Pippa: Palitoy.

1975   Paul: Matchbox: Lesney Products & Co. Ltd.
      Picnic Playset: Lesney Products & Co. Ltd.

1976   Poppet 23: Palitoy.

1977   Peter and Sundancer: Pedigree.

STU

1840   Salmon Pedlar dolls at Stratford upon Avon.

1850   Santy: Made wax dolls.
      Townsend, George: Made china toys and figures.

1852   Shields, John, & Mrs. M.: Made composition dolls.

1855   Snowball, Mrs. S.: Made wax dolls.

1856   Scott, William: Made Gutta-percha dolls.
      Teather, George: Made wax dolls.
      Thorpe, Joseph: Wax doll maker.

1867   Tilson, William: Doll maker.

1870   Thompson, Henry: Made dolls.

1880   Simpson, Jessie Worthing: Painted fabric dolls.
      Smith, Edward: Handles wax dolls.

1881   Spratt, Miss H. Made Dolls.
      Stiff, Walter: Made and exported wax dolls and
        figures.

1882   Shoolbred & Co.: Shop sold dolls.

1887   Simpson W. S.: Patent doll on musical wheels.
      Star Mfg. Co.: Manufacturers and exporters of dolls.

1889   Standers, W. & Perry J. J.: Patent moving dolls.

1892   Strome & Co.: Made dolls, and merchants.

1893   Statham, Samuel Edward: Rubber doll patent.
      Tuck, Raphael: Paper doll patent.

1895   Schmidt, Richard: Importer and distributor of dolls.
      Sindall, Frederick: Wholesaler and exporter of rag
        dolls and wool toys.
      Trufant, Bertha: Cardboard doll and toy patent.

1898   Thompson, R. A. & Freeman, W. S.: Mechanical doll
        patent.

1903   Turnbull & Co., Chas. Edward: Made dolls, golliwogs and toys.

1905   Stallard & Co.: Kismi trademark dolls.

1910   Sherwood, Katherine Mary: Mechanical doll trademarks.

1911   Thompson, Bernard Home: Trademark Peek-a-Boo for dolls.

1912   Sandow, Eugene: Patent exercise doll.
Sunshine Girl: Bings Ltd.
Sunshine Kid: Bings Ltd.
Teddie: Grace Wiederseim.
Toddles: Eisenmann & Co.

1913   Shynall Rag Doll Co.: Manufacturer.
Speights Ltd.: Dolls and dolls wig manufacturers.
Terry, William J.: Soft dolls and toy manufacturer.
Textile Novelty Co. The: Art Toy Mfg. Co. Ltd.
Tru-to-Life dolls: Dean's Rag Book Co. Ltd.

1914   Sarah Starter: Dean's Rag Book Co. Ltd.
Shrieking Susan: Dean's Rag Book Co. Ltd.
Soldier Boy in Khaki: Whyte, Ridsdale & Co.
Soldier's Baby, The: Elizabeth Boase.
Tommy Atkins: Whyte, Ridsdale & Co.
Tommy Fuzbuz: Dean's Rag Book Co. Ltd.
Torrington, W. J.: Patent umbrella doll.

1915   Sea Baby: Tarpey, Jessie Toler Kingsley.
Shanklin Toy Industry: Doll manufacturer.
Short, S. & A. Ltd.: Doll and toy mfg.
Simpson Fawcett & Co. Ltd. Toy and doll manufacturers.
Smith & Hoyle: Made porcelain dolls.
Sunlight Sieve & Co.: Wholesale, export and manufacture of dolls and toys.
Tarpey, Jessie Toler Kingsley: Sea Baby trademark.
Thorne Bros.: Doll and toy manufacturers.
Tinkerbill: Laurie Hansen & Co. Ltd.
Tipperary Tommy: Harwin & Co. Ltd.
Toddler, The: Shanklin Toy Industry.
Tumble-it Dolls: Thorne Bros.
Turton, W. S.: Doll and toy manufacture.

1916   Sloan & Co.: Made felt dolls and animals.
Smith, W. H.: Doll and toy manufacture.
South Wales Toy Mfg. Co. Ltd.: Soft toy and doll manufacture.
Spencer & Co.: Composition doll manufacturers.
Staffordshire Doll Co.: Made undressed dolls.
Tah Toys Ltd.: Toy and doll manufacturers.
Union Jack Baby: Leon Rees.

1917   Salisbury, Thos. Chas.: Trademark Leda for dolls.
Sissons Bros. & Co. Ltd.: Dolac manufacturers.
Smith, R. H. Made dolls' wigs.
Snow Baby: G. L. Kirby.
Stratton Doll: Stratton Doll Industry.
Sun Tan Doll: G. L. Kirby.
Tam O'Shanter: S. Hancock & Son.
Ta-Ta dolls: Dean's Rag Book Co. Ltd.
Telma Mfg. Co.: Woollen dolls.
Three Arts Womens Employment Fund Toy Industry: Soft toy and doll mfg.
Toyland Toys: W. H. Smith & Sons.

1918   Shirley: E. E. Houghton.
Shortland, J. W.: Doll's eye patent.
Silver series: Elite Doll Co.
Steevans Mfg. Co. Ltd.: Doll and toy manufacturers.
Stoke-on-Trent Dolls Supplies Ltd.: Dolls' limbs.
Sutherland Doll Co.: Manufacturer of China dolls.

Tyneside Toys Ltd.: China and unbreakable doll manufacturers.

1919   Snow Boy: Harwin & Co. Ltd.
Southport Mfg.: Co.: Manufacturers of dolls and dolls parts.
Speciality Toy Co.: Doll manufacturers.
Syer, Ernest: Doll importer.
Tattersall, J. Ltd.: Dealers and manufacturer of dolls.
Tinkles: Harwin & Co. Ltd.

1920   Sammie: Fairyland Toy Mfg. Co. Ltd.
Seaside Girl: Speights Ltd.
Storm Girl: Speights Ltd.
Suner: Hewitt Bros.
Susie: Fairyland Toy Mfg. Co. Ltd.
Tumbling Doll: East London (Federation) Toy Factory.

1921   Slymphs: S. H. Burgess.

1923   Sonia: Chad Valley Co.
Steinman-Beyencenet, Maurice: Trademark Wob-li-gob.
Sunbonnet Baby: Dean's Rag Book Co. Ltd.

1924   Sabo: Trademark of S. Ranson.
Salome: Miniature dolls.
Sant, J. S. Ltd.: Manufacturers and importers.
Slater, M. H.: Patent rubber doll.

1925   Sambo: Dean's Rag Book Co. Ltd.
Seelig, William.
Trixie: Dean's Rag Book Co. Ltd.

1926   S. & L. Mfg. Co.: Doll and soft toy manufacture, dolls furniture etc.
Seyfarth, N.: Patent dolls eye.
Todhunter, M. E.: Patent doll.

1928   Sandy: John Sear Ltd.
Smart Set dolls: Dean's Rag Book Co. Ltd.

1929   Sonny Boy: Trademark for dolls, Cowan De Groot & Co.
Trike Toys: Dean's Rag Book Co. Ltd.
Turner, Ernest: Kalutu doll patent.

1930   Silvie dolls: Dean's Rag Book Co. Ltd.

1932   Tich: Daily Mirror and Sunday Pictorial.

1934   Sunshine Babs: British National Dolls Ltd.
Teddy Toy Co.: Soft toy and doll manufacturer.
Tennant, W. J.: Doll patent.
Toitz, I.: Doll manufacturing.

1935   Sear, J. Ltd.: Soft toy and doll manufacturing.
Simple Simon: Chad Valley.
Sofa dolls: Chad Valley.
Superior: Chad Valley.

1936   Sam: Dean's Rag Book Co. Ltd.
Saucy Joyce: Austin Gray Ltd.
Shirley Temple doll: Richards, Son & Allwin.

1937   Sabu The Elephant Boy: J. K. Farnell & Co. Ltd.
Sambo The Turk: J. K. Farnell & Co. Ltd.
Spaniard: J. K. Farnell & Co. Ltd.
Todd, Daniel G.: Doll manufacturer.

1938   Shorter, E. A.: Doll patent.
Snow White: Chad Valley.
Stevens, Lanher, Parry & Rollinson: Patent rubber doll.

1939   Service dolls: Chad Valley.
Smilers: J. K. Farnell & Co. Ltd.
Twins: Cascelloid.

1941   Softanlite: Teddy Toy Co. Ltd.
Timpo Toys: Toy Importers Ltd.
Toy Importers Ltd.: Doll and toy manufacturers.

1945   Thomas Industries (London) Ltd.: Doll and toy manufacturers.

1946   Silbertson, L. & Sons Ltd.: Trademark Marvo for dolls.

Stamford Doll Co.: Composition heads and limbs.

Tocoly Dolls: Thomas Industries (London) Ltd.

Unity Pack Co.: Doll manufacture.

1947   Skintex: British National Dolls Ltd.

Smith, T. Eric: Rosebud dolls.

1948   Tiny Belle: Toys (Components) Ltd.

Toys (Components) Ltd: Doll manufacturers.

1949   Spraytex: Britoy Ltd.

Sweetheart Doll: Drials Products Ltd.

Tommy: Playplastic Toy Co. Ltd.

Trixie: Playplastic Toy Co. Ltd.

1950   Sarold Mfg. Co. Ltd.: Plastic dolls.

Sleepa Doll Co.: Doll manufacturers.

Stevens Sales Co. Ltd.: Unbreakable dolls.

Tiny Tot Toy Co.: Doll and soft toy manufacturers.

1952   Saucy Walkers: Pedigree Soft Toys Ltd.

1955   Shirley Dolls: Castle Toy Co. Ltd.

True Life Dolls: Palitoy.

1956   Simon & Susan: The Mettoy Co. Ltd.

Sunshine: Mettoy Co. Ltd.

Sweet Sue: Palitoy.

Sylvia: Palitoy.

1957   Sunday Best Dolls: Cascelloid.

Topsy: Palitoy.

1958   Story Book: Mettoy Co. Ltd.

Thomas, Garrie: Cariad trademark.

Upperton, Patricia G. W.: Doll manufacturer.

1959   Sieki, Masa Roy: Doll and puppet manufacturer.

1960   Theda: Pedigree Soft Toys Ltd.

1962   Semco Ltd.: Doll manufacturer.

Talkative Jane: Pedigree Soft Toys Ltd.

Tiny Talker: Pedigree Soft Toys Ltd.

1963   Sindy Dolls: Pedigree Soft Toys Ltd.

1964   Topper Toys: De Luxe Toy Co. Ltd.

1965   Tina: Hook & Franks Ltd.

Tiny Tears: Palitoy.

Toots: Palitoy.

1966   Teeny Tiny Tears: Palitoy.

Tommy Gunn: Pedigree.

Trevor Toys Ltd.: Toy and doll manufacturer.

1967   Tearful Tammy: D. G. Todd & Co. Ltd.

1968   Sally Happytalk: Pedigree.

Slipsy Skiddle: Rosebud Mattel Ltd.

Story Book Kiddles: Rosebud Mattel Ltd.

Swinging Sweetie: D. G. Todd & Co. Ltd.

Tippy Toes: Palitoy.

1969   Stroll with Me Doll: Rosebud Mattel Ltd.

Suzie Sing-A-Song: Pedigree.

Thernglade Ltd.: Assembled German dolls.

Tippy Tumbles: Palitoy.

Tip Tap: Rosebud Mattel.

Trixie Ride A Trike: D. G. Todd & Co. Ltd.

Turtle dolls: Thernglade Ltd.

1970   Sally Says: Palitoy.

Toddle Talks: Pedigree.

1972   Tia: Lesney Products & Co. Ltd.

Tickles: Pedigree Soft Toys Ltd.

Ting-A-Ling Trudy: Palitoy.

Tony: Lesney Products & Co. Ltd.

Tracy: Palitoy.

1974   Sheena: Palitoy.

Tammee: Palitoy.

1975   Sandy: Lesney Products & Co. Ltd.

Suky Dolls: Matchbox.

Tina: Lesney Products & Co. Ltd.

1976   Sweet Dreams: Airfix Products Ltd.

1977   Summertime Girls: Airfix Products Ltd.

VWXYZ

1812   Wallis Paper cut out dolls: St. Julien.

1850   White's: Houndsditch wholesaler.

1852   Wicks, H. & J.: Composition dolls.

1857   Wheelhouse, W. & C.: Wax dolls.

1860   White, C. & H. Milton: Portsmouth: Pedlar dolls.

1879   Wheeler, J.: Dolls with Crown trademark.

1882   Xylolith: Composition for doll making.

1884   Wild, Lewis: London Importer.

1891   Willshur, C.: Doll bodies.

1894   Weber, W. & H.: Patent for doll head.

Wilson, G.: Rubber doll hot water bottle.

1897   Wynne, W. R.: Bubble blowing doll patent.

1899   Weigel, R.: Hopping dolls.

1904   Worcester, I. D.: Doll patent.

1909   Young England: Hughes, Jeffrey & Son.

1911   Wiederseim, Grace: Designer for Dean's.

1913   Vera Dolls: Kohnstam, J. & Keen Co.

1914   Whyte, Ridsdale Co.: Dolly Dimple: Tommy Atkins.

1915   Wilkins, F.: Patent Doll.

Wholesale Toy Co.: Ross Dolls.

Whistling Boy: Imperial Toy Co.

1916   Union Jack Baby: Leon Rees.

Webb, Florence: Kid Leather doll.

Wee Willie Winkie: Harwin & Co.

Wu-Wu: Hamley.

Worthitt & Co.: Soft dolls.

1917   Victory dolls: H. J. Benjamin.

Wheeldon, H. L.: Patent for Dean's.

1918   Vogue Dolls: Nottingham Toy Industry Ltd.

Watts Bros.: Wigs.

1919   Wellings, Norah: Doll Designer.

Welsh Toy Industries: We-to Dolls.

Wobbler: Harwin & Co.

Whiteley Ltd.: Sandow.

Zazz: Harwin & Co.

1920   Weeks & Co. Ltd.: Nellie Dolls.

Woolam, S. Mfg. Co.: Cathedral dolls.

Zobeide: Aldon Studios.

1921   Woolly Wally: Deans Golliwog.

Wonderland Toymaking Co.: Art Dolls.

Wolstan Doll Co. Ltd.: Pottery dolls.

1922   Wilson Bros Ltd.: Character dolls.

Winter Sports girl: Leon Rees.

1923   Wendy and her Wardrobe: Cut out, Dean's Rag Book Co. Ltd.

1924   Wembley Willie: Dean's Rag Book Co. Ltd.

Wendy: Dean's Tru-to-Life Doll.

1925   Wheelhouse, Miss M: Dolls.

William and Mary: Chloe Preston.

1927   Willow Pattern: Dolls Dean's Rag Book Co. Ltd.
        Wonder Toy Co.: Skipping Doll.
1928   Winston Churchill: J. S. Sant Ltd.
1930   Zulu, Zuzu: Norah Wellings.
1936   Walkaway Dolls: Chad Valley.
        Woombo: Black Dolls, Dean's Rag Book Co. Ltd.
1941   Williams, S. F.: Unbreakable dolls.
        Wynjoy: Colonial and Overseas Exporters.
1944   Webbers Dolls Ltd.
1947   Williams, K. B.: Patent eyes.
1949   Walkie Talkie: Doll Industries Ltd.
        Williams, S. F. and Stear Mfg. Co.: Mignon Radio
            doll.
1950   Wendy Wonder: Sleepa Doll Co.
1951   Washey Dolly: East London (Federation) Toy
            Factory.
1952   Watson K. E. K.: Dolls' eyes patent.
1955   Walking Princess: D. G. Todd & Co. Ltd.
        Wendy Boston Play Safe dolls.
        Yvonne: Palitoy.
        Young and Fogg Rubber Co.: Dolls.
1959   Wendy: Palitoy Petalskin.
1962   Wonder Gift Baby doll: Rosebud.
1969   Wendy: Bluebell Range Doll by D. G. Todd & Co.
1972   Wig World: Dolly Locks Doll Wigs.
1975   Yawnie: Palitoy.
        Walking Baby Loves You: Airfix.
        Walking and Talking Liza: W. H. Cornelius.
1977   Winky Blinky Moppit: Lesney.

ACKNOWLEDGEMENTS

In addition to those photographs acknowledged in the text, the authors and publishers wish to thank the following for kindly granting them permission to reproduce material in this book:

Sue Atkinson, Bethnal Green Museum, Bob Croxford, Jenny Croxford who designed the alphabetical title pages, Dolls in Wonderland, Melvyn Gill, Guildhall Library, Christiane Hermelink, Mary Hillier, Lesney Products & Co. Ltd., Luton Museum, Susan Macfarlane, Manchester Public Library, National Film Archive, Old Cottage Toys, Pelham Puppets, Pollock's Toy Theatres Ltd., Myrtle Smith, Sotheby & Co., Tunbridge Wells Museum, Victoria and Albert Museum, Welsh Folk Museum, Helen Whateley, and Worthing Museum.